LINGUISTIC THEORY
IN AMERICA

Second Edition

LINGUISTIC THEORY
IN AMERICA

Second Edition

Frederick J. Newmeyer

DEPARTMENT OF LINGUISTICS
UNIVERSITY OF WASHINGTON
SEATTLE, WASHINGTON

1986

ACADEMIC PRESS, INC.
Harcourt Brace Jovanovich, Publishers

Orlando   San Diego   New York   Austin
Boston   London   Sydney   Tokyo   Toronto

ACADEMIC PRESS, INC.
Orlando, Florida 32887

United Kingdom Edition published by
ACADEMIC PRESS INC. (LONDON) LTD.
24–28 Oval Road, London NW1 7DX

Library of Congress Cataloging in Publication Data

Newmeyer, Frederick J.
   Linguistic theory in America.

   Bibliography: p.
   Includes indexes.
   1. Generative grammar—History.   2. Linguistics—
United States—History.   I. Title.
P158.N4   1986   415   86-10802
ISBN 0–12–517151–X (hardcover) (alk. paper)
ISBN 0–12–517152–8 (paperback) (alk. paper)

PRINTED IN THE UNITED STATES OF AMERICA

86 87 88 89   9 8 7 6 5 4 3 2 1

Contents

Preface to the Second Edition

Though I had no way of knowing it at the time, I wrote the first edition of *Linguistic Theory in America* during the only major lull in syntactic research between the mid 1950s and the present. As I was preparing the book in the late 1970s, it had become unquestionably clear that generative semantics had collapsed, yet no other worked-out alternative to the Extended Standard Theory had presented itself as a pole of opposition to it. At the same time, the EST itself, which was bogged down in its "Filters and Control" phase, seemed too unappealing to too many linguists to be able to benefit to any great extent from its lack of competition. This lull afforded me a golden opportunity to undertake a quarter-century retrospective without having to worry that the contents of the next issue of *Linguistic Inquiry* might render obsolete my overview of current work in the field.

But within months after the appearance of the first edition, the theories of government-binding, generalized phrase structure grammar, and lexical-functional grammar were introduced. The resultant explosion in work devoted to syntactic theory exceeded anything the field had ever seen, surpassing even the late 1960s boom that followed the publication of *Aspects of the Theory of Syntax*. More has been published in syntactic theory and analysis in the past half-dozen years than the previous two dozen.

I think that the dust has settled sufficiently on the new frameworks to make the time right for a second edition providing an account of their origins and development; I have therefore devoted most of the last chapter to outlining these exciting recent trends in syntax. I have restructured the other chapters as well, most importantly by adding a section on morphology and greatly expanding the discussion of work in pragmatics. In order to keep the book to roughly the same length, I truncated the possibly overly detailed account of the rise of abstract syntax and generative semantics in the late 1960s.

I would like to acknowledge the helpful advice I received from a number of persons, in particular Ron Amundson, Avery Andrews, Noam Chomsky, Donald Foss, John Fought, Morris Halle, Laurence Horn, James McCawley, Donna Jo Napoli, Ivan Sag, Karl Teeter, and Alice ter Meulen. I owe a special debt of gratitude to Timothy Stowell, Pauline Jacobson, and Annie Zaenen, who read and commented on portions of the new material.

Preface to the First Edition

In this book I attempt to document the origins, birth, and development of the theory of transformational generative grammar. Despite the fact that it is now 25 years since Noam Chomsky completed his *Logical Structure of Linguistic Theory,* what I have written is, to my knowledge, the only work that combines a comprehensive account of the forging of modern linguistic theory with a detailed elaboration and explanation of its development. I have not intended the book to be an introduction to linguistics, and it cannot substitute for one. A minimal understanding of modern linguistic theory is presupposed throughout. Fortunately, there is no dearth of texts in print whose purpose is to acquaint the reader with fundamentals of theory. To my mind, the best is Neil Smith and Deirdre Wilson's lucid *Modern Linguistics: The Results of Chomsky's Revolution,* which I can recommend without reservation to the beginning student and advanced scholar alike.

To keep this book to a manageable size, I have had to slight developments in generative phonology. In fact, there is no discussion of developments in phonology since the early 1960s. My omission is compensated for in part by the existence of Alan Sommerstein's *Modern Phonology*, which covers the recent history of phonology in some detail.

The reader may be puzzled by the "in America" in the title. Why should the discussion of a scientific theory be constrained by a national boundary? In part this is a reflection of the immaturity of our science: It is a sad commentary on the state of the field that we can still talk realistically of "American linguistics," "French linguistics," and "Soviet linguistics." But more positively, my choice of title was dictated by the fact that transformational grammar HAS begun to internationalize; "in America" was necessary lest I appear to be slighting recent work of theoretical importance in Japanese, Finnish, Arabic, and other languages unknown to me.

Since there is no such thing as totally unbiased historiography, it would be utopian to imagine that an author could be free from background assumptions or beliefs that might color his or her perception of events. As a PARTICIPANT (however noncentral) in the history I describe, I might be particularly open to charges of bias. However, I feel that my participation has given me a real advantage: It has permitted me an inside view of the field that would be denied to the more displaced historian. I hope that the reader will find this to be to the book's advantage.

For those who may be interested in my background, I have been in linguistics since 1965, the year I received a B.A. in geology from the University of Rochester. Fortunately, a senior year course taught by the late William A. Coates, called "The Languages of the World," so intrigued me that I gave up any dreams I may have harbored of a career in petroleum engineering (or worse). I received a Master's in linguistics from Rochester the following year and would have stayed there longer had I not attended Chomsky's lectures at the LSA Institute at UCLA in the summer of 1966. They convinced me to transfer as soon as possible to a transformational grammar-oriented department. In 1967 I was admitted to the Ph.D. program at the University of Illinois, where I studied syntax with Robert B. Lees, Arnold Zwicky, and Michael Geis, and phonology with Theodore Lightner. My last year of graduate work was spent as a guest at MIT. After receiving a Ph.D. from Illinois in 1969, I was hired by the University of Washington, where I have been teaching ever since, with the exception of leave time spent at the University of Edinburgh, Wayne State University, and the University of London.

My earliest theoretical commitment was to generative semantics, and I contributed several uninfluential publications in defense of a deep-structureless model of grammar (1970, 1971, 1975). By 1972 or 1973, I began to have serious reservations about the direction generative semantics was taking. Since then, I have identified myself loosely as an interpretivist, without committing myself to any one particular model in that framework.

Some who know me as a Marxist may be surprised and, perhaps, disappointed that there is no obvious "Marxist analysis" given to the events I describe. For this I make no apology. There is simply no evidence that language structure (outside of limited aspects of the lexicon) is, in the Marxist sense, a superstructural phenomenon. Even if it were, however, it seems inconceivable that events taking place in such a short period of time and involving so few, so sociologically homogeneous, participants could lend themselves to such an analysis. Those interested in my views on the relationship between Marxist theory and linguistic theory may find useful my review of Rossi-Landi's *Linguistics and Economics,* published in *Language* in 1977.

A final word on chronology. Throughout the text, I cite books and articles by the year of their first publication, not by the year that they were written. Since publishing delays are uneven, this has resulted in some cases in replies appearing to be older than the publications to which they are addressed and in other possibly confusing aspects of dating. When delays are extreme or when the time lag is significant in some respect, the year of writing (in parentheses) appears after the year of publication in the reference list.

Chapter 1

The State of American Linguistics in the Mid 1950s

1.1. A PERIOD OF OPTIMISM

If American linguistics was in a state of crisis in the mid 1950s, few of its practitioners seemed aware of it. Einar Haugen (1951), in his overview of the field, wrote that "American linguistics is today in a more flourishing state than at any time since the founding of the Republic" (p. 211). Commentators boasted of the "great progress" (Hall 1951:101), "far reaching advances" (Allen 1958:v), and "definitive results" (Gleason 1955:11) achieved by linguistics, which was "compared in method with field physics, quantum mechanics, discrete mathematics, and Gestalt psychology" (Whitehall 1951:v). Even Kenneth Pike (1958), often critical of many of the assumptions of the dominant American linguistic theorists, felt moved to write that "theirs [Harris's and Bloch's] is an attempt to reduce language to a formal analysis of great simplicity, elegance, and mathematical rigor, and they have come astonishingly close to succeeding" (p. 204).

More than self-congratulation was going on. The psychologist John B. Carroll (1953) wrote that linguistics was the most advanced of all the social sciences, with a close resemblance to physics and chemistry. And Claude Lévi-Strauss, probably the world's foremost anthropologist, compared the discovery that language consists of phonemes and morphemes to the Newtonian revolution in physics (Lévi-Strauss 1953:350–351).

There was a widespread feeling among American linguists in the 1950s that the fundamental problems of linguistic analysis had been solved and that all that was left was to fill in the details. The basic theoretical–methodological statements of Bloch's "A Set of Postulates for Phonemic Analysis" (1948) and Harris's *Methods in Structural Linguistics* (1951) seemed to render any more basic theoretical work unnecessary. In fact, many linguists felt that the procedures had been so well worked out that computers could take over the drudgery of linguistic analysis. The time was near at hand when all one would have to do would be to punch the data into the computer and out would come the grammar!

There was also a feeling that computers could solve another traditional linguistic problem—translation. The idea of machine translation had been first suggested (in a memorandum by Warren Weaver) only in 1949. By 1955, such translation work was going on in three countries at half-a-dozen institutions. These six years were enough to convert the skeptics, as William N. Locke put it in an enthusiastic review article written in that year (Locke 1955:109).

Other postwar scientific developments seemed to be especially promising for linguistics. A new field called "information theory" proposed methods of measuring the efficiency of communication channels in terms of information and redundancy. Shannon and Weaver (1949) in their pioneering study of information theory pointed out the possible linguistic implications of the theory:

> The concept of the information to be associated with a source leads directly, as we have seen, to a study of the statistical structure of language; and this study reveals about the English language, as an example, information which seems surely significant to students of every phase of language and communication. (p. 117)

Shannon and Weaver's ideas were enthusiastically received by a large number of linguists; prominent among these was Charles Hockett (1953, 1955), who set out to apply the results of information theory in the construction of a Markov-process model of human language.

Progress in acoustic phonetics also contributed to the general optimism. The spectrograph, first made public in 1945, had replaced the inconvenient oscilloscope as the most important tool for linguists in the physical recording of speech sounds. There was a general feeling that spectrograms would help decide between competing phonemicizations of a given language, the existence of which had posed a perennial problem.

Finally, the synthesis of linguistics and psychology was adding a new dimension to the study of language. The behaviorist theory of psychology developed by Clark Hull (see Hull 1943) provided the linguists of the period with the theoretical apparatus they needed to link their approach to linguistic description with theories of language acquisition, speech perception, and communication. By the early 1950s, an interdisciplinary field of psycholinguistics had emerged, with important seminars being held at Cornell in 1951 and Indiana in 1953. The progress reports from the latter seminar were published in the first volume of papers dealing with language and psychology, Osgood and Sebeok (1954), a work hailed by one reviewer as "a scientific event of great importance" (Olmsted 1955:59). Among many other topics, the book dealt with issues such as the psychological verification of the phoneme and the psychological criteria that would help decide between competing linguistic analyses. The book itself inspired work conferences on many related subjects, which themselves resulted in influential publications on content analysis (Pool

1959), stylistics (Sebeok 1960), aphasia (Osgood and Miron 1963), and language universals (Greenberg 1963).

Linguistics seemed so successful that it was being consciously imitated by the social sciences.[1] The anthropologist A. L. Kroeber (1952:124) asked "What is the cultural equivalent of the phoneme?" and Kenneth Pike had an answer: the "behavioreme." Pike (1954) was in the process of constructing a comprehensive theory in which "verbal and non-verbal activity is a unified whole, and theory and methodology should be organized to treat it as such" (p. 2). Not only was it a cliché "that what mathematics already is for the physical sciences, linguistics can be for the social sciences" (LaBarre 1958:74; Le Page 1964:1), but many even held the view that "as no science can go beyond mathematics, no criticism can go beyond its linguistics" (Whitehall 1951:v). In this period the "linguistic method" was being applied to the study of kinesics, folkloric texts, the analysis of the political content of agitational leaflets, and much more.

1.2. STRUCTURAL LINGUISTICS

1.2.1. The Saussurean Heritage

The linguistics practiced in the United States in the 1950s, along with that in much of Europe, owed an intellectual debt to the great Swiss linguist Ferdinand de Saussure (1857–1913). Saussure's lecture notes, published posthumously as the *Cours de Linguistique Générale,* represent a turning point in the history of linguistics. The central principle of the *Cours* is that a well-defined subpart of language can be abstracted from the totality of speech. This subpart Saussure called "*langue,*" which he contrasted with "*parole,*" or "speech." *Langue* represents the abstract system of structural relationships inherent in language, relationships that are held in common by all members of a speech community. *Parole,* on the other hand, represents the individual act of speaking, which is never performed exactly the same way twice. Saussure compared language to a symphony. *Langue* represents the unvarying score, *parole* the actual performance, no two of which are alike.

Since in the Saussurean view, *langue* forms a coherent structural system, any approach to language devoted to explicating the internal workings of this system has come to be known as "structural linguistics." A structuralist description of a language has typically taken the form of an inventory of the linguistic elements of the language under analysis along with a statement of the positions in which these elements occur. The point of such a rather taxonomic approach to *langue* was made explicit in the *Cours:*

> It would be interesting from a practical viewpoint to begin with units, to determine what they are and to account for their diversity by classifying them. . . . Next we would have to classify the subunits,

[1]This point is argued at length in Greenberg (1973).

then the larger units, etc. By determining in this way the elements that it manipulates, synchronic linguistics would completely fulfill its task, for it would relate all synchronic phenomena to their fundamental principle. (Saussure 1959:111)

Structural linguistics grew slowly in the first two decades after Saussure's death. But by the late 1930s, it was flourishing in a variety of Western academic centers, in particular, in Prague,[2] Copenhagen, Paris, Geneva, London, Chicago, and New Haven. While it had never been a unified movement, the fragmentation of structural linguistics accelerated in the war-torn 1940s, with the consequence that the particular form it took largely became a function of the country in which it was practiced. It was in the 1940s that American structuralism took on its distinctive cast and entered the period of its great success.

1.2.2. American Structural Linguistics[3]

The two pioneers of structural linguistics in America were Edward Sapir and Leonard Bloomfield. Sapir, in fact, had worked out the basic principles of structuralism even before Saussure's *Cours* had been published, as is evidenced by his Takelma grammar of 1911 (published as Sapir 1922). Sapir's interests were far-ranging; in addition to grammatical analysis, he concerned himself with the humanistic and cultural aspects of language and published papers on the functioning of language in creative literature, mythology, and religion. Indeed, the scope of his interests extended far beyond language, and he is still regarded as one of the greatest American cultural anthropologists. Sapir could be classified as a "mentalist," that is, he conceived of linguistic structure as having an underlying mental reality that could be probed by studying native speakers' overt judgments about their language as well as their unguarded use of it. He also believed that linguistic structure plays a role in shaping our perception of reality, an idea that was developed further by his student Benjamin Whorf (hence the "Sapir-Whorf Hypothesis.") Finally, Sapir was perhaps the greatest fieldworker in the history of linguistics: he not only published analyses of a number of American Indian languages that are still valuable today, but trained more than a dozen students who themselves would achieve prominence for their work on the indigenous languages of North America.

Leonard Bloomfield also published analyses of particular languages based on his fieldwork, but his greatest impact on the course of American linguistics resulted from those sections of his book *Language* (1933) that outlined his theoretical perspective on language. While he had earlier been a mentalist too, by 1933 Bloomfield had become convinced that it was unscientific to posit mental constructs within linguistic theory. That is, he had become an empiricist—he had adopted a view of

---

[2]The work done by the Prague School was of such great importance to the development of transformational generative grammar that it merits a section of its own (see Section 2.4.1.).

[3]For a comprehensive overview of the development of structural linguistics in the United States, see Hymes and Fought (1981). Anderson (1985) presents a thorough discussion of its approach to phonology, which he contrasts to approaches prevalent in Europe.

linguistic science that allowed only statements based on direct observation of the phenomena under investigation or generalizations that could be drawn from observables by a set of mechanical procedures. As he put it, "The only useful generalizations about language are inductive generalizations. Features which we think ought to be universal may be absent from the very next language that becomes accessible" (1933:20). Bloomfield's empiricist orientation also affected his approach to the study of meaning. While he recognized that a central function of language was to convey meaning, he nevertheless was skeptical that meaning could be studied scientifically. This is because "[t]he situations which prompt people to utter speech include every object and happening in their universe. In order to give a scientifically accurate definition of meaning for every form of language, we should have to have a scientifically accurate knowledge of everything in the speaker's world" (p. 139). Since this goal was, of course, unattainable, recourse to meaning was to be avoided wherever possible.

The essence of the intellectual differences between Sapir and Bloomfield can be captured nicely by Bloomfield's sobriquet for Sapir, "medicine man," and by Sapir's references to "Bloomfield's sophomoric psychology" (Jakobson, 1979:170).

By the early 1950s, both Sapir and Bloomfield had a considerable following among American structuralists (Sapir had died in 1939, Bloomfield in 1948). But it was Bloomfield's intellectual heirs, the "post-Bloomfieldians",[4] who predominated both in numbers and influence.[5] The leading post-Bloomfieldian linguists, Bernard Bloch, Zellig Harris, Charles Hockett, George Trager, Henry Lee Smith, Archibald Hill, and Robert Hall, were committed to reconstituting linguistic theory along strict empiricist lines. Sapir's students, whose ranks included Morris Swadesh, Stanley Newman, Mary Haas, and C. F. Voegelin, retained the mentalistic outlook of their teacher, though it must be said that they had no comprehensive alternative theory to offer to the post-Bloomfieldians' empiricist one. The Sapirean group is noteworthy for the many careful descriptive studies of native American languages that they published in that period (and continue to publish).

The predominance of the Bloomfieldian wing of American structural linguistics was a function of the wide appeal of empiricist philosophy in the American intellectual community in the 1930s and 1940s. And this appeal in turn was undoubtedly related to the fact that there was no period in American history in which there was greater respect for the methods and results of science. Social scientists and philosophers, envious of the dramatic achievements in nineteenth- and early twentieth-century natural science and (temporarily) innocent of the ethical issues that would be raised by the atomic bomb, counterinsurgency technology, and genetic experi-

---

[4]Confusingly, some commentators have applied the term "post-Bloomfieldian" to all American structuralists of the 1940s and 1950s. However, in this work its use will be confined to those committed to Bloomfield's empiricist program for linguistics.

[5]There were other structuralists in America at that time who were independent sociologically and intellectually of both the Sapireans and post-Bloomfieldians. Foremost among them were the Christian missionary linguists, the two most prominent of whom were (and are) Kenneth Pike and Eugene Nida.

mentation, asked: "How can we be scientific too? How can we rid ourselves of the fuzzy speculation that has often characterized theorizing about language?" Empiricism appeared to provide an answer. By hitching his fortunes to the then-popular conception of "science," Bloomfield assured that he and his followers would come to dominate structural linguistics in America. Those who resisted the empiricist tide, like Sapir and his students, found themselves increasingly peripheral in the field.

The post-Bloomfieldians' insistence that linguistics could be assimilated to the natural sciences is partly responsible for the fact that American structural linguists prospered in the 1940s and 1950s, while their European counterparts declined in relative importance.[6] Since their empiricist outlook dissuaded them from raising the broad philosophical questions about the underlying nature of language, the Americans kept to a single-minded focus on developing procedures for phonemic and morphemic analysis. Hence a group of specialists arose in this country, whose only professional loyalty was to the field of linguistics and its particular techniques. European structuralists, by contrast, all had interdisciplinary interests, which paradoxically diminished their commitment to building linguistics as an independent discipline.

Nowhere were the practical consequences of the Bloomfieldian empiricist stance more evident than in the treatment of meaning. To the Europeans, understanding the role of language in conveying meaning was paramount; consequently they devoted considerable attention to the semantic function of the units they arrived at in their structural analysis. Their preoccupation with meaning meant that they were constantly abutting on fields like philosophy, psychology, and criticism, which also studied meaning. Some followers of Bloomfield, on the other hand, attempted to expunge the study of meaning altogether from the field of linguistics! They felt uncomfortable even addressing a concept so notoriously difficult to quantify and operationalize. Yet the very limitation of their vision helped them to create a distinct field with clearly defined boundaries.

To those American structuralist theoreticians most committed to an empiricist approach to language, European linguistic scholarship seemed more akin to mysticism than to science. Robert Hall expressed such an idea with a particular intensity of feeling:

> The present-day intellectual atmosphere of Europe is influenced by an essentially reactionary hostility to objective science, and by a return to doctrines of "spiritual activity," "creativity of the human soul," and socially biased value-judgments which European scholarship has inherited from the aristocratic, theological background of mediaeval and Renaissance intellectualism. This reactionary attitude is present in the theorizing of many modern European students of language, who sacrifice positive analysis of concrete data to discussion of purely imaginary, non-demonstrable fictions like "thought" and "spirit" as supposedly reflected in language. In American work on language, the burning question at present is whether this same anti-scientific attitude is to be allowed to block the

[6]Other factors boosted the fortunes of the Americans with respect to the Europeans. In particular, the former benefited from governmental support during the Second World War while the latter did not, and the commitment of the former to the principle of "egalitarianism" gave them an issue around which they could rally to crystalize their professional identity. For more discussion, see Newmeyer (in press).

further development of linguistics and its contribution to our understanding of human affairs, especially in our teaching. (Hall 1946:33–34)

Leo Spitzer, a European exile then teaching in the United States, in turn accused Hall of desiring to set up an "academic F.B.I." to stifle views departing from those then current in America (1946:499).

By the end of the 1940s, however, as a result of increased cross-Atlantic scholarly contact after World War II, signs of rapprochement appeared on both sides. In 1951, the American Charles Hockett wrote an extremely favorable review of a book by the leading French structuralist André Martinet, and Martinet in turn wrote that terminological differences alone were the major impediments to Americans and Europeans understanding each other's work (see Hockett 1951; Martinet 1953).

1.2.3. Post-Bloomfieldian Methodology

In this section, I attempt to synthesize the approach to linguistic methodology of the post-Bloomfieldian school. While, as one might expect, its members had differences with each other over certain theoretical issues (some of importance), basic agreements, which far outweighed their disagreements, make such a synthesis possible.

The goal of post-Bloomfieldian linguistics was to "discover" a grammar by performing a set of operations on a corpus of data. Each successive operation was one step farther removed from the corpus. Since the physical record of the flow of speech itself was the only data considered objective enough to serve as a starting point, it followed that the levels of a grammatical description had to be arrived at in the following order:

I. Phonemics
II. Morphemics
III. Syntax
IV. Discourse

Since morphemes could be discovered only after the phonemes of which they were composed were extracted from the flow of speech, it followed that morphemic (or syntactic) information could not enter a phonemic description: "There must be no circularity; phonological analysis is assumed for grammatical analysis and so must not assume any part of the latter. The line of demarcation between the two must be sharp" (Hockett 1942:19). This procedural constraint became known as the prohibition against "mixing levels" in a grammatical description.

These conditions were intended to guarantee that a linguistic description be a catalog of observables and statements in principle extractable directly from observables by a set of mechanical procedures: "The over-all purpose of work in descriptive linguistics is to obtain a compact one–one representation of the stock of utterances in the corpus" (Harris 1951:366). The subjectivity of language consultants' judgments necessarily ruled them inadmissible as data, and any description employing unobservable "process" notions such as deletion, metathesis, and insertion were found to be incompatible with empiricist strictures. As a matter of fact, the descriptive work of Bloomfield himself often had been stated in a process framework, complete with rule ordering statements (see Bloomfield 1939b). But after the discrepancies between Bloomfield's theory and his practice were pointed out, process statements disappeared from the literature. Hockett (1954) wrote that he could not even conceive of any meaning to "ordering" but an historical one.

The first step in the process of grammar construction was to divide the speech flow itself into a series of phones, the basic units of sound. Phones were eligible to be members of the same phoneme if they did not contrast, that is, if they were in complementary distribution or free variation in an environment. In the earliest structuralist work, meaning contrast was used as a criterion for establishing the separate phonemic status of two phones. (For example, [ɪ] and [æ] result in meaning differences in the context /b . . . d/. Hence they were to be assigned to two separate phonemes.) However, many post-Bloomfieldians explored the use of operational tests that did not rely on judgments of meaning differences in order to put the notion of contrast on a more objective footing (see, for example, Harris 1951.)

After the phonemes were discovered, the next step was to group them into "morphs," the minimal recurrent sequences of phonemes. Since the cues for the existence of morph boundaries had to exist in an already-discovered level, this was no easy task. One method was proposed by Harris (1955), who suggested that morph boundaries might be arrived at by a procedure whose first step was the calculation of the number of phonemes that could conceivably follow a sequence of phonemes in a string. Harris used by way of illustration the English sentence *he's clever*, phonemicized as /hiyzklevər/. He estimated that 9 phonemes can follow utterance-initial /h/, 14 utterance-initial /hi/, 29 /hiy/, 29 /hiyz/, 11 /hiyzk/, 7 /hiyzkl/, 8 /hiyzkle/, 1 /hiyzklev/, 1 /hiyzklevə/, and 28 /hiyzklevər/. Harris theorized that morph boundaries followed peaks, that is, that they were to be posited after /y/, /z/, and /r/.

The procedure for classifying morphs into morphemes was similar to that for classifying phones into phonemes. Two morphs were eligible to be members of the same morpheme if (in the simplest case) they were in complementary distribution and were phonemically similar. Hence, a morphemic description consisted of statements like "The morpheme {ed} has members /ed/ (in a particular environment) and /t/ (in a particular environment)." Irregularity, particularly if it was reflected by vowel alternations, was a troublesome point in post-Bloomfieldian morphemics. There were several different morphemic analyses of /tuk/, for example, all of which attempted to be consistent with the classificatory principle of linguistic analysis and to avoid a process description like "/ey/ goes to /u/ in the past tense of /teyk/."

The principle of complementary distribution led to a different set of procedures in syntax, since one wanted to say that two morphemes were of the same syntactic type if they were NOT in complementary distribution. One set of procedures for assigning elements to syntactic categories was Harris's (1946) "bottom-up" morpheme-to-utterance approach; another was Wells's (1947) "top-down" immediate-constituent analysis. Harris classified individual morphemes into syntactic categories on the basis of their distributions. For example, any morpheme that occurred before the plural {-s} morpheme (itself arrived at via bottom-up distributional analysis) would be classified as a noun. Lower-level syntactic categories were grouped into higher ones by analogous procedures. Wells, on the other hand, started from the sentence as a whole, and by substitution procedures divided it into smaller and smaller constituents. Since in the sentence *the King of England opened Parliament,* the sequences of morphemes *the King of England* and *opened Parliament* had greater substitutive possibilities than any other sequences in the sentence, the major immediate constituent break was drawn between *England* and *opened.* This procedure was followed down to the level of the individual morphemes.

In the 1950s, Harris began to work out procedures for stating syntactic relations between sentences. Harris's work developed out of his attempt to analyze the structure of extended discourse. The problem was that sentences could exist in many different surface forms, and the usual substitution procedures did not seem to be of much help in stating the obvious systematic relatedness that existed between their various types. Hence he worked out procedures (1952a, 1952b; 1957; 1965) for "normalizing" complex sentence types to simpler "kernel" ones. He noted, for example, that corresponding to sentences of the form

$$N_1 V N_2$$

there often existed sentences of the form

$$N_2 \text{ is V-ed by } N_1$$

or

$$\text{it is } N_2 \text{ that } N_1 V.$$

Provided that the cooccurrence relations between N_1, V, and N_2 in the three sentence types were the same, Harris set up TRANSFORMATIONS relating them. They might be stated as follows:

$$N_1 V N_2 \leftrightarrow N_2 \text{ is V-ed by } N_1 \qquad \text{(Passive Transformation)}$$
$$N_1 V N_2 \leftrightarrow \text{it is } N_2 \text{ that } N_1 V \qquad \text{(Cleft Transformation)}$$

Despite the work of Harris and a few others, the post-Bloomfieldians published relatively few syntactic analyses. Robert Hall (1951) explained why: "Descriptive syntactic studies have also been rather rare; but, since they normally come at the end of one's analysis, the tendency is perhaps to hold them for incorporation into a more complete description" (p. 120). In fact, the little syntactic work that was done necessarily bypassed the procedures to a greater or lesser extent, since a complete morphemic analysis had never been worked out even for English (for the most ambitious attempts to present one, see Trager and Smith, 1951, Francis 1958).

Actually, the structuralist procedures were bypassed in many ways. It was therefore necessary to have some checks that could be applied to any description to ensure that it could have been arrived at operationally. The most comprehensive

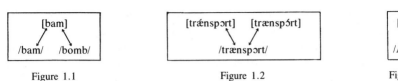

Figure 1.1   Figure 1.2

Figure 1.3

was that there be a BIUNIQUE relationship between elements of one level and those of the next higher level (Harris 1951; Hockett 1951). Let us take the relationship between phones and phonemes as an illustration. Biuniqueness entails that any sequence of phones in a description has to be associated with a unique sequence of phonemes and that any sequence of phonemes has to be associated with a unique sequence of phones, ignoring free variation. Hence, descriptions involving neutralization at either the phonetic level (Figure 1.1) or the phonemic level (Figure 1.2) were automatically ruled out.

It is easy to see how both situations are incompatible with an empiricist-based requirement that phonemes be literally extractable from the sequence of phones by mechanical procedures.

Operational considerations also demanded that a condition later termed "linearity" be placed on adjacent levels in a linguistic description. Linearity requires that the linear order of elements at one level match the linear order of the corresponding elements at the next level. Analyses representable by Figure 1.3 were therefore ruled out, assuming that phone [b] belongs to the phoneme /B/ and phone [c] belongs to the phoneme /C/.

Another necessary check was that an invariant relation hold between phones and phonemes: that a phonetic segment in a given environment be invariantly assignable to a given phoneme. The weak form of invariance allowed partial intersection (overlapping) of two phonemes. Biuniqueness was not violated if, say, the [D] of [θDow] *throw* (in the dialect described in Bloch 1941) was assigned to the phoneme /r/ and the [D] of [bɛDiy] *Betty* assigned to /t/, since the environment for the identical phonetic manifestation of the two phonemes could (in principle) be recoverable from the acoustic signal. However, some post-Bloomfieldians (Hockett 1942; Wells 1945) disallowed even partial overlapping, which resulted in the two occurrences of [D] being assigned to the same phoneme. This requirement of "once a phoneme, always a phoneme" seems to have been a consequence of the desire to raise the principle of complementary distribution to an inviolable strategy.

While empiricist assumptions necessitate a biunique relationship between levels within one description, it does not follow that there is necessarily a biunique relationship between the corpus of data and a description of it. The reason is that there were an indefinite number of procedures of segmentation and classification applicable to a given body of data, each consistent with empiricist methodology. This nonuniqueness of phonemic analyses (see Chao 1934) was a constant source of dismay to the post-Bloomfieldians. For example, at least three different phonemicizations of the vowel nucleus in the word *bay* were proposed: /bej/ (Trager and Bloch 1941), /bee/ (Swadesh 1947), and /bei/ (Pike 1947b). The criterion of "pattern congruity" was often applied when a choice was made between alternatives. That is, the phonemicization was chosen which led to the greatest overall symmetry in the language's phonemic system. The Trager-Bloch analysis was selected as preferable by means of this criterion.

1.3. CLOUDS ON THE HORIZON

So far, the picture painted of the self-perceived state of American linguistics in the mid 1950s has been a uniformly rosy one. Yet, hardly 10 years later, the advocates of post-Bloomfieldian structuralism were hard pressed to find an audience. And 20 years later, that approach was typically encountered by the student in a history of linguistics class, not in a survey of contemporary theory. How did it fall so far so fast? In this section, I begin to answer this question by pointing both to the changing intellectual climate in America and to some of the weaknesses of post-Bloomfieldian theorizing that had already become evident.

1.3.1. Crisis in Empiricist Philosophy

The downfall of post-Bloomfieldian linguistics was hastened by dramatic changes of outlook in the philosophy of science. Little by little, the post-Bloomfieldians found the philosophical props knocked out from their conception of scientific methodology. And since more than anything else they felt they had scientific justification for their theory, when they lost that justification they had very little to appeal to.

For years, philosophers had been grappling with the criteria for determining whether a statement is meaningful, and hence proper in scientific discourse. An extremely strong empiricist position known as "the principle of complete verification" had considerable support in the 1930s. According to this principle, the meaning of a statement is simply a description of the ways in which it might be verified: "Whenever we ask about a sentence 'what does it mean?' . . . we want a description of the conditions under which the sentence will form a true proposition, and of those which will make it false. . . . The meaning of a proposition is the method of its verification" (Schlick 1936:341). Strict verificationism was abandoned very early as untenable by philosophers (though not by behavioral psychologists). Various weaker forms of verificationism were put forth in the late 1930s and in the 1940s. The criteria for significance were weakened still further to the "principle of falsifiability," by which a statement was to be considered meaningful if it was falsifiable in principle. But still there were problems—many meaningful statements (such as any containing an existential quantifier) simply did not meet this condition. Yet it seemed counterintuitive to call them "unscientific."

By the late 1940s it was widely believed in the United States that a sentence could be considered meaningful if its constituent terms could be given what is often known as an "operational definition." That is, all terms in a scientific statement would have to be linkable directly to observables by an operation (or series of operations) performable by the investigator. Notice that the theoretical terms in structural linguistics (such as "phoneme" and "noun") had just this quality. If anybody wanted to know why the claim had been made that /k/, for example, was a phoneme of English, that person could (in principle) be provided with a list of the operations performed on the raw data to arrive at that conclusion.

In two important papers (partly surveying earlier work, partly original in nature), the philosopher Carl Hempel (1950, 1951) laid to rest any hope for an empiricist criterion for cognitive significance.[7] After reviewing the earlier, more inadequate theories of meaninglessness, he pointed out that even the more permissive empiricist approaches to this question failed to capture the essence of what it takes for a statement to be considered scientific. There is simply no direct connection between a scientific term or statement and the empirical confirmation of a theory containing that term or statement. For example,

> the hypothesis that the agent of tuberculosis is rod-shaped does not by itself entail the consequence that upon looking at a tubercular sputum specimen through a microscope, rod-like shapes will be observed: a large number of subsidiary hypotheses, including the theory of the microscope, have to be used as additional premises in deducing that prediction. (Hempel 1950:58–59)

Moreover, many fundamental scientific notions, such as "gravitational potential," "absolute temperature," and "electric field," have no operational definitions at all.

How then might a statement be judged as meaningful or not? The problem, according to Hempel, lies in attempting to ascribe meaningfulness to statements themselves in isolation. Science is more in the business of comparing theories than in evaluating statements. A theory is simply an axiomatized system which as a whole has an empirical interpretation. We can compare competing theoretical systems in regard to such characteristics as these:

> a. the clarity and precision with which the theories are formulated, and with which the logical relationships of their elements to each other and to expressions couched in observational terms have been made explicit;
> b. the systematic, i.e., explanatory and predictive, power of the systems in regard to observable phenomena;
> c. the formal simplicity of the theoretical system with which a certain systematic power is attained;
> d. the extent to which the theories have been confirmed by experimental evidence. (Hempel 1951:74)

Hempel went on to write:

> Many of the speculative philosophical approaches to cosmology, biology, or history, for example, would make a poor showing on practically all of these counts and would thus prove no matches to available rival theories, or would be recognized as so unpromising as not to warrant further study or development. (p. 74)

Statements like these signaled the demise of empiricism as a significant force in the philosophy of science. As its philosophical props gave way, post-Bloomfieldian

---

[7]These two papers were later merged in Hempel (1965).

structuralism found itself in a distinctly unstable posture. Not surprisingly, it was relatively simple for a new theory, defective by any empiricist standards, yet nevertheless highly valued according to Hempel's four criteria, to topple it completely.

1.3.2. Unresolved Problems in Structural Linguistics

The most penetrating challenges to the post-Bloomfieldians in the early 1950s came from those who accepted the basic principles of structuralism yet had no commitment to an empiricist program. Since these latter linguists had no well-worked-out alternative, the most they could do was point out the failings of the dominant procedural approach. Nevertheless, their doing so helped to create an accelerating atmosphere of uncertainty around the entire post-Bloomfieldian enterprise.

The contemporary critics of the post-Bloomfieldians had no trouble in pointing out the failure of this approach to present a half-convincing account of suprasegmental phenomena: stress, pitch, and juncture. Alternative analyses abounded, and no one was able to argue successfully that their phonemicization was latent in the acoustic signal, as empiricist constraints demanded that it be. James Sledd, in his 1955 review of Trager and Smith's influential *Outline of English Structure* (1951), told the truth more openly than it had ever been told before. Sledd, who had a reputation as an iconoclast, said that he simply did not hear the neat distribution of stress, pitch, and juncture phonemes of the Trager-Smith analysis, strongly implying that the authors had done nothing less than cheat.

Another persistent critic of the post-Bloomfieldians, Kenneth Pike, pointed out many of the same problems (see Pike 1947a, 1952). But Pike went farther than other critics; he said that in order to assign juncture correctly one had to mix levels—to do at least part of the grammatical analysis first. Pike's alternative did not really represent a break from operationalism since he outlined (very vaguely) some mechanical procedures for identifying morphemes before doing a phonemic analysis. But it is noteworthy for its clear statement of the dilemma facing competent linguistics of the period: they knew what to do to get the right grammatical analysis, but their theory would not let them do it. According to Pike (1947a:159): "There must be something wrong with present-day phonemic theory if workers agree on the practical value of a procedure (and of evidence) in the field which they then rule out in theoretical discussion and in presentation."

By 1958, the inability of the post-Bloomfieldians to handle suprasegmentals had become so obvious that even their own followers had to acknowledge it openly. Archibald Hill admitted that

> until a few years ago, it was an assumption almost universal among linguists that a speaker, even without special training, would infallibly and automatically hear the contrasts in his own speech and that the only things he would not hear would be sounds which are not contrastive. Consequently, it would at that time have been necessary to say that any speaker who had trouble in hearing four grades of stress would be one who had only three contrasts. We have taken the position that there are

speakers who have four contrasts but who still have difficulty in hearing all the distinctions they make. Such difficulties occur not only in the system of stresses, but with other sounds as well. (Hill 1958:17–18)

There are a number of examples in the literature where their empiricist outlook forced the post-Bloomfieldians to adopt analyses that they themselves seemed to recognize were inelegant and uninsightful. Two examples of this sort involve Bernard Bloch. Bloch (1947) worked out detailed procedures for assigning morphs to morphemes. After disposing of the bulk of regular and irregular verbs in English, he noted the variant phonemic shapes of the word *have* in four pronunciations of the sentence *I have seen it:*

/ày hæv síyn it/
/ày v síyn it/
/ày həv síyn it/
/ày əv síyn it/

Since /hæv/, /v/, /həv/, and /əv/ are neither in complementary distribution nor in free variation (they differ in their "social flavor"), Bloch (1947) could not escape the conclusion that they belong to four separate morphemes. He wrote, "Reluctant as we may be to allow the multiplication of elements, we cannot escape the conclusion that the verb forms /həv/ and /əv/ belong to none of the morphemes mentioned so far" (p. 417).

An even better example can be found in Bloch's two phonological studies of Japanese (1946, 1950). The earlier paper gave an extremely elegant (though informal) description of the sound patterning of that language. But in 1950 he revised his analysis in the direction of complexity and lack of generalization. Why? Because earlier he had "confused phonemes with morphophonemes"; the earlier insightful analysis had violated biuniqueness. Hockett (1951) comments on this: "What is deceptively simple in [Bloch's] earlier treatment turns out to be quite complicated in the later—but the more complicated treatment is also obviously more accurate" (p. 341). Bloch and Hockett could not have been undisturbed by having to reject simple treatments for complicated but accurate ones.

By 1955, even Hockett had to agree reluctantly that one could not do an analysis of a language objectively—one had to empathize with the informant (Hockett 1955:147). But if that were the case, then what theoretical validity could operational procedures have which were designed to guarantee the correct description of a language?

Finally, in 1957, at least one observer noted a growing decline in dogmatism and confidence among practicing structural linguists:

In the intervening years [since the early 1940s], however, it seems to me that the attitudes and behavior-patterns of linguists have changed. Naturally the fervor of that generation has waned, but even among the younger linguists there seem to be a few [sic] who are either as chauvinistic, as passionate, or as confident that they have discovered the whole truth. . . . Dogmatism also appears to have declined, though, to be sure, it has not vanished (and presumably never will). (Householder 1957:156)

As events in that year were to prove, they had very little to be dogmatic or confident about.

Chapter 2

The Chomskyan Revolution

2.1. OVERVIEW

Early in 1957, Noam Chomsky's *Syntactic Structures* was released by Mouton Publishers in The Hague. This book, which introduced the theory of transformational generative grammar, did not share the fate of most first books by unknown authors distributed by obscure publishers. Within weeks, a review by Robert B. Lees appeared in *Language*. Lees, who enjoyed a modest reputation in the field, left no doubt that the book would change linguistics. Such praise for a new approach to the study of language and such derogation of the contemporary paradigm had never been seen before in the pages of that journal. Lees (1957) wrote that Chomsky's book was "one of the first serious attempts on the part of a linguist to construct within the tradition of scientific theory-construction a comprehensive theory of language which may be understood in the same sense that a chemical, biological theory is ordinarily understood by experts in those fields" (p. 377).

Actually, the tone of the review as a whole made it clear that Lees regarded it as the only serious attempt, and a completely successful one at that. And C. F. Voegelin (1958), in another review, noted that even if *Syntactic Structures* managed to accomplish only part of its goals, "it will have accomplished a Copernican revolution" (p. 229). The distinguished British linguist, C. E. Bazell, after one reading of the book, remarked to a student that "linguistics will never be the same" and immediately initiated a continuing correspondence with Chomsky.

By the mid 1960s, after the full implications of transformational generative grammar had become evident, counterattacks by the score were directed against this "theory spawned by a generation of vipers" (Charles Hockett, quoted in Mehta 1971:175). But the challenge to the new theory was not successful. In the mid and late 1960s, American universities underwent their greatest expansion in history.

17

New linguistics departments sprang up in a dozen locations, and some existing ones literally quadrupled in size. The reputation of Chomsky's theory had grown to the point where, by and large, its partisans were sought to fill the new positions. In fact, the growth of linguistics outpaced that of most other fields, a testament to the intellectual appeal of the theory.

Even as early as 1964, transformational generative grammar was being described as having "established itself as the reference point for discussion of linguistic theory" (Hymes 1964:25). An obvious indicator of the rapid success of the theory is that, by the late 1960s, its advocates had stopped replying to criticism from linguists in the post-Bloomfieldian structuralist tradition. They had no further need to answer the Old Guard. Chomsky and others turned their attention to assaults on the fundamentals of the theory by psychologists and philosophers. But the increased stature of cognitive psychology and rationalist philosophy within their respective disciplines in recent years points to the impact that generativist theory has had outside of linguistics proper and to the indifferent success of the psychological and philosophical critique. The 1970s also saw the unprecedented internationalization of a linguistic theory; by the 1980s transformational generative grammar had at least as many practitioners outside the United States as inside.

In the 1980s there has been an undeniable fragmentation of the once-monolithic theory. Many alternative models of linguistic description have been proposed, some heralded as making as much of a break from mainstream transformational grammar as this theory made from the varieties of structural linguistics that were practiced in 1957. But, by and large, the debate has taken place well within the general framework of theoretical assumptions first articulated in *Syntactic Structures*. A truly alternative conception of grammar with general credibility or widespread support has yet to emerge.

2.2. *SYNTACTIC STRUCTURES*

2.2.1. The Revolutionary Import of *Syntactic Structures*

What made *Syntactic Structures* revolutionary was its conception of a grammar as a theory of a language, subject to the same constraints on construction and evaluation as any theory in the natural sciences.[1] Prior to 1957, it was widely thought, not just in linguistics but throughout the humanities and social sciences, that a formal, yet nonempiricist, theory of a human attribute was impossible. Chomsky showed

---

[1]Many European structuralists, Saussure among them, have explicitly regarded themselves as doing "scientific" linguistics, though it is fairly clear that they have not seen themselves as paralleling natural scientists in their goals and methodology. For many, the term "scientific" seems to have meant little more than "objective" or "nonprescriptive." Consider for example, the following passage from Martinet: "Une étude est dite scientifique lorsqu'elle se fonde sur l'observation des faits et s'abstient de proposer un choix parmi ces faits au nom de certains principes esthétiques ou moraux. 'Scientifique' s'oppose donc à 'prescriptif' " (Martinet 1960:9).

that such a theory was possible. Indeed, he devotes the central chapter of *Syntactic Structures*, "On the Goals of Linguistic Theory," to demonstrating the parallels between linguistic theory, as he conceived it, and what uncontroversially would be taken to be scientific theories. Still, *Syntactic Structures* would not have made a revolution simply by presenting a novel theory of the nature of grammar. The book had revolutionary consequences because it was not merely an exercise in speculative philosophy of science. On the contrary, *Syntactic Structures* demonstrates the practical possibility of a nonempiricist theory of linguistic structure: half of the volume is devoted to the presentation and defense of a formal fragment of English grammar.

Chomsky's conception of a grammar as a theory of a language allowed him to derive the major insight of earlier theorizing about language: the *langue/parole* (later competence/performance) distinction. For Saussure, who conceived of linguistics as a branch of social psychology, the distinction was merely stipulated; surely, for him there was no necessary reason why *langue* should be "a well-defined object in the heterogeneous mass of speech facts" (Saussure 1959:14). One can easily imagine a social system of verbal exchange in which such a "well-defined object" is absent. For Chomsky, however, the distinction followed as a logical consequence of the assimilation of linguistics to the natural sciences. Just as physics seeks to specify precisely the class of physical processes and biology the class of biological processes, it follows that a task of linguistics is to provide "a precise specification of the class of formalized grammars" (Chomsky 1962a:534). Interestingly, Chomsky's empiricist antecendents in American structural linguistics, who were in principle incapable of postulating a sharp dichotomy on the basis of observationally graded data, were forced to negate the *langue–parole* distinction by regarding the former as no more than a set of habits deducible directly from speech behavior (Hockett 1952). Not surprisingly then, Hockett's major attempt to rebut Chomsky (1968) recognized that the question of whether the grammar of a language is a well-defined system was the central issue separating his view of language from Chomsky's.

The publication of *Syntactic Structures* represented a revolutionary event in the history of linguistics for a second reason: it placed syntactic relations at the center of *langue*. By focusing on syntax, Chomsky was able to lay the groundwork for an explanation of the most distinctive aspect of human language—its creativity. The revolutionary importance of the centrality of syntax cannot be overstated. Phonological and morphological systems are essentially closed finite ones; whatever their complexity or intrinsic interest, their study does not lead to an understanding of a speaker's capacity for linguistic novelty nor to an explanation of the infinitude of language. Yet earlier accounts had typically excluded syntax from *langue* altogether. For Saussure, most syntagmatic relations were consigned to *parole*, as they were for the linguists of the Prague School, who treated them from the point of view of "functional sentence perspective." Zellig Harris, it is true, had begun in the 1940s to undertake a formal analysis of intersentential syntactic relations, but his empiricist commitment to developing mechanical procedures for grammatical analysis led him to miss the implications that the study of these relations had for an understanding of linguistic creativity.

Chomsky attacked the empiricist conception of linguistic theory held by the post-Bloomfieldians for imposing a condition on theory formation that prevented the development of an insightful account of language, namely the condition that the description must be mechanically extractable from the primary data. But such a condition, Chomsky argued, is not to be found in any science. In his view, the most a linguistic theory can be expected to provide is an evaluation procedure for grammars—a mechanical way of deciding between alternative grammars within a particular theory. And, as Chomsky pointed out, even an evaluation procedure is more than most sciences would hope to accomplish: "There are few areas of science in which one would seriously consider the possibility of developing a general, practical, mechanical method for choosing among several theories, each compatible with the available data" (p. 53).

Given the abandonment of the aim of literally "discovering" a grammar, there need be no concern about a description that mixes levels. Since a grammar would no longer result from a cookbooklike set of directions that tells the linguist to "find the phonemes first," the rules and the inventory of phonemes, morphemes, and other components might be arrived at "by intuition, guesswork, all sorts of partial methodological hints, reliance on past experience, etc." (p. 56). In the resultant description, if syntactic information, say, entered into the statement of a phonological rule, there would be no cause for concern: the question of the interdependence of levels is to be answered by empirical investigation rather than by methodological fiat.

While Chomsky's conception of the nature of grammatical theory was a revolutionary one, there are, needless to say, numerous respects in which *Syntactic Structures* retains crucial conceptions of its historical antecedents. Foremost among them is Saussure's great insight that at the heart of language lies a structured interrelationship of elements characterizable as an autonomous system. Such an insight is the essence of "structuralism" and, since it is assumed throughout *Syntactic Structures* and Chomsky's subsequent work, one can, with good reason, refer to Chomsky as a "structuralist."[2] Some commentators have pointed to this fact in order to dismiss the idea that there could have been a Chomskyan revolution. Since structuralism was well established years before the publication of *Syntactic Structures,* by what criteria, such individuals ask, could it be correct to refer to a "Chomskyan" revolution? George Lakoff, for example, concluded from Chomsky's commitment to structural analysis that early transformational grammar, rather than representing a revolutionary development, "was a natural outgrowth of

[2]The structuralism issue is confused by the fact that in the early 1960s Chomsky and his followers began to reserve the label "structuralist" just for those synchronic approaches in the Saussurean tradition that did not share their views on theory construction. The result is that now within linguistics, when one speaks of a "structuralist," it is normally understood that one is referring to a pre-Chomskyan or an anti-Chomskyan. Interestingly, commentators from outside the field have always labeled Chomsky a "structuralist," and we find his ideas discussed in most overviews of twentieth century structuralism (see, for example, Lane 1970:28–29; De George and De George 1972:xx).

American structural linguistics'' (Lakoff 1971a:267–268). The same point has been made more recently by Stephen Murray, who finds ''the base of Chomsky's early work . . . in American structural linguistics, especially as developed by Zellig Harris'' (1980:76); by Dell Hymes and John Fought, who regard *Syntactic Structures* as showing ''no evidence of basic revolutionary change'' (1981:241); and by Konrad Koerner, who feels that ''TGG is basically post-Saussurean structuralism, characterized by excessive concern with 'langue' . . . to the detriment of 'parole' '' (Koerner 1983:152).

Chomsky's structuralism, however, no more disqualifies his theory from being revolutionary than does Einstein's Newton-like search for physical laws undermine the revolutionary nature of relativity theory. Saussure's victory was the victory of structuralism, just as Newton's victory was the victory of a lawful universe. We would no more expect the next revolution in linguistics to be an antistructuralist one than we would expect the next revolution in physics to return to divine intervention as an explanatory device. Chomsky's revolution was a revolution within structural linguistics, a revolution that profoundly altered our conceptions of the nature of linguistic structure and opened the way to an understanding of how its nature bears on the workings of the human mind.

When Charles Hockett wrote that ''Chomsky's outlook . . . is so radically different from Bloomfield's and from my own that there is, at present, no available frame of reference external to both within which they can be compared'' (Hockett 1966:156), one presumes that he was (correctly) ignoring the fact that the approaches of the three linguists share the property of ''structuralism.''

2.2.2. Simplicity and the Evaluation of Grammars

To say that a theory provides an evaluation procedure for grammars obviously invites the question: By what criteria are grammars to be evaluated? Clearly, the nature of a successful linguistic description had to be made explicit. Chomsky termed the criteria of evaluation ''external conditions of adequacy'' and in *Syntactic Structures* outlined four of them:

1. The sentences generated are acceptable to the native speaker.
2. Every case of a ''constructional homonymity'' (the assignment of more than one structural description to a sentence) describes a real ambiguity; every case of ambiguity is represented by constructional homonymity.
3. Differential interpretations of superficially similar sentences are represented by different derivational histories. (His example involved the sentences *the picture was painted by a new technique* and *the picture was painted by a real artist.*)
4. Sentences understood in similar ways are represented in similar ways at one level of description.

But it is not sufficient that a grammatical analysis in isolation meet the external conditions of adequacy. In addition, it is necessary to posit ''a CONDITION OF

GENERALITY on grammars; we require that the grammar of a given language be constructed in accord with a specific theory of linguistic structure in which such terms as 'phoneme' and 'phrase' are defined independently of any particular language'' (p. 50). The ''condition of generality'' (Chomsky used this term only once) corresponds to what were later called ''linguistic universals'' and comprises those theoretical terms, notational conventions, etc., that interact in such a way as to allow the external conditions of adequacy to be met in the most linguistically revealing way. For example, since a grammar without transformational rules presumably could not meet the external conditions, the condition on generality demands the incorporation of such rules into the descriptive apparatus of the theory. But what of a case where there appeared to be two grammars, each meeting the external conditions? Here the evaluation procedure alluded to above would come into play. Chomsky hoped the condition of generality might be formulable so that, given two alternative descriptions, the shorter one (as measured in terms of absolute length, number of symbols, or some such criterion) would always be the one of maximum generality as well.

2.2.3. Three Models of Linguistic Description

Chomsky had two major goals in *Syntactic Structures*. First, he had the general goal of motivating linguistic theory and its formalization by means of generative grammars that were subject to certain conditions of adequacy. But also, he had the more narrow goal of demonstrating that only a specific type of generative grammar had the ability to meet these conditions, namely a generative grammar embodying transformational as well as phrase structure rules. The former were inspired by, and are essentially generative reinterpretations of, the identically named rules proposed by his teacher Zellig Harris in his attempt to apply the methods of structural linguistics to the analysis of discourse.

Chomsky was in the peculiar position of having to argue against two generative grammatical models—finite state grammars and phrase structure grammars—which had very few outspoken adherents. He had to do this because these models were the closest generative interpretations of the views of language current in the 1950s. Finite state grammars bore a close resemblance to (or were identical to, as in the case of Hockett 1955) the type of device promoted by communications theorists. The sorts of descriptions which phrase structure grammars provided were (for all practical purposes) identical to those that resulted from the post-Bloomfieldians' procedures. So Chomsky's demonstration of the inadequacy of these two models in Chapters 3, 4, and 5 of *Syntactic Structures* was directed to—and was most convincing to—those linguists who might have been won over to his general goal of constructing a formal nonempiricist linguistic theory but still clung to the generative analogs of earlier views of language. Clearly, a linguist who rejected the need for generative rules, external conditions of adequacy, etc., would not have been terribly impressed by Chomsky's demonstration of the superiority of transformational grammar over phrase structure grammar.

Chomsky contrasted the three models in terms of their "weak generative capacity" and their "strong generative capacity," to use terms that appeared a few years later. The former refers to their string-generating ability, the latter to their ability to assign structural descriptions to these strings. Since a grammar unable to generate all and only the sentences of a language is of no further empirical interest, the demonstration of the defect of a model in terms of weak generative capacity makes any discussion of its strong capacity unnecessary. Chomsky proved that finite state grammars could not even weakly generate the sentences of English in an argument taking the following form:

First Premise: No finite state grammar is capable of generating a language containing an infinite set of strings with nested dependencies while simultaneously excluding the infinite set of strings that contradict these dependencies.

Second Premise: A subpart of English is a language as described in the First Premise.

Conclusion: All and only the sentences of English cannot be generated by a finite state grammar.

Chomsky proved the first premise in his 1956 paper, "Three Models for the Description of Language." The second depends crucially on the assumption that sentences of the form *if* _____ *then* _____, *either* _____ *or*, _____ etc., can be embedded in each other without limit. Although it is probably the case that the degree of nesting is quite restricted in actual speech, speakers (with paper and pencil) can normally interpret highly complex nested constructions such as the following one cited in Chomsky and Miller (1963) (a dependent relation holds between like-subscripted elements):

Anyone$_1$ who feels that if$_2$ so-many$_3$ more$_4$ students$_5$ whom we$_6$ haven't$_6$ actually admitted are$_5$ sitting in on the course than$_4$ ones we have that$_3$ the room had to be changed, then$_2$ probably auditors will have to be excluded, is$_1$ likely to agree that the curriculum needs revision. (p. 286).

Given that there is no principled limit to the nesting possibilities, it follows that English (and, by extension, language in general) cannot be described in finite state terms. There was no need for Chomsky even to mention the more serious defects of finite state grammars in terms of their strong generative capacity.

Chomsky did not question in *Syntactic Structures* that phrase structure grammars are capable of weakly generating the sentences of English.[3] He rather argued that

[3]Chomsky later (1959a) proved that the language consisting of all and only the strings [*XX*] is not a context-free language where *X* varies over an infinite set of strings in an alphabet of two or more symbols. Postal (1964b) then demonstrated that Mohawk, an Iroquoian language, contains, as a subpart, an infinite set of sentences with this property. While his proof demonstrated only that Mohawk sentences could not be weakly generated by a context-free phrase structure grammar, he also argued that a phrase structure grammar containing context-sensitive rules would require at least thirty-six million symbols.

The question of the context-freeness of natural language has become a major theoretical issue in recent years (see Section 8.3).

they can do so only in a cumbersome fashion and, furthermore, do not come close to assigning the correct structural descriptions to the sentences generated. His examples of the defects of phrase structure grammars were illustrated simultaneously with the demonstration that grammars containing the more powerful transformational rules can handle the same phenomena in an elegant and revealing manner. By far his most persuasive demonstration involved the English verbal auxiliary system. While Chomsky did not attempt to state the phrase structure rules that would be involved in generating all of the possible combinations of auxiliary verbs in English (and excluding the impossible ones), it was generally accepted at that time that such rules would have to be enormously complex. The *Syntactic Structures* analysis, however, treated the superficially discontinuous auxiliary morphemes *have . . . en* and *be . . . ing* as unit constituents generated by the phrase structure rules and posited a simple transformational rule to permute the affixal and verbal elements into their surface positions, thus predicting the basic distribution of auxiliaries in simple declarative sentences. Moreover, Chomsky was able to show that the permutation rule, "the Auxiliary transformation" (later called "Affix Hopping" by other linguists), interacts with rules forming simple negatives and simple yes-no questions to specify neatly the exact locations where "supportive" *do* appears. The ingenuity of this analysis probably did more to win supporters for Chomsky than all of his metatheoretical statements about discovery and evaluation procedures and immediately led to some linguists' proposing generative-transformational analyses of particular phenomena despite a lack of enthusiasm for the foundations of the theory itself (see, for example, Gleason 1961:171–194 and the suspiciously Chomskyan analysis in Joos 1964:53ff.).

Chomsky's motivation of the Passive transformation was analogous to that of the Auxiliary transformation. He argued that the contextual restrictions holding between the passive morpheme, the passive *by*-phrase, and the transitive verb would be extraordinarily difficult to state by means of phrase structure rules. However, one transformational rule permuting the subject and the object and adding the morphemes that are characteristic of the passive construction (*be . . . en* and *by*) eliminates the need for any of these special restrictions.

Chomsky's arguments for transformational rules in *Syntactic Structures* were all simplicity arguments, that is, arguments appealing to weak generative capacity. They all involved showing that a grammar with phrase structure rules alone required great complexity, a complexity that could be avoided only by the positing of a transformational rule. Chomsky felt that analyses motivated strictly in terms of simplicity would invariably turn out to be the optimal ones in terms of strong generative capacity as well. For example, Chomsky did not posit a transformational analysis of the auxiliary system because of the inability of phrase structure grammar to generate discontinuous morphemes as the unitary elements that they intuitively are. He based his analysis on formal simplicity alone, opting for a simple phrase structure rule and a simple transformational rule over a large number of cumbersome phrase structure rules. However, as he demonstrated, the generation of these morphemes as constituents turned out to be an important by-product of the analysis, which was motivated on purely formal grounds. Likewise, Chomsky was unwilling to point to the undeniable semantic correspondences between declaratives and inter- rogatives, affirmatives and negatives, actives and passives, etc., as evidence for setting up transformations relating them. He felt that to use such evidence would have led merely to a stipulation of the correspondences rather than to an explanation of them. Hence, the relevant transformations were motivated on the grounds of formal simplicity alone (for further discussion of this point see Section 2.2.4).

The transformational model of *Syntactic Structures* contained three levels: phrase structure, transformational structure, and morphophonemics. The rules of the phrase structure level generated a finite set of "underlying terminal strings," that is, strings with phrase structure interpretations. This set was finite because there were no recursive rules applying at the phrase structure level.[4] Most phrase structure rules were context free, such as Rule (2.1), which expands the Auxiliary node:

(2.1)   Aux → Tense (Modal) (*have* + *en*) (*be* + *en*)

However, it was necessary to posit context-sensitive phrase structure rules as well as to account for lexical subcategorization. The following rule (taken from Chomsky 1962b:138), which subcategorizes verbs with respect to their cooccur- rences within the verb phrase, is an example:

$$
(2.2)\ V \rightarrow \left\{ \begin{array}{l} \left\{ \begin{array}{l} V_s \\ become \end{array} \right\} \text{in env.} \underline{\hspace{2cm}} \text{Pred} \\ V_t \text{ in env.} \underline{\hspace{1cm}} \text{NP} \\ V_i \text{ in env.} \left\{ \begin{array}{l} \# \\ \text{Adv} \end{array} \right\} \end{array} \right\}
$$

Phrase structure rules (ordinarily context free) then introduce the lexical items themselves:

(2.3) V_s → *feel, seem, . . .*

Transformational rules then map these underlying terminal strings into other strings, each derived string being assigned a new constituent structure. Chomsky had no term for the output of the transformational rules more technical than "a string of words." Transformations were of two fundamentally distinct types: singu- lary (simple) and generalized (double-based). Singulary transformations, such as Passive, the Auxiliary transformation, and the Negative transformation, applied within the simple phrase markers generated by the branching rules. Generalized

---

[4]Strictly speaking, this is not correct. Chomsky (p. 73) envisaged handling some very marginal recursive processes, such as the unlimited successive appearances of the modifier *very*, by phrase structure rules. Technically, then, the output of this component is an infinite set of terminal strings in the *Syntactic Structures* model.

transformations embedded into each other or joined with each other these derived phrase markers without limit, thereby capturing the recursive property of human language. Similarly transformations could apply after embedding, as well as before.

Many have wondered why Chomsky did not, from the very beginning, handle recursion by the device of recursive phrase structure rules—an approach both conceptually simpler and more constrained, in that base recursion limits the class of possible grammars.[5] The reason is that the interaction of the singulary and generalized transformations was a complete mystery at the time. The more conservative approach chosen by Chomsky, that of positing embedding transformations, left open the possibility that singulary transformations might apply in a matrix clause before another sentence was embedded into it. Certainly there was no evidence that such might not be the case. A multiclausal base structure would have made this possibility difficult, if not impossible, to state formally. I discuss this problem in some detail in the next chapter.

Chomsky further argued that at least some transformations had to be extrinsically ordered with respect to each other in the grammar. For example, the transformation that assigned number to the verb based on the number of the subject had to be specified to follow the passive transformation to avoid *the boy* (singular) *sees the girls* (plural) from being mapped into **the girls* (plural) *is seen by the boy* (singular).

Chomsky also drew a distinction between obligatory and optional transformations. The former had to apply whenever their structural description was met. The Auxiliary transformation and the *Do* transformation (which inserted the morpheme *do* before a stranded tense affix) are examples. The class of optional transformations was quite large: negatives, *wh-* and yes-no questions, and imperatives were all formed by optional rules. Hence, the terminal string *you*-Pres-*will-light-the-fire* underlay all of *you will light the fire, light the fire, you will not light the fire, will you light the fire? what will you light? who will light the fire?* etc.

Those sentences derived only by the application of obligatory transformations had a special name: "kernel strings." The kernel of the language corresponded exactly to the set of simple (i.e., uniclausal) declarative affirmatives.

The derivation of a sentence was complete after the string of words was converted into a string of phonemes by the morphophonemic rules. Each derivation in the pre-1965 model was graphically represented by its unique transformation marker. Such markers consisted of the specification of the phrase markers associated with each underlying terminal string and those singulary and generalized transformations that applied in the derivation, in the order in which they applied.

2.2.4. Grammar and Meaning

Superficially, the relationship between syntax and semantics seems quite straightforward in *Syntactic Structures* and can be captured by the following quote: ''I think

---

[5]But see Bach (1977b) for a defense of the view that generalized transformations are in principle more constraining than base recursion.

that we are forced to conclude that grammar is autonomous and independent of meaning'' (p. 17). The independence of grammar and meaning is stressed so many times in that book that many commentators have assumed that Chomsky simply took over the position of Harris and Bloch, an assumption often going hand-in-hand with the implication that this demonstrates that he had not really broken completely from post-Bloomfieldian structuralism. But a careful reading of *Syntactic Structures* clearly falsifies this conclusion. First of all, the independence of grammar in no way followed from his methodology, as it did for the post-Bloomfieldians. Chomsky was clear that the question of the relation of grammar and meaning is an empirical one. He gave example after example to illustrate his position: Speakers have intuitions that cannot be expressed in semantic terms; neither phonemic distinctness nor morpheme identity is wholly semantic; notions like ''subject'' and ''object'' defy strict semantic characterization; etc. In fact, Chomsky used the apparent non-paraphrase relationship between sentences like *everyone in the room knows at least two languages* and *at least two languages are known by everyone in the room* as evidence that Passive (and transformations in general) cannot be defined strictly in terms of meaning. In other words, he was arguing that the assumption that syntax is semantically based is false and any theory built on this assumption must therefore be fundamentally deficient.

Second, an understanding of how Chomsky regarded the notion ''meaning'' at that time helps put many of his comments in a different light. While his theory of meaning was fairly eclectic (in footnote 10 on page 103 he seems to imply that much of meaning can be reduced to reference), he was then very much under the influence of the Oxford philosophers and their use theory of meaning. In fact, the words ''meaning'' and ''use'' are used almost interchangeably throughout *Syntactic Structures:*

> There is no aspect of linguistic study more subject to confusion and more in need of clear and careful formulation than that which deals with the points of connection between syntax and semantics. The real question that should be asked is: ''How are the syntactic devices available in a given language put to work in the actual use of this language?'' (p. 93)

In other words, many of Chomsky's arguments in *Syntactic Structures* for the autonomy of syntax were in reality arguments for (what he would call a few years later) the competence–performance dichotomy. Many aspects of meaning, in his view at the time, were part of performance.

Third, he regarded as theoretically significant a number of systematic connections between syntax and semantics. For example, he pointed out that the popular view that syntax is semantically-based, though empirically false, does contain a considerable element of truth. Yet, he went on to say, there is no possibility of explaining the considerable fit between syntax and semantics if one takes a semantically-based syntax as a starting point. He noted other systematic connections, as in the following passage in which deep structure interpretation was foreshadowed (note again the ''performance'' terminology): ''The general problem of analyzing the process of 'understanding' is thus reduced, in a sense, to the problem of explaining how kernel sentences are understood, these being considered the basic 'content elements' from which the usual, more complex sentences of real life are formed by transformational development'' (p. 92). Likewise, later claims about the relationship of T-rules and meaning were foreshadowed in statements like ''we find, however, that the transformations are, by and large, meaning-preserving'' (p. 123), a fact that would have never come to light if transformations ''had been investigated exclusively in terms of such notions as synonymity'' (p. 101).

Finally and most importantly, Chomsky proposed that grammars be evaluated on the basis of their ability to lead to insights about the meanings of sentences:

> We can judge formal theories in terms of their ability to explain and clarify a variety of facts about the way in which sentences are used and understood. In other words, we should like the syntactic framework of the language that is isolated and exhibited by the grammar to be able to support semantic description, and we shall naturally rate more highly a theory of formal structure that leads to grammars that meet this requirement more fully. (p. 102)

Recall that two of the external conditions of adequacy to be imposed on grammars were their ability to handle ambiguity and paraphrase—semantic notions par excellence. Chomsky was completely explicit about the direct syntactic capturing of ambiguity:

> If the grammar of a language is to provide insight into the way the language is understood, it must be true, in particular, that if a sentence is ambiguous (understood in more than one way), then this sentence is provided with alternative analyses by the grammar. In other words, if a certain sentence S is ambiguous, we can test the adequacy of a given linguistic theory by asking whether or not the simplest grammar constructible in terms of this theory for the language in question automatically provides distinct ways of generating the sentence S. (p. 123)

This quotation shows clearly that Chomsky felt that analyses motivated on purely formal grounds would have the property of capturing semantic ambiguity directly. We see in later chapters of this volume how the discovery that many T-rules motivated in this way do not have this property was to lead to radically different analyses of the same phenomena.

2.3. NOAM CHOMSKY

The Chomskyan revolution in linguistics was very much a revolution from the inside. Chomsky was immersed from childhood in an environment where language and its scientific study were constant topics of discussion. He was born in Philadelphia on December 7, 1928, and through his father, William, a noted Hebrew philologist, he developed an interest in language structure. At the age of 10, he was reading the proofs of his father's *David Kimhi's Hebrew Grammar*. Chomsky attributes his early interest in explaining linguistic phenomena, as opposed to simply describing them, to his childhood exposure to historical linguistics. In a period when leading theorists tended to look upon the desire for explanation as a sort of infantile aberration,[6] historians of language like his father, either ignorant of or

---

[6]In the words of the post-Bloomfieldian Martin Joos, ''Children want explanations, and there is a child in each of us; descriptivism makes a virtue of not pampering that child'' (Joos 1958:96).

indifferent to the contemporary "scientific" wisdom in the field, clung to a nine-teenth-century desire to explain why a particular distribution of forms existed at a particular point in time.

As an undergraduate at the University of Pennsylvania, Chomsky's main interest was Middle East politics. In fact, he had considered leaving his studies entirely "to live on a Kibbutz and work for Arab-Jewish cooperation" (quoted in Mehta 1971:186). In an effort to discourage him from going to Palestine, his parents introduced him to Zellig Harris, who taught at Pennsylvania and shared Chomsky's views on Zionism—and was able to function as a productive scholar at the same time. The ploy worked. Harris immediately took the 18-year-old Chomsky under his wing and gave him the proofs of his *Methods in Structural Linguistics* to examine—before Chomsky had even taken his first linguistics class! As he later remarked, "That's how I learned linguistics, by proofreading Harris' book—which was fine for me, I really learned the field" (Sklar 1968:215).

At Harris's suggestion, Chomsky began to work on a grammar of Hebrew. The combination of his thorough understanding of historical process, the striking un-suitability of the Hebrew language to description in post-Bloomfieldian terms, and the intangible factor of his own genius made him realize almost immediately that a revealing account of that language in terms of a taxonomic inventory of elements was hopeless:

> I started right off, without even asking any questions, working within the framework of generative grammar, which seemed to be the only conceivable thing, namely, trying to find a system of rules which would enable you to characterize all of the sentence structures of the language. I very quickly discovered that if you wanted to do this properly you had to have a long sequence of ordered rules. I also noticed right off that the logical order corresponded to some extent to the historical order which I knew of. I found that if you gave it the right kind of logical order then you could explain a lot of phenomena which otherwise seemed very inexplicable. I worked on this for a couple of years in really total isolation. (quoted in Sklar 1968:214)

"Total isolation" is no exaggeration. While Chomsky's Hebrew work developed into his 1949 undergraduate thesis and his 1951 M.A. thesis, "Morphophonemics of Modern Hebrew," there is no evidence that Harris, who "didn't pay any atten-tion to what anybody else was doing in linguistics or in anything else" (Chomsky, quoted in Mehta 1971:187), took it at all seriously. With the exception of Henry Hoenigswald, few linguists were then even willing to call what Chomsky was doing "linguistics," a feeling which reinforced the lingering doubts in his own mind about the fruitfulness of his approach.

Thanks to the impression he made upon the philosopher Nelson Goodman, with whom he took philosophy courses as an M.A. student at Pennsylvania, Chomsky won a prestigious Junior Fellowship in the Society of Fellows at Harvard, where he worked from 1951 to 1955. Ironically, his project was to improve the techniques of structural linguistics; he even published one paper with this goal in mind (Chomsky 1953). But, little by little, his work in generative grammar became his central focus. Two individuals, the philosopher Yehoshua Bar-Hillel and the linguist Morris Hal-le, stand out above all others in their encouragement of Chomsky to pursue his ideas along these lines. It was Bar-Hillel who convinced him to put aside all hestitations

and postulate (as his intuitions had already told him was correct) something very
much like the reconstructed historical forms at the abstract morphophonemic level.
And it was Halle, whom Chomsky met in the fall of 1951, who, as a result of their
constant discussions, was the most decisive factor in causing him to abandon any
hope of a procedural approach to linguistic analysis. Here is Chomsky's own
account of his moment of truth:

> By 1953, I came to the same conclusion [as Halle]: if the discovery procedures did not work, it was
> not because I had failed to formulate them correctly but because the entire approach was wrong. In
> retrospect I cannot understand why it took me so long to reach this conclusion—I remember exactly
> the moment when I finally felt convinced. On board ship in mid-Atlantic, aided by a bout of
> seasickness, on a rickety tub that was listing noticeably—it had been sunk by the Germans and was
> now making its first voyage after having been salvaged. It suddenly seemed that there was a good
> reason—the obvious reason—why several years of intense effort devoted to improving discovery
> procedures had come to naught, while the work I had been doing during the same period on generative
> grammars and explanatory theory, in almost complete isolation, seemed to be consistently yielding
> interesting results. (1979:131)

With post-Bloomfieldian structural linguistics now permanently in his past,
Chomsky began writing *The Logical Structure of Linguistic Theory* (*LSLT*), his
exposition of the goals, assumptions, and methodology of transformational generative grammar (one chapter of which earned him his Ph.D from Pennsylvania). A
truly incredible work of the highest degree of creativity, *LSLT* completely shattered
all contemporary conceptions of linguistic theory. This 900-page volume contains
the initial proposals for the formalization and evaluation of grammars that would
underlie all subsequent generative research. But the American linguistic community
in 1955 was not impressed. *LSLT*'s rejection by MIT Press (the only publisher
whom Chomsky felt might take the work seriously) came practically by return mail.
Likewise, in the next two years his dissertation and an article on simplicity and
explanation submitted to *Word* were turned down almost as rapidly. Since the only
job offer he could muster at the end of the tenure of his fellowship was to teach
Hebrew at Brandeis at a salary of $3500, he decided to stay at Harvard for another
year.

But fortunately for Chomsky, Halle was teaching at MIT and was able to arrange
for him to be hired in the Modern Language Department, with a joint appointment
in the Research Laboratory of Electronics. (His responsibilities at first included
teaching scientific French and German and some undergraduate linguistics, philosophy, and logic courses.) But he was able to find time to write up the notes to his
introductory linguistics course, which Halle encouraged him to submit to Mouton
Publishers (Mouton had just published Jakobson and Halle's *Fundamentals of Language*). By May of 1957, *Syntactic Structures* was off the presses.

As a result of Lees's review, Chomsky began to receive invitation after invitation
to present his ideas, the most important of which was to the 1958 Third Texas
Conference on Problems of Linguistic Analysis of English (see Chomsky 1962b).
Here he scored his first important coup: he succeeded in winning over the prominent
young structuralist Robert Stockwell, who soon became a vigorous campaigner for

the new model. While the other papers at this conference are not memorable and the content of Chomsky's is little more than an elaboration of some points in *Syntactic Structures,* the proceedings of the conference (Hill 1962) are nevertheless wonderful reading. The reason is that they faithfully transcribe the discussion sessions at the end of each paper. Here we can see linguistic history documented as nowhere else: Chomsky, the enfant terrible, taking on some of the giants of the field and making them look like rather confused students in a beginning linguistics course. The Chomskyan Revolution was now in full motion. I chart its progress in Section 2.5.

2.4. GENERATIVE PHONOLOGY

2.4.1. The Prague School

One structuralist school of language, the Prague School, had such an important influence on generative grammar that it seems appropriate to discuss it in this chapter. Broadly, the name describes the circle of scholars active in Prague and Vienna in the 1920s and 1930s. One leading member, Prince N. S. Trubetskoi, contributed *Grundzüge der Phonologie* (1939), the basic Prague School statement of phonology, the area in which it had the greatest impact on modern linguistic theory. Prague School phonology was brought to the United States in the 1940s and further elaborated by Trubetskoi's colleague Roman Jakobson.

The Prague School phonologists shared with their American counterparts the fundamental assumption of pre-Chomskyan structuralism that a linguistic description consists of an inventory of elements meeting the condition of biuniqueness. But in crucial respects, their theoretical outlook was diametrically opposed to that of the post-Bloomfieldians. Most importantly, they made it perfectly clear that their overall goal was explanation rather than taxonomy. Their requirement of biuniqueness, then, which guaranteed that a description would be a taxonomy, was regarded as an empirical hypothesis rather than (as it was to the Americans) an a priori assumption. For this reason they were not obsessed with developing the "correct" set of operational procedures by which an analysis might be obtained.[7] Furthermore, since they had no hesitation about imputing psychological reality to their linguistic descriptions, native-speaker judgments were not ruled out as admissible evidence. This enabled them to develop phonetic theory to a rather sophisticated degree. While the Bloomfieldians had always been suspicious of phonetics, given its essentially impressionistic basis, the Pragueans, not shrinking from impressionistic data, were able to make important cross-language generalizations about phonetic universals. Jakobson insightfully incorporated these results in the first major theoretical study

---

[7]On the other hand, the attraction of most of the leading Prague School members to phenomenology made them suspicious of formalism and dubious that the goals and methods of linguistic theory could be identified with those of the natural sciences.

of language acquisition, his remarkable *Kindersprache, Aphasie, und allgemeine Lautgesetze* (1941).

For Jakobson and other members of the Prague School, the phoneme was not simply a notational device but, rather, a complex phonological unit consisting of a set of distinctive features. This concept of the phoneme represented an important advance for several reasons. First, because it turned out that the phonemic systems of every language in the world are characterizable in terms of a small number of binary feature oppositions. Second, because features allow the formulation of generalizations impossible to state in other structuralist models. For example, the assimilation of nasals to following stops in English could be described by positing an abstract nasal "archiphoneme" before stops and a general rule which then filled in the redundant features. Third, features make possible the development of a mechanical evaluation procedure: since redundant features could be left unspecified in the basic feature matrix (which would be filled in by rules), the most highly valued analysis would be regarded as the one with the minimal number of feature specifications per phoneme.

A great amount of work took place in the 1950s to characterize precisely those features relevant for description of all human languages. The results were reported in two important books: Jakobson, Fant, and Halle's *Preliminaries to Speech Analysis* (1952) and Jakobson and Halle's *Fundamentals of Language* (1956). The universal inventory was reduced to 12 binary distinctive features, some defined in absolute acousitc terms (e.g., vocalic versus nonvocalic) and some in relative acoustic terms (e.g., grave versus acute).

From the above discussion it should be clear to anyone with the slightest familiarity with generative phonology how great a debt is owed to the Prague School phonologists. Roman Jakobson probably exerted a greater influence on transformational grammar than any other linguist. However, he himself was never to embrace without fundamental reservations the generativist view of linguistic theory. This was left to his student, Morris Halle, who began his collaboration with Chomsky in 1953. Together they developed the theory of generative phonology within a comprehensive theory of human language.

2.4.2. Morris Halle

Even before his collaboration with Chomsky began, Halle had built a reputation for himself in linguistics. The publication of *Preliminaries to Speech Analysis* (the research for which was carried out at the Acoustics Laboratory at MIT) made Halle a public figure in the field. Halle, who was born and educated in Latvia, emigrated to the United States in 1940. He studied engineering at the City College of New York before being drafted in 1943. After the war, he received a degree in linguistics from the University of Chicago. At the urging of Giuliano Bonfante (who was then at Chicago) he went to Columbia University to study with Roman Jakobson in 1948 and followed Jakobson to Harvard a year later. His Harvard Ph.D., which he received in 1955, was awarded on the basis of his dissertation "The Russian Consonants: A Phonemic and Acoustical Study." In somewhat revised form, this later appeared as the second half of *The Sound Pattern of Russian* (1959).

Halle had worked on the MIT Research Laboratory of Electronics acoustics project while a student, and he was hired by that university's Modern Language Department (to teach German and Russian) in 1951. In addition to his scholarly activities, he was instrumental in initiating the Ph.D. program in linguistics at MIT, which he supervised from 1960 until he stepped down in 1977.

Halle combines in a rare fashion the qualities of productive scholar and organizer-administrator. While transformational generative grammar would no doubt have succeeded had he lacked one of these two attributes, it does not seem too farfetched to say that its history would have been very different had he lacked both.

2.4.3. Early Generative Phonology

Generative phonology, in essence, synthesized three contemporary trends in linguistics. First, it incorporated the unformalized insights about phonological processes that characterized the work of Edward Sapir and his students. Second, it drew from the post-Bloomfieldians the practice of explicit formalization of all rules. And, finally, it owed to the Prague School the overall explanatory goals of phonological theory as well as some specific insights (e.g., distinctive features).

Chomsky and Halle teamed with Fred Lukoff in 1956 to publish the first generative phonological analysis, "On Accent and Juncture in English." This paper, which proposed a retreatment of English suprasegmentals, hit the post-Bloomfieldians where they were weakest. In place of the four degrees of phonemic stress that previous treatments hypothesized, they were able to predict the full range of phonetic stress possibilities with only a simple phonemic accented–unaccented distinction. They achieved this economy by assuming a set of ordered rules sensitive to underlying junctures placed at certain morpheme boundaries. Since their analysis resulted in a nonbiunique relation between phonemics and phonetics and violated the prohibition against mixing levels, it was incompatible with post-Bloomfieldian methodology. But, they argued, four important benefits resulted from abandoning these methodological constraints: the constituent organization imposed to state the stress rules most simply coincided with that required for other levels of description; the binary phonemic feature of accent made special suprasegmental phonemes unnecessary; the simplicity and symmetry of the rules proposed contrasted markedly with the inelegant earlier account; and the rules predicted how native speakers could assign stress patterns to new utterances in a consistent and uniform manner.

The first major work of generative phonology was Halle's *The Sound Pattern of Russian* (1959). While his specific rules for Russian would be modified many times, the book is remembered primarily for its argument against the structuralist concept of the phoneme. This argument not only was regarded as the most compelling one for generative phonology at the time, but even reappeared in its broad

TABLE 2.1

Gloss	A	B	C
was he getting wet	{m′ok 1,i}	/m′ok 1,i/	[m′ok 1,i]
were he getting wet	{m′ok bi}	/m′og bi/	[m′og bɨ]
should one burn	{ž′eč 1,i}	/ž′eč 1,i/	[ž′eč 1,i]
were one to burn	{ž′eč bi}	/ž′eč bi/	[ž′eǯ bɨ]

structural outline 10 years later to be used against the level of syntactic deep structure (see Section 4.3.1). Hence, it is worth paraphrasing:

> Consider the phonetic representations (C in Table 2.1) and the morphophonemic representations (A in Table 2.1) of four Russian phrases. Since there are instances where the velar stops ([k] and [g]) are in contrast, the relationship between A and C violates biuniqueness. Structuralists would therefore have to set up an intermediate phonemic level (B) to insure a biunique relation holding between all levels of description. On the other hand, [č] and [ǯ] never contrast, and in structuralist grammar would have to be identical at phonemic level B. But consider the consequences of this. A grammar with level B has no choice but to break down the generalization that obstruents are voiced before voiced obstruents into two distinct statements: once as a morphophonemic (A to B) rule applying to {k}; once as an allophonic (B to C) rule applying to /č/. Only by abandoning biuniqueness, and with it level B, can we capture this generalization by one unitary rule statement.

In Chomsky and Halle (1960), the analysis of English stress was simplified still further. By incorporating syntactic categorical information into the stress rules, they were able to dispense with underlying phonemic accent entirely and, at the same time, eliminate the phonemic /ɨ/ required in the 1956 paper. That year also saw the publication of Stockwell (1960), the first attempt to incorporate pitch into a generative description.

The major theoretical discussion of generative phonology prior to Chomsky and Halle's *The Sound Pattern of English* (1968) was Halle's "Phonology in Generative Grammar" (1962). Halle gave the first clear statement of the economy gained by formulating phonological rules in terms of distinctive features rather than in terms of indivisible phonemes. He pointed out that in the latter approach, despite the fact that Rule (2.4) represents a natural phonological process and (2.5) an unnatural one, the two rules would be equally complex:

$$(2.4) \quad /a/ \rightarrow /æ/ \text{ in the env. } — \left\{ \begin{array}{c} /i/ \\ /e/ \\ /æ/ \end{array} \right\}$$

$$(2.5) \quad /a/ \rightarrow /æ/ \text{ in the env. } — \left\{ \begin{array}{c} /i/ \\ /p/ \\ /z/ \end{array} \right\}$$

But under an analysis in which rules are stated in terms of features, Rule (2.4) would be vastly simpler to state than Rule (2.5)—a clear demonstration of how feature theory can provide a definition of the intuitive notions "natural class" and "natural phonological process." He further argued (using an example based on Sanskrit vowel sandhi) that the ordering of rule statements would, at one and the same time, lead to both a minimization of feature specifications and an analysis that intuitively was the most insightful as well. While this was by no means the first example given of phonological rule ordering, it was the first concrete illustration of the theoretical interrelatedness of this concept with that of distinctive features and the simplicity criterion for evaluating alternative analyses.

Halle broke ground in three other important areas in this article. First, he explained how differences between dialects could be explained by hypothesizing that they contain the same set of rules applying in different orders. Second, he gave a broad overview of how generative phonology was suited to the description of language change. He suggested that rule addition characteristically takes place at the end of the grammar (or at the end of natural subdivisions in it). Hence, it is no accident that the synchronic order of rules characteristically mirrors their relative chronology, a point first observed by Bloomfield (1939b) in his study of Menomini. He went on to give what he claimed was an example of a case (from the history of English) where two phonemes that had merged later reappeared, the reemerging phonemes corresponding exactly to their historical antecendents. Since such a phenomenon would be utterly inexplicable under an account of phonology that assumed biuniqueness, Halle's example pointed to the need for an abstract level of representation not simply extractable from the superficial phonetic data.

Finally, Halle (1962) gave the first theoretical explanation of the diminished language learning ability of the adult:

> I propose to explain this as being due to deterioration or loss in the adult of the ability to construct optimal (simplest) grammars on the basis of a restricted corpus of examples. The language of the adult—and hence also the grammar that he has internalized—need not, however, remain static: it can and does, in fact, change. I conjecture that changes in later life are restricted to the addition of a few rules in the grammar and that the elimination of rules and hence a wholesale restructuring of his grammar is beyond the capabilities of the average adult. (p. 64)

While few of Halle's specific theoretical claims stand unaltered today, except in the most general terms, the importance of "Phonology in Generative Grammar" should not be underestimated. This article was the closest thing to a "*Syntactic Structures* of phonology"—the basic theoretical statement that would direct research in this area of linguistics for years.

2.5. WINNING THE REVOLUTION

2.5.1. Robert B. Lees

Any discussion of the revolutionary period of transformational generative grammar must begin with a portrait of Robert B. Lees. I have already noted the impact of his review of *Syntactic Structures*. But the debt that linguistic theory owes him far exceeds that one piece of writing. Lees's book *The Grammar of English Nomi-*

nalizations (1960) (see Section 3.2.1) was to linguistic analysis what *Syntactic Structures* was to linguistic theory. It meant that the opponents of the theory had the burden of responding to (and finding alternatives to) highly detailed analyses of many central syntactic phenomena in English. But most importantly of all, Lees was a campaigner. At every conference, at every forum, there was Lees—to champion the generative view of language in as articulate and methodical a manner as is humanly imaginable. Nobody who was around linguistics in the late 1950s and early 1960s can talk about that period without recalling Lees's colorful style and unyielding determination to win victories for the new theory, and without recalling how moved they were by his charismatic presence—whichever position in factional debate they held then or hold now.

Lees's undergraduate studies in chemical engineering were interrupted by World War II (in which he was trained as a meteorologist). The four postwar years in which he worked at the Argonne National Laboratories were influential to his future linguistic research. He was involved in a project whose goal was to develop a methodology for counting carbon isotopes—the same project that led to Willard Libby's discovery of carbon-14 dating. As a voracious reader in linguistics in his spare time, Lees was led to see in Morris Swadesh's observations about lexical loss in Salish a process which could be described by a familiar first-order rate-equation; as a result he worked out the mathematical equations involved in glottochronology (Lees 1953). While Lees soon saw the limitations of the method, the fame he gained through his work in glottochronology was indispensible in giving him the credibility he needed as "Chomsky's Huxley" several years later.

Disenchanted with chemistry, Lees entered the University of Chicago Linguistics Department in 1947; he received his M.A. in 1950. After editing a book on English for Turkish speakers and working at several other jobs, Lees in 1956 accepted Victor Yngve's invitation to come to MIT to work on his machine translation project. While the project held little interest for him (in fact, Yngve fired him in short order), it was there he began his collaboration with Chomsky, whose views he began to champion and develop creatively in his own right. *The Grammar of English Nominalizations* earned him his MIT Ph.D. in 1959 in the Department of Electrical Engineering (there was no Linguistics Department there at the time). After a brief stint at IBM, he accepted a position at the University of Illinois, where he built one of the leading linguistics programs in the United States. Since 1969, he has taught at Tel Aviv University, where he has also built a successful program.

2.5.2. The Ascendancy of Transformational Generative Grammar

The established leaders of American structuralism recognized from the outset that Chomsky's theory represented a profound challenge to contemporary ideas about how to carry on linguistic research. And they recognized as well that the essence of the challenge lay in Chomsky's ideas about how language might be studied scientifically. Charles Hockett, for example, in his presidential address to the Linguistic

Society of America in 1964 (published as Hockett 1965), went so far as to characterize the publication of *Syntactic Structures* as one of "only four major breakthroughs" in the history of modern linguistics (Hockett 1965:185). In Hockett's words:

> Between Sir William [Jones's] address and the present Thirty-Ninth Annual Meeting of the Linguistic Society of America there is a span of 178 years. Half of 178 is 89, a prime number. If we add that to 1786 [the date of Jones's address] we reach the year 1875, in which appeared Karl Verner's 'Eine Ausnahme der ersten Lautverschiebung'. Thereafter, two successive steps of 41 years each . . . bring us to the posthumous publication of Ferdinand de Saussure's *Cours de linguistique générale* and then to Noam Chomsky's *Syntactic Structures*.
>
> I have allowed myself this bit of numerology because I know none of you will take it seriously. But behind this persiflage there is a sober intent. Our fraternity has accomplished a great deal in the short span of 178 years; yet, in my opinion, there have been only four major breakthroughs. All else that we have done relates to these four in one way or another. (p. 185)

Hockett recognized that the major breakthrough of *Syntactic Structures* was its abandonment of empiricist constraints on theory formation and evaluation, which, as he noted, involved distinguishing between discovery and evaluation procedures and between practical description and formal theory and required setting the formal requirements that a theory must meet. Hockett referred the various components of nonempiricist theory collectively as the "accountability hypothesis" and wrote "that it is a breakthrough I am certain" (p. 196). Later in his address he confessed:

> I know how I would have reacted to [the abrasive style of the Junggrammatiker], because I know my reaction to the similar tone of Robert B. Lees's review, which appeared in 1957, of Chomsky's *Syntactic Structures*, and of the introductory remarks in his *Grammar of English Nominalizations*, published in 1960. We do not enjoy being told that we are fools. We can shrug off an imprecation from a religious fanatic, because it does not particularly worry us that every such nut is sure he holds the only key to salvation. But when a respected colleague holds our cherished opinions up to ridicule, there is always the sneaking suspicion that he may be right. (p. 187)

Similarly, while Martin Joos recognized the "structuralist" core of generative grammar, he also recognized that it differed from other structuralist approaches in a fundamental way. Hence, he identified Chomsky's theory as a "heresy within the neo-Saussurean tradition rather than as a competitor to it" (Joos 1961:17). Why was it heretical? Because it

> ignores . . . something which has been either taken for granted or circumvented for many years . . . this is the neo-Saussurean axiom which we may try to state in these words: 'Text signals its own structure.' From this tacit assumption there follows automatically the most troublesome rule of neo-Bloomfieldian methodology: the rule demanding 'separation of levels'. . . . But [the generativist] leaders are able to point out that NO OTHER SCIENCE HAS A PARALLEL RULE. (17–18, emphasis added)

In short, Joos recognized that the rejection of empiricist constraints on theory formation was at the heart of the Chomskyan movement and that Chomsky's thrust was to bring linguistics into accord with the natural sciences.

The post-Bloomfieldian establishment not only recognized the importance of Chomsky's theory, but concretely abetted it in a number of ways. For example, Archibald A. Hill provided Chomsky with an important forum at the Third Texas

Conference alluded to in Section 2.3. While many feel that Hill's primary intent in inviting Chomsky was to exorcise the demon of generative grammar, the theory nevertheless benefited immensely from the exposure the conference provided.

Bernard Bloch, arguably the most influential post-Bloomfieldian in the mid 1950s, went out of his way to help Chomsky. While Bloch never publicly endorsed the new theory, he did confide to at least two colleagues, "Chomsky really seems to be on the right track. If I were younger, I'd be on his bandwagon too."[8] Bloch's actions certainly bear out the attitude expressed in this quotation. As editor of *Language,* he unhesitatingly published the crucial Lees review of *Syntactic Structures.* And several years later, in an unprecedented action, he inserted an editorial comment in a published review in that journal. The review was Paul Postal's (1966) uncompromising attack on R. M. W. Dixon's *Linguistic Science and Logic* (1963a), a book filled with polemics against generative grammar. Bloch's comment added insult to injury by bolstering Postal's case against Dixon.[9] Bloch also was responsible for placing *The Morphophonemics of Modern Hebrew* and *The Logical Structure of Linguistic Theory* in the Yale University linguistics library as early as 1958.

To digress for a moment: Chomsky's ease at gaining a hearing has been preferred as an argument that instead of a genuine "Chomskyan revolution," the field saw only a power grab by him and his supporters in the mid 1960s. Stephen Murray (1980), for example, questions whether Bloch and other prominent structuralists would have accorded Chomsky easy access to the public organs of the field if they had seen his ideas as an intellectual threat to post-Bloomfieldianism or had regarded him as likely to form a sociological pole of attraction. Murray's case is built implicitly on the idea that no rational individual would willingly help to undermine his or her own dominant position; hence the field's leaders (being rational) must have viewed Chomsky's ideas as quite congenial to their own.

It is difficult to ascertain whether reasoning such as Murray's has its roots in anything other than a thoroughly dismal view of human nature, but I suspect that it might be attributable to a misreading of those passages in Kuhn (1970) that take on the question of the transition of power from one paradigm to the next. In his discussion of this question, Kuhn points out that it is very often the case that older workers in a scientific field do not accept revolutionary developments, and to support this idea he cites examples of the nonadoption of the theories of Newton, Priestly, Kelvin, and others by the establishment in their respective fields. But Kuhn never implies that the Old Guard attempt to suppress revolutionary new ideas, nor do they even fail to encourage such ideas (however much they may disagree with them). It is easy to fall prey to the romantic (and pessimistic) idea that in order to win a voice, a young innovator in a field must struggle heroically against the obstructionist establishment. But such a scenario does not correspond to reality,

---

[8]Personal communication, Donald Foss and Sol Saporta.
[9]Dixon was later to become a productive contributor to generative grammar (see, for example, Dixon 1970, 1972, 1977).

either within linguistics or within science in general. And Kuhn's point about establishment figures not adopting new theories themselves is borne out completely by the Chomskyan revolution. With the exception of Sol Saporta and Robert Stockwell, both of whom were quite young at the time, and only a very few others, the leading structural linguists of the late 1950s did not become generative grammarians.

Interestingly, most of the very earliest published attacks on the theory were by non-Americans (see Reichling 1961; Uhlenbeck 1963; Dixon 1963a, 1963b, 1964; Winter 1965; and the responses in Chomsky 1966b). This fact should not seem surprising: while Chomsky shared with the post-Bloomfieldians the commitment to building a formal scientific theory of language (albeit their conceptions of "science" differed drastically), many Europeans have traditionally taken the position that language, as a human institution, is not amenable to scientific study. Hence they saw in generative grammar a further move away from their humanistic concerns.

By the mid 1960s, however, the post-Bloomfieldians, as well as the Europeans, had joined in the polemical assault against generative grammar. There are several reasons why their hostile reaction to the new theory was delayed by half a decade. Most importantly, they were appalled by the openly rationalist underlying assumptions of Chomsky's *Aspects of the Theory of Syntax,* published in 1965 but presented in public lectures for several years prior to that date. Chapter One of this book, which points to Cartesian rationalism as an intellectual antecedent of generative grammar, so repelled Hockett that he felt compelled to revise the preface of his book *Language, Mathematics, and Linguistics* for the express purpose of condemning it. Hockett (1966) wrote: "This chapter is a *reductio ad incredible* of the mistakes we have been making in linguistics for the last thirty or forty years; my study of it, after the present essay was completed, was responsible for the radical change of view reported in this Preface" (p. 8). By 1971, Hockett had come to regard studies within the framework of generative grammar as "as worthless as horoscopes" (quoted in Mehta 1971:218).

Another reason that the post-Bloomfieldian rebuttal was delayed comes from the fact that the generativists turned their full attention to phonology only several years after the publication of *Syntactic Structures.* Since the post-Bloomfieldians never had much to say about syntax, they felt no immediate threat from a new approach to that aspect of grammar. But they reacted with horror to Halle's and Chomsky's assaults on their approach to phonology. Indeed, the debate over generative phonology continued to rage long after transformational syntax had won a significant degree of acceptance (see Chomsky 1964a; Chomsky and Halle's 1965 reply to Householder; and Postal's 1968 reply to Lamb). As Archibald Hill put it, "I could stay with the transformationalists pretty well, until they attacked my darling, the phoneme" (Hill 1980:75).

To a certain extent, the generativist leaders provoked the attack from the post-Bloomfieldians in the mid 1960s. While the latter frequently showed signs of genuine willingness to compromise, Chomsky and Halle felt that intellectual principles were at stake—principles that admitted no compromise. As a consequence, the post-Bloomfieldians had become so antagonized by that time that they felt they had no alternative but to launch a frontal assault on the new theory. Their antagonism was increased by the behavior of the partisans of generative grammar, particularly the younger ones. Halle and Chomsky had the policy of encouraging their students to integrate themselves into American linguistic life from the moment they entered MIT. It was not unusual in the early 1960s to see even first-year graduate students from that institution presenting and commenting on papers at meetings. But their combative spirit surely got out of hand at times, as even undergraduate advocates of the theory embarrassed their teachers by ruthlessly lighting into linguists old enough to be their grandparents.

A final explanation for the delay in the post-Bloomfieldian counterattack is impossible to document but has a good deal of plausibility nevertheless. By the mid 1960s, many post-Bloomfieldians must have felt that their own power in the field, both intellectual and political, was gradually slipping away. One can assume that their marshalling of their forces at that time was in part a response to what must have seemed to them to be a very alarming development.

One of the earliest criticisms of generative grammar, and one that has survived to the present day (see Hagège 1976; Hall 1977), is the supposed English-language orientation of the theoretical work within this model. American structuralists, whose roots are in the Boas tradition that gave priority to the description of indigenous languages, and European scholars have united to condemn what many have implied is at best poor linguistics, at worst a reflection of American chauvinism and arrogance. Yet even the earliest work was not as English-centered as many believe. For example, of the six faculty members in the MIT Linguistics Department in the late 1960s, four were known primarily for their work in languages other than English: Kenneth Hale for Amerindian and Australian; G. Hubert Matthews for Amerindian; Paul Kiparsky for general Indo-European; and Morris Halle for Russian. In addition, it will be recalled that Chomsky wrote a partial generative grammar of Hebrew before attacking English. And of the 28 doctoral dissertations written in linguistics at MIT in the 1960s, 17 (or 61%) dealt primarily with languages other than English, including those by Stephen Anderson (West Scandinavian), George Bedell (Japanese), Thomas Bever (Menomini), James Fidelholtz (Micmac), James Foley (Spanish), James Harris (Spanish), Richard Kayne (French), Paul Kiparsky (various languages), Sige-Yuki Kuroda (Japanese), Theodore Lightner (Russian), James McCawley (Japanese), Anthony Naro (Portuguese), David Perlmutter (various languages), Sanford Schane (French), Richard Stanley (Navajo), Nancy Woo (various languages), and Arnold Zwicky (Sanskrit).

It goes without saying, of course, that the majority of published syntactic analyses have dealt with English. This is an inevitable consequence of the American origins of the theory and the value placed on native-speaker judgments as data. But as more and more non-English speakers have adopted transformational generative grammar, the percentage of work involving English has steadily declined, and by now generativist studies have appeared on literally hundreds of languages. It might also be pointed out that the first concerted attempt to train American Indians as professional linguists was undertaken at MIT (under the impetus of Kenneth Hale), where in recent years Navajo and Hopi speakers have received Ph.D's.

By the middle years of the 1960s, commentators were already speaking of Chomsky's revolutionary effect on the field (see, for example, Bach 1965:111–112; Levin 1965:92; Thorne 1965:74). How was this feat accomplished less than a decade after the publication of *Syntactic Structures?* While the early encouragement of the post-Bloomfieldians was an important factor, there were many others as well. From the beginning, Chomsky and Halle were able to attract some of the brightest young scholars in the United States to the new way of doing linguistics. Not only Lees, but also G. Hubert Matthews, Fred Lukoff, Edward Klima, Keith Percival, and John Viertel were part of Victor Yngve's machine translation project when they came into contact with generative grammar, a fact which exacerbated the theoretical differences which already existed between Chomsky and Yngve (see Yngve 1960, 1961; Miller and Chomsky 1963). Jerrold Katz and Jerry Fodor, philosophy students at Princeton, were won over and hired by MIT around 1960, as were Paul Postal and Jay Keyser from Yale. As Searle (1972) put it, "Chomsky did not convince the established leaders of the field but he did something more important, he convinced their graduate students" (p. 17). Many of the earliest transformationalists, such as Emmon Bach, Carlota Smith, Charles Fillmore, and Kenneth Hale, were students or recent Ph.D's who adopted the new theory despite the indifference or open hostility of their teachers.

The quality of the first two classes to enter MIT (in 1961 and 1962) was instrumental to the early success that the theory achieved. Not one individual who has failed to contribute to linguistic theory is found in its list, which includes Thomas Bever, James Foley, Bruce Fraser, Jeffrey Gruber, Paul Kiparsky, S.-Y. Kuroda, Terence Langendoen, Theodore Lightner, James McCawley, Barbara Hall Partee, Peter Rosenbaum, Sanford Schane, and Arnold Zwicky. None found difficulty in finding jobs upon graduation; during the 1960s, Illinois, California-San Diego, UCLA, Texas, Washington, and Ohio State joined MIT as universities in which transformational grammar predominated.

This decade was also a decade of rebellion, and the intellectual and political ferment going on in American universities at that time provided an ideal atmosphere for the intellectual movement sweeping linguistics, which was bent on overthrowing the rigid dogmas of American structuralism. Just as students began en masse to question the "common sense" political assumptions of their upbringing, which they felt were rationalizing an imperialist foreign policy and oppressive domestic policy by the American government, they began to question the "common sense" pseudoscientific assumptions of empiricism in linguistics. The appeal of nonobvious explanatory ideas in linguistics at this time was a reflection of the openness of students to such ideas in politics as well.

Far from substituting one dogma for another, as Hagège (1976) would have it, the transformationalists encouraged—in fact, rewarded—students for questioning every assumption of linguistics, including those of transformational generative grammar itself. Paul Newman (1978) has.stressed:

> While there was a general consensus that "the other guys" were wrong and that the basic linguistic/philosophical tenets of generative grammar were essentially right, there was a singular absence of dogma or rigidity. Everyone was encouraged to test the theory on a new language, to explore linguistic areas not yet treated, and to experiment with different kinds of formal devices—always with the freedom to modify or reject the then-standing TG theory as necessary. Of great importance in understanding the growth and spread of generative grammar is the fact that this freedom extended to students who, in key places, were permitted to follow their own lines of research, challenge the views of their teachers (generativist or not), take part in the continual discussion and debate, and otherwise participate actively in the creation and dissemination of this new theory. In the final analysis, generative grammar was a creative, liberating movement, which freed linguistics as a discipline and as a profession from the straitjacket of the post-Bloomfieldian period. Whatever the other factors involved, a great part of its success must be ascribed to this. (pp. 928–929)

The missionary zeal with which "the other guys" were attacked may have led some linguists, along with Wallace Chafe (1970), to be "repelled by the arrogance with which [the generativists'] ideas were propounded" (p. 2), but overall the effect was positive. Seeing the leaders of the field constantly on the defensive at every professional meeting helped recruit younger linguists far more successfully and rapidly than would have been the case if the debate had been confined to the journals. Lees and Postal, in particular, became legends as a result of their uncompromising attacks on every post-Bloomfieldian paper at every meeting.

Postal's fame derived in large part from his book *Constituent Structure*, published in 1964. He attempted to show that each of the models of grammatical description in competition with the transformational generative model was equivalent in weak generative power to phrase structure grammar and was therefore inadequate as a model of human language. This involved reinterpreting the goals of the formulators of these models as being identical to those of the transformationalists, opening Postal to charges of gross distortion and rewriting history (for interesting commentary on this point, see Thorne 1965). Needless to say, Postal's approach had the effect of strengthening the resolution of established non-Chomskyan linguists to resist the new model. But their students were profoundly impressed; no single publication was more instrumental in drawing students into the transformationalist camp.

There were other factors that contributed to the theory's rapid success. First, the field in the late 1950s was very small. For example, the Linguistic Society of America in 1957 had only about 1300 members in the entire world, the vast majority of whom would not have identified themselves as linguists. Simultaneous sessions were not instituted at its meetings until 1968. This meant that a new idea could be disseminated rapidly to the entire profession.

Second, by sheer coincidence, the Ninth International Congress of Linguists was held in Cambridge, Massachusetts in 1962, with Halle and William Locke (who was Chairman of the Modern Languages Department at MIT) on the Local Arrangements Committee. After Zellig Harris turned down his invitation to present one of the five major papers at the plenary session (the others were by Kurylowicz, Benveniste, Martinet, and Andreyev), there was no trouble in replacing him with Chomsky. Chomsky's paper, "The Logical Basis of Linguistic Theory" (1964b), thus reached an international audience, giving him the appearance of being the principal spokesperson for linguistics in the United States. There was no question in the mind of anybody at MIT that transformational generative grammar would prove a lasting success after that point.

Third, transformational grammar was blessed from the beginning with extraordinarily gifted teachers, writers, and explicators:

> [A] number of the early generativists were extremely good teachers. The outsider—outraged by the belligerent polemics of generative lectures and writings—could not know that, in the classroom, a Halle at MIT or a Stockwell at UCLA functioned as a sympathetic and dedicated teacher, prepared to spend long hours explaining the intricacies and nuances of the new model. Students were attracted to generative grammar because, among other reasons, their teachers made it intellectually challenging and exciting. (Newman 1978:928)

Two pieces of pedagogical writing greatly advanced the theory in this period: Emmon Bach's *An Introduction to Transformational Grammars* (1964a), which made it accessible and interpretable to beginning students, and Paul Postal's "Underlying and Superficial Linguistic Structure," published in the *Harvard Educational Review* in 1964, which acquainted educators and psychologists with its basic goals.

And finally, there was enough money available in the late 1960s in America for university expansion that young transformationalists did not have to contend with Old Guard-dominated departments before or after finding employment. It did not matter that Hockett and Hall were at Cornell, Trager and Smith at Buffalo, or Harris and Hiż at Pennsylvania. New departments could always be founded to serve as academic bases for generative grammar from the very beginning. MIT was particularly favored in this respect. Chomsky (1979) has commented:

> We were able to develop our program at MIT because, in a sense, MIT was outside the American university system. There were no large departments of humanities or the related social sciences at MIT. Consequently, we could build up a linguistics department without coming up against problems of rivalry and academic bureaucracy. Here we were really part of the Research Laboratory of Electronics. That permitted us to develop a program very different from any other and quite independent. (p. 134)

The affiliation with the Research Laboratory of Electronics arose as a result of the classification of linguistics at MIT as a "communication science," thus placing it under the purview of the laboratory. This affiliation guaranteed that vast sums of money (largely military in origin) would trickle down into the department, enabling the kind of support for a linguistics program that no other university could hope to match.[10]

---

[10]Newmeyer and Emonds (1971) and Newmeyer (in press) discuss at length the funding of linguistic research in the United States. The point is made that while the source of funding may be irrelevant to the ultimate correctness of a theory, it is by no means irrelevant to a (partial) explanation of one's acceptance. It is tempting to speculate on the speed with which generative grammar would have won general

TABLE 2.2
Linguistic Society of American Membership, 1950–1984

December	Active LSA membership	December	Active LSA membership
1950	829	1968	4166
1951	822	1969	4231
1952	914	1970	4383
1953	978	1971	4723
1954	1022	1972	4263
1955	1090	1973	4258
1956	1178	1974	4148
1957	1354	1975	4279
1958	1501	1976	4112
1959	1633	1977	4108
1960	1768	1978	4258
1961	1951	1979	4268
1962	2180	1980	4303
1963	2602	1981	4267
1964	2918	1982	4248
1965	3263	1983	4222
1966	3495	1984	4168
1967	3814		

Source: LSA Bulletins.

2.6. THE GROWTH OF THE FIELD

The period of the Chomskyan Revolution was one of unprecedented growth in the field of linguistics in the United States. Measured by every imaginable statistic, the discipline grew by enormous proportions throughout the 1960s. Tables 2.2 through 2.6 provide documentation of this fact: LSA membership grew (Table 2.2); the number of departments and programs increased (Table 2.3); more institutions offered degrees (Table 2.4); enrollments increased (Table 2.5); and more degrees were conferred (Table 2.6).[11]

Table 2.2 shows that since around 1971 growth of LSA membership has leveled off and has actually declined. This has gone hand-in-hand with an employment picture aptly described by Levy, Carroll, and Hood (1976:14) as "bleak." It is my impression that reduced funding to higher education rather than disenchantment with linguistics is primarily responsible for this, and that the field has suffered less than others oriented toward basic scholarly research. By way of confirmation, it is worth pointing out that between 1970 and 1975, while the number of first-year

---

acceptance had Chomsky and Halle's students had to contend with today's more austere conditions, in which not just military, but most other sources of funding, have been curtailed, and new positions are a rarity.

[11]Tables 2.3–2.6 and 2.8–2.12 report United States' statistics only.

TABLE 2.3
Organization of Linguistics Departments and Programs, 1963–1984

Organizational arrangement	1963	1966	1969–1970	1971–1972	1984
Department of linguistics	13	23	31	42	51
Department of linguistics and languages (or other subject)	4	8	10	12	14
Interdepartmental program or committee	14	25	52	78	73
Linguistics courses offered in other departments	43	29	30	39	n.a.
Languages	(7)	(4)	(4)	(2)	
English	(14)	(14)	(17)	(24)	
Anthropology	(4)	(7)	(5)	(4)	
Other	(18)	(4)	(4)	(9)	
Interdepartmental courses only	3	1	11	2	n.a.
Total	77	86	134	173	n.a.

Source: Levy *et al.* (1976:114) and *Directory of Programs in Linguistics in the United States and Canada.*

graduate students in physics declined by 41%, in English by 35%, and in history by 31%, linguistics actually saw an increase of 49%.

Of course it is well known that the 1960s saw the expansion of almost every area of American higher education. But the growth rate of linguistics was considerably above the average, suggesting that it is to a large extent the appeal of transformational generative grammar rather than economic growth alone to which this expansion must be attributed. For example, in 1956–1957, 16 doctorates were awarded in linguistics out of a total of 8752 in all fields in American universities—that is .18%. But by the years 1972–1973, the percentage had almost tripled to .51% (177 out of 34,790).

TABLE 2.4
Number of Institutions Offering Each Linguistics Degree, 1963–1984

Degree offered	1963	1966	1969–1970	1971–1972	1974–1975	1984
Ph.D. in linguistics	25	29	39	45	45	47
Ph.D.: linguistics concentration	9	16	17	13	19	28
MA/MS in linguistics	26	38	49	66	70	86
MA/MS: linguistics concentration	9	27	34	37	33	36
BA/BS in linguistics	16	22	40	49	66	106
BA/BS: linguistics concentration	4	16	27	35	46	57

Source: Levy *et al.* (1976:116); *Guide to Programs in Linguistics: 1974–1975; Directory of Programs in Linguistics in the United States and Canada.*

TABLE 2.5
Enrollment for Advanced Degrees in Linguistics,
1960–1975

Year	Enrollment	Increase	Percentage increase
1960	407		
1961	558	151	37.1
1962	739	181	32.4
1963	882	143	19.4
1964	1083	201	22.8
1965	1298	215	19.9
1966	1482	184	14.2
1967	1567	85	5.7
1968	1740	173	11.0
1969	1846	106	6.1
1970	1884	38	2.1
1971	2043	159	8.4
1972	2220	177	8.7
1973	2294	74	3.3
1974	2316	22	1.0
1975	2597	281	12.1

Source: Levy et al. (1976:119); U.S. Department
of Health, Education, and Welfare, Enrollment for
Advanced Degrees.

It is much more difficult of course to document the growth of transformational generative grammar within the field of linguistics. Many articles and presented papers reflect diverse (and sometimes contradictory) influences and assumptions, while individuals and departments often resist such categorizations as "transformationalist" or "stratificationalist." Table 2.7 represents my estimation of the percentage of papers at winter LSA meetings from 1961–1966 that either presuppose or defend transformational generative grammar. After about 1966 such attempts at quantification become quite impossible, given the questioning of certain theoretical fundamentals by many generativists (see Chapters 4 and 5) and the concomitant adoption by nongenerativists of many of the assumptions of the dominant theory. Yet even so, William Bright, editor of *Language,* could remark in the March 1975 *LSA Bulletin:* "It is clear that the overwhelming majority of papers submitted [to *Language*], and of those published, take for granted certain principles of generative grammar" (p. 12).

It is an unfortunate fact that women and racial minorities have not fared much better in linguistics (whether pre- or post-generativist) than in other disciplines. As Table 2.8 illustrates, female students in linguistics have consistently tended to drop out of the field at a greater rate than male students. Linguistics B.A.'s have always gone to a higher percentage of women than M.A.'s, and M.A.'s to a higher

TABLE 2.6
Degrees Conferred in Linguistics, 1955–1981, by
Level

Year	Bachelor's	Master's	Ph.D
1955–1956	38	41	18
1956–1957	25	31	16
1957–1958	20	73	30
1958–1959	31	72	21
1959–1960	57	70	26
1960–1961	41	90	31
1961–1962	64	105	33
1962–1963	54	103	38
1963–1964	57	114	48
1964–1965	67	173	60
1965–1966	113	229	84
1966–1967	132	232	70
1967–1968	126	340	97
1968–1969	192	343	90
1969–1970	220	338	109
1970–1971	254	352	150
1971–1972	296	373	139
1972–1973	443	452	177
1973–1974	431	455	145
1974–1975	434	506	166
1975–1976	534	523	151
1976–1977	564	552	174
1977–1978	596	522	159
1978–1979	585	502	143
1979–1980	552	521	162
1980–1981	551	498	166

Source: U.S. Department of Health, Education,
and Welfare, *Earned Degrees Conferred.*

percentage than Ph.D.'s, suggesting a channeling of women out of the field. However, this situation seems to be improving faster in linguistics than elsewhere. At the Ph.D. level, women are closing the gap on men more rapidly in linguistics than in academia as a whole.

As far as academic hiring is concerned, conditions have been improving for women over the past decade, to the point where they are being hired roughly in the proportion that they are receiving Ph.D.'s.[12] Nevertheless, as Table 2.9 illustrates, in 1982 women were still far outnumbered by men in linguistics positions at American universities and were heavily concentrated in the lower (nontenured) rungs of

[12]In a study commissioned by the Linguistic Society of America, Price (1983) finds that women are more poorly represented at the 12 leading linguistics departments in the United States, as ranked in a survey carried out by the National Research Council (Jones, Lindzey, and Coggeshell 1982), than they are at other departments.

TABLE 2.7
Papers at Winter LSA Meetings Presupposing
or Defending Transformational Generative
Grammar, 1961–1966

Year	Number of papers	Number of generativist papers	Percentage of generativist papers
1961	31	4	13
1962	33	2	6
1963	45	8	18
1964	52	16	31
1965	37	14	38
1966	40	22	55

TABLE 2.8
Percentage of Degrees Awarded to Women, 1955–1981, by Level

Year	Linguistics			Ph.D.'s awarded to women, all fields
	Bachelor's	Master's	Ph.D.	
1955–1956	45	39	6	10
1956–1957	56	55	6	11
1957–1958	60	38	27	11
1958–1959	55	43	33	11
1959–1960	28	30	12	11
1960–1961	44	38	23	11
1961–1962	36	35	19	11
1962–1963	35	45	26	11
1963–1964	35	39	21	11
1964–1965	45	36	15	11
1965–1966	43	39	33	12
1966–1967	56	39	30	12
1967–1968	62	40	21	13
1968–1969	61	46	24	13
1969–1970	62	52	21	13
1970–1971	67	51	25	14
1971–1972	63	53	24	16
1972–1973	65	50	29	18
1973–1974	73	55	42	19
1974–1975	70	55	36	21
1975–1976	69	60	48	23
1976–1977	71	59	36	24
1977–1978	68	60	39	26
1978–1979	70	59	48	28
1979–1980	76	60	43	30
1980–1981	74	62	41	31

Source: U.S. Department of Health, Education, and Welfare, *Earned Degrees Conferred.*

TABLE 2.9
Composition by Sex and Rank of Linguistics Faculties, 1964–1982

Year	Number of programs surveyed	Below assistant professor			Assistant professor			Associate professor			Full professor		
		Male	Female	Percentage female	Male	Female	Percentage female	Male	Female	Percentage female	Male	Female	Percentage female
1964–1965	27	36	5	12	89	6	6	59	5	8	130	4	3
1974–1975	45	28	23	45	116	43	27	103	22	18	215	18	8
1978–1979	40	7	6	46	64	49	43	106	24	18	196	16	8
1982	123	26	27	51	143	103	42	270	73	21	356	43	11

Source: 1964–1965: *University Resources in the United States for Linguistics and Teacher Training in English as a Foreign Language: 1965; 1974–1975: Guide to Programs in Linguistics: 1974–1975; 1978–1979: LSA Bulletins. Nos. 80 and 94.*

TABLE 2.10
Percentage of Unemployment and Underemployment (Combined) in Linguistics,
by Sex, 1973

Degree level	Men	Women
Ph.D.	5.5	16.4
Ph.D. candidate	8.0	31.3
Master's	30.4	21.1
Overall	7.8	19.2

Source: Levy *et al.* (1976:249).

the academic ladder. As tenure is becoming increasingly difficult to obtain, there is a real danger that the gains that women have made will be reversed in the coming years. A 1973 survey (see Table 2.10) indicated as well that unemployment and underemployment were considerably more acute among women in linguistics than among men. I suspect (but can provide no documentation) that things were worse in the mid 1980s.

The most overt forms of discrimination are, for obvious reasons, impossible to document. Perhaps the best example of antifemale (and anti-Asian) bias among linguists, and one that seemingly disallows any alternative conclusions, is reflected in an admission in the March 1974 *LSA Bulletin* that "the number of females and Orientals participating in the [LSA] meetings increased significantly when the abstracts were read masked, and they have been so read ever since" (Friedrich 1974:15). By the same token, the first year that Chicago Linguistic Society abstracts were read anonymously, the percentage of women presenting papers rose from 25 to 34.

A 1972 survey (Table 2.11) shows an insignificant number of minority-group faculty members in linguistics. While I know of no more recent tabulations of

TABLE 2.11
Minority Group Members as Percentage of Linguistics Faculty, by Rank, 1972

| Minority group | Rank | | | | | |
	Instructor/ lecturer	Assistant professor	Associate professor	Full professor	Total	Total number
Black	—	2.3%	1.5%	.5%	1.4%	10
Spanish speaking	4.6%	1.5	4.4	2.7	2.9	21
Asian	2.3	5.0	4.4	3.1	4.1	30
American Indian	—	—	.5	—	.1	1
Total	7.0	8.9	10.8	6.3	8.5	
Total number	3	23	22	14		62

Source: Levy *et al.* (1976:229).

TABLE 2.12
Ph.D.'s in Linguistics Awarded to Minority Group Members 1974–1983

	Total number	Blacks	Asian-Americans	Hispanics	American Indians
1974	145	1	2	4	2
1975	166	4	0	0	1
1976	151	2	1	0	0
1977	190	4	7	4	0
1978	175	3	4	3	2
1979	155	2	9	6	1
1980	182	9	6	6	1
1981	176	2	5	3	0
1982	191	3	8	5	0
1983	164	4	5	3	1

Source: National Research Council, Commission on Human Resources, *Summary Report, Doctorate Recipients from United States Universities.*

minority hiring, the percentage of minorities receiving Ph.D.'s in linguistics continues to be tiny (see Table 2.12). It seems to be the case that most black linguists in the United States are involved in work that might be considered "race-related": pidgins and creoles, African languages, and Black English.

2.7. THE EARLY IMPACT OF GENERATIVE GRAMMAR ON OTHER FIELDS[13]

The great appeal of *Syntactic Structures* cannot be explained exclusively by the fact that it presented a convincing theory of grammatical description. After all, the correct form of the theory of grammar is a topic of little interest to the nonspecialist. No, the theory presented in that book captured the imagination of scholars and pedagogues in numerous fields because it seemed likely to promote solutions to long-standing problems in every area in which language plays a role.

Chomsky himself did not bring up the question of the psychological implications of transformational generative grammar in either *LSLT* or *Syntactic Structures;* as he wrote later, it would have been "too audacious" for him to have done so (Chomsky 1975a:35). But Lees in his review did not shrink from this. He closed the review with a frontal attack on inductivist learning theory, arguing that there could be no alternative but to conclude that the grammar the linguist constructed was "in the head" of the speaker. But if that were the case, then how could these highly abstract principles possibly be learned inductively? "It would seem," he wrote, "that our notions of human learning are due for some considerable sophistication" (1957:408).

---

[13]For a more detailed discussion of much of the material in this section, see Newmeyer (1983).

It was Chomsky's 1959 review of B. F. Skinner's *Verbal Behavior* that drove home the fact that his theory of language was more than a neat manipulation of arcane symbols—it was a psychological model of an aspect of human knowledge. Chomsky's review represents, even after the passage of 20 years, the basic refutation of behaviorist psychology. The review takes in turn each basic construct of behaviorism and demonstrates that either it leads to false predictions or is simply devoid of content:

> a critical account of his book must show that . . . with a literal reading (where the terms of the descriptive system have something like the technical meanings given in Skinner's definitions) the book covers almost no aspect of linguistic behavior, and that with a metaphoric reading, it is no more scientific than the traditional approaches to this subject matter, and rarely as clear and careful. (Chomsky 1959b:31)

How then is verbal behavior to be explained? While its complexities defy any simplistic treatment, Chomsky wrote that

> the actual observed ability of a speaker to distinguish sentences from nonsentences, detect ambiguities, etc., apparently forces us to the conclusion that this grammar is of an extremely complex and abstract character, and that the young child has succeeded in carrying out what from the formal point of view, at least, seems to be a remarkable type of theory construction. (p. 57)

Chomsky went on to argue that this ability indicates that rather than being born "blank slates," children have a genetic predisposition to structure the acquisition of linguistic knowledge in a highly specific way: "The fact that all normal children acquire essentially comparable grammars of great complexity with remarkable rapidity suggests that human beings are somehow specially designed to do this, with data-handling or 'hypothesis-formulating' ability of unknown character and complexity" (p. 57).

Since Chomsky's review was published in a linguistics journal, its immediate impact on the field of psychology was minor. However, it did attract the attention of George A. Miller, Eugene Galanter, and Karl Pribram, three researchers at the forefront of the young discipline of cognitive psychology, who immediately realized the relevance of Chomsky's work to their interests. Miller, Galanter, and Pribram made extensive reference to generative grammar in their ensuing book *Plans and the Structure of Behavior* (1960). They saw in Chomsky's approach to syntax a model example of their claim that behavior must be organized simultaneously at several levels of complexity and require a complex planning device to coordinate the interplay between the various levels. As a result of their book (and the Skinner review, which by the mid 1960s had become well known among psychologists), Chomsky had come to be regarded as a leading figure in American psychology. As Judith Greene put it: "Chomsky's theory of generative transformational grammar was the first to force psychologists to reconsider their whole approach to the study of language behavior, and so heralded the psycholinguistic 'revolution'" (1972:15).[14]

---

[14]Maclay (1973) is an interesting discussion of the attitudes of psycholinguists before, during, and after the Chomskyan revolution.

Language teachers as well found transformational generative grammar to be relevant to their concerns. Disillusioned with behaviorist-inspired teaching methods like the audiolingual method and programmed instruction, many welcomed Chomsky's theory, whose emphasis on the creative aspect of language and its freedom from stimulus control seemed to encourage a more active role for the learner. By 1965, many agreed with Owen Thomas that "transformational grammar has significant application to the teaching of all languages, including English, at all grade levels and to both native and nonnative speakers" (1965:1). In the late 1960s, while generativist concepts had only rarely filtered down into the classroom itself, the journals of applied linguistics routinely discussed the application of the theory for some pedagogical purpose (for an historical overview of this period of second language research, see Newmeyer and Weinberger, forthcoming).

Finally, Chomsky's early work had an impact on philosophy, particularly the philosophy of science, even before the publication of his *Cartesian Linguistics* in 1966. While the success of generative grammar benefited from the retreat of empiricist philosophy, it helped contribute to that retreat as well. Indeed, Israel Scheffler's book *The Anatomy of Inquiry* (1963), a classic in the philosophy of science, cited Chomsky's results in *Syntactic Structures* to bolster his case for a nonempiricist analysis of scientific investigation. He pointed out that since Chomsky demonstrated the need to define such theoretical notions as "noun" and "morpheme" independently of particular languages, so philosophers should concern themselves with the general nature of scientific laws, rather than take an atomistic empiricist approach.

Chapter 3

From *Syntactic Structures* to *Aspects of the Theory of Syntax*

3.1. INTRODUCTION

In this chapter, I sketch the progress made in linguistic theory in the years following the writing of *Syntactic Structures*. This period was characterized by close to total agreement by generative grammarians on all the major issues and was capped by three complementary works, which collectively would define the next decade's research strategy: Katz and Fodor (1963), which took the initial steps to incorporate semantics into generative grammar; Katz and Postal (1964), which hypothesized that underlying structures alone serve as input to the semantic component; and Chomsky (1965), which, by eliminating generalized transformations in favor of phrase structure recursion, allowed, for the first time, a level of "deep structure" to be defined.

3.2. REVISIONS IN THE SYNTACTIC COMPONENT: 1957–1965

3.2.1. Early Publications

The first booklength study of syntax giving extensive rule motivations and derivations was Robert B. Lees's *The Grammar of English Nominalizations* (1960). Since virtually all of Lees's specific analyses have long since been revised, it is hard to appreciate the importance the book had at the time. By working out in fine detail the embedding transformations involved in the derivation of the various subordinate and relatival structures in English, Lees succeeded in demonstrating that the theory of transformational generative grammar could be applied insightfully to the analysis of a huge body of material. To a skeptical audience of linguists, this was an achievement of the highest order. Today, many remember *The Grammar of English Nominalizations* primarily for its comprehensive analysis of English compound nouns, which would not undergo substantial revision for almost 20 years.[1]

No important booklength studies of syntax appeared between Lees (1960) and Katz and Postal (1964), to which we turn in Section 3.3.2. Those five years, however, saw groundbreaking studies of the following topics: comparatives (Lees 1961); indirect object constructions (Fillmore 1965); German word order (Bach 1962); cleft sentences (Lees 1963); pronouns (Lees and Klima 1963); passives and imperatives (Lees 1964); negatives (Klima 1964); and determiners, adjectives, and relative clauses (Smith 1964).

3.2.2. The "Traffic Rule" Problem

While Chomsky, in *Syntactic Structures,* had given several examples to illustrate that singularly transformations were ordered with respect to each other, he left open many important questions about rule ordering. For example, do the generalized transformations also obey ordering restrictions? Can singulary transformations apply in a matrix ("higher") sentence before a generalized transformation embeds a constituent ("lower") sentence into it? What other factors determine ordering relations among transformations? The complexity of the ordering restrictions became evident from the discovery that a transformation can reapply to structures created by its own application. For example, Lees (1960) pointed out that a passive sentence can be nominalized, and then this nominalization itself can undergo a second application of Passive:

(3.1)   a. *The invader destroyed the citadel* (underlying constituent sentence)
        b. *The citadel was destroyed by the invader* (after Passive)
        c. *The people regretted the citadel's destruction by the invader* (after Nominalization and Embedding)

---

[1]*The Grammar of English Nominalizations* contains the first published use of the asterisk to designate ungrammatical sentences. Fred Householder (1973) takes credit for the notation:

> I suppose that I may be somehow responsible myself for the spread of this notation; in the summer of 1958 I taught a course in "morphology-syntax" at the Michigan Linguistic Institute, in which I complained that the problems we had to solve . . . never included specification of ungrammatical strings. For one or two special problems we did get some sample ungrammatical strings and listed them, using the asterisk to mark them. Andreas Koutsoudas and R. B. Lees were auditors in that class, and both of them adopted the asterisk (as well as the double-arrow notation for transformations, which was devised in the same class), as did Emmon Bach in his text (though I don't think he was in that 1958 class). (p. 366).

It took editors of linguistics texts several years to accommodate themselves to ill-formed sentences. The first proofs of Katz and Postal's *An Integrated Theory of Linguistic Descriptions* (1964) were returned to them with all the ungrammatical sentences "corrected" to the closest grammatical equivalents!

d. *The citadel's destruction by the invader was regretted by the people*
(after Passive)

Lees made two proposals regarding ordering relations among transformations that
are of particular historical interest. The first is his claim that all obligatory transformations are ordered to follow all optional transformations. Lees believed that such
an ordering would help explain how a grammar was utilized in speech production,
since, in such a view, only the optional rules would need to be provided with
external inputs. Lees himself recognized that delaying the application of the obligatory rules would lead to complications. For example, Reflexive, an obligatory rule,
would be required to "look back" to an earlier stage in the derivation before
various optional transformations had applied, since only at that point could the
restriction of that transformation to apply within simple clauses be stated: "The
only alternative is to use the full power of transformational rules to look back into
the derivational history of complex strings and identify all the simplexes within
them" (p. 101). Lees dropped the segregation of optional and obligatory rules a few
years later, pointing out (in the Preface to the 1964 edition) that it was based on the
mistaken notion that the grammar could be conceived of directly as a processing and
perception model. He also pointed out that the fact that certain rules seemed both to
precede and follow other rules would make his proposal impossible to formulate.
However, Lees, in segregating the two rule types into distinct blocks, had not only
anticipated similar proposals for grammatical organization that would be advanced
many years later by supporters of trace theory (see Chapter 6), but had also been
forced to propose the first global rule in transformational syntax (see Chapter 4).

Lees proposed a second ordering restriction that would soon be abandoned, yet
reintroduced (without acknowledgment) many years later, namely that all ellipsis
transformations be ordered at the very end of the grammar. At that time, such rules
were allowed to delete any element freely. For example, one rule of Lees's, Pseudo-
Intransitive, optionally deleted any nominal following a verb like *breathe, eat,
hammer, read,* and *steal.* Hence, *the boy steals* was derived from all of *the boy
steals books, the boy steals money, the boy steals food,* etc. As a consequence,
deletions were unrecoverable and the grammar therefore undecidable: given the
output of the T-rule and the rule's formal statement, it was impossible to recover the
input uniquely. Lees proposed that by segregating ellipsis rules in this way, at least
the rest of the grammar would be decidable. While his proposal was soon abandoned in favor of a general prohibition against nonrecoverable deletion (see Section
3.2.6), recent work has revived the segregation of ellipsis rules (see Section 6.5.3).

The traffic rule problem was given a general solution in Fillmore (1963), a
solution that in its essentials is still assumed in all transformational accounts of
syntax. Fillmore began by making three observations about the ordering of transformations: first, no cases were known of ordering among the generalized transformations, although the theory allowed such ordering; second, there was no evidence
that a singular transformation ever had to apply to a matrix sentence before another
sentence was embedded into it by a generalized transformation; and third, there

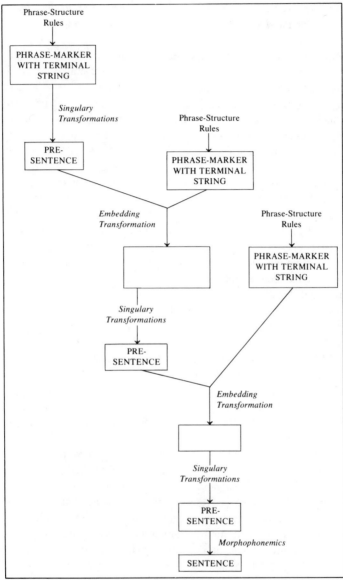

Figure 3.1

were many examples of singulary transformations having to apply to a constituent sentence before embedding and then again to the entire matrix-constituent complex after embedding. These facts suggested to Fillmore that the singulary transformations should apply to the most deeply embedded sentence first. Then this sentence would itself be embedded by a generalized transformation into a matrix sentence. Singulary transformations would then apply to the phrase marker resulting from this embedding, and, depending on the number of constituent sentences, the recycling of embedding and singulary transformations would continue until the sentence in its entirety was generated (see Figure 3.1).

The predictability of ordering between embedding and singulary transformations and the nonordering of embedding transformations with respect to each other was to be a major motivation for Chomsky's (1965) proposal to eliminate embedding transformations entirely (see Section 3.5).

3.2.3. The Derived Constituent Structure Problem

Since it was generally the case that a string created by the application of a transformational rule itself could serve as input to another transformation, it was necessary that constituent structure be mechanically assigned to the derived string. For simple permutations, deletions, substitutions, and adjunctions this was no great problem. Postal (1962:26–31) gave an improved version of the original Chomsky (1955) proposal for breaking down each transformation into the elementary transformational operations it performed, each of which was associated with a simple algorithm for derived constituent structure imposition.

But special problems remained. The first had to do with the assignment of constituent structure to elements that were believed to be created by the application of a transformation: the *be* + *en* and *by* of passive, the *for* of *for John to go,* the expletive *it* of *it's good to be here,* and the *of* of *the refusal of the offer* are examples. To deal with this problem, Chomsky (1957:73–74) had proposed that the passive *by*-phrase be automatically assigned to the category "Prepositional Phrase" by virtue of its formal resemblance to *by*-phrases generated by the phrase structure rules. By implication, the constituent structure of the other examples would be handled in a like manner. Yet no one considered Chomsky's solution satisfactory; indeed, he himself was later to describe it as ad hoc (1965:104). The difficulty of finding a non-ad hoc principle for assigning constituent structure to transformationally inserted elements was to lead many linguists to propose that most (or all) of such elements be generated instead by the base rules.

A much more serious problem had to do with the assignment of derived constituent structure to sentences formed by generalized transformations. In the earliest work, as much of the assignment as possible was built into the embedding transformation itself. For example, in the derivation of *we persuaded him to play the flute,* the generalized transformation not only embedded *he play the flute* into *we persuaded* COMP *him,* but also deleted the embedded subject *he.* The reason that embedding and deletion were accomplished simultaneously was that since so little was known about ordering relations among the various types of transformations, it was considered desirable to avoid postulating a deletion transformation that would apply after embedding and have both matrix and constituent sentences as its domain. Hence, the embedding transformation had to perform two operations at once, leading to complications in the precise specification of its structural output.

Once the traffic rule problem had been solved by Fillmore, the derived constituent structure difficulty resolved itself almost instantaneously. We find proposals in Chomsky and Miller (1963) and Katz and Postal (1964) that all embedding take place at unexpanded nodes in the matrix sentence and that the constituent sentence keep the node label ''S'' after embedding. Given that, there was no difficulty in formulating a transformational rule such as Equi-Noun Phrase Deletion, which, though singularly (nonembedding), has to apply across clause boundaries.

Since in such an analysis constituent sentences were to keep their internal structure intact after embedding, the embedding transformations were left with a rather restricted syntactic role to play, thus providing another argument for their elimination (see Section 3.5).

3.2.4. Underlying Trigger Morphemes

Beginning in the early 1960s, transformations that had previously been regarded as optional were reanalyzed as obligatory, their application triggered by the presence of optionally generated morphemes in the underlying string. For example, Lees (1964) proposed that the *be* + *en* and the *by*-phrase of the passive construction be generated by optional phrase structure rules, whose presence would trigger obligatory passivization. While Lees's motivation was the desire to avoid the derived constituent structure problem described in the previous section, syntactic motivation was found as well (see for example, Katz and Postal 1964:72–73; Chomsky 1965:103). More importantly, arguments were put forward for introducing the negative (Neg), imperative (I), and question (Q) morphemes by optional phrase structure rules and for deriving negatives, imperatives, and questions by obligatory transformations that would apply if the appropriate morpheme were present.

Lees (1960) was the first to suggest generating Neg in the base, arguing that such a morpheme was necessary to the statement of the co-occurrence restrictions against double negatives such as **not never*. Klima (1964), in his extensive analysis of English negation, also gave co-occurrence arguments for a base-generated Neg. His arguments rested on the many similar syntactic properties of the word *not* and words in the class of negative preverbal adverbs, such as *never, scarcely, hardly, rarely, seldom,* and *barely.* As Klima pointed out, *not even* requires negation in the preceding clause:

(3.2)   a. *Max won't come, not even if you beg him*
          b.**Max will come, not even if you beg him*

But this negation can be manifested by a negative adverb as well as by the word *not:*

(3.3)   *Max will never come, not even if you beg him*

Klima explained these and other facts by positing an abstract negative morpheme in the underlying structures of sentences containing negative adverbials, making possible a single statement of the identical co-occurrence restrictions that these elements share.

Lees (1964) proposed an underlying imperative morpheme based on the special co-occurrence restrictions within imperative sentences. For example, while *be* in declaratives does not allow *do*-support, *do* does appear before *be* in negative imperatives:

(3.4)   a.*He doesn't be silly*
         b. *Don't be silly*

Furthermore, imperatives have a number of restrictions not found in declaratives: They allow neither *have + en,* modals, nor tensed verbs. Lees proposed capturing these facts by positing an imperative morpheme that would be positioned in the auxiliary to trigger *do*-support in appropriate contexts.

Katz and Postal, in *An Integrated Theory of Linguistic Descriptions* also argued for an underlying imperative morpheme (and a question morpheme as well) on the basis of co-occurrence. In previous analyses, *you will drive the car, drive the car,* and *will you drive the car?* had been derived from the same underlying structure. But they noted that the distributions of the three sentence types differ: neither imperatives nor questions co-occur with sentence adverbials:

(3.5) $\left\{ \begin{array}{l} Maybe \\ Yes \\ Perhaps \\ Certainly \end{array} \right\}$ *you will drive the car*

(3.6) $\left\{ \begin{array}{l} {*Maybe} \\ {*Yes} \\ {*Perhaps} \\ {*Certainly} \end{array} \right\}$ *drive the car*

(3.7) $\left\{ \begin{array}{l} {*Maybe} \\ {*Yes} \\ {*Perhaps} \\ {*Certainly} \end{array} \right\}$ *will you drive the car?*

How could such a restriction be captured in the grammar? Only, they reasoned, by assuming that the morphemes I and Q occur in underlying structure and are prohibited at that level from co-occurring with sentence adverbials.

3.2.5. The Abandonment of the Notion "Kernel Sentence"

In the *Syntactic Structures* model, the notion "kernel sentence" had a certain intuitive appeal, since the class of sentences formed by the application of only obligatory transformations corresponded exactly to the class of uniclausal declarative affirmatives. But as we have seen, more and more transformations were made obligatory in the early 1960s, a fact that had the undesirable result that negatives, questions, and imperatives had now become kernels. Furthermore, Lees suggested (in the Preface to the 1964 edition of *The Grammar of English Nomi-nalizations*) that in German it was probably the case that one rule out of a particular set of rules had to be chosen in the derivation of every sentence. (He unfortunately did not give any data in support of this.) But since not one of the relevant rules was itself obligatory, German would have, strictly speaking, no kernel sentences at all.

For these reasons, the notion "kernel sentence" was simply dropped from the technical vocabulary of linguistic theory by the mid 1960s.[2]

3.2.6. Recoverability of Deletion

Chomsky (1964a:39–40) observed that interrogative pronouns that replace (i.e., delete) an entire noun phrase can be derived only from those noun phrases that are singular and indefinite. Thus (3.8a) and (3.8b) are well formed, while (3.8c) (de-rived from a definite) and (3.8d) (derived from a plural) are rather odd:

(3.8)   a. *Who do I know with a scar?*
          b. *Who do I know who was expelled?*
          c.*Who do I know with the scar?*
          d.*Who do I know who were expelled?*

Relative clauses and nondeleting interrogatives, however, are not subject to this restriction:

(3.9)   a. *You know the boy with the scar*
          b. *You know the boys who were expelled*

(3.10)   a. *Which boy has the scar?*
          b. *Which boys were expelled?*

Chomsky further noted that the distribution of deleting interrogatives corresponds precisely to the distribution of the indefinite singular pronouns *someone* and *something*. But why should this be the case, and why should nondeleting interrogatives and relatives have different distributions? Chomsky suggested that this could be explained if it were assumed that each category has associated with it a "designated element" that could be realized phonologically (as with the pro-verb *do*) or be an abstract "dummy element." Furthermore, he hypothesized that if a transformation deletes an element not structurally identical to another in the phrase marker, then that element could be only a designated element of a category. It thereby follows that interrogatives formed by deletion of a noun phrase are more restricted in their distribution than relative pronouns (which occur in structures with head nouns identical to the deleted element) and interrogatives, in which no deletion at all takes place.

Chomsky's hypothesis, the "Condition on Recoverability of Deletion," was

---

[2]There was also a persistent tendency on the part of many to confuse kernel sentences with underlying terminal strings. This confusion is found even in Lees (1960:2), if I read him correctly.

extended by Katz and Postal (1964:81) to allow deletion of terminal symbols mentioned in the structural description of the rule, as, for example, the deletion of *you* and *will* in a popular formulation of the Imperative transformation.

Matthews (1961) had proposed the same condition for a different reason. He noted that free deletion results in the set of sentences generated by the syntactic component not being decidable. But how then, he asked, could a grammar ever be learned or an utterance processed? To avoid this consequence, he proposed a recoverability condition. Chomsky's purely syntactic arguments gave Matthews's proposal the empirical support it had lacked.

There were other reasons for adopting the condition on recoverability of deletion. Early syntactic analyses tended to bear out the idea that there is direct correlation between the number of underlying sources a sentence has and its degree of ambiguity. On independent syntactic grounds, for example, two underlying structures had been motivated for *flying planes can be dangerous* and *John doesn't know how good meat tastes*, each structure corresponding to one of the interpretations. But nonrecoverable deletion of the object noun phrase in the derivation of *John is eating* results in an infinite number of underlying structures for this sentence. As Chomsky pointed out, however, this sentence is simply vague, not infinitely ambiguous; speakers interpret the understood object of *eating* roughly in the sense of the indefinite pronoun *something*. Since this indefinite pronoun is what was motivated independently as the designated element for the category "Noun Phrase," the condition on recoverability of deletion seemed to have semantic as well as syntactic motivation.

3.2.7. Subcategorization and the Lexicon

In the earliest work in transformational generative grammar, phrase structure rules both introduced lexical categories and subcategorized them (i.e., they divided nouns into subclasses of humans and nonhumans, verbs into subclasses of transitives and intransitives, and so on). It was pointed out as early as 1957 (by G. H. Matthews, in class lectures) that because subcategories typically cross classify, branching rules are not the appropriate devices for introducing them. For example, nouns in English can be either common or proper, human or nonhuman; Figure 3.2 shows how these classes themselves intersect to create four subclasses. This situation can be described by two sets of phrase structure rules of equal complexity:

(3.11) a. N → $\left\{ \begin{array}{l} \text{N human} \\ \text{N nonhuman} \end{array} \right\}$

b. N human → $\left\{ \begin{array}{l} \text{N human and common} \\ \text{N human and proper} \end{array} \right\}$

c. N nonhuman → $\left\{ \begin{array}{l} \text{N nonhuman and common} \\ \text{N nonhuman and proper} \end{array} \right\}$

d. N human and common → *boy*, . . .

e. N human and proper → *Charlie*, . . .

	HUMAN	NONHUMAN
COMMON	*boy*	*book*
PROPER	*Charlie*	*Egypt*

Figure 3.2

   f. N nonhuman and common → *book,* . . .
   g. N nonhuman and proper → *Egypt,* . . .

(3.12)

   a. N → $\left\{ \begin{array}{l} \text{N common} \\ \text{N proper} \end{array} \right\}$

   b. N common → $\left\{ \begin{array}{l} \text{N common and human} \\ \text{N common and nonhuman} \end{array} \right\}$

   c. N proper → $\left\{ \begin{array}{l} \text{N proper and human} \\ \text{N proper and nonhuman} \end{array} \right\}$

   d. N common and human → *boy,* . . .
   e. N common and nonhuman → *book,* . . .
   f. N proper and human → *Charlie,* . . .
   g. N proper and nonhuman → *Egypt,* . . .

Matthews argued that such subcategorization rules miss important generalizations. The root of the problem is that (3.11) and (3.12), while containing the same number of symbols, differ in their empirical claims. Rule set (3.12) makes the claim that common nouns and proper nouns form natural classes in English, since they can be referred to by one symbol, but not the classes of human nouns and nonhuman nouns. Rule set (3.11) makes the opposite claim. It allows the classes of human nouns and nonhuman nouns to be referred to by one symbol, but not the classes of common nouns and proper nouns. Yet, clearly, both binary classes are natural and should not have to be characterized by a conjunction of symbols. For example, the class of human nouns must be referred to by the rule that accounts for the distribution of the relative and interrogative pronouns *who, whom,* and *whose.* The common–proper distinction is relevant to the statement of the occurrence of the determiner. But since these distinctions themselves cross classify with a large number of others (e.g., count–mass; masculine–feminine; concrete–abstract), it is obvious that a phrase structure treatment of subcategorization would require literally thousands of separate branching rules and sublexical categories.

Various suggestions were made for dealing with this problem in the early 1960s (Schachter 1962; Stockwell and Schachter 1962; Bach 1964b), but these had little impact. Chomsky (1965), however, noted that a similar problem occurs in phonology, where subcategorization typically involves cross classification rather than hierarchy. For example, some rules must refer to the class of all obstruents, others to the (overlapping) class of all alveolars. The solution in phonology is to consider each segment to be composed of a set of binary distinctive features, thereby allowing a simple and elegant characterization of both classes. Chomsky suggested that an analogous solution could be applied to syntactic subcategorization by supplementing the categorial phrase structure rules with a set of feature-introducing lexical subcategorization rules. Thus (3.13) would replace (3.11a–c) and (3.12a–c):

(3.13)   N → [±N, ±Human, ±Common]

(3.13) is not only formally simpler than either (3.11a–c) or (3.12a–c), but it also allows the classes of both human nouns and common nouns to be referred to by a single symbol.

The removal of the subcategorization function from the phrase structure rules led naturally to the conclusion that phrase structure rules should not introduce lexical items either. Chomsky proposed instead a distinct lexicon containing the words (or, possibly, morphemes) of the language and rules for inserting them into the phrase marker. This lexicon would need to specify for each word entered those aspects of its phonetic structure not predictable by general rule, its behavior with respect to the transformational rules, its meaning, and the conditions under which it could be inserted into the structure created by the phrase structure and subcategorization rules (Chomsky 1965:87).

3.3. THE INCORPORATION OF SEMANTICS INTO THE MODEL

Hardly a mention was made of semantics during the first five years after the publication of *Syntactic Structures*. Yet it was never forgotten that an adequate grammatical theory would have to provide syntactic structures that formed a suitable basis for semantic interpretation. Indeed, the syntactically motivated underlying structures in this period almost without exception captured important aspects of the meaning of the sentences under investigation. Chomsky took note of this fact: "In general, as syntactic description becomes deeper, what appear to be semantic questions fall increasingly within its scope" (Chomsky 1964b:936). For the first time within generative grammar, Chomsky went on to raise the possibility of an independent semantic theory:

[I]t is not entirely obvious whether or where one can draw a natural bound between grammar and "logical grammar" in the sense of Wittgenstein and the Oxford philosophers. Nevertheless, it seems clear that explanatory adequacy for descriptive semantics requires, beyond this, the development of an independent semantic theory (analogous, perhaps, to the general theory of grammar as described above) that deals with questions of a kind that can scarcely be formulated today, in particular, with the question: what are the substantive and formal constraints on systems of concepts that are constructed by humans on the basis of presented data? (Chomsky 1964b:936)

The task of developing this theory was undertaken not by Chomsky, but by two young Princeton philosophers, Jerrold Katz and Jerry Fodor, who had come to MIT to help develop the theory of transformational generative grammar.

3.3.1. "The Structure of a Semantic Theory"

The number of fundamental questions that Katz and Fodor had to answer in their ensuing paper "The Structure of a Semantic Theory" (1963) was simply overwhelming. First, they had to address the question of the goals of the theory itself. What is its lower bound? Its upper bound? Second, they not only had to posit a set of primitives for the theory, but they also had at least to attempt to answer the question of their epistemological character. Are all semantic constructs universal and, by implication, innate? And if not all, then which? Finally, there was still the unresolved problem of the relationship between semantic theory and grammatical theory. This problem not only involved the question of how transformational rules affect meaning, but also the question of which traditionally semantic problems had purely syntactic solutions and which required special semantic rules of a still unknown character.

Katz and Fodor concluded that a line had to be drawn between those aspects of sentence interpretation deriving from linguistic knowledge and those deriving from beliefs about the world. As they pointed out, while world knowledge might typically limit the number of interpretations actually assigned to an utterance by participants in a discourse, the full range of possible interpretations is part of the speaker's linguistic ability and therefore has to be accounted for by the semantic theory. A concrete example involved the sentences *our store sells horse shoes* and *our store sells alligator shoes*. In actual usage, these sentences are not taken ambiguously—the former is typically interpreted as '. . . shoes for horses,' the latter as '. . . shoes from alligator skin.' Now, surely, Katz and Fodor argued, it is not the job of a semantic theory to incorporate the purely cultural, possibly temporary, facts that shoes are made for horses but not for alligators, and that shoes are made out of alligator skin but not out of horsehide. Semantic theory, then, characterizes both sentences as ambiguous. The only alternative, as they saw it, would be for semantic theory to incorporate all of human culture.

As for the lower bound of the theory, they asserted that its goals are to describe and explain speakers' ability to (a) determine the number and content of the readings of a sentence; (b) detect semantic anomalies; (c) decide on paraphrase relations between sentences; and (d) mark "every other semantic property that plays a role in this ability" (Katz and Fodor 1963:176).

Katz and Fodor posited two interrelated components to characterize this ability. The first they called the "dictionary," which contained, for each lexical item, a characterization of the role it played in semantic interpretation (Chomsky's "lexicon" was to incorporate this aspect of the Katz–Fodor dictionary). The second component was a set of "projection rules," which determined how the structured combinations of lexical items assigned a meaning to the sentence as a whole.

The dictionary entry for each item consisted of a grammatical portion (grammatical markers) and a semantic portion containing semantic markers, distinguishers, and selectional restrictions. The grammatical markers were simply the lexical (and sublexical—this paper was written before the introduction of syntactic features) categories to which the lexical item belonged. The semantic markers

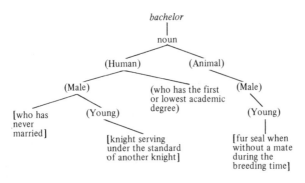

Figure 3.3

assigned to a lexical item the systematic relations holding between that item and the rest of the vocabulary of the language, while the distinguishers reflected purely idiosyncratic aspects of meaning. Figure 3.3 represents the Katz-Fodor entry for the word *bachelor,* with markers in parentheses and distinguishers in square brackets:

The first step in the interpretation of a sentence was to plug into the syntactically generated phrase marker the lexical items from the dictionary. After insertion, projection rules applied upward from the bottom of the tree, amalgamating the readings of adjacent nodes to specify the reading of the node that immediately dominated them. As an example, consider the phrase marker represented by (3.14) (in this example, the dictionary entries have already been inserted into the phrase marker):

(3.14)

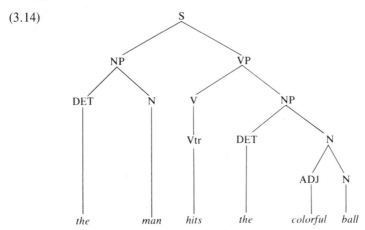

First, the projection rule operating on heads and modifiers combined the readings of *colorful* and *ball* to give the reading of *colorful ball*. The projection rules for articles and nouns then applied twice, amalgamating the readings of *the* and *man*, and *the* and *colorful ball*. The operation of the Main Verb-Object Projection Rule resulted in a reading of the verb phrase *hits the colorful ball*, and, finally, the reading of the entire sentence was attained by the application of the Subject-Verb Phrase Projection Rule.

Since any lexical item might have more than one reading if the projection rules were to apply in an unconstrained fashion, the number of readings of a node would simply have been the product of the number of readings of those nodes that it dominated. However, the selectional restrictions forming part of the dictionary entry of each lexical item served to limit the amalgamatory possibilities. For example, the verb *hit* contains a selectional restriction limiting its occurrence to objects with the marker (Physical Object). The sentence *the man hits the colorful ball* would thus be interpreted as meaning '. . . strikes the brightly colored round object,' but not as having the anomalous reading '. . . strikes the gala dance,' since *dance* does not contain the marker (Physical Object).

While Katz and Fodor's proposals regarding the general goals of a semantic theory were generally accepted by theoretical linguists and were to underlie most of the work done by generative grammarians in semantics for years afterward, their specific claims about the structure of the semantic component were largely ignored. This is because many linguists regarded their projection rules as utterly trivial. Katz and Fodor hypothesized four distinct projection rules, but, in reality, all had the identical function of combining readings of adjacent nodes without regard to their category or to the internal syntactic or semantic structure of the nodes being combined. Since structural information was lost as the projection rules applied, the reading of an entire sentence actually contained less semantic information than the phrase marker before the first application of a projection rule. Given the final semantically interpreted sentence, there was no way to tell where the reading of one subpart of the sentence stopped and another started.[3]

In the years following the appearance of Katz and Fodor's work, attention turned from the question of the character of the semantic rules to that of the syntactic level most relevant to their application.

3.3.2. Levels of Syntactic Structure, Transformations, and Meaning

The first paper to make a specific claim about the relationship between transformations and meaning was Fodor (1961). Fodor was aware that, given the contemporary formulation of the syntactic rules, the relationship had to be a fairly indirect one. For example, while many transformational rules preserved meaning, not all did: *John swept the floor* and *John did not sweep the floor* were related by an optional transformation. Likewise, while sentences whose derivations included the same set of phrase structure rules were often paraphrases, there were a number of cases where they were not, as the preceding example also illustrates. Fodor therefore put forward a rather weak claim about the relation of transformations and

---

[3]Katz was to refine the projection rules considerably in later publications (1967, 1972). For a useful discussion of this work, see J. D. Fodor (1977).

meaning, though it was the strongest that seemed feasible at the time: If two sentences are paraphrases and the same transformation is applied to each, then the resultant transforms are also paraphrases. In a reply to Fodor, Katz (1962) showed that even this exceedingly weak claim was deficient, pointing out that a single embedding rule could transform *the man hit the man* into the nonparaphrases *the old man hit the man* and *the man hit the old man*.

Katz and Fodor devoted very little space to this problem in their 1963 paper. They recognized that there was no single level at which their projection rules seemed suited to apply with maximum generality. On the one hand, they did not want the rules to apply to the output of the transformations alone, since that would render unpredictable the ambiguity inherent in a sentence derived from more than one underlying source. On the other hand, it would not do for the projection rules to apply before the transformations, since transformations not only changed meaning, but actually introduced elements with semantic content. They therefore arrived at the compromise of positing two types of projection rules. The first type, P1 rules, interpreted sentences produced without the aid of optional transformations (i.e., kernel sentences). The second type, P2 rules, introduced to the final interpretation the contribution of the optional transformational rules. Katz and Fodor never made the P2 rules precise.

An attractive solution to the problem of the interaction of syntax and semantics followed with the publication of Katz and Postal's *An Integrated Theory of Linguistic Descriptions* (1964). Katz and Postal concluded that all information necessary for the application of the projection rules is present in the underlying syntactic structure, or, alternatively stated, that transformational rules do not affect meaning. This conclusion became known to all linguists simply as the "Katz-Postal Hypothesis."

Katz and Postal first attempted to motivate the meaning-preserving nature of the singularly transformations. (This was necessary, of course, only for the optional transformations—what could it mean to claim that the input to and output of an obligatory rule had different interpretations?) They pointed out three ways that such rules might behave with respect to meaning:

1. No singular transformations affect semantic interpretation.
2. All singular transformations affect semantic interpretation.
3. Some singular transformations affect semantic interpretation and some do not.

Katz and Postal argued that simply on a priori methodological grounds, 1 was preferable to 2, just as both were preferable to 3. On empirical grounds 1 also seemed to have the most support. According to this alternative, it is the underlying structure of a sentence that is most suited to semantic interpretation. For a number of reasons, this appeared to be correct. First, rules such as Passive distort the underlying grammatical relations, relations that quite plausibly affect the semantic interpretation of the sentence. Hence, it seemed logical that the projection rules should apply to structures before the application of Passive. Second, it was typically the case that discontinuities were created by transformational rules (*look . . . up, have . . . en,* etc.) and never the case that a discontinuous underlying construction became continuous by the application of a transformation. Naturally, then, it made sense to interpret such constructions at an underlying level where their semantic unity was reflected by syntactic continuity. Finally, while there were many motivated examples of transformations that deleted elements contributing to the meaning of the sentence (the transformations forming imperatives and comparatives, for example), none had been proposed that inserted such elements. The rule that Chomsky (1957) had proposed to insert meaningless supportive *do* was typical in this respect.

There were, however, a number of apparent counterexamples to the Katz-Postal hypothesis. Consider Passive first. Recall from Section 2.2.4 that Chomsky had actually used the apparent meaning-changing property of this rule as evidence that transformations could not be defined in terms of synonymy. Katz and Postal reconsidered the data and called attention to the fact that both *everyone in the room knows at least two languages* and *at least two languages are known by everyone in the room* could be supplied with two interpretations, and hence Passive was meaning-preserving after all.[4]

Other examples of meaning-changing singulary transformations in *Syntactic Structures* were those that formed negatives, imperatives, and questions. But given the existence of the meaning-bearing morphemes Neg, I, and Q in the underlying structure (see Section 3.2.4), these transformations no longer had an effect on semantic interpretation. Thus there appeared to be no further counterexamples to the Katz-Postal hypothesis among the singulary transformations (but see Section 4.5.2).

Finally, they argued that those generalized transformations that, in the past, had been hypothesized to change meaning, in reality did not do so. Most of their attention was centered on the derivation of nominalizations. Both the factive and the manner readings of sentences such as *I don't approve of his drinking* had been derived from the same underlying phrase markers, roughly *I don't approve of it* and *he drinks.* Different generalized transformations then carried these identical underlying structures through different derivational paths to the surface. Katz and Postal argued at length for deriving each nominalization from a structure containing a head noun representing its abstract semantic quality, such as "act," "fact," "manner." Given such an analysis, each of the two readings of *I don't approve of John's drinking* would be derived from a different underlying structure, so the generalized transformations involved would not violate their hypotheses.

Their arguments for an abstract underlying structure for nominalizations are too detailed for discussion here. But these, and many of the other arguments in their book, utilized a novel heuristic for motivating rules and structures. They outlined the principle as follows:

---

[4]Newmeyer (1983:58–60) discusses how theoretical issues have contributed to judgments about the number of readings possessed by these sentences.

Given a sentence for which a syntactic derivation is needed; look for simple paraphrases of the sentence which are not paraphrases by virtue of synonymous expressions; on finding them, construct grammatical rules that relate the original sentence and its paraphrases in such a way that each of these sentences has the same sequence of underlying P-markers. Of course, having constructed such rules, it is still necessary to find INDEPENDENT SYNTACTIC JUSTIFICATION for them. (Katz and Postal 1964:157, emphasis in original)

The Katz-Postal hypothesis and the accompanying heuristic of motivating syntactic structure by appeal to meaning seemed so attractive that both were soon adopted by a large majority of practicing syntacticians. The consequences of this novel blurring of the boundary between syntax and semantics is discussed in depth in Chapters 4 and 5 of this volume.

3.4. SOME ASSUMPTIONS MADE EXPLICIT[5]

Several notions were implicit in the very earliest work in transformational generative grammar: the competence–performance dichotomy and the concepts "linguistic universal" and "level of adequacy." However, since they were not made precise until the early 1960s (or at least not given their familiar labels until then), I have saved discussion of them for this section.

3.4.1. Competence and Performance

Chomsky (1964b:915), in coining the terms "competence" and "performance" to refer to language knowledge and language use, respectively, was (as he explicitly acknowledged) giving a modern reinterpretation to the Saussurean notions of *langue* and *parole*. But it is just as well that Chomsky avoided Saussure's terms, given the differences in how the two linguists viewed the constructs. For Saussure, *langue* was an inventory of elements, not a system of generative rules. Moreover, to Saussure most syntactic relations were part of *parole*, rather than *langue*.

Chomsky's notion of "competence" encompasses the nonreducible core of language—those aspects that form the autonomous, purely linguistic, system characterized by a formal grammar. He defined the term "performance" to refer to "the actual use of language in concrete situations" (1965:4). Thus, competence is one of many systems that contribute to performance. As Chomsky put it, "To study actual linguistic performance, we must consider the interaction of a variety of factors, of which the underlying competence of the speaker–hearer is only one. In this respect, study of language is no different from empirical investigation of other complex phenomena" (1965:4).

In the 1970s, "competence" began to be used in a much broadened sense to refer to any systematic knowledge about language, not just grammatical knowledge (see

---

[5]The issues in this section are treated in greater detail in Newmeyer (1983).

Chapter 5). And Dell Hymes has "communicative competence" as "the most general term for the speaking and hearing capabilities of a person" (1971:16). Many generative grammarians have objected to these latter-day uses of the term "competence," since they seem to downplay (or dismiss altogether) the importance of the existence of a strictly grammatical linguistic faculty (for further discussion of this point, see Newmeyer 1983:35–38).

3.4.2. Linguistic Universals

As has already been noted, Chomsky in *Syntactic Structures* referred to the "condition of generality" that must be posed by the theory: "We require that the grammar of a given language be constructed in accord with a specific theory of linguistic structure in which such terms as 'phoneme' and 'phrase' are defined independently of any particular language" (p. 50). While he left no room for doubt in this and other passages that the general form of linguistic rules and the vocabulary of the theory itself were universal, he was not actually to use the term "universal" until around 1962. One can only speculate that the atmosphere of the 1950s, suspicious of any but "inductive" generalizations, made him discreet enough to avoid that emotionally charged term.

By the late 1960s, Chomsky had come to equate linguistic universals with that which is true of language by biological necessity, i.e., that which is innate. Thus he has used the term "universal grammar" to refer to "the set of properties, conditions, or whatever that constitute the 'initial state' of the language learner, hence the basis on which knowledge of language develops" (Chomsky 1980b:69). Generativists have typically motivated particular aspects of universal grammar by reference to the poverty of the stimulus available to the child language learner. How could the child have learned such-and-such a principle inductively, the argument goes, given its abstractness, the meager amount of relevant information provided, and the speed of acquisition?

Katz and Postal (1964:160–161) and Chomsky (1965:27–30) classified universals into two types: substantive and formal. The substantive universals are those concepts out of which particular statements in a linguistic description are constructed, as, for example, the syntactic categories, phonological distinctive features, and semantic markers. Traditional grammar, insofar as it claimed (or assumed) that all the languages in the world could be described by the same set of phonetic features or syntactic categories, embodied a theory of substantive universals.

Formal universals are more abstract. They specify the formal conditions that every grammatical description must meet, including the character of the rules that appear in grammars and the ways in which they can be interconnected. Thus, the Katz-Postal hypothesis is an example of a formal universal.

3.4.3. Levels of Adequacy

Chomsky (1964b and subsequent work) outlined the levels of success that might be attained by a grammatical description. The lower, the level of observational adequacy, is attained "if the grammar presents the primary data correctly" (p. 924). The higher, the level of descriptive adequacy, is achieved "when the grammar gives a correct account of the linguistic intuition of the native speaker, and specifies the observed data (in particular) in terms of significant generalizations that express underlying regularities in the language" (p. 924). The level of explanatory adequacy is attainable by the theory itself, not by a particular description within it. A theory is considered explanatorily adequate if it is capable of selecting one of a competing set of descriptively adequate grammars on the basis of a well-motivated theory of linguistic universals grounded in the human linguistic faculty.

Chomsky illustrated the various levels of adequacy by giving several examples from syntax and phonology. One of them involved the alternate phonetic shapes of the element *telegraph,* which appears as (3.15a), (3.15b), and (3.15c), in the contexts ♯   ♯, *-ic, -y,* respectively:

(3.15)   a. téligræf
           b. tèligræf
           c. tilégrif

Observational adequacy would be achieved by any grammar that simply stated the above facts. To achieve the level of descriptive adequacy, the grammar would have to treat these variant shapes as special cases of general rules applying to many other items. Explanatory adequacy would be attained by a theory able to select one of the descriptively adequate grammars as preferable, on principled grounds.

3.5. THE *ASPECTS* MODEL

The two most important theoretical innovations of Chomsky's *Aspects of the Theory of Syntax* (1965) were the abandonment of generalized transformations in favor of phrase structure recursion and the separation of the subcategorization and lexical rules from the phrase structure rules. Three findings led Chomsky to discard generalized transformations:

1. There is no order among embedding transformations. A singulary transformation never applies in a matrix sentence before a constituent sentence is embedded into it (see Section 3.2.2).
2. Constituent sentences keep their internal structure intact after embedding (see Section 3.2.3).
3. Generalized transformations themselves contribute nothing to the interpretation of the sentence (see Section 3.3.2).

Figure 3.4 illustrates the resultant organization of the *Aspects* model:

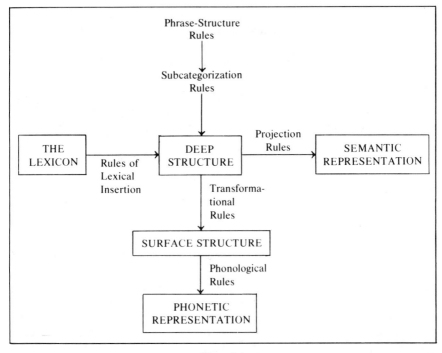

Figure 3.4

Since all recursion in this model is handled by the phrase structure rules, it follows that each derivation contains a single formal object, consisting of a lexically specified phrase marker, serving as input to the transformational rules. This formal object Chomsky named the "deep structure" of the sentence. The term "deep structure," like so much of the technical vocabulary of transformational generative grammar, has its historical antecedents. For example, in the nineteenth century Wilhelm von Humboldt (1836:119) had used the term *innere Form* in a similar way, as did the philosopher Ludwig Wittgenstein (1953:168) in his remarks on *Tiefengrammatik*. Even Charles Hockett (1958:246) had (uncharacteristically) referred to the "deep grammar" of a sentence, as distinct from its "surface grammar." Nevertheless, the term "deep structure" has had the unfortunate effect of inviting a metaphorical interpretation by the linguistically unsophisticated. As Chomsky later (1975c) complained, "[the term] has led a number of people to suppose that it is the deep structure and their properties that are truly 'deep,' in the nontechnical sense of the word, while the rest is superficial, unimportant, variable across languages, and so on. This was never intended" (p. 82). Even practicing linguists have confused deep structure, which is simply a level of grammatical description, with the innate linguistic mechanisms common to all humans: "Besides being explicit, generative grammars propose to include an underlying or deep structure which reflects innate patterns controlled by the brain'' (Lehmann 1978:50). Such profound misunderstandings have been only too common.

In any event, given the choice of the term "deep structure" for the level prior to the application of the transformational rules, "surface structure" was the obvious name for the level following their application.

3.5.1. The Level of Deep Structure

The level of deep structure in *Aspects* is defined by the application of three sets of rules: phrase structure rules, subcategorization rules, and rules of lexical insertion. Chomsky referred to the first two collectively as the "base rules."

The provision of categorial information is the task of the phrase structure rules, which generate a phrase marker, each node of which is labeled with a particular category symbol. Grammatical relations are then defined as wholly derivative relations between categories. For example, Chomsky (1965:71)[6] defines the following grammatical relations:

Subject-of: [NP immediately dominated by S]
Predicate-of: [VP immediately dominated by S]
Direct-Object-of: [NP immediately dominated by VP]
Main-Verb-of: [V immediately dominated by VP]

Chomsky suggested that while these definitions are adequate for deep structure grammatical relations, sentences with topicalized noun phrases, such as *this book I really enjoy,* in which two NP's occur in sentence-initial position, point to the need for supplementary definitions for surface structure relations. He mentioned, but did not expand on, a proposal by Paul Kiparsky that the relations "Topic-of" and "Comment-of" might be the appropriate ones for surface structure.

Chomsky attributed universality to the above definitions of grammatical relations: "These definitions must be thought of as belonging to general linguistic theory; in other words, they form part of the general procedure for assigning a full structural description to a sentence, given a grammar" (pp. 71–72)

Dozens of densely written pages of *Aspects* are devoted to the mechanics of subcategorization and lexical insertion. Many of them contrast alternative formats and formalizations, often without concluding firmly in favor of one alternative or the other. While such issues were regarded as important at the time, given the novelty of feature-introducing subcategorization rules and rules of lexical insertion, the specific form of these rules has proven to have little impact on subsequent theoretical debate. Hence, I outline them only sketchily.

The *Aspects* model embodied three types of subcategorization rules: context-free subcategorization rules, context-sensitive subcategorization rules (called "strict

---

[6]All references to Chomsky (1965) in this chapter are reprinted from *Aspects of the Theory of Syntax* by Noam Chomsky by permission of MIT Press, Cambridge, Massachusetts. Copyright © 1965.

subcategorization'' rules), and selectional rules. The first type of subcategorization rule has already been illustrated in Section 3.2.7 (see example 3.13). The second type subcategorized lexical categories in terms of the syntactic frames in which they occurred. That is, a verb occurring before a noun phrase would automatically be assigned the feature +[__NP], a noun after a determiner would take the feature +[DET__], and so on. Selectional rules subcategorized verbs on the basis of the features of the nouns with which they co-occurred. Thus a verb occurring after a subject noun with the feature +[HUMAN] would be assigned the feature +[+HUMAN__].

Finally, lexical items were insertable into the base phrase marker if their syntactic features matched those generated by the base rules. Hence, since the lexical entry of *discuss* contains the features +[__NP] and +[+HUMAN__], it could be inserted into the following phrase marker in the derivation of the sentence *the boy discussed the problem:*

(3.16)

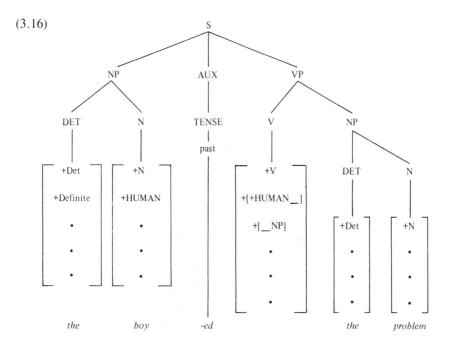

The *Aspects* approach thus treated selectional restrictions as syntactic restrictions holding between lexical items. The deviance of *the rock discussed the problem,* for example, was accounted for at the syntactic level of deep structure by virtue of a feature mismatch between the lexical entry of *discuss* and that of *rock*. In this way, *Aspects* departed from the Katz–Fodor approach to selectional restrictions, which handled them in the semantic component. The question of whether selectional violations are semantic or syntactic would emerge as a major controversy in the late 1960s (see Section 4.5.3).

3.5.2. The Transformational Component

The ordered set of transformational rules applied to the output of the base rules and lexical insertion rules. Chomsky incorporated Fillmore's proposal that the set of singular transformations "recycle" after each embedding by proposing that the transformational rules apply cyclically (preserving their linear order) from the most deeply embedded S to the highest S. That is, given a deep structure like (3.17), transformational rules apply first on the domain S_4, then on S_3, then on S_2, and finally on S_1:

(3.17)

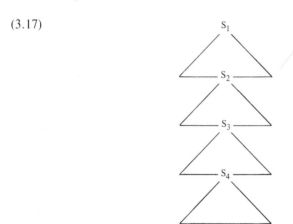

In other words, any transformation might have as many applications as there are levels of deep structure embedding.

Since the principle of cyclic application is not logically entailed by base recursion, a number of linguists in the years following the publication of *Aspects* set out to demonstrate that the principle had more to recommend it than elegance alone, that it was necessary for the generatiion of all and only the sentences of the language under investigation. The best-known argument for the cycle was constructed by George Lakoff (1968b), who showed that a noncyclic grammar would have to be nonfinite (Lakoff's argument may be found in published form in Grinder and Elgin 1973).[7]

---

[7]For other defenses of the transformational cycle, see Akmajian and Heny (1975), Jacobson and Neubauer (1976), and Pullum (1979a). Many variants of the cyclic hypothesis have been proposed, including the idea that there exist pre-cyclic rules that apply to the entire phrase marker before the first application of a cyclic rule and post-cyclic rules that apply to the entire phrase marker after the last cyclic rule. For discussion and an exhaustive review of the literature, see Pullum (1979a).

The principle of cyclic application remains one of the most solid results in transformational syntax. Every current approach to grammar that posits transformational rules at all assumes that they apply in cyclic fashion.

Aspects imputed to transformational rules a filtering function by which they could prevent certain well-formed base structures from being realized as grammatical sentences. For example, in the *Aspects* model, both (3.18) and (3.19) were well formed at the level of deep structure (ignoring irrelevant details):

(3.18)

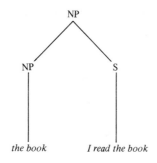

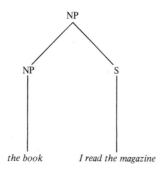

(3.18) is mapped into the phrase *the book which I read* by the Relative Clause Transformation, which fronts *the book,* deletes it, and replaces it with the relative pronoun *which*. (3.19), on the other hand, underlies no well-formed phrase. *Aspects* attributed its deviance to a violation of the Condition on Recoverability of Deletion, which filters out the structure based on (3.19) by preventing the deletion of *the magazine.*

There were, however, two other options available in the *Aspects* model for blocking a derivation involving (3.19). Chomsky could have eliminated (3.19) at the level of deep structure through a selectional restriction requiring that the head noun phrase of a relative clause select an identical noun phrase in the relative clause itself. Or he could have left the task of explaining the deviance to the semantic rules. Since (3.19) receives no interpretation, seemingly the semantic rules would have to block it anyway.

Perlmutter (1971:1–3) pointed out that Chomsky had two reasons for choosing the transformational over the deep structural filtering solution. First, while conditions governing deletion were well understood for transformations, identity conditions had never been claimed to be operative in the base. Second, there were no other clear examples of selectional restrictions holding between items in separate clauses. Chomsky's not even considering the semantic alternative simply illustrates the reluctance of most generativists at that time to attribute any nontrivial role to that poorly understood component.

Before *Aspects,* syntactic relatedness between sentences was expressible only in transformational terms. But as Chomsky pointed out (1965:219), the adoption of a separate lexicon and syntactic features made it possible to enter forms in the lexicon that had previously been related transformationally. For example, it was no longer necessary to derive a phrase like *John's proof of the theorem* transformationally from the sentence *John proved the theorem.* Rather, both *prove* and *proof* could be entered in the lexicon and related by a lexical rule handling verbs and their corresponding nominalizations.

What criteria, then, would determine whether a process was lexical or transformational? In *Aspects,* Chomsky appealed to only one: productivity. In keeping with the idea that ''all properties of a formative that are essentially idiosyncratic will be specified in the lexicon'' (p. 87), Chomsky proposed to handle lexically those quasi-productive processes that would necessarily have been considered transformational at an earlier time; he gave as examples sets of forms such as *horror, horrid, horrify; terror, (*terrid), terrify;* and *candor, candid, (*candify).*

In retrospect, it is interesting to recall that in *Aspects* Chomsky considered productive the processes involved in the formation of *destruction, refusal,* etc., and hence felt that ''clearly'' (p. 184) they were to be derived transformationally. Soon, however, his criteria for productivity were to become more stringent, and he would opt for a lexical treatment of all nominalizations exhibiting derivational morphology (see Chapters 4 and 6).

3.5.3. Syntax and Semantics

Chomsky's views in *Aspects* on the relationship between grammar and meaning are decidedly peculiar, perhaps even contradictory. In one passage, for example, he restated his earlier position on the independence of the two notions:

> For the moment, I see no reason to modify the view, expressed in Chomsky (1957) and elsewhere, that although, obviously, semantic considerations are relevant to the construction of a general linguistic theory (that is, obviously the theory of syntax should be designed so that the syntactic structures exhibited for particular languages will support semantic interpretation), there is, at present, no way to show that semantic considerations play a role in the choice of the syntactic or phonological

component of a grammar or that semantic features (in any significant sense of this term) play a role in the functioning of the syntactic or phonological rules. (Chomsky 1965:226)

But in another, he uncritically adopted the Katz–Postal hypothesis with its assumption that everything necessary for semantic interpretation is present in the deep structure. Assuming Katz-Postal, semantic considerations clearly "play a role in the choice of the syntactic component"—a syntactic analysis that resulted in an ambiguous sentence having only one deep structure would necessarily have to be rejected.

Furthermore, he avoided taking a position on the question of whether semantic features play a role in the functioning of the syntactic rules: "We call a feature 'semantic' if it is not mentioned in any syntactic rule, thus begging the question of whether semantics is involved in syntax" (Chomsky 1965:142). If, as Chomsky seemed to imply, any semantic feature that appeared in a syntactic rule was to be considered syntactic by definition, then it seems fair to conclude that in 1965 he could not have regarded the independence of grammar as a very strong empirical hypothesis.

The overall impression that one gets about Chomsky's position on this question is one of agnosticism. For example, he was quite open to the possibility that selection might be handled by the semantic rules, rather than at the level of deep structure. Going to the other extreme, he even considered plausible an alternative that later would be called "generative semantics" and set forth the first published proposal along these lines: "Alternatively, one might raise the question whether the functions of the semantic component as described earlier should not be taken over, *in toto*, by the generative syntactic rules" (Chomsky 1965:158). While Chomsky did not advocate this position, he certainly considered it reasonable.

Aspects of the Theory of Syntax, as the most ambitious general exposition of syntactic theory since *Syntactic Structures,* for a time played the role of the Bible of grammatical theory. An old saying about the other Bible (the holy one) is that even the devil could use it for his own purposes. As we will shortly see, every approach to syntax of the following decade, whether on the side of the angels or on the side of the devil, found Chomsky's remarks about the relationship of syntax and semantics in that book vague enough to suit its own purposes.

Chapter 4

The Rise of Generative Semantics

4.1. THE SYNTAX EXPLOSION

The years immediately following the publication of *Aspects* saw the greatest outpouring of work in syntax in the history of the field. For the first time ever in theoretical linguistics, the number of journal submissions, conference papers, and dissertations devoted to syntax exceeded those devoted to phonology. A general feeling arose that not being current in syntax was not being fully a linguist.

James McCawley (1976b) has attributed the creative outburst in syntax in the late 1960s in part to the fact that *Aspects* had "brought semantics out of the closet" (p. 6). By incorporating a semantic theory, the *Aspects* model promised insights into the nature of language as a medium of concept formation and communication. And the Katz-Postal hypothesis, which by now had become firmly entrenched, invited the conclusion that, as syntactic investigation became deeper, semantics would automatically fall into place.

As McCawley also pointed out, the *Aspects* model was far more systematic and intuitively appealing than either the *Syntactic Structures* model or any existing nontransformational model. Principles such as base recursion, the separation of subcategorization from the phrase structure rules, a distinct lexicon, the transformational cycle, and the meaning-preserving nature of transformations seemed naturally designed to extract an order and symmetry from what had always been regarded as the most chaotic aspect of language. *Aspects* made doing syntax fun, and more and more linguists wanted to be in on the fun. Moreover, in the late 1960s a number of studies demonstrated that the theory could be applied insightfully to the analysis of the most complex linguistic phenomena. The most noteworthy was Peter Rosenbaum's 1965 MIT dissertation, *The Grammar of English Predicate Complement Constructions* (Rosenbaum 1967). Rosenbaum did for *Aspects* what Lees had done for *Syntactic Structures,* showing that base recursion and cyclic transformations provided a satisfactory framework for the analysis of the fundamental syntactic processes in English.

The great majority of generative syntacticians in the late 1960s were MIT faculty and students or MIT graduates and their students. Indeed, virtually all knew each other personally. This meant that new ideas could be transmitted rapidly and the theory could undergo modification at a correspondingly rapid pace. But it also meant that many generativists came for a time to rely more on word of mouth or on informally circulated papers than on conventional publication as a means of disseminating their ideas.[1] As a consequence, those who were not part of the ingroup felt more and more isolated and developed a resentment toward the more strategically placed group of linguists, which in some cases led ultimately to hostility to generative grammar itself. But for those who were at the center of the developments in linguistic theory—and by 1970 they numbered in the dozens—this was a time of unbridled enthusiasm and unparalleled conviction that the frontiers of knowledge were being pushed back daily.

4.2. THE STEPS TO GENERATIVE SEMANTICS

4.2.1. An Unstable Situation

Until around 1965, generative theoreticians had been united on virtually every important issue. In one sense, this is hardly surprising. *Aspects* was written by Chomsky with constant feedback from the faculty and students at MIT, who made up at least 90% of the transformational grammarians in the world at that time. Yet, even by late 1965, the first public signs of division had appeared. In the fall of that year, Paul Postal argued at a colloquium at MIT that adjectives were members of the category "verb," a conclusion quite uncongenial to Chomsky's view of English syntax. The following spring, John Robert Ross, a graduate student and instructor at MIT, and George Lakoff, a part-time instructor at Harvard and associate in its computation laboratory, organized a series of Friday afternoon seminars in Harvard's William James Building, devoted to challenging analyses then favored by Chomsky. In the fall of 1966, with Chomsky on leave in Berkeley, Ross and Lakoff brought their opposition into the open in their classes. Ross's class in universal grammar at MIT drew dozens of students; Lakoff's in syntactic theory at Harvard well over 100.

The real fight began upon Chomsky's return early in 1967. For several years, however, the sides were very uneven. The large majority of theoretical linguists held positions very much at odds with those of Chomsky and his current students at MIT (most of whom speedily reconverted from their infatuation with the Ross–

---

[1]Some of the most important early papers were not published until 1976, when they were collected into an anthology by James McCawley (see McCawley 1976d).

Lakoff approach). And throughout the late 1960s the rift grew, as measured both by the intensity of the feeling of the participants and by the number of theoretical issues at stake.

The primary point of contention at that time centered around the abstractness of underlying syntactic structure. While all grammatical structures are "abstract," the notion "degree of abstractness" came to be identified with "degree of distance of deep structure from surface structure," or as contemporary eyes saw the issue, with "degree of closeness of deep structure to semantic representation." By this criterion the deep structures posited by many linguists were becoming very abstract indeed. To give one typical (and much discussed) example, Ross and Lakoff argued that the deep structure of (4.1) was not (4.2), as an analysis along the lines sketched in *Aspects* would suggest, but rather the highly abstract (4.4):

(4.1)   *Floyd broke the glass*

(4.2)

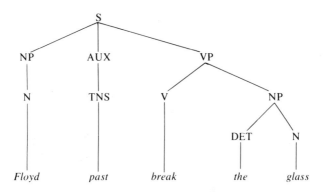

Going hand in hand with abstract deep structures was a drastic reduction in the inventory of grammatical categories. For example, abstract syntacticians argued that adjectives, prepositions, auxiliaries, and negative elements were all members of the category "Verb" in deep structure. In addition, numerous arguments were adduced for "lexical decomposition," the structural representation of a word's component elements in the underlying phrase marker. Example (4.4) illustrates lexical decomposition. The verb *break* is derived from (roughly) '*cause* + *come about* + *be* + *broken.*' Under abstract syntax, sentences with radically different surface structures were typically analyzed as identical at the deepest level of syntactic representation, as was the case with (4.3a) and (4.3b):

(4.3)   a. *Seymour sliced the salami with a knife*
          b. *Seymour used a knife to slice the salami*

Before the end of the decade, abstract syntacticians had come to abandon the concept of an independent level of deep structure entirely; this level had been driven back so far that it made no theoretical sense to distinguish it from semantic represen-

(4.4)

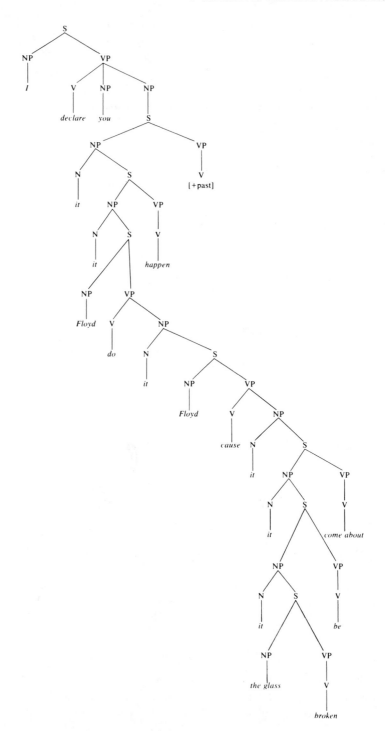

tation. The new deep structureless model of grammar, dubbed "generative semantics" by its practitioners, won virtually all abstract syntacticians to its banner.

As we will see, these radical conclusions were arrived at almost entirely by recourse to the assumptions of Katz and Postal's *Integrated Theory of Linguistic Descriptions* and Chomsky's *Aspects*. This fact alone, needless to say, accounts in large part for their widespread acceptance. The counterattack, initiated by Chomsky's lectures in the spring of 1967 (published as Chomsky 1970), required an abandonment of certain of these assumptions, and for that reason, if for no other, Chomsky was faced with an uphill struggle. It was not until the mid 1970s, in fact, that the nonabstract alternative was to reassert itself as the dominant model of syntactic description (for an outline of its development, see Chapter 6).

In the remainder of this section, I outline in some detail the reasoning that led to the conclusion that deep structures were highly abstract. I have often chosen the expository device of presenting these arguments by paraphrasing the authors' own words, without providing immediate critical commentary on their adequacy. The reader should not, however, conclude from my doing so that I either endorse the assumptions underlying the arguments or feel that the arguments go through, even granting the assumptions. In fact, I do neither. For the sake of historical continuity, however, it seems best to delay their evaluation until subsequent sections.

4.2.2. The Katz–Postal Contribution to Generative Semantics

By far, the main impetus for the adoption of highly abstract deep structures came from the Katz–Postal hypothesis. This might seem surprising. There is nothing in the notion that all interpretation takes place at deep structure that, per se, leads to abstractness. One can imagine a model consistent with Katz–Postal in which deep structures are quite shallow, and are mapped onto their respective meanings by a rich set of interpretive rules. In fact, the possibility of semantic rules actually contributing to meaning is not ruled out under the Katz–Postal hypothesis. But recall the trivial nature of the projection rules as proposed in the seminal Katz–Fodor paper. Their triviality led syntacticians simply to ignore them and invited the search for a syntactic solution to every semantic problem. Furthermore, whatever Chomsky's actual views may have been in 1965, many interpreted his comment that "the syntactic component of a grammar must specify, for each sentence, a DEEP STRUCTURE that determines its semantic interpretation" (Reprinted from *Aspects of the Theory of Syntax*, p. 16, by Noam Chomsky by permission of MIT Press, Cambridge, Massachusetts. Copyright © 1965.) as an endorsement of the position that it was reasonable to appeal to meaning in constructing syntactic rules and representations. Hence syntacticians began to posit deep structures that represented every aspect of the meaning of the sentence under investigation, a practice that led to ever more abstract deep structures.

It follows logically from the Katz–Postal hypothesis and the Katz–Fodor conception of the projection rules that every ambiguity must be represented by a deep structure difference. A few arguments for abstract deep structures motivated by the assumption that such structures should be semantically unique are paraphrased below. In all cases, previous analyses would have derived the sentence in question from only a single deep structure.

Sentences like (4.5a), which contain both a reason adverbial and a negative, are ambiguous between one reading in which the adverbial has wider scope and another in which the negative has wider scope. A natural way of representing this ambiguity in deep structure is by phrase markers (4.5b) and (4.5c), respectively:

(4.5)   a. *I don't steal from John because I like him*

b.

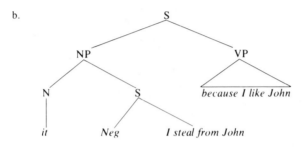

c.

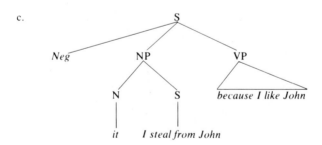

[PARAPHRASING G. LAKOFF 1970b, 169 –171]

Sentences like (4.6) are ambiguous between one reading in which *John* and *Mary* left jointly and another in which they left separately. Therefore two deep structures must be posited for such sentences, one capturing the joint reading (4.7a) and one capturing the separate reading (4.7b):

(4.6)   *John and Mary left*

(4.7)   a.

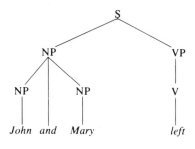

   b.

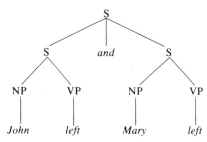

[PARAPHRASING LAKOFF AND PETERS 1969, 113–120]

It also followed that since projection rules did not supply any aspect of the meaning, anything understood as part of the meaning had to occur in the deep structure. Two examples follow of arguments constructed to represent syntactically a semantically understood element.

(4.8) contains a nonovert but understood verbal sense of performing some activity with respect to the book. (4.9), in which this verbal sense in syntactically encoded, is a reasonable candidate for the deep structure of (4.8).

(4.8)   *John began the book*

(4.9)

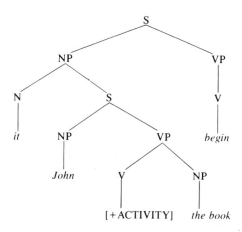

[PARAPHRASING NEWMEYER 1975, 40–44]

Consider (4.10):

(4.10)   *John agreed that Harry was an idiot*

One cannot simply agree; one must agree with SOMEONE. Hence, the deep structure of (4.10) is
roughly (4.11).

(4.11)

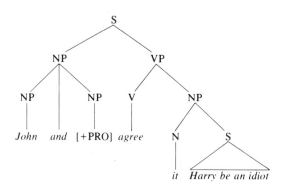

[PARAPHRASING LAKOFF and PETERS 1969, 118–119]

4.2.3. The *Aspects* Contribution to Generative Semantics

Even the assumptions of Katz–Postal and Katz–Fodor, taken together, were not
sufficient to secure the generative semantic conclusion that there exists no level of
deep structure distinct from semantic representation. This is because there is nothing in them that demands that if two sentences are paraphrases, they must have
identical deep structures. Take for example the following two sentences, which, for
purposes of illustration, are assumed to be perfect paraphrases:

(4.12)   a. *Mary sold the book to John*
           b. *John bought the book from Mary*

It is consistent with Katz–Postal and Katz–Fodor that these sentences could have
strikingly different deep structures, yet could be mapped onto identical semantic
representations by the projection rules.

Ironically, it was a proposal that Chomsky himself put forward in *Aspects* (however hesitantly) that facilitated the final step to generative semantics. He suggested
that selectional restrictions be handled at the level of deep structure by means of
subcategorization features of lexical entries. That is, a verb like *persuade* might be
entered with a feature requiring it to co-occur with a human subject and a complement sequence consisting of a human direct object followed by a clause denoting a
concept. As it turns out, the great majority of syntacticians in the late 1960s

accepted the idea of deep structure selection without question and found that, carried to its logical conclusion, it led to the virtual annihilation of deep structure as an independent level. Typically, arguments constructed on the basis of selectional restrictions took the following form:

The selectional restrictions holding between A and B in sentence S and between C and D in sentence S′ are essentially the same. We can capture this within the *Aspects* framework by positing substructures within S and S′ where A and C, and B and D, have the same representation. The restriction now need be stated only once.

Here are two examples:

Consider sentences (4.13a) and (4.13b). Prior analyses would most likely have derived them from deep structures (4.14a) and (4.14b), respectively:

(4.13) a. *Seymour sliced the salami with a knife*
  b. *Seymour used a knife to slice the salami*

(4.14)

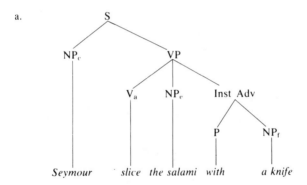

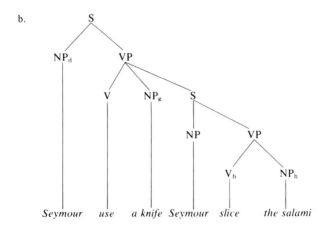

But notice the internal selectional correspondences that the two sentences share. The class V_a that occurs before instrumental adverbs is identical to the class V_b, which can occur as the main verb of the complement to *use*. Animate nouns alone can be NP_c in (4.14a); likewise only animates can be NP_d in (4.14b). The same coreferentiality restrictions that block $NP_e = NP_f$ and $NP_c = NP_f$ in (4.14a) seem to block $NP_g = NP_h$ and $NP_d = NP_g$ in (4.14b). And so on. Clearly, it would be undesirable to have to state these restrictions once for structures like (4.14a) and again for structures like (4.14b). Yet this is what would be necessary if the sentences were derived from two different deep structures. Therefore both (4.13a) and (4.13b) are derived from (4.14b), and the selectional restrictions need to be stated but once.

[PARAPHRASING G. LAKOFF 1968b, 4–29]

Observe the parallels between (4.15a), (4.15b), and (4.15c):

(4.15)   a. *America attacked Cuba*
            b. *The American attack on Cuba (was outrageous)*
            c. *America's attack on Cuba (was outrageous)*

Clearly, the possible noun phrase subjects of the verb *attack* in sentences like (4.15a) and the possible prenominal pseudo-adjectives and possessives in sentences like (4.15b) and (4.15c) respectively are, in an intuitive sense, the same. In other words, the verb *attack* and the noun *attack* share selectional restrictions. Yet a nonabstract approach to syntax would treat the restriction in (4.15a) as one between a noun phrase and a verb, in (4.15b) as one between an adjective and a noun, and in (4.15c) as one between a noun phrase and a noun. How can the statement of three separate selectional restrictions be avoided? Quite simply, by deriving them all from the same deep structure. The noun *attack* should be derived from its homophonous verb and the pseudo-adjective *American* from the noun *America*. In such an analysis, the selectional restriction would need to be stated only once, as a subject–verb restriction.

[PARAPHRASING POSTAL 1969, 219–224]

Arguments based on selectional restrictions led irrevocably to the conclusion that every meaning identity had to be represented as a deep structure identity. To see why, let us consider sentences (4.12a) and (4.12b) once again. Clearly, if the sentences are true paraphrases, the possible subjects of *buy* are identical to the possible indirect objects of *sell*, the possible subjects of *sell* are identical to the possible indirect objects of *buy*, and so on. In other words, these sentences manifest identical selectional restrictions. The obvious way to capture this generalization seemed to be to derive both sentences from the same deep structure, so that the selectional restrictions would require only one statement.

In other words, two conclusions had been reached: meaning differences were reflected by deep structure differences, and meaning similarities were reflected by deep structure similarities. These two conclusions invited a third: there was no appreciable difference between a deep structure representation and a semantic representation, and hence little reason to continue positing an independent syntactic level of deep structure.

4.2.4. The Birth of Generative Semantics

Up to about 1967, a battery of arguments had led consistently in one direction— to deep structures that exhibited semantic relations far more straightforwardly than the rather shallow ones of earlier work. Yet in no way had the fundamental assumptions of Katz and Postal (1964) and Chomsky (1965) been challenged. Quite the contrary, in fact; as we have seen, the abstract analyses arrived at were based explicitly on the theory put forward in those works. But paradoxically, the more abstract deep structures became, the more difficulties were created for another well-accepted proposal put forward in *Aspects,* namely the hypothesis that deep structure is the level at which lexical items enter the derivation. The seriousness of this problem became evident as a result of George Lakoff's conclusion (1970b) that if the theory were to account for the selectional restrictions holding between lexical items, it would also have to account for those within lexical items. For example, Lakoff argued that since selectional arguments demanded deriving *John thickened the sauce* from (roughly) *John caused – the sauce thicken,* it was necessary to derive *John killed Bill* from (roughly) *John caused – Bill die.* Otherwise, two separate (and unrelated) projection rules would be necessary to interpret causative sentences. But since Lakoff had not yet questioned the *Aspects* assumption that lexical items were inserted at deep structure, he had no choice but to posit the following deep structure for *John killed Bill.*

(4.16)

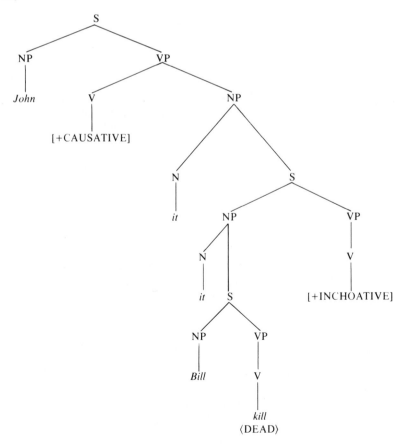

Since lexical items were assumed to be in the phrase marker before the first application of a transformation, *kill* had to be inserted in the deep structure prior to the transformations collapsing the triclausal structure into a uniclausal one. Furthermore, it was necessary to enter the word *kill* with the meaning 'dead' (where else would that meaning be represented?) and supply it with a feature to ensure that in such a circumstance it would obligatorily undergo the collapsing transformations. Such consequences made it clear that the presence of *kill* in the deep structure prior to the application of the collapsing rules was undesirable.

The obvious solution was to formulate deep structure representations strictly in terms of semantic features and to insert *kill* and other lexical items only after the collapsing rule (soon to be christened "Predicate Raising") applied. The fact that, by 1967, deep structure had come virtually to represent meaning anyway made this step a completely natural one to take.

The idea of getting rid of deep structure as an independent level was first suggested in a widely circulated letter that George Lakoff and John R. Ross wrote to Arnold Zwicky in March 1967 (now published as Lakoff and Ross 1976).[2] As they saw it, the level of deep structure, as defined in *Aspects,* possessed four properties. Deep structure was

1. the base of the simplest syntactic component;
2. the place where subcategorization and selectional restrictions were defined;
3. the place where basic grammatical relations were defined;
4. the place where lexical items were inserted from the lexicon.

But, they argued, all the evidence pointed to 1, 2, and 3 being properties of semantic representation, not of some intermediate level of deep structure. And as far as 4 was concerned, they pointed to examples like those discussed above to illustrate that some transformations had to apply before lexical items entered the derivation.[3]

With the abandonment of an independent deep structure, the first major rift among generative grammarians was firmly established.

4.3. EARLY GENERATIVE SEMANTICS

By rejecting the level of deep structure, generative semantics had rejected an assumption that had gone unchallenged since the inception of transformational generative grammar, the assumption that syntactic and semantic processes are fundamentally distinct. Indeed, generative semanticists saw no aspect of meaning that could not be represented in phrase-marker form. Figure 4.1 represents the initial generative semantic model put forward by Lakoff, Ross, and McCawley in 1967.

---

[2]George Lakoff had actually proposed as early as 1963 that the rules of the base generate semantic structures. However, the not very widely circulated mimeographed paper in which he proposed this (now published as G. Lakoff 1976b) was largely forgotten during the later years of the decade.

[3]Lakoff and Ross's specific example of post-transformational lexical insertion involved idioms, not causatives.

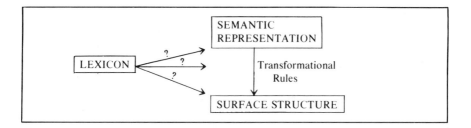

Figure 4.1

As Figure 4.1 indicates, the question of where lexical items were to enter the derivation was still to be worked out. McCawley (1968b) dealt with this problem by treating lexical entries themselves as structured composites of semantic material.[4] Thus he offered (4.17) as the entry for *kill:*

(4.17)

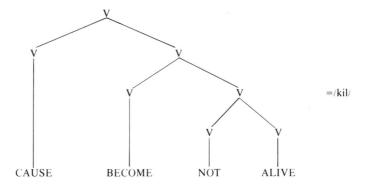

After the transformational rules had created a substructure in the derivation that matched the structure of a lexical entry, the phonological matrix of that entry would be insertable into the derivation. McCawley in 1968 hesitantly suggested that lexical-insertion transformations might apply in a block at the level of shallow structure (the point between the cyclic and post-cyclic rules) and later (1974) proposed cyclic insertion. However, generative semanticists never did agree on the locus of lexical insertion, nor even whether it occurred at some independently definable level at all.

The remainder of this section develops further the case that was made for generative semantics and charts its progress during the half-dozen years in which it flourished. The later development of this model is treated in Section 5.2.

---

[4]The idea that lexical items have their own internal syntax that mirrors sentence-level syntax was first put forward in Weinreich (1966).

4.3.1. Against the Level of Deep Structure

Generative semanticists realized that their rejection of the level of deep structure would be little more than word playing if the transformational mapping from semantic representation to surface structure turned out to be characterized by a major break before the application of the familiar cyclic rules, particularly if the natural location for the insertion of lexical items was precisely at this break. They therefore constructed a number of arguments, some quite ingenious, to show that no such break existed. The most compelling were modeled after Halle's argument (see Section 2.4.3) that an independent phonemic level demanded that one general process be stated as two separate, but nearly identical, rules. Below is an example from Paul Postal designed to illustrate that a consequence of a syntactic level of deep structure is just such a double-rule statement.

> Given a theory that posits such a level, the deep structures of (4.18a) and (4.18b) would have to be (4.19a) and (4.19b) respectively.

(4.18)   a. *John likes pork*
           b. *John likes meat from pigs*

(4.19)

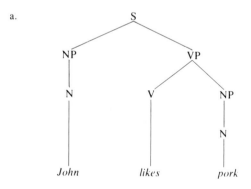

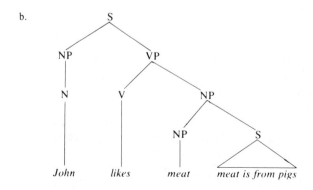

The transformations involved in forming and reducing relative clauses would apply to (4.19b) to derive (4.18b). However, given that (4.19a) underlies (4.18a), the same two rules would have to apply in reverse in the semantics to map (4.19a) into its semantic representation, something like MEAT WHICH COMES FROM PIGS. The only way to avoid such a double-rule statement is to take this semantic representation as the initial representation in the derivation and form (4.18a) by transforming it (by a lexical insertion rule) into the noun *pork*. Since this lexical transformation is optional, its nonapplication would yield (4.18b).

[PARAPHRASING POSTAL 1970b, 106–108]

Many arguments were constructed to show that cyclic rules have to precede lexical insertion, thereby depriving deep structure of what Chomsky (1971) saw as its crucial defining feature—the locus of lexical insertion. For example, Postal (1970b), who took (4.20b) to be the underlying syntactic structure of (4.20a),[5] argued that *Max* could become the surface structure subject only by being raised by the cyclic rule of Subject Raising, which itself must have applied prior to the lexical insertion of *remind*.

(4.20)   a. *Max reminded me of Pete*

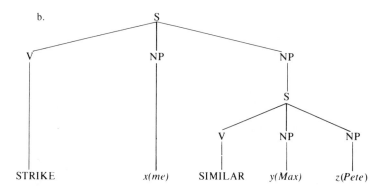

Analogously, G. Lakoff (1971a) argued that the lexical item *dissuade* could be inserted only after the application of Passive, and McCawley (1970b) suggested that the meanings of *suicide* ('killing oneself'), *malinger* ('pretend to be sick'), and *under surveillance* ('being watched') pointed to the application of Reflexive, Equi, and Passive, respectively, prior to their insertion.

Below are two more arguments in favor of lexical decomposition (and therefore against the level of deep structure):

Word-internal structures can be modified externally. Note that (4.21) is ambiguous between (4.22a) and (4.22b):

---

[5]While the question is logically independent of other assumptions, most generative semanticists assumed underlying verb–subject–object order for English (see McCawley 1970a). The refutation of this assumption by Berman (1974) is well accepted, though it has been subjected to an interesting critique by Anderson and Chung (1977).

(4.21)   *I almost killed John*

(4.22)   a. *I almost caused John to die*
          b. *I caused John to almost die*

Such facts fall out automatically from a treatment in which *kill* is syntactically decomposed into 'cause to die.'

[PARAPHRASING MORGAN 1969a, 49–52]

Syntactic lexical decomposition combined with the restriction that lexical items replace only constituents allows us to characterize the notion "possible lexical item." No lexical item could correspond to the circled material in (4.23), since it does not form a constituent.

(4.23)

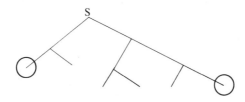

In contrast, the nonexistence of a lexical item meaning 'cause to become not obnoxious' is predicted to be an accidental gap, since the rule of Predicate Raising creates a structure that represents a (nonoccurring) lexical item with this meaning.

[PARAPHRASING MCCAWLEY 1968b, 71–76]

4.3.2. Global Rules

Since the cornerstone of generative semantics was the Katz–Postal hypothesis, any examples that tended to discredit the hypothesis presented a profound challenge. Yet such examples had long been known to exist. We have already seen (Sections 2.2.4 and 3.3.2) that a case could be made that passive sentences containing multiple quantifiers differ in meaning from their corresponding actives. The scope differences between (4.24a) and (4.24b), for example, might be taken to suggest that Passive is a meaning-changing transformation:

(4.24)   a. *Many men read few books*
          b. *Few books were read by many men*

Generative semanticists had no problem in constructing underlying structures for (4.24a) and (4.24b) that represented their different meanings. All of the usual arguments for abstract structures led them to posit something like (4.25a) and (4.25b), respectively, as their semantic representations, although there was disagreement as to the details.

(4.25) a.

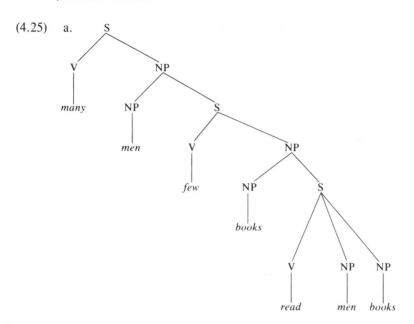

b.

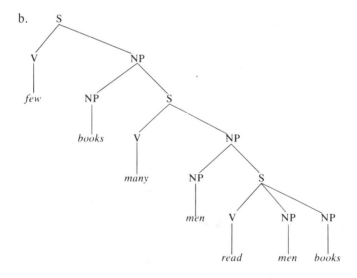

The problem, as Partee (1970) succinctly pointed out, was in insuring that (4.25a) would not be mapped into (4.24b) by undesired passivization and that (4.25b) would undergo this rule to guarantee that it not underlie (4.24a). The solution arrived at by G. Lakoff (1971a) was to let the rules of Passive and Quantifier Lowering apply freely to (4.25a) and (4.25b). By the end of the transformational derivation, then, each would have been mapped into both (4.24a) and (4.24b).

However, Lakoff suggested that the strict transformational derivation be supplemented by another type of rule—a global rule (or global derivational constraint), to be stated roughly as follows: if one logical predicate "asymmetrically commands" (roughly, "is in a higher sentence than") another in semantic representation, then it must precede it in derived structure. In this way (4.24a) and (4.24b) are filtered out as sentences derivable from (4.25b) and (4.25a), respectively.

The proposed global rule had the virtue of allowing both the Katz–Postal hypothesis and the hypothesis that the deepest syntactic level is semantic representation to be technically maintained.

Soon many examples of other types of processes were found that could not be stated in strict transformational terms, but seemed instead to involve conditions holding between derivationally nonadjacent phrase markers (i.e., were global). Many of these involved presupposition. Morgan (1969b), using standard abstract syntactic argumentation, postulated that the presuppositions of a sentence are represented in semantic representation as complements of an abstract performative verb of presupposing conjoined to the left of the sentence. The semantic representation of (4.26a), then, would be roughly (4.26b).

(4.26)   a. *John doesn't realize that his fly is open*

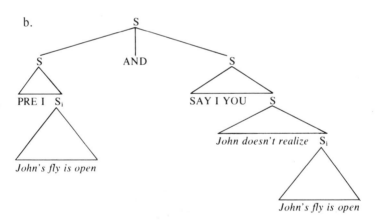

G. Lakoff (1971a) gave several examples of grammatical processes that seemed to refer, globally, to the presuppositions of the sentence. For example, he argued that the well-formedness of (4.27b) beside ill-formed (4.28b) indicates that the rule of *Will*-Deletion can apply only "if it is presupposed that the speaker is sure that the event will happen" (G. Lakoff 1971a:260).

(4.27)   a. *The Red Sox will play the Yankees tomorrow*
          b. *The Red Sox play the Yankees tomorrow*

(4.28)   a. *The Red Sox will beat the Yankees tomorrow*
          b. **The Red Sox beat the Yankees tomorrow*

He argued that lexical insertion transformations as well have to refer globally to presuppositions. Drawing on work by Fillmore (1969b, 1971c), he suggested that the meanings of lexical items contain both assertions and presuppositions. In this view, *assassinate* asserts 'kill' and presupposes that its object is an important public figure. Hence, Lakoff argued, the insertion transformation for *assassinate* differs from that for *kill* only in that in the former case this rule is conditioned globally by the above presupposition.

The first global rules proposed all referred to a level of syntactic structure and a level of semantic structure. This left their proponents open to the charge that global rules were no more than a maneuver to comply with the letter of the Katz-Postal hypothesis. In response to such an accusation, George Lakoff wrote his famous "Global Rules" paper (1970a), in which he attempted to establish that global rules had purely syntactic motivation. Below are briefly (and inadequately!) paraphrased two much-discussed global rules of this type:

> In Classical Greek, the agreement in case of adjectives and participles with their subjects cannot be stated by a simple transformational rule of Case Agreement. The reason is that these elements agree with the derived case of what had been their subject at an earlier stage in the derivation. Hence, Case Agreement must be stated as a global rule that applies late in the derivation but has the power to "look back" to see what grammatical relations had existed previously.
>
> [PARAPHRASING G. LAKOFF 1970a, 628–629; ANDREWS 1971, 127–152]

Be in English contracts regularly under reduced stress:

(4.29)   a. *There is this much wine in the bottle*
         b. *There's this much wine in the bottle*

(4.30)   a. *The concert is here at two o'clock*
         b. *The concert's here at two o'clock*

But note:

(4.31)   a. *I wonder how much wine there is in the bottle*
         b. **I wonder how much wine there's in the bottle*

(4.32)   a. *Tell Harry where the concert is at two o'clock*
         b. **Tell Harry where the concert's at two o'clock*

> (4.31b) and (4.32b) are ungrammatical because stress lowering (and subsequent contraction) have occurred immediately preceding a place where movement or deletion took place. Stress lowering, which is in the phonology, must therefore be stated with a global condition blocking it from applying before a deletion site.
>
> [PARAPHRASING KING 1970, 134–136; G. LAKOFF 1970a, 631–632]

Lakoff's definition of "global rule" was broad enough to encompass almost any conceivable grammatical process that was not a transformation:[6]

> Those of us who have tried to make transformational grammar work have attempted to patch up the classical theory with one ad hoc device after another: my theory of exceptions [G. Lakoff 1970b],

---

[6] I have updated the references in the quotation. Lakoff (1971a) also described extrinsic rule-ordering statements as global constraints.

Ross' constraints on movement transformations [1968], the Ross [1968]–Perlmutter [1971] output conditions, Postal's crossover principle [1971] and anaphoric island constraints (1969), Jackendoff's surface interpretation rules [1972], Chomsky's lexical redundancy rules and his analogy component [1970], and so on. In a recent paper . . . [G. Lakoff 1971a], I suggested that most, if not all, of these ad hoc patching attempts were special cases of a single general phenomenon: global derivational constraints . . . constraints [stating] well-formedness conditions on configurations of corresponding notes in non-adjacent trees in a derivation. (G. Lakoff 1970a:627–628)

The only attempt to constrain the power of global rules involved limiting the points in a derivation to which they might make reference: "It is assumed that derivational constraints will be restricted to hold either at particular levels in a derivation (semantic representation, surface structure, shallow structure and deep structure, if such exists), or to range over entire derivations or parts of derivations holding between levels" (G. Lakoff 1971a:234). At first it was suggested that any particular global rule could refer to at most two nodes (G. Lakoff 1971a:234). This was later increased to "hopefully no more than three or four" (G. Lakoff 1972a:87).

4.3.3. Logic and Semantic Representation

In the late 1960s, the generative semanticists began to realize that as the inventory of syntactic categories became more and more reduced, those remaining bore a close correspondence to the categories of symbolic logic. The three categories whose existence generative semanticists were certain of in this period—sentence, noun phrase, and verb—seemed to correspond directly to the proposition, argument, and predicate of logic (logical connectives were incorporated into the class of predicates, as were quantifiers).[7] This was an exhilarating discovery for generative semanticists and indicated to them more than anything else that they were on the right track. For, now, the deepest level of representation had a "natural" language-independent basis, rooted in what Boole (1854) had called "The Laws of Thought." What is more, syntactic work in languages other than English was leading to the same three basic categories for all languages. This "universal base hypothesis," not surprisingly, was seen as one of the most attractive features of generative semantics.

By around 1970, generative semanticists, particularly George Lakoff, had raised the term "natural logic" to the level of a slogan for generative semantics. However, the meaning of the term was never fully clarified. In some cases it seemed to refer to a field of inquiry: "Natural logic is the study of reasoning in natural language" (G. Lakoff 1974a:162); in others to a set of conditions on a successful linguistic description (G. Lakoff 1972e:589); and in still others to a new logical system to replace the inadequate arbitrary ones of the logicians (McCawley 1971:285–286).[8]

---

[7]McCawley later (1970b:230ff, 1970c:173) listed many other respects in which his ideas about the nature of semantic representation differed from the more usual variants of symbolic logic.

[8]These three uses of the term are not necessarily incompatible, although they may be. Stalker (1973) describes at length the difficulty in interpreting precisely what generative semanticists meant by the term "natural logic."

Generally, examples cited to illustrate the need for natural logic involved subtle interactions of grammatical and logical phenomena. The following is typical:

The expression *would rather* is a positive polarity item:

(4.33)   a. *I would rather go*
           b. **I wouldn't rather go*

But note the acceptability of (4.34):

(4.34)   *I didn't meet anyone who wouldn't rather go*

One might suppose, then, that it is the even number of negatives that renders (4.34) acceptable. But this is not so, since (4.35) is ungrammatical:

(4.35)   **I didn't meet the man who wouldn't rather go*

Double negatives are permissible only when they result in a sentence that is logically equivalent to a positive. This shows the inseparability of grammar and logic and the hopelessness of any model that attempts to maintain a strict separation of the two.

[PARAPHRASING G. LAKOFF, 1972e, 588–599, based on work by BAKER 1970a]

4.3.4. The Appeal of Generative Semantics

I have already pointed to the reasons for the widespread acceptance of generative semantics. Its characterization of the relation between syntax and semantics was both familiar, in that it was based on pre-*Aspects* assumptions, and conceptually simple. Traditionally, grammarians have set as their goal explicating the relation between form and content; generative semantics set out to capture this relation in as direct (and therefore in as an intuitively plausible, or commonsensical) way as possible. As Kuroda (1972:3) pointed out: "One seems to witness here [in generative semantics] a more faithful reemergence of the time-honored view of language that it is a correlation of the inner content of meaning and outer form of sound representation."[9]

In an influential essay, Paul Postal (1972a) elevated to principle the desirability of the generative semantic view of uniform homogeneous derivations:

What I wish to suggest briefly is that because of its a priori logical and conceptual properties, [generative semantics] is the basic [theory] which generative linguists should operate from as an investigatory framework, and that it should be abandoned, if at all, only under the strongest pressures of empirical disconfirmation. In short, I suggest that [this] framework has a rather special logical position vis-a-vis its possible competitors within the generative framework, a position which makes the choice of this theory obligatory in the absence of direct empirical disconfirmation. (p. 135)

---

[9]Interestingly, Chomsky (personal communication) has offered the opinion that the history of transformational grammar would have been more "rational" if generative semantics had been the original position, with interpretivism a subsequent development, given the fact that the former more directly captures the grammarian's classic goal. Along the same lines, he suggests that the only valid criticism of his research into the Port-Royal grammar (see Chomsky 1966a) comes from commentators like H. E. Brekle (1969) who have implied that this seventeenth century linguistic model is more directly an antecedent of generative semantics than of the *Aspects* theory.

In short, Postal's view that generative semantics was an a priori desirable theory was widely accepted at the time.

There were sociological reasons as well for the success of generative semantics. Many of the earliest transformational grammarians, at home with the Katz–Postal hypothesis, naturally adopted this framework in the late 1960s. But by then, they had radiated into teaching positions all over the United States, while almost all of Chomsky's supporters were at MIT. This not only gave generative semantics the aura of a national "movement," but it meant that 10 times as many students were being taught generative semantics as were being taught the alternative. The clubby ingroup atmosphere that then characterized (and still, to a certain extent, characterizes) the MIT Linguistics Department contrasted sharply with the missionary zeal of the generative semanticists and further helped to guarantee a slow, arduous reassertion of MIT hegemony within transformational grammar.

The allusion to generative semantics as a "movement" is not simply a figure of speech. The public lectures given by Lakoff, Ross, McCawley, Postal, and others resembled political rallies as much as academic seminars. The 1968 Linguistic Institute at the University of Illinois, at which Lakoff, Ross, and McCawley preached the new gospel to hundreds, stands out not only as a high-water mark in the ascendant tide of generative semantics, but also as the epitome of the mixing of reasoned argument with pure showmanship and pure salesmanship.

The epicenter of generative semantics was the Department of Linguistics at the University of Chicago, where James McCawley (and later Jerrold Sadock and Noriko Akatsuka McCawley) taught. McCawley's charisma was an important factor in spreading the model. Many of the "second generation" of generative semanticists—including Jerry Morgan, Georgia Green, Robert Binnick, and Alice Davison—were McCawley's students. Also instrumental in this regard was the Chicago Linguistic Society, whose published proceedings (particularly in the 1968–1972 period) provided a vehicle for the rapid dissemination of the latest generative semantic hypotheses. The CLS, which holds yearly meetings organized by Chicago students, helped to give generative semantics a national (and later international) presence, for which Chomsky and his supporters in that period had no match.

The excitement that pervaded the early Chicago meetings is impossible to characterize adequately in print. Linguists traveled from across the United States just to hear about the latest developments in generative semantics. CLS papers like the ones in Table 4.1 were to define a research strategy for the majority of the theoretical linguists in America.

The CLS itself was not officially committed to generative semantics any more than it was officially committed to generative grammar. In fact, each volume contained one or two Chomskyan papers, and even an occasional paper from completely outside the generative tradition was presented at the meetings. But the combination of the commitment of the CLS organizers to generative semantics and the insularity of the Chomskyans guaranteed that the views of generative semanticists would dominate the meetings.

TABLE 4.1

CLS volume	Author and date	Title of paper
4	James McCawley (1968b)	Lexical Insertion in a Transformational Grammar without Deep Structure
5	Laurence Horn (1969)	A Presuppositional Analysis of *only* and *even*
5	George Lakoff (1969b)	On Derivational Constraints
5	Jerry Morgan (1969b)	On the Treatment of Presupposition in Transformational Grammar
5	Paul Postal (1969)	Anaphoric Islands
5	John R. Ross (1969c)	Guess Who?
7	David Gordon and George Lakoff (1971)	Conversational Postulates

4.4. CASE GRAMMAR

In the late 1960s, the relatively shallow deep structures of the *Aspects* model were attacked from another quarter. In a number of important papers, Charles Fillmore (1966, 1968, 1969a, 1971b, 1971c) developed an alternative model of grammar whose distinguishing feature is that, at the deepest syntactic level, a sentence consists of a verb and an unordered series of semantically characterizable thematic roles, or, as he called them, cases, which are drawn from a universal vocabulary.

Fillmore took as his starting point the seeming inability of the *Aspects* model to represent categorial and thematic information simultaneously. It seemed evident, for example, that *Aspects* could not adequately capture the fact that expressions such as *in the room, toward the moon, on the next day, in a careless way, with a sharp knife,* and *by my brother* are simultaneously prepositional phrases and indicators of location, direction, time, manner, instrument, and agent respectively. His solution was to reanalyze prepositional phrases in underlying syntactic structure as a sequence of a noun phrase and an associated prepositional ''case-marker,'' both dominated by a case symbol denoting the thematic role of that prepositional phrase. For the sake of generality, he analyzed every element in the sentence bearing a thematic role, whether PP or NP, in an analogous fashion. Thus even noun phrase subjects were to be associated with case markers and case symbols.

Fillmore's methodology, then, was analogous to that of the generative semanticists'. Both appealed to meaning to motivate syntactic structure, and, as a consequence, both were led to models of grammar in which the deepest level of syntactic structure was close to semantic structure.

While the specific set of cases (and their definitions) varied from paper to paper, the following list (from Fillmore 1971a) is typical (LOCATIVE has been added from Fillmore 1968):

(4.36)   a. AGENT (A), the instigator of the event
         b. COUNTERAGENT (C), the force or resistance against which the action is carried out

    c. OBJECT (O), the entity that moves or changes or whose position or existence is in consideration

    d. RESULT (R), the entity that comes into existence as a result of the action

    e. INSTRUMENT (I), the stimulus or immediate cause of an event

    f. SOURCE (S), the place from which something moves

    g. GOAL (G), the place to which something moves

    h. EXPERIENCER (E), the entity that receives or accepts or experiences or undergoes the effect of an action (earlier called "Dative")

    i. LOCATIVE (L), the case that identifies the location or spatial orientation of the state or action identified by the verb

Below are Fillmore's arguments for the benefits accrued by considering case to be a primitive notion.

    I. Semantic benefits. The theory of *Aspects* claims that deep structure is an adequate base for semantic interpretation. This is clearly false. In each of the sentences of (4.37), the noun phrase *the door* bears the same semantic relation to the verb, yet it would be considered a deep structure subject in (4.37a) and a deep structure object in (4.37b–d). Conversely, *the door* in (4.37a), *John* in (4.37b and d), and *the wind* in (4.37c) all manifest different semantic relations with respect to the verb. Yet in the *Aspects* model, all would be treated as deep structure subjects.

(4.37)   a. *The door opened*
          b. *John opened the door*
          c. *The wind opened the door*
          d. *John opened the door with a chisel*

Case grammar can capture these relationships straightforwardly. *Open* is a verb which takes an obligatory OBJECT and an optional AGENT and/or INSTRUMENT. Hence, at the deepest syntactic level the relevant semantic information is presented directly.

                             [Paraphrasing Fillmore 1969a, 363–369]

    II. Syntactic benefits. The surface subject of a sentence can be predicted on the basis of case information. Let us posit the following case hierarchy for English:

    a. AGENT
    b. EXPERIENCER
    c. INSTRUMENT
    d. OBJECT
    e. SOURCE
    f. GOAL
    g. LOCATION
    h. TIME

If more than one noun phrase is present in the sentence, the highest one in the hierarchy becomes subject. For example, since AGENT is higher than OBJECT, (4.37b) is grammatical, not (4.38a); since INSTRUMENT is higher than OBJECT, (4.37c) is grammatical, not (4.38b):

(4.38)   a. **The door opened by John*
          b. **The door opened with/by the wind*

    Rules such as Passive, which lead to violations of the hierarchy, "register" their violation by means of special morphological elements (hence the *be* + *en* of Passive).[10]

                              [Paraphrasing Fillmore 1971b, 42]

---

[10]Some violations of the hierarchy, however, are not registered morphologically. Sentences such as *The play pleased me,* in which an OBJECT was chosen subject instead of a higher ranked EXPERIENCER, had to be treated by an exception mechanism.

III. Lexical benefits. By entering verbs and their associated case frames in the lexicon, considerable simplification in that component can be attained. *Like* and *please,* for example, can be treated as synonymous, each bearing the case frame +[_____O + E]; they differ only in their subject-selection features. Along the same lines, *show* has the same semantic representation as *see;* their entries differ only in that the frame feature for *show* contains an A, while that for *see* does not:

(4.39)   a. *see;* +[_____O + E]
           b. *show;* +[_____O + E + A]

[PARAPHRASING FILLMORE 1968, 30–31]

Case grammar, in a certain respect, was a more fundamental departure from the *Aspects* model than the abstract syntactic model that developed alongside it in the late 1960s. Abstract syntacticians explicitly based their conclusions on the theory as outlined in *Aspects;* case grammarians, on the other hand, took as a starting point the perceived inadequacies of *Aspects.* Hence, Fillmore broke with that theory even before abstract syntacticians had become generative semanticists. In Fillmore's words, deep structure "is an artificial intermediate level between the empirically discoverable 'semantic deep structure' and the observationally accessible surface structure, a level the properties of which have more to do with the methodological commitments of grammarians than with the nature of human languages" (Fillmore 1968:88).

One might conclude from the above remarks that Fillmore was in the vanguard of the generative semantic movement. Nothing could be farther from the truth, however. Despite Fillmore's rhetorical abandonment of deep structure, the case structures he posited were more shallow even than those posited under abstract syntax, much less generative semantics.[11] For Fillmore (1968), a sentence consisted of a "proposition," the tenseless set of verb–case relationships, and a "modality" constituent consisting of such items as negation, tense, mood, and aspect. But by that time, generative semanticists had concluded that not only were the modalities deprepositional, but the cases, "semantic primitives" in Fillmore's view, were themselves decomposable into more basic units.

Fillmore, to be sure, drew case grammar somewhat closer to generative semantics by analyzing the former BENEFACTIVE case preposition *for* as a higher predicate (1971b). But this hardly satisfied generative semanticists, who pointed out (correctly) that the same argumentation should lead to an analogous treatment for all cases—that is, to an abandonment of case grammar in favor of generative semantics.

While generative semanticists attacked case grammar for not being semantically revealing, others concentrated on its syntactic shortcomings (see especially Dougherty 1970b; Chomsky 1972a; Mellema 1974). Most importantly, they pointed out flaws in the subject-selection hierarchy. The subject-selection rules at best, it was argued, would simply supplement the familiar movement transformations, which in itself would not lend any special support to case grammar. But at worst, the subject-

---

[11]The relative shallowness of the level of case structure is indicated by the fact Stockwell, Schachter, and Partee (1973), an ambitious attempt to construct a complete grammar of English, is based on the compatibility of case grammar and Chomsky's nonabstract lexicalist hypothesis.

selection rules would complicate the transformational component considerably, the correct alternative depending on the interpretation of the rather vague statements about how and where the subject-selection rules function in the grammar.

Work in case grammar has always been somewhat outside of "mainstream" generative syntax. Nevertheless, the theory has attracted quite a number of adherents over the years, and its possibilities continue to be explored. Two adaptations that deserve mention are the "lexicase" approach of Starosta (1971, 1973) and the "localist" hypothesis of J. Anderson (1971, 1977). Fillmore himself later (1977) developed a more functionalist approach to subject selection in particular and case grammar in general. In fact, the theory has been taken in well over a dozen different directions, with its proponents differing among themselves over such fundamental questions as the number of cases (from three to over a dozen have been proposed) and the criteria by which they might be identified.

Despite the lack of success of case grammar itself, most generative syntacticians would agree today that any adequate theory must include a characterization of semantic cases (or, as they are more commonly termed, "thematic roles") and relate them to other aspects of syntactic patterning. Indeed, in the current government–binding theory (see Section 8.2.3), thematic roles are at the center of one of the subsystems of the theory. Fillmore and the case grammarians deserve credit for impressing upon the linguistic community the importance of these roles.[12]

4.5. THE EMERGING OPPOSITION TO GENERATIVE SEMANTICS

While most syntacticians in the late 1960s became generative semanticists, not all did. In particular, Chomsky and his current students resisted the generative semantic tide. Before the end of that decade this latter group of linguists had adduced evidence that raised serious doubts about the generative semantic direction: their lexicalist hypothesis pointed to a loss of generality if an important class of sentences were to be derived transformationally (Section 4.5.1), and they constructed counterexample after counterexample to the Katz–Postal hypothesis, which had played such a crucial role in the development of generative semantics (Section 4.5.2). Furthermore, the *Aspects* assumptions about selectional restrictions, which had also spurred generative semantics, began to be questioned as well (Section 4.5.3). While few hardcore generative semanticists were moved by any of the above, the fact that their conclusions were being called into question helped contribute to the formation of a pool of "undecideds," which would facilitate the victory of nonabstract syntax in the 1970s.

---

[12]Other foundational work in this period was contributed by Jeffrey Gruber (1976). Gruber's work attracted little contemporary attention (but see Jackendoff 1972) but later became as influential as Fillmore's on 1980s approaches to thematic relations.

4.5.1. The Lexicalist Hypothesis

Chomsky launched his counteroffensive to abstract syntax upon his return from Berkeley at the beginning of 1967, at about the same time that its practitioners had begun to regard themselves as generative semanticists. The principal document of this counteroffensive, his paper "Remarks on Nominalization" (Chomsky 1970), argued that fundamental syntactic generalizations can be captured only if the syntactic deep structure level exists and is moreover much less abstract than it had ever been previously regarded.

The "Remarks" paper is devoted to arguing for what Chomsky, borrowing a term from Chapin (1967), called the "lexicalist hypothesis." Essentially, the hypothesis bans category-changing transformational rules from the grammar. That is, it disallows a verb or an adjective from being transformed into a noun, a verb from being transformed into an adjective, and so on. "Remarks" centers on the analysis of derived nominals,[13] those words illustrated in boldface in (4.40). The paper argues that they should be entered in the lexicon directly as nouns, rather than derived by a transformational rule from their related verbs (or adjectives), as Chomsky himself had proposed in earlier work:

(4.40) a. *John's **refusal** of the offer*
  b. *Mary's great **skill** at tennis*
  c. *the **payment** of one hundred dollars to the fund*
  d. *Helen's **marriage** to Terry*
  e. *an itinerant **laborer***

Chomsky's three principal arguments for the lexicalist hypothesis are outlined below:

Argument I: Derived nominals (DN's) occur in sentences corresponding to base structures, but never to transformationally derived structures (contrast the (c) phrases with the (d) phrases below). This fact follows from the treatment of DN's as deep structure nouns. Transformations such as Raising-to-Object (4.41), Particle Movement (4.42), and Dative Movement (4.43) apply to verbs, not nouns, thus rendering the (d) phrases underivable.

(4.41) a. *John believed that Bill was a fool* → RAISING-TO-OBJECT
  b. *John believed Bill to be a fool*
  c. *John's belief that Bill was a fool* ↛
  d. **John's belief of Bill to be a fool*

(4.42) a. *John looked up the answer* → PARTICLE MOVEMENT
  b. *John looked the answer up*
  c. *John's looking up of the answer* ↛
  d. **John's looking of the answer up*

---

[13]The term "derived nominal" created no end of confusion, since Chomsky applied the term just to those nominalizations which he argued were NOT derived transformationally. Presumably the name comes from the fact that they exhibit derivational (as opposed to inflectional) morphology.

(4.43)   a. *John gave the book to Bill* → DATIVE MOVEMENT
          b. *John gave Bill the book*
          c. *John's gift of the book to Bill* ↛
          d. **John's gift of Bill of the book*

Argument II: A transformational rule should capture a regular productive relationship. But the relationship between DN's and their corresponding verbs is highly irregular. Not only does every verb not have a corresponding DN, but every DN does not have a corresponding verb. Furthermore, the meaning relation between verbs and DN's is an idiosyncratic one (consider, for example, the relation between *do* and *deed, marry* and *marriage, ignore* and *ignorance*). In those cases in which no verb corresponding to a DN exists, a transformational account would have to invent an abstract verb whose only function would be to undergo the nominalization transformation. On the other hand, a lexicalist treatment of DN's captures their irregularity in a natural manner. We can capture lexically the shared features of the verb *refuse* and the noun *refusal,* for example, by considering *refuse* to be lexically neutral between N and V, and allowing its entry in the lexicon to contain a N branch and a V branch. The properties common to *refuse* and *refusal* need to be represented only once in the neutral entry, while their distinct properties can be represented on the appropriate branch.

We are still left with the problem of accounting for the fact that the co-occurrence restrictions that hold within sentences are similar to those that hold within noun phrases. For example, consider (4.44a) and (4.44b):

(4.44)   a. *John proved the theorem*
          b. *John's proof of the theorem*

The noun phrase subject of *prove* corresponds to the noun phrase in the determiner of *proof,* and the noun phrase object of *prove* corresponds to the noun phrase in the prepositional phrase following *proof.* A transformational account of DN's handles these facts automatically by deriving phrases like (4.44b) from full sentences, thus necessitating only one statement of the co-occurrence restrictions.

A lexicalist account can handle these facts as well, given a formalism like the following that exploits the internal similarities of the major categories. Assume rules (4.45a–c) as the core phrase structure rules of English (where X can be a Noun, Adjective, or Verb):

(4.45)   a. $\underline{S} → \bar{\bar{N}} \; \bar{\bar{V}}$
          b. $\bar{\bar{X}} → [\text{Specifier-of-}\bar{X}] \; \bar{X}$
          c. $\bar{X} → X \ldots$

Now the deep structure of (4.44a–b) will be (4.46a–b), respectively:

(4.46)

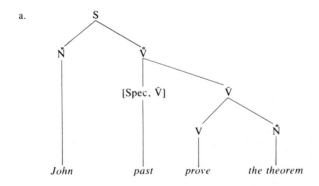

a.

b.

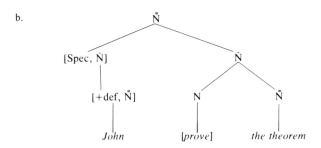

Notice the structural similarities between the nominal phrase (4.44b) and the sentence (4.44a). Thus the neutral entry for *prove* can be specified with co-occurrence features that apply equally in phrases and sentences.

Put simply, the "X-bar convention" (as it came to be called) allows the co-occurrence restrictions holding within sentences to be generalized to hold within noun phrases as well, thereby eliminating what is perhaps the major motivation for a transformational treatment of DN's.[14]

Argument III: The structures in which DN's occur resemble noun phrases in every way. They can contain determiners, prenominal adjectives, and prepositional phrase complements, but not adverbs, negation, aspect, nor tense. This follows automatically if DN's are nouns in the lexicon and are inserted as such in deep structure: a lexicalist treatment predicts them to have the same distribution as ordinary nouns. A transformational analysis, on the other hand, would be forced to posit ad hoc conditions on the nominalization transformation to ensure that the underlying sentences end up looking like surface noun phrases.

Chomsky was quite unsuccessful in his initial attempt to win general support for the lexicalist alternative to generative semantics. There are several reasons for this. First, there was the half-hearted nature of his counterattack. Whereas the abstract syntacticians proselytized for their model with the zeal of born-again Christians (in the fall of 1966, Ross lectured for 18 hours in 3 days at the University of Illinois), Chomsky confined his rebuttal to lectures at MIT and the "Remarks" paper. This is hardly surprising; in the late 1960s he had far weightier issues on his mind than the abstractness of syntactic structure. As the American war against Vietnam escalated, Chomsky found more and more of his time devoted to political rather than linguistic activism.

Second, Chomsky's adoption of the terms "lexicalism" and "lexicalist hypothesis" to describe his position had unfortunate consequences. Since these terms contrasted with "transformationalism" and "transformationalist hypothesis," they had built-in negative emotional overtones. Indeed, to the unsophisticated, it seemed that Chomsky was leading an astonishing rearguard attack on transformational grammar itself. Many felt that Chomsky was actually advocating unilluminating

---

[14]The X-bar convention was seen to provide a solution to the long-standing problem of characterizing the notion "head of a phrase." Lyons (1968) had pointed out that the *Aspects* model was unable to capture the generalization that noun phrases have nouns as heads, verb phrases have verbs as heads. etc. (that is, that such constructions are endocentric). The rules of (4.45), by formally capturing this relationship, were seen as lending support to the lexicalist approach. For interesting early discussions of the problem of endocentricity, see Postal (1964a) and the reply in Robinson (1970).

solutions to problems over motivated ones, since a decade of propaganda for transformational grammar had resulted in a general feeling that phrase structural solutions were devoid of interest and that the transformational component was the explanatory component of the grammar. While such a confused reaction may have been inevitable whatever terminology Chomsky had chosen, the negative consequences would have been lessened in intensity had he taken greater care in this regard.

Finally, enough problems were found in the lexicalist theory as outlined in the *Remarks* paper to deter many generative semanticists from abandoning their views. Chomsky himself pointed to a problem for the claim that DN's cannot be formed from transformationally derived structures: a passive sentence appears to be nominalized in a phrase like *John's rejection by the committee.*[15] Chomsky attempted to circumvent this problem by allowing the rule of Passive to apply within noun phrases as well as within sentences. Thus, Passive would apply within the phrase *the committee's rejection of John,* resulting in the derivation of *John's rejection by the committee* without a Nominalization transformation. But this move was perceived as ad hoc by many linguists (see McCawley 1975). If Passive applies within noun phrases, it was asked, then why don't the other cyclic transformations apply as well? What principle determines that the domain of Dative Movement, say, is only S, but that of Passive is both S and NP?

Chomsky's arguments for the lexicalist hypothesis based on the irregularity of the verb–DN relation were also at first found to be unconvincing. For one thing, once generative semanticists had hypothesized that lexical items were to be inserted after transformations such as Nominalization had applied, there was no longer a need for the abstract verbs that Chomsky had seen as so injurious to the transformational account. And for another, since Chomsky made no specific proposal for accounting for the paraphrase relationship between, say, *John's refusal was unexpected* and *the fact that John refused was unexpected,* few generative semanticists saw any reason to give up their Nominalization transformation, which, though no doubt messy, would account implicitly for the relationship.

Finally, the initial response to the preliminary "Remarks" version of the X-bar notation was not positive. While Chomsky needed a formalism that imputed parallel internal structures to noun phrases and sentences, in schema (4.45) the S node is outside the system altogether. And it was difficult to find a set of parallels that are predicted by (4.45): those between adjective, noun phrase, and verb phrase "specifiers," i.e., between degree phrases, determiners, and auxiliaries. Generative semantics, rather than attempting to solve these problems, simply dismissed the X-bar system altogether as one more example of the inherent difficulties of a lexicalist account.

It is hardly surprising, then, that when it appeared, "Remarks on Nominalization" had little impact outside MIT. In 1967, generative semantics appeared to be the wave of the future, and lexicalism nothing but a dead end.

---

[15]For discussion of other rules that seem to feed Nominalization, see Newmeyer (1971, 1976a), Ross (1973b), Postal (1974), and Pullum (1979b).

4.5.2. Problems with the Katz–Postal Hypothesis

So intuitively appealing was the Katz–Postal hypothesis that few linguists in the mid 1960s questioned it. And as we have seen, it was this hypothesis that, more than anything else, lay at the root of generative semantics. Yet there were lingering doubts throughout this period that transformational rules were without semantic effect. Chomsky expressed these doubts in a footnote in *Aspects* (1965:224), where he reiterated his feeling that *everyone in the room knows at least two languages* and *at least two languages are known by everyone in the room* differ in meaning. Yet he conceded that both interpretations might be latent in each sentence. A couple of years later he gave his doubts even stronger voice, though he neither gave specific examples nor made specific proposals: "In fact, I think that a reasonable explication of the term 'semantic interpretation' would lead to the conclusion that surface structure also contributed in a restricted but important way to semantic interpretation, but I will say no more about that matter here" (Chomsky 1967:407).

In the last few years of the 1960s there was a great outpouring of examples from Chomsky and his students to illustrate superficial levels of syntactic structure playing an important role in determining semantic interpretation. Taken as a whole, they seemed to indicate that any strong form of the Katz–Postal hypothesis had to be false—everything needed for semantic interpretation was not present in the deep structure. And, while these facts might still allow one (legalistically) to maintain that transformations did not change meaning, the conclusion was inescapable that all of meaning was not determined before the application of the transformational rules. Some examples:

> The following two sentences clearly differ in meaning, suggesting that Passive is a meaning-changing transformation:

(4.47)   a. *Many arrows did not hit the target*
           b. *The target was not hit by many arrows*

> Klima's (1964) rule placing negatives also changes meaning:

(4.48)   a. *Not much shrapnel hit the soldier*
           b. *Much shrapnel did not hit the soldier*

> In (4.47) and (4.48) it is the surface order of quantifier and negative that determines the interpretation. The element on the left in surface structure is interpreted as having the wider scope.
> [PARAPHRASING JACKENDOFF 1969, 222–225]

> The scope of elements like *only* and *even* is determined by their surface structure position:

(4.49)   a. *Only John reads books on politics*
           b. *John only reads books on politics*
           c. *John reads only books on politics*
> [PARAPHRASING KURODA 1969, 333–341]

> Consider questions (4.50a–c) and their natural responses (4.51a–c), respectively:

(4.50)   a. *Was John told to look out for an ex-convict with a red **shirt**?*
           b. *Was John told to look out for a red-shirted ex-**convict**?*
           c. *Was John told to look out for an ex-convict with a shirt that is **red**?*

(4.51)   a. *No, John was told to look out for an ex-convict with a red **tie**.*
           b. *No, John was told to look out for a red-shirted **car salesman**.*
           c. *No, John was told to look out for an ex-convict with a shirt that is **green**.*

The focused (questioned) element seems to be part of the phrase that contains the intonation center, and the presupposition inherent in the sentence is the remainder of the sentence. Crucially, focusable phrases are surface structure phrases. This point can be illustrated by question (4.52) and its natural responses (4.53a–c). In each case, the focused element is in a phrase that did not even exist at the level of deep structure, but rather was formed by the application of a transformational rule. Therefore the interpretation of focus and presupposition must take place at surface structure:

(4.52)   *Is John certain to win?*

(4.53)   a. *No, he is certain to **lose**.*
           b. *No, he's likely not to be **nominated**.*
           c. *No, the election won't ever **happen**.*
                                                      [PARAPHRASING CHOMSKY 1971, 199–206]

Consider the sentence *John hit Bill and then George hit him.* If *him* is unstressed, it refers to *Bill.* If *him* is stressed, it refers to *John.* This suggests that the interpretation of anaphoric expressions must follow stress placement and therefore cannot possibly take place at deep structure.
          [PARAPHRASING CHOMSKY 1971, 211, who cites ADRIAN AKMAJIAN and RAY DOUGHTERY]

Consider the meaning differences between (4.54a) and (4.54b):

(4.54)   a. *It is certain that nobody will pass the test*
           b. *Nobody is certain to pass the test*

We must conclude that either Subject Raising is a meaning-changing transformation or (more naturally) that the relative scope of *certain* and *nobody* is determined after the application of this rule.
                                                           [PARAPHRASING PARTEE 1971, 18–20]

One might think that the discovery that surface structure plays an important role in semantic interpretation would have led to the abandonment of the idea that it was possible to motivate underlying syntactic structure by appealing to meaning. That is, one might think that the discovery would have led to the abandonment of generative semantics. But that is not what happened at all. By the end of the 1960s, generative semanticists had raised the Katz-Postal hypothesis to axiomatic status. As the cornerstone of their way of doing syntax, it had become literally unfalsifiable. Any phenomenon that seemed to indicate an intrinsic connection between a superficial level of syntactic structure and meaning they simply reanalyzed as a global rule, a solution that allowed them to keep their abstract analyses intact and comply with the letter, if not the spirit, of the Katz–Postal hypothesis.

On the other hand, the discovery that surface structure was relevant to semantic interpretation dovetailed nicely with Chomsky's faltering lexicalist hypothesis. While surface interpretation and lexicalism are logically independent, the realization that close-to-the-surface syntax has interesting implications for semantics naturally encouraged linguists to look more seriously at lexicalism, which also attributes interesting properties to nonabstract syntax. The framework resulting from the merger of the lexicalist hypothesis and surface structure semantic interpretation, the "Extended Standard Theory," is developed in Chapter 6.

4.5.3. The Question of Selectional Restrictions

Jackendoff (1972) and McCawley (1968a, 1968c) independently put forward arguments that selectional restrictions are defined, not at some intermediate level of syntactic deep structure, but directly at the level of semantic representation.

Jackendoff's most convincing examples involved sentences such as the following:

(4.55)   a.   *I ate something that was the result of what Bill acknowledged to be a new baking process*

   b.   **I ate something that was the result of what Bill acknowledged to be a syntactic transformation*

As Jackendoff pointed out, (4.55b) seems ill formed because *a syntactic transformation* is an abstraction and therefore not capable of being eaten. Yet this noun phrase is not the direct object of *eat* in the deep structure of (4.55b); rather it is deeply embedded inside the full direct object phrase. Hence, Jackendoff argued, the deviance of this sentence is uncapturable by the selectional machinery proposed in *Aspects,* which would not be capable of distinguishing the full direct object phrases of (4.55a) and (4.55b) in terms of abstractness. However, if selection were to be handled semantically, the restriction of *eat* to nonabstract objects could be stated simply after the projection rules had amalgamated the readings of the material in the object of *eat,* resulting in the characterization of the object phrase of (4.55a) as nonabstract and that of (4.55b) as abstract.

McCawley argued that handling selection at the level of deep structure would require an unacceptably large number of syntactic features. As he pointed out, if a sentence such as *John ate the idea* is to be blocked at that level, then so should be those of (4.56). Yet each would require a separate idiosyncratic syntactic feature. This problem, McCawley concluded, could be avoided by attributing their deviance to semantic or pragmatic factors, rather than syntactic:

(4.56)   a.   **The verb is in the indicative tense*

   b.   **Bernstein's theorem is nondenumerable*

   c.   **John diagonalized that differentiable manifold*

   d.   **That election is green*

   e.   **I ate three phonemes for breakfast*

   f.   **He pronounces diffuseness too loud*

   g.   **My hair is bleeding*

   h.   **That unicorn's left horn is black*

McCawley also based his case for semantic selection on the fact that paraphrases have the same selectional restrictions. For example, any verb in English that can take *bachelor* as its subject can take *unmarried man* as well. By the same token, (4.57b) is deviant for the same reason as (4.57a):

(4.57)   a.   **My sister is the father of two*

   b.   **My buxom neighbor is the father of two*

Furthermore, whenever grammatical features and semantic features are in conflict, selection is based on the latter, not the former. There are many verbs in German, for example, that occur with only semantically female subjects, but none that take only grammatically feminine subjects.

The *Aspects* approach, McCawley concluded, which considers selectional restrictions as restrictions holding between lexical items, is unable to account for these facts. Yet they lend themselves quite naturally to a restriction stated at the level of semantic representation.

One might have expected the widely accepted conclusion that selection is semantic to be perceived as weakening the case for abstract approaches to syntax. After all, if selectional restrictions are not defined syntactically, then it is hardly appropriate to refer to them as evidence that such-and-such a construction should have such-and-such a syntactic deep structure. If selectional restrictions are semantic, then any arguments for a deep structure for a particular sentence based on them are going to end up motivating something close to the semantic representation as the deep structure. Put simply, arguments for deep structure based on selectional restrictions are going to lead inevitably to generative semantics.

This point seemed to be lost on generative semanticists, who regarded semantic selection as independent evidence for their framework (see Lakoff and Ross 1976). They reasoned that one less generalization definable at deep structure was one more argument for scrapping that level entirely. But at the same time, they failed to reevaluate their many arguments for abstract deep structures that had been based on the assumption that selectional restrictions were defined at an independent syntactic level.[16]

Generative semanticists simply took it for granted that strict subcategorization restrictions were also semantic (see R. Lakoff 1968:17; McCawley 1968c:136; Lakoff and Ross 1976:160). Naturally, analogous reasoning led them to regard that as one more reason for abandoning deep structure. But the case for a semantic treatment of strict subcategorization was never made as persuasively as for selection. Wasow (1976) and Oehrle (1977) were later to cite numerous examples of strict subcategorization restrictions that were not predictable from the meaning of the items involved. As Wasow (p. 282) pointed out, *dine, devour* and *eat* differ with respect to transitivity: *dine* is intransitive, *devour* requires an object, and *eat* takes an optional object. Yet there is nothing in the meanings of these words that predicts this difference in strict subcategorization, since all seem to designate two-place predicates involving both some sort of food and a consumer of food.

4.6. SYNTACTIC THEORY IN 1970: A SYNOPSIS

Syntactic theory entered the 1970s very much under generative semantic hegemony. Generative semantics wore the mantle of orthodoxy, and that more than

---

[16]Chomsky has continued to maintain (in class lectures) that at least some selection is syntactic, citing as evidence sentences like *the boy who was turned by magic into a swarm of bees dispersed*. For a critical evaluation of the arguments against syntactic selection, see Seegmiller (1974).

anything else explains its phenomenal success. Katz and Postal's conclusion that underlying structure fully determines meaning and Chomsky's that selectional restrictions are defined at the deepest syntactic level seemed too intuitively pleasing to be seriously questioned. While Chomsky had succeeded in building at MIT a committed core of nongenerative semanticists, he found himself, for the first time since the founding of transformational generative grammar, in a distinct minority in the field that he himself had created. It took several years of the most acrimonious battles linguistics had seen in over a decade before the nonabstract current was again dominant in syntax. Those battles are the subject of Chapter 5.

The Linguistic Wars

5.1. INTRODUCTION

This chapter gets its title from Paul Postal's apt term for the state of hostility that existed between the two rival camps of theoreticians in the late 1960s and early 1970s. But it could just as easily have been called ''The Fall of Generative Semantics.'' In 1968, there was hardly a syntactician who was not committed to, or at least attracted to, this new model. Around 1970 and 1971 many commentators saw generative semantics as being as important and dramatic a break from classical transformational grammar as the latter was from post-Bloomfieldian structural linguistics. George Lakoff traveled around the world speaking on ''Why Transformational Grammar Died'' and wrote with confidence about the ''crumbling foundations'' of Chomskyan syntax (1972b).

But Lakoff's state of euphoria must have been short-lived. Even by 1972, to judge from the quantity and tone of the papers that took sides in factional debate, generative semantics was on the defensive. Most significantly, its own adherents began to abandon ship. A dramatic indicator of this fact is a remarkable paper by generative semanticist Jerry Morgan (1973a), which demolished step by step many of the fundamental hypotheses of the model, hypotheses that Morgan himself had played a key role in fashioning. Today many of these hypotheses have no public adherents at all, and the term ''generative semantics'' itself evokes nostalgia rather than partisan fervor.

5.2. LATE GENERATIVE SEMANTICS

Generative semantics continued to develop beyond the stage outlined in Section 4.3. A number of linguists working in this model, particularly George Lakoff,

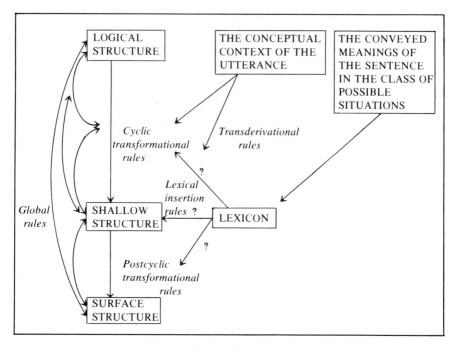

Figure 5.1

continued to elaborate and enrich the theoretical devices that it employed in grammatical description. While it must be stressed that not all generative semanticists followed Lakoff, his stature guaranteed that his own proposals would be regarded by most linguists as defining the model. By 1972, Lakoff's conception of grammatical organization appeared as in Figure 5.1 (an oversimplified diagram based on the discussion in G. Lakoff 1974a).

5.2.1. Beyond Global Rules

In the 1970s, the generative semanticists began proposing grammatical mechanisms that far exceeded the power of global rules. This was necessitated by the steady expansion of the type of phenomena that generative semanticists felt required a grammatical treatment. As the scope of formal grammar expanded, so did the number of formal devices and their power. Arguments motivating such devices invariably took the following form:

1. Phenomenon P has in the past been considered to be simply pragmatic, that is, part of performance and hence not requiring treatment within formal grammar.
2. But P is reflected both in morpheme distribution and in the grammaticality judgments that speakers are able to provide.

3. If anything is the task of the grammarian, it is the explanation of native-speaker judgments and the distribution of morphemes in a language. Therefore, P must be handled in the grammar.
4. But the grammatical devices now available are insufficient for this task. Therefore, new devices of greater power must be added.

John Ross (1970) and Jerrold Sadock (1969, 1970) were the first to argue that what in the past had been considered to be pragmatic phenomena were amenable to grammatical treatment. Both linguists, for example, argued that the type of speech act that a sentence represents should be encoded directly in its semantic representation (i.e., its underlying syntactic structure). Ross argued on syntactic grounds that all declarative sentences contain in semantic representation a topmost performative clause (i.e., a clause that indicates what type of speech act is being performed) with *I* for a subject, *you* for an indirect object, and a main verb with the features [+V, +PERFORMATIVE, +COMMUNICATION, +LINGUISTIC, +DECLARATIVE]. The following argument was typical of the many adduced by Ross for such a claim:

Consider the sentences of (5.1).

(5.1)

a. *I told Albert that physicists like* $\left\{ \begin{array}{l} myself \\ himself \\ *yourself \\ *themselves \end{array} \right\}$ *are hard to find*

b. *Physicists like* $\left\{ \begin{array}{l} myself \\ yourself \\ *himself \\ *themselves \end{array} \right\}$ *are hard to find*

(5.1a) illustrates that reflexives in the *like . . . -self* construction must agree in person, number, and gender with a noun phrase in a higher sentence. This suggests that a simple uniclausal declarative like (5.1b) is derived from an underlying structure containing an additional higher performative sentence with the noun phrases *I* and *you*.

[PARAPHRASING ROSS 1970, 229–230]

Sadock's arguments for a higher performative clause were typically based on the observation that the acceptability of a sentence is often dependent upon certain properties of the participants in the discourse. For example, Sadock (1969) called attention to the "clearly ungrammatical" [p. 297] German imperative sentence (5.2), in which the command to the addressee mixes polite and familiar forms. He thus concluded that underlying syntactic structure should encode the speaker and hearer and their relative social status as well.

(5.2)   *Machen Sie deinen Koffer zu!*
close (polite) your (familiar) suitcase

Sadock (1970, 1972, 1974) extended the performative analysis to indirect speech acts as well. He began one argument for this extension by pointing out that while the

words *please* and vocative *someone* typically occur in imperative utterances, paren-
thetical *tell me* never occurs with true imperatives:

(5.3)   a. *Give me a drink, please*
         b. *Give me a drink, someone*
         c. **Tell me, give me a drink*

He then noted that sentences superficially mimicking questions but conveying an
imperative sense behave identically to true imperatives:

(5.4)   a. *Would you give me a drink, please*
         b. *Would you give me a drink, someone*
         c. **Tell me, would you give me a drink*

This fact suggested to Sadock a deep structure for (5.5a) roughly like (5.5b), which
contains a conjunction of imperative and interrogative performative verbs.

(5.5)   a. *Would you give me a drink*

b.

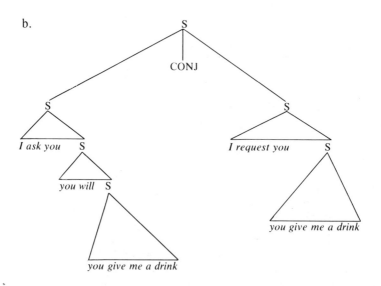

Sadock never took step 4, above; he felt that the existing syntactic mechanisms
sufficed to handle the phenomena in question. But the work of George Lakoff in the
early 1970s was largely devoted to motivating new, more powerful, grammatical
devices. For example, in one paper (G. Lakoff 1971b), he arrived at the conclusion
that a speaker's beliefs about the world needed to be encoded into syntactic structure. His conclusion was based on the attempt to account syntactically for judgments such as those illustrated in (5.6), which he explicitly regarded as grammaticality judgments.

(5.6)   a. *John told Mary that she was ugly and then shé insúlted hím*
      b. **John told Mary that she was beautiful and then shé insúlted hím*

He noted that the grammaticality of (5.6a) and the ungrammaticality of (5.6b) are relative to our culture, which praises beauty and denigrates ugliness—"those with other beliefs may disagree" (G. Lakoff 1971b:333). Since "one's judgment of the well-formedness of sentences seems to vary with one's beliefs or assumptions" (p. 332), he concluded that rules of stress placement had to make reference to such beliefs or assumptions, an ability clearly beyond the bounds of the grammar as they were conceived in 1970. He also argued that in order to provide a full account of the possible antecedents of anaphoric expressions, even deductive reasoning had to enter into grammatical description (1971c). As Lakoff pointed out, the antecedent of *too* in (5.7), "the major is honest," is not present in the logical structure of the sentence but must be deduced from it and its associated presupposition "Republicans are honest".

(5.7)   *The mayor is a Republican and the used-car dealer is honest too*

The deduction, then, was to be performed in the grammar itself.

    The attempt to handle all aspects of conveyed meaning grammatically led Lakoff to develop a mechanism of great expressive power, the transderivational constraint, a constraint on one derivation subject to properties of another. Such constraints were first suggested (in unpublished work) around 1970 by David Perlmutter and Paul Postal, who were puzzled by the fact that the rule of Extraposition-from-NP seems to apply to (5.8a) to derive (5.8b), but not to (5.9a) to derive (5.9b).

(5.8)   a. *A woman that was pregnant took the job*
      b. *A woman took the job that was pregnant*

(5.9)   a. *A woman that was attractive took the job*
      b. *A woman took the job that was attractive*

Perlmutter and Postal suggested that the incorrect reading of (5.9b) was blocked by a transderivational constraint sensitive to the fact that this sentence, but not (5.8b), is ambiguous.[1]

    Lakoff (1971a, 1972e) further developed transderivational constraints to handle presuppositions, suggesting that they need not be part of the logical structure of a sentence if rules dependent on presuppositional information were endowed with transderivational power. Such power became crucial after he had decided that conversationally conveyed aspects of meaning (such as indirect speech acts) should be treated as context-dependent entailments. Consider, for example, his treatment of Searle's (1975) observation that one can convey a request by either asserting one's sincerity to have that request carried out or by questioning the hearer's ability to carry out the request (note that (5.10b) and (5.10c) can both convey (5.10a)).

---

[1]The Perlmutter–Postal conception of transderivational constraints was developed in several papers by Judith Aissen and Jorge Hankamer (see Aissen and Hankamer 1972; Hankamer 1972, 1973; Aissen 1973).

(5.10)   a. *Pass the salt*
         b. *I'd like the salt*
         c. *Can you pass the salt?*

He and his collaborator David Gordon (see Gordon and Lakoff 1971; G. Lakoff 1975b) formalized Searle's observation by treating conveyed meanings as logical entailments. Just as the entailment relation between (5.11a) and (5.11b) could be stated by meaning postulate (5.12), Searle's observation was to be captured by the transderivational conversational postulates represented in (5.13), which were to be considered as entailments with respect to a particular context and speaker intention.

(5.11)   a. *It is certain that Harry will lose*
         b. *It is possible that Harry will lose*

(5.12)   CERTAIN (S_1) → POSSIBLE (S_1)

(5.13)   a. SAY (a, b, WANT (a, Q)) → REQUEST (a, b, Q)
         b. ASK (a, b, CAN (b, Q)) → REQUEST (a, b, Q)

In Lakoff's opinion, the outstanding benefit of such an approach was its integration of one of the least-understood aspects of language into a familiar framework: "What we have done is to largely, if not entirely, eliminate pragmatics, reducing it to garden variety semantics" (Lakoff 1972e:655).

A major early 1970s debate within generative semantics involved Sadock (1975) and Green (1975) on one side and George Lakoff on the other on the issue of whether indirect illocutionary force should be encoded directly into the underlying syntactic structure (à la Sadock) or should be handled transderivationally (à la Lakoff). Sadock was quick to point out that transderivational rules undermine the basis of the performative analysis; given such devices there could be no principled objection to a transderivational rule of performative addition, which could operate on representations in which no performative clause was present. Green (1975) stated the case in even stronger terms: "In fact, the possibility of having global syntactic rules that refer to conversational entailments of deep structures removes the basis for all arguments in favor of generative semantics and makes 'generative semantics' an interpretive theory" (p. 131).

However, the debate was dropped as more and more problems were discovered with any solution to these phenomena within the domain of formal grammar (see Section 5.3.5).

As generative semanticists extended the domain of syntactic analysis, they not surprisingly uncovered a multitude of cases pointing to an intimate interaction between syntax and pragmatic phenomena. Two are paraphrased below:

> Sentences like (5.14a–b) can be interpreted in three ways: as *yes-no* questions, as requests for information, or as rhetorical exclamations.

(5.14)   a. *Have you seen John lately?*
          b. *Do you have any idea how much that vase was worth?*

> But if a rule that deletes the subject and auxiliary applies, such sentences may be interpreted only as requests for information.

(5.15)   a. *Seen John lately?*
           b. *Any idea how much that vase was worth?*
                                                    [PARAPHRASING SCHMERLING 1973, 577–586]

The verbal element in a comparative clause may optionally be replaced by the pro-verb *do*, or be deleted.

(5.16)   a. *John is taller than Bill (is)*
           b. *John runs faster than Bill (runs, does)*
           c. *John walks like his father (walks, does)*

Comparatives have a sense in which they are used as conventionalized hyperbole.

(5.17)   a. *Mary is bigger than a house*
           b. *John runs as fast as a deer*
           c. *Hans leaps like a gazelle*

But in order to convey a figurative sense, the deletion rule *must* take place. (5.18a–c) are not understood as hyperbolic.

(5.18)   a. *Mary is bigger than a house is*
           b. *John runs as fast as a deer runs*
           c. *Hans leaps like a gazelle does*
                                                    [PARAPHRASING MORGAN 1975, 300]

5.2.2. Fuzzy Grammar

As is well known, a speaker's judgment about the acceptability of a sentence is generally not an either–or matter. Some sentences are more acceptable than others. George Lakoff (1973) concluded that the graded nature of speaker judgments falsifies the notion that sentences should be either generated (i.e., be considered grammatical) or not generated (i.e., be treated as ungrammatical). Lakoff suggested instead that a mechanism be devised to assign grammaticality to a certain degree. He took by way of illustration sentences (5.19a–f), which he felt grow gradually less acceptable from (a) to (f).

(5.19)   a. *John is the kinda fella that accidents naturally happen to him*
           b. *John is the kinda fella that it's likely that accidents'll happen to him*
           c. *John is the kinda fella that people think accidents naturally happen to him*
           d. *John is the kinda fella that I know that accidents happen to him*
           e. *John is the kinda fella that I realize that accidents happen to him*
           f. *John is the kinda fella that you find out that accidents happen to him*

On the basis of his own subjective judgment, he posited the following well-formedness ratings to be assigned to these sentences by the grammar:[2]

---

[2]When assigning graded grammaticality judgments, generative semanticists tended to forget their assertion that the grammaticality of a sentence was dependent on its external context.

Sentence	(5.19a)	(5.19b)	(5.19c)	(5.19d)	(5.19e)	(5.19f)
Rating	.8	.7	.6	.5	.4	.3

Lakoff considered his fuzzy grammars, that is, grammars capable of generating sentences with specific degrees of assigned grammaticality, to involve only a slight extension of the mechanisms already available to generative semantics.

Between 1972 and 1974, a number of generative semanticists, most notably John Ross, argued that all of the constructs of linguistic theory are nondiscrete (or "squishy"). For example, Ross (1973b) found no discrete boundary between the category "Sentence" and the category "Noun." Constructions at the left end of the "nouniness squish" (5.20) appear to be more sentencelike; those at the right end more nounlike. The squish is further elaborated in (5.21).

(5.20)   *that* > *for–to* > *Q* > *Acc Ing* > *Poss Ing* > Action Nominal > Derived Nominal > Noun

(5.21)   a. *that* = *that*-clause (*that Max gave the letters to Frieda*)
          b. *for-to* = *for* NP *to* VX (*for Max to have given the letters to Frieda*)
          c. *Q* = embedded questions (*how willingly Max gave the letters to Frieda*)
          d. *Acc Ing* = [$_{+ACC}^{NP}$] V + *ing* X (*Max giving the letters to Frieda*)
          e. *Poss Ing* = NP's V + *ing* X (*Max's giving the letters to Frieda*)

          f. Action Nominal $\left(\left\{ \begin{matrix} Max's \\ the \end{matrix} \right\} giving\ of\ the\ letters\ to\ Frieda \right)$

          g. Derived Nominal $\left(\left\{ \begin{matrix} Max's \\ the \end{matrix} \right\} gift\ of\ the\ letters\ to\ Frieda \right)$

          h. Noun (*spatula*)

To illustrate the hierarchy implicit in (5.20), Ross gave examples of phenomena that apply, say, to (5.21a–d), but not to (5.21e–h); to (5.21c–f), but not to (5.21a–b) or to (5.21g–h); to (5.21d–h), but not to (5.21a–c); and so on. For example, as illustrated in (5.22), the rule of Preposition Deletion, which deletes the *at* of *surprised at,* must apply before *that* complements and *for–to* complements, may apply before embedded questions, and may not apply before complements of greater nouniness (an asterisk inside parentheses indicates that the enclosed material must not occur; an asterisk outside parentheses that it must occur).

(5.22)   a. *I was surprised (*at) that you had hives*
          b. *I was surprised (at) how far you could throw the ball*
          c. *I was surprised *(at) Jim's victory*

Ross (1973b) proposed to capture these generalizations formally in the following manner:

I propose that the previously used node S, sentence, be replaced by a feature [αS], where α ranges over the real numbers in [0,1]. Each of the complement types in [(5.20)] would be given a basic value of α, and rules, filters, and other types of semantactic [*sic*] processes, would be given upper and lower threshold values of α between which they operate. (p. 188).

In addition to the notions of ''grammaticality'' and ''category membership,'' it was also argued that rule applicability (Ross 1974), island strength (Rodman 1975), grammatical relation (Lawler 1977), and the basic constructs of semantics (G. Lakoff 1972d, 1973) are also fuzzy.[3]

5.2.3. The End of Grammatical Theory

Not surprisingly, as the class of ''grammatical'' phenomena increased, the competence–performance dichotomy became correspondingly cloudy. As early as 1972, McCawley had used the term ''competence'' with a meaning that encompassed much of what had previously been considered part of performance: ''I take 'linguistic competence' here as referring to a speaker's internalized system for relating meanings to possible ways of expressing them and the characteristics of linguistic and extra-linguistic contexts under which particular ways of expressing them are appropriate'' (McCawley 1972:np).

George Lakoff (1974a) made it explicit that the domain of grammatical theory was no less than the domain of linguistics itself. Grammar, for Lakoff, was to

specify the CONDITIONS under which sentences can be APPROPRIATELY used. . . . One thing that one might ask is whether there is anything that does NOT enter into rules of grammar. For example, there are certain concepts from the study of social interaction that are part of grammar, e.g., relative social status, politeness, formality, etc. Even such an abstract notion as FREE GOODS enters into rules of grammar. Free goods are things (including information) that everyone in a group has a right to. (pp. 159–161, emphasis in original)

Since it is hard to imagine what might not affect the appropriateness of an utterance in actual discourse, the generative semantic program with great rapidity moved from the task of grammar construction to that of observing language in its external setting. By the mid 1970s, most generative semanticists had ceased proposing explicit grammatical rules altogether. The idea that any conceivable phenomenon might influence such rules made doing so a thorough impracticality. And before long, the next logical step was taken as grammatical theory itself was abandoned. Lakoff (and his collaborator, Henry Thompson) came to characterize the constructs of grammatical theory as nothing but ''convenient fictions,'' lacking separate mental reality (Lakoff and Thompson 1975:295). Indeed, by now such constructs had become so intertwined with all of human experience and awareness that their characterization as a distinct entity was out of the question. A generative semanticist might study language as a sociocultural phenomenon or explore its processing by the brain. There was no longer a place, however, for generative grammar.

---

[3]Lakoff and Ross acknowledged their debt for the notion of fuzzy grammar to the logician Lofti Zadeh and his work in ''fuzzy set theory'' (Zadeh 1965, 1971). They also derived psychological support for fuzzy grammar from the work of Eleanor Rosch (1973) on the structure of categories.

5.2.4. On the Inevitability of These Developments

It is worth asking whether or not the course that generative semantics took was an inevitable one. The fact that not all generative semanticists followed Lakoff to the end suggests that the answer is "no." Yet, in retrospect, it seems clear that events could not have turned out otherwise. The cornerstone of generative semantic argumentation was the Katz–Postal hypothesis, which led to the strategy of motivating underlying structures by appealing to the meaning of the sentence. But there are few constructs in linguistics as fuzzy as "meaning of a sentence." And to make matters worse, the boundary between semantics and pragmatics was barely understood in the early 1970s. As a consequence, convenience and familiarity conspired to expand the domain of meaning to include virtually any construct relevant to understanding, from quantifier scope to strategies for indicating sarcasm. As the scope of grammatical theory expanded (and with it the amount of information needed to be encoded into underlying structure), the content of the theory declined correspondingly. The Lakoff and Thompson view of grammatical constructs as "fictions" is no more than the Katz-Postal hypothesis carried to its logical conclusion.

5.3. GENERATIVE SEMANTICS UNDER ATTACK

5.3.1. A Period of Acrimony

It is hard in retrospect to appreciate the vehemence with which the debate between generative semanticists and partisans of the Extended Standard Theory (interpretivists) was carried out in the late 1960s and early 1970s. At times, its heat grew so intense that even in print the rhetoric exceeded the bounds of normal partisan scholarship—witness Doughtery's (1974:267) description of a paper of McCawley's as "Machiavellian" and George Lakoff's (1972f:70L) accusation that Chomsky "fights dirty when he argues. He uses every trick in the book." As can easily be imagined, the discussion sessions after conference papers provided an arena for far stronger sentiments. The high point (or low point) surely followed the presentation of George Lakoff's "Global Rules" paper at the 1969 Linguistic Society of America meeting, when for several minutes he and Ray Jackendoff hurled amplified obscenities at each other before 200 embarrassed onlookers. There is hardly a need to mention the personal animosities engendered, some of which smolder still.

As might be expected, hiring-decision controversies provided a particularly bitter aspect of the internecine warfare. For example, the replacement of two generative semanticists at the University of Massachusetts by interpretivists served to solidify partisans of the former model in their opposition to interpretivism. On the other side of the fence, the hiring of a noninterpretivist by MIT in 1970 to fill a vacant position had an analogous effect on the students at that institution, who almost unanimously would have preferred an interpretivist.

In the following pages, I attempt to identify the more substantive issues of the debate and explain why generative semantics came away very much the loser.

5.3.2. The Question of Category Membership

The generative semantic arguments that were by far the most vulnerable (and therefore the first to be attacked by their opponents) were those that led to the conclusion that the inventory of syntactic categories could be reduced to three. Yet such a conclusion was vital to generative semantics, given its commitment to identifying syntactic categories with those of predicate logic. It was easy to show that generative semanticists succeeded in eliminating categories by recognizing only sufficient conditions for conflating two categories into one, never necessary conditions (a point acknowledged by McCawley 1977b). To take a typical example, Ross (1969a), making the then well-accepted assumption that definite pronouns refer only to full noun phrases, concluded on the basis of sentence (5.23) that adjective phrases are really members of the category NP:

(5.23)   *John is happy, but he doesn't look it*

For Ross, (5.23) provided sufficient justification for *happy* being an NP. He felt no obligation to discuss the prima facie counterexamples (5.24a–c), in which *it* does not refer to *happy*.

(5.24)   a. **John is happy, but I can't imagine why he is it*
         b. **John isn't happy, but he hopes to become it*
         c. **John is happy and I'm it, too*

In any event, Chomsky (1971) later demonstrated that the antecedent of *it* need not even be a constituent, much less a noun phrase (see section 6.1.1).

The assumption that if two categories share some syntactic feature then they are in reality members of the same category also contributed to the generative semantic reduction in the inventory of syntactic categories. For example, G. Lakoff (1970b) subsumed adjectives into the class of verbs on the basis of their both being subcategorized for the features [±STATIVE] and ±[____S] (the ability to occur before a sentential complement). But Chomsky (1970) and Culicover (1977) pointed out in response that not just adjectives and verbs share the feature stative; nouns can be stative or nonstative as well:

(5.25)   *Be a hero*   [−STATIVE]

(5.26)   **Be a person*   [+STATIVE]

Analogous reasoning should have led logically to placing nouns, adjectives, and verbs in the same category. While such a conclusion was not necessarily repellent to generative semanticists—Bach (1968), in fact, had proposed it on independent grounds—the same type of test could have been used to conflate all categories into one, a conclusion that few, if any, would have found acceptable.

Finally, it was pointed out that even if generative semantics had been successful in reducing the underlying set of categories to three members, it did not succeed in reducing the total number to three. There is a difference between nouns, verbs, adjectives, adverbs, quantifiers, prepositions, and so on in surface structure, regardless of what is needed at the most underlying level. Hence, there seemed to be no substance to the generative semantic claim that it had succeeded in reducing the inventory of substantive universals. How would generative semantics distinguish nouns from verbs? McCawley (1970c) explained: "The difference between nouns and verbs is that nouns but not verbs are subject to a transformation which replaces a relative clause by its predicate element" (pp. 169–170). But as Bresnan (1972b:198) pointed out, such an approach is really nothing more than using a class of transformations as categories in disguise. Nothing is gained by replacing ad hoc (if such they be) categories by ad hoc transformations. Bresnan discussed the problem at length, arguing that an approach positing deep structure and a variety of categories makes an important prediction that the generative semantic approach does not, namely, that syntactic properties should cluster around the distinct categories. Given the generative semantic approach, such a clustering is not predicted to occur.

5.3.3. The Question of Deep Structure

Needless to say, the generative semantic abandonment of deep structure was an issue that caused its share of rancor. Since the most persuasive refutations of the existence of this level involved arguments for syntactic lexical decomposition, it was on lexical decomposition that the interpretivists most frequently trained their guns. They claimed to be able to show, and by and large were perceived as successful in doing so, that the syntactic and semantic behavior of lexical items does not match those of their supposed syntactic sources, thereby invalidating the strongest argument for lexical decomposition.

For example, J. A. Fodor (1970) argued that if transitive *melt* were derived from something like 'cause to melt,' (5.27b) should be grammatical and a paraphrase of (5.27a).

(5.27)   a.   *Floyd caused the glass to melt on Sunday by heating it on Saturday*
          b.   **Floyd melted the glass on Sunday by heating it on Saturday*

Yet, contrary to the prediction implicit in an analysis involving lexical decomposition, (5.27b) is unacceptable.

Analogously, Bowers (1970) pointed out that Postal's treatment of *remind* (see (4.20b)) predicts that the contradictory nature of (5.28a) should entail (5.28b) being contradictory as well. But it is not, as (5.28c) (in which modifiers have been added for clarity) illustrates.

(5.28)   a.   *I perceive that Larry is similar to Winston Churchill, although I perceive that Larry is not similar to Winston Churchill*
          b.   *Larry reminds me of Winston Churchill, although I perceive that Larry is not similar to Winston Churchill*

    c. *For some reason Larry reminds me of Winston Churchill, although I perceive that Larry is not really similar to him at all*

Many more arguments of a similar nature were constructed against lexical decomposition. The generative semanticists' only recourse was to say that the lexical items *melt, remind*, etc., do not have exactly the same semantic representations as *cause to melt, perceive to be similar*, etc., but have meanings that are either more or less restricted. While nobody denied that such was the case, having to posit distinct structures for lexical items and their phrasal near-paraphrases undercut the justification for having lexical decomposition in the first place.

Generative semanticists also attempted to motivate syntactic lexical decomposition by pointing to the fact that their crucial rule of Predicate Raising applied uncontroversially in languages as diverse as Japanese, Eskimo, and Blackfoot (see Frantz 1974). Hence, they claimed, it followed that English should also have the rule. But such reasoning was not regarded as compelling. Indeed, it seemed to be the case that whenever generative semanticists needed a prelexical transformation to collapse two clauses, they postulated Predicate Raising at work; to raise a noun phrase to a higher clause, Subject Raising; to make an object a subject, Passive. No motivation for the application of these rules was ever given, aside from the need to get from Point A (semantic representation) to Point B (a constituent that a lexical item could replace). But as many linguists came to realize in the mid 1970s, given enough ingenuity and enough rules for whose application no formal statement nor external motivation was required, and whose application could be assumed to be optional or obligatory at will, there would never be a problem in getting from A to B.

The internal modification arguments for lexical decomposition fared little better than the others. Chomsky (1972a) and Kac (1972) pointed out that lexical decomposition predicts far more ambiguities than actually occur. If the ambiguity of *John almost killed Bill* is an argument for the decomposition of *kill*, then the fact that the sentence is not obviously four (or more) ways ambiguous should count as an argument against it, since, for generative semanticists, the semantic representation of *kill* contained (at least) *cause-become-not-alive*, each of which was in principle modifiable by *almost*.

But by far the most intractable problem for the generative semanticists was accounting for the primary function of the renounced level of deep structure, the specification of morpheme order. As most syntacticians soon realized, the order of articles, adjectives, negatives, numerals, nouns, and noun complements within a noun phrase is not predictable (or even stable) on semantic grounds. How then could generative semantics state morpheme order? Only, it seemed, by supplementing the transformational rules with a close-to-the-surface filter that functioned to mimic the phrase structure rules of a theory with the level of deep structure. Thus, despite its rhetorical abandonment of deep structure, generative semantics would end up slipping that level in through the back door.[4]

---

[4]For later work directly addressing the question of the mismatch between syntactic and semantic regularity, see Grimshaw (1979a), Williams (1980), Newmeyer (1983:5–11), and Akmajian (1984).

5.3.4. The Question of Globality

One of the most emotional issues between generative semanticists and interpretivists involved the question of the existence of global rules. This might seem strange, since even prior to the birth of generative semantics it had been taken for granted that the history of the derivation often played a role in determining the applicability of a transformation (recall the Lees proposal outlined in Section 3.2.2). Indeed, as recently as 1968, Chomsky had discussed in some detail a "rather abstract condition that takes into account not only the structure to which the operation applies but also the history of derivation of this structure" (p. 28). And even during the debate over global rules, nobody denied that transformations needed to be supplemented with rules of a different formal nature. Why then did the claim that some rules were global engender such heated controversy?

Global rules were controversial because their thrust was an entirely negative one. George Lakoff (whose positions, for better or worse, came to be identified with the "official" generative semantic line) repeatedly implied that to claim that a phenomenon was to be handled by a global rule was to make no claim at all about it, other than the negative one that a transformational rule could not handle it. Since neither Lakoff nor any other generative semanticists made a serious attempt to constrain global rules, the expression "global rule" became a catchall phrase for a disparate collection of mysterious phenomena that defied ready explanation. More and more, it seemed, when a generative semanticist invoked globality, he or she had simply given up on trying to explain what was going on.

It is instructive to contrast the alternative interpretivist account of global phenomena. As far as Greek case agreement is concerned, Baker and Brame (1972) and Quicoli (1972, 1982) proposed the following solution: An index that indicates they are in the same simple S is assigned to an NP and its modifiers; a late rule assigns case to the modifer based on that of its co-indexed NP. And for *be*-contraction, Selkirk (1972) proposed that transformations that move or delete constituents do not move or delete the word boundaries associated with them and that the presence of these word boundaries blocks stress reduction and contraction.

In one sense, the above proposals were little more than formalizations of the global rules they were intended to replace. After all, they recognized that standard transformational approaches were insufficient for handling the phenomena and, in their own distinct ways, allowed generalizations to be stated involving nonadjacent phrase markers. But at a more metatheoretical level, they were profoundly different from global solutions and came to be seen as preferable to them. Devices such as co-indexing between heads and modifiers and special conventions regarding the deletion of word boundaries involve the most minimal extensions of already-existing mechanisms. Solutions involving them, it seemed, could be achieved without increasing the power of the theory. Whatever unclarities an indexing–word boundary approach might contain, such an approach came to be more and more favored, since, if nothing else, it at least enabled the phenomenon under investigation to be concretized and, in many cases, it pointed the way to a principled solution.

5.3.5. The Question of Grammatical Theory and Pragmatics

By the mid 1980s virtually nobody accepted a strictly grammatical explanation of all pragmatic phenomena. The mid and late 1970s saw an accelerating number of papers and books that convincingly cast into doubt the possibility of one homogeneous syntax–semantics–pragmatics and the consequent abandonment of the competence–performance distinction.

The syntactic arguments for the performative hypothesis were challenged very early and in many papers (see S. Anderson 1971a; Banfield 1973a; Fraser 1974; Heal 1977; Gildin 1978; Gazdar 1979a).[5] All concluded that there was no syntactic motivation for positing an abstract performative verb of declaring, requesting, commanding, or whatever at the deepest level of syntactic representation. Fraser, for example, pointed out that Ross's argument based on the distribution of reflexive pronouns (see Section 5.2.1) was invalidated by the possibility of a reflexive occuring in the performative clause itself:

(5.29) a. *You are hereby authorized by John and myself to buy that ship*
       b. *You are hereby advised by Mary and myself that we are married*
       c. *The court rejects any such remarks directed at the other jurors and myself*

Others challenged Lakoff's view that conversationally implied aspects of meaning could be analyzed as entailments. For example, Gazdar (1979a) demonstrated that there is no relationship of semantic entailment betwen a speech act and its felicity conditions. If Lakoff were right, he argued, (5.30a) should entail (5.30b):

(5.30) a. *Sue requested of Tom that he meet Harry*
       b. *Sue attempted to get Tom to meet Harry*

But if there were such an entailment relation, Gazdar argued, (5.31a) should make Sue sound irrational, and (5.31b) should be contradictory:

(5.31) a. *Sue requested of Tom that he meet Harry, because it was the only way she knew of preventing him from doing so*
       b. *Sue requested of Tom that he meet Harry, but she was only attempting to shock him*

Since (5.31a–b) do not behave as predicted by Lakoff, it follows that the relationship between a speech act and its felicity conditions cannot be one of entailment. Thus a pragmatic rather than a grammatical treatment of such phenomena is preferable.

Morgan (1977) discussed at length the problems of treating indirect speech acts (and conversational implicature in general) in terms of semantic entailment. He pointed out that while, indeed, (5.32a) is often used to convey (5.32b), (5.32a) does not entail (5.32b):

---

[5]There have also been objections to grammatical approaches to performatives from a philosophical standpoint, for example, Searle (1976b) and Pelletier (1977).

(5.32)   a. *Can you open the door?*
         b. *Open the door*

If the relationship were one of entailment, then there could be no possibility of a cooperative individual ever interpreting (5.32a) as a questioning of his or her ability to open the door. But this sentence could be interpreted in just such a way. As Morgan concluded, "The very property of implicature that makes it so useful as a conversational ploy is that it is not entailed, but merely suggested or hinted at" (Morgan 1977:279–280).

Kempson (1975) carried the attack on grammatical treatments of pragmatics a step farther, arguing that any attempt to include speaker-relative concepts (such as intentions or assumptions) in a grammatical statement is doomed to failure. Focusing on Robin Lakoff's (1971) analysis of conjunction, which involves taking "presupposed common topic" as a grammatical notion, she demonstrated that any mechanism able to predict the required sentence–presupposition pairs would need to be embodied with unconstrainable power. From this, she concluded that speaker assumptions and the like cannot be part of a formal semantic theory.

By around 1973, all of the issues discussed in this section had been debated at conferences, in unpublished (and some published) work, and at a personal level. Generative semantics was on the retreat.

5.4. THE COLLAPSE OF GENERATIVE SEMANTICS

In this section, we probe farther the amazing rapid decline of generative semantics. We still have not arrived at an adequate explanation for the fact that a model whose followers were "motivated only by personal loyalty to Chomsky" (as popular wisdom had it in 1967) would a dozen years later become the predominant syntactic theory, with a corresponding decline of its rival.

This is not to say that all generative semanticists abandoned their beliefs, and certainly not to say that all became interpretivists (although some did; examples are Emmon Bach, D. Terence Langendoen, and David Lightfoot). Many adopted newer frameworks of analysis with rather different assumptions from both, like relational grammar. Many others ceased to involve themselves altogether in the defense of a particular framework. But most significantly, students entering linguistics from around 1971 or 1972 on turned away from generative semantics. And this is the fact that is need of explanation.

5.4.1. The Generative Semantic Dynamic

It is tempting to think that it was the weight of the interpretivist counterattack that led to the demise of generative semantics. While it played an important role, it was not the deciding factor. For one thing, generative semanticists saw enough defects in the interpretive model (some of which are outlined in Chapter 6) for the interpretivist critique to lose some of its force. For another, the majority of the published critiques of generative semantics, including the most comprehensive ones (Brame 1976; Wasow 1976; Oehrle 1977), did not appear until after that model had begun to crumble.

No, the fact is that generative semantics destroyed itself. Its internal dynamic led to a state of affairs in which it could no longer be taken seriously by anyone interested in the scientific study of human language. Generative semantics simply gave up on attempting to explain grammatical phenomena, leaving the field open to its competitors.

The dynamic that led generative semantics to abandon explanation flowed irrevocably from its practice of regarding any speaker judgment and any fact about morpheme distribution as a de facto matter for grammatical analysis. In retrospect, it is easy to appreciate the a priori nature of the practice of reducing all linguistic facts to grammatical facts. It is no more logically necessary that, say, the proper use of *please* in English and the surface order of clitic pronouns in Spanish be treated within the same general framework than it is that any two physical phenomena be necessarily derivable from the same set of equations. Other sciences take a modular approach to their subject matter: They take it for granted that a complex phenomenon is best explained by regarding it as a product of the interaction of a number of autonomously functioning systems, each governed by its own general principles. Generative semantics, on the other hand, attempted to force all phenomena into one and only one system.

Attributing the same theoretical weight to each and every fact about language had disastrous consequences. Since the number of facts is, of course, absolutely overwhelming, simply describing the incredible complexities of language became the all-consuming task, with formal explanation postponed to some future data. Fillmore (1972) explicitly noted the data-collecting consequences of the generative semantic view of language: "The ordinary working grammarian," he observed, "finds himself in the age of what we might call the New Taxonomy, an era of a new and exuberant cataloging of the enormous range of facts that linguists need eventually to find theories to deal with" (p. 16).

This "exuberant cataloging of . . . facts" became a hallmark of generative semantics, as every counterexample to a claim (real or apparent) was greeted as an excuse to broaden still further the domain of grammatical analysis. Its data fetishism reached its apogee in fuzzy grammar. Many staunch generative semanticists who had followed every step of Lakoff and Ross up to that point turned away from fuzzy theoretical constructs. "Of course there's a squish," they objected. "There's always a squish. It's the nature of data to be squishy. And it's the purpose of a theory to extract order from squishy data." Generative semantics, it became all too clear, was not such a theory.[6]

---

[6]Apparently Ross's mid 1970s squishes lacked significance even when evaluated on their own terms. Gazdar and Klein (1978) point out that "it is crucial to Ross' argument [for squishes] in this paper [Ross 1975], as in his others, that the matrices exhibit statistically significant scalar properties that would not typically show up on an arbitrary matrix. He does not subject his matrices to any kind of significance test, nor does he seem to be aware that any such testing is necessary" (p. 666). After applying the appropriate statistical technique (Guttman scaling) to Ross's major clausemateness "squishoid," they conclude from

The substitution of "squishy" lists of sentences for rules and derivations took on a life of its own. Generative semanticists squealed with delight at the "horrors," "monstrosities," "mind snappers," and "wonders" (Postal 1976b) that no theory seemed to be able to explain. Bill Darden (1974) captured the nihilistic outlook of his generative semanticist co-thinkers admirably (referring specifically to natural phonology): "The multitude of views can be taken as evidence that we have reached that happy state when no one can be sure that he knows anything—except that everyone else is wrong" (np).

It needs to be pointed out that very few interpretivists in the early 1970s were either formalizing rules or presenting grammar fragments. But for generative semanticists, not doing so became a matter of principle: "I think that the time has come to return to the tradition of informal descriptions of exotic languages" (G. Lakoff 1974a:153). To students entering theoretical linguistics in the early 1970s, increasingly trained in the sciences, mathematics, and philosophy, the generative semantic positions on theory construction and formalization were anathema. It is little wonder that they found nothing of interest in this model.[7]

At the same time, generative semantics was co-opted from the opposite direction by sociolinguistics. Sociolinguists looked with amazement at the generative semantic program of attempting to treat societal phenomena in a framework originally designed to handle such sentence-level properties as morpheme order and vowel alternations. They found no difficulty in convincing those generative semanticists most committed to studying language in its social context to drop whatever lingering pretense they still might have of doing a grammatical analysis and to approach the subject matter instead from the traditional perspective of the social sciences.

Not surprisingly, commentators began to see in generative semantics the seeds of a structuralist–empiricist counterrevolution. The first to make this point explicit, Ronat (1972), compared Postal's (1970b) heavy reliance on selectional co-occurrence to support his analysis of the verb *remind* to the methodology of Zellig Harris and other post-Bloomfieldians, to whom surface distribution of morphemes was also the primary criterion for positing a particular linguistic structure (for a similar critique, see Dougherty 1974). By the time that the consummate critique of the philosophical implications of late generative semantics, Katz and Bever (1976), had been published, that model had been abandoned by most of its erstwhile supporters. Nevertheless, the following passage from their article is worth quoting, since it was the realization of its point that led many linguists to turn their backs on generative semantics:

---

the results that "Ross' squishoid provides no backing whatever for his claim that grammars require a quantifiable predicate of clausematiness" (p. 666).

For arguments that fuzzy logic is formally unsuitable for the linguistic goals to which Lakoff and Ross wish to apply it, see Morgan and Pelletier (1977).

[7]Robin Lakoff (1974) has attempted to provide the generative semantic rejection of formalism with explicit political motivation, arguing that "undue obeisance to formalism" (xiv–23) discourages women from the field. While she did not state whether mathematics and the sciences should also abandon formalism as a step toward sexual equality, she did, astonishingly, explicitly leave open the possibility that the "indisposition toward formalism among women" might be inherent!

[G]enerative semantics has distorted grammar by including within its goals a complete theory of acceptability. This assimilation of the phenomenon of performance into the domain of grammaticality has come about as a consequence of an empiricist criterion for determining what counts as grammatical. In almost every paper Lakoff makes explicit his assumption that the explanatory goal of a grammar is to state all the factors that influence the distributions of morphemes in speech. On this view, any phenomenon systematically related to cooccurrence is *ipso facto* something to be explained in the grammar. Since in actual speech almost anything can influence cooccurrence relations, it is no wonder that Lakoff repeatedly discovers more and more new kinds of "grammatical phenomena." In fact, the generative semanticist program for linguistic theory represents, if anything, a more extreme approach than even Bloomfieldian structuralism, which recognized that a variety of phenomena concerning language are extragrammatical. (Katz and Bever 1976:58)

5.4.2. "The Best Theory"

Probably no metatheoretical statement by a generative semanticist did more to undermine confidence in that model than Paul Postal's paper "The Best Theory" (1972a), to which I alluded in Section 4.3.4. Interpreted at one level, this paper is no more than a routine plea for a theory without unneeded apparatus and with as tight constraints as possible on the apparatus it does have. But that is not how "The Best Theory" was generally interpreted. Postal contrasted two hypothetical models, one with just A's and another with both B's and C's, where A, B, and C are distinct components or rule types. Surely, Postal argued, the first, more "homogeneous" theory is preferable. Generative semantics would then be preferable to its interpretivist competitor, since it is more homogeneous: generative semantics postulates a single mapping from semantic representation to surface structure without the level of deep structure intervening, whereas the latter has (at least) two distinct rule types and an extra level.

If for Postal, A, B, and C had been constructs of equal complexity and generality, then no one would have objected to his characterization. But for Postal and the other generative semanticists, A came more and more to be nothing but an unconstrained rule of grammar, while for the interpretivists, B and C were highly constrained rule types of definite form and specific function. Thus, the latter alternative was seen to be preferable, not the former. In the early 1970s, interpretivists were committed to constraining (or at least characterizing) B and C, while generative semanticists steadily weakened the content of A by ever increasing the type of data for which it was responsible. Postal's paper was more successful than any interpretivist critique in impressing upon the linguistic community that generative semantics had constructed a more homogeneous theory only by ceasing to make concrete claims about language.

A generative semantic response to such criticism was to deny that the two rival frameworks were even comparable, due to the differing conceptual status of their primitives. In generative semantics, such primitives were all "natural" ones:

> The same considerations of naturalness obtain in syntax [as in phonology]. The theory of generative semantics claims that the linguistic elements used in grammar have an independent natural basis in the human conceptual system. . . . In generative semantics, possible grammars are limited by the requirement [*sic*] that the nonphonological elements used have a natural semantic basis, independent of the rules of the grammar of any particular natural language. (G. Lakoff 1972a:77–78)

But such argumentation did not get very far. Many saw through its transparently aprioristic character. Emonds (1973) wrote: "Lakoff refuses to consider the merits of [the interpretivist] analysis, which employs categories which are well-motivated internal to language (syntactically). This refusal seems to me like requiring that philosophy define a priori the notions of science, in which case we never would have gotten to gravity, relativity, etc." (p. 56).

But even more important, the naturalness requirement was seen as little more than a terminological trick. Taken literally, it embodied the claim that all syntactic behavior could be expressed in "natural" semantic terms. But thus stated, nobody ever held such a position: how could one possibly explain the radically different syntactic behavior of the adjective *possible* and the modal *may* on the basis of their meanings, for example? In other words, all of the "natural" categories of generative semantics would have to be supplemented by a set of "unnatural" categories, rules, or whatever to explain all of the regularities (and irregularities) of language that could not be formulated in strictly semantic terms.

All the appeal to naturalness did, in effect, was bequeath to the interpretivists the task of searching for syntactic regularity.

5.4.3. Generative Semantic Style[8]

One last characteristic trait of generative semantics that speeded its downfall was the whimsical style of presentation that pervaded so much written in that framework. This is not to say that all generative semanticists were prone to such practice, nor that partisans of that model alone were, but the free introduction of humor into scholarly writing became more and more identified with generative semantics. The practice manifested itself in titles of papers and books (5.33), names of rules and constraints (5.34), example sentences (5.35), and in the prose itself (5.36):

(5.33)   a. *You Take the High Node and I'll Take the Low Node* (Corum, Smith-Stark, and Weiser 1973)
         b. "If You Hiss or Anything, I'll Do It Back" (Cantrall 1970)
         c. "Tracking the Generic Toad" (Lawler 1973)

(5.34)   a. "Richard" (Rogers 1974)
         b. "Q-Magic" (Carden 1968)
         c. "Stuffing" (Ross 1972b)

(5.35)   a. *Norbert the narc only reports potheads* (Lawler 1973)
         b. *Tums's taste is wall-to-wall Yucksville* (Ross 1973a)
         c. *Symbolic logic—and, by the way, who invented it?—isn't my cup of Postum* (Sadock 1974)

(5.36)   a. "The winner gets to say 'Nyaah, nyaah!' to the loser." (G. Lakoff 1973:286)

[8] I am indebted to Ann Banfield and Joseph Emonds for first making me aware of the issue discussed in this section. For remarks in a similar vein, see Percival (1971), Sampson (1976), and Hagège (1976).

b. "In summing up this awesome display of cosmic mysteries with scarcely a hint here and there of a denouement, we are reminded of the immortal words of Harry Reasoner." (L. Horn 1970:326)

c. "It is no longer necessary to assume that instrumental verb formation occurs in one swell foop." (Green 1972:84)

Such stylistic traits were undoubtedly grounded in youthful enthusiasm (the average age of generative semanticists in 1970 was well below 30) and in the rambunctious personalities of several prominent generative semanticists who served as role models for their students. Nevertheless, the whimsical style of generative semantic papers served to give extra credibility to the charge of lack of seriousness to which generative semanticists had opened themselves by downplaying and then abandoning the task of constructing a formalized theory of language. Indeed, it is tempting to regard generative semantic style as a classic example of content both shaping form and dominating it. Certainly not all generative semanticists would agree with one expartisan that "we went out of our way to be funny in our papers so that once our ideas were refuted we could get ourselves off the hook by saying, 'Oh, did you take us seriously? Couldn't you see that we were just fooling around?'" [personal communication]. But most, I suspect, would acknowledge a kernel of truth in it.

In addition to the way this stylistic practice reflected on generative semantics itself, many linguists from outside of American culture found it offensive. Even highly fluent nonnative speakers of English found many generative semantic papers impossible to read by virtue of the culture-bound slang and topical examples that permeated them. In at least one instance, a native speaker was baffled. Stephen Isard, an American linguist resident in Britain, recalls that he had to serve as interpreter for a colleague to help him through Ross's example sentence *It is said that the tacos Judge Bean won't go for* (Ross 1973d:164). *Tacos, Judge Bean,* and *go for* were all unfamiliar to him. As it turns out, the sentence *It is said that the oranges John won't ask for* would have served just as well to make the relevant theoretical point.

5.4.4. The Generative Semanticists' Organizational Problems

Generative semanticists were never able to take full advantage of the numerical and geographical head start they had over the interpretivists. Of the leading members of that tendency, only James McCawley was able to build a stable base and following. Paul Postal, working for IBM, had no students at all, while John Ross was always very much under Chomsky's shadow at MIT, a fact that for obvious reasons deterred students at that university from becoming generative semanticists. And George Lakoff, by associating himself with four different institutions (Harvard, Michigan, The Center for Advanced Studies in the Behavioral Sciences, and The University of California, Berkeley) during the crucial years of 1969–1972, relinquished any possibility of building the kind of program that Halle and Chomsky had succeeded in building at MIT.

Once at Berkeley, Lakoff did attempt this. But in 1972 it was already too late. Neither the linguistics department there nor the Berkeley Linguistics Society (over which he exerted considerable influence at first) ever became major vehicles for the dissemination of his ideas. And by coming out almost yearly with a newly named theory, from "fuzzy grammar" (1973) to "global transderivational well-formedness grammar" (1974b) to "cognitive grammar" (Lakoff and Thompson 1975) to "dual-hierarchy grammar" (1975a) to "linguistic gestalt theory" and "experiental linguistics" (1977), Lakoff did not present himself to the linguistic world as a consistent theoretician.

5.5. THE LEGACY OF GENERATIVE SEMANTICS

While generative semantics no longer is regarded as a viable model of grammar, there are innumerable ways in which it left its mark on its successors. Most importantly, its view that sentences must at one level have a representation in a formalism isomorphic to that of symbolic logic is now widely accepted by interpretivists, and in particular by Chomsky. It was generative semanticists who first undertook an intensive investigation of syntactic phenomena that defied formalization by means of transformational rules as they were then understood. This led to the plethora of mechanisms, such as indexing devices, traces, and filters that are now part of the interpretivists' theoretical store. Even the idea of lexical decomposition, for which generative semanticists were much scorned, has turned up in the semantic theories of several interpretativists. Furthermore, many proposals originally mooted by generative semanticists, such as the nonexistence of extrinsic rule ordering, postcyclic lexical insertion, and treating anaphoric pronouns as bound variables, have since appeared in the interpertivist literature, virtually always without acknowledgment.

While late generative semantics may have proven itself theoretically bankrupt, the important initial studies it inspired on the logical and sublogical properties of lexical items, on speech acts both direct and indirect, and on the more general pragmatic aspects of language become more and more appreciated as linguistic theory develops means to incorporate them. The wealth of information and interesting generalizations they contain have barely begun to be tapped by current researchers.

Chapter 6

The Extended Standard Theory

6.1. THE 1970 INTERPRETIVE MODEL

During the period in which generative semantics was flourishing, Chomsky and his students set to work to develop a lexicalist grammatical model that did not embody the Katz–Postal hypothesis. By 1970, they had come to view the organization of the grammar as depicted in Figure 6.1. Three principal features distinguished this model from that presented in *Aspects of the Theory of Syntax:* deep structures had become shallower (closer to the surface) as a result of the lexicalist hypothesis (see Sections 4.5.1 and 6.1.1); the cases that were problematic for the Katz–Postal hypothesis were handled by surface structure rules of interpretation (see Sections 4.5.2 and 6.1.2); a rich set of rules applied in the lexicon to relate constructions that had previously been related transformationally (see Sections 4.5.1 and 7.1.3).

Since Chomsky had for several years been referring to the *Aspects* model, correctly if immodestly, as the "standard theory," it was logical for him to dub this revised model the "extended standard theory" (EST). Its advocates were known from the beginning as "interpretivists" (short for "interpretive semanticists") due to the importance they attributed to rules of semantic interpretation. But terminology became rather muddled over the years. For example, the terms "lexicalism," "interpretive semantics" (or simply "interpretivism"), and the "Extended Standard Theory" have often been used interchangeably. This is unfortunate, since strictly speaking they are distinct in their referents. "Lexicalism" has a narrow sense in which it refers to the idea that derived nominals do not have a deverbal derivation and a (more common) broad sense in which it refers to the idea that there are no transformations that change category labels. Interpretive semantics in its broad sense refers to the idea that interpretive semantic rules take syntactic structures as their input. Lexicalism (in both senses) entails interpretivism

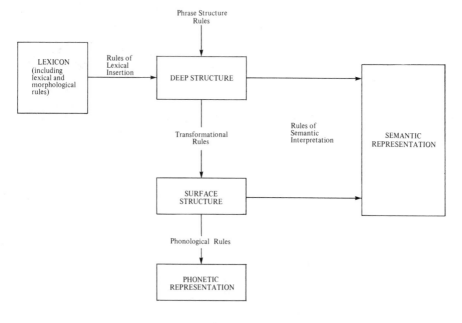

Figure 6.1

in its broad sense, since if transformations themselves do not refer to semantic structure, then they must be supplemented by interpretive rules that relate syntactic structure and semantic structure. However, "interpretivism" developed a narrow sense to refer to the idea that interpretive rules apply to superficial syntactic structures as well as to deep structures. Lexicalism does not entail such an idea: Katz (1972), for example, combines lexicalism with interpretive rules applying only to deep structures. In any event, the term "Extended Standard Theory" has generally been used (and is used in this book) to refer to any model incorporating a set of transformational rules, the lexicalist hypothesis, and surface structure rules of semantic interpretation.[1]

6.1.1. Deep Structure and the Lexicalist Hypothesis

A great deal of interpretivist work in the late 1960s and early 1970s was patterned on Chomsky's "Remarks on Nominalization" paper. That is, it attempted to refute transformational analyses of syntactic relationships that had long been assumed best

---

[1]For further remarks on the logical independence of the referents of these various terms and an interesting discussion of the mixed positions that have been adopted, see Partee (1971). An example of the chaotic state of terminology is provided in Jackendoff (1977:4), where the trace theory of movement rules (see Section 6.5) is referred to as an "alternative" to the EST, even though most would regard trace theory as the most important development within the EST.

handled by means of such rules and argued instead that the relationships could best be treated by means of lexical or interpretive semantic rules. Such conclusions typically demanded enrichment of the phrase structure component, since constructions that had once been transformationally derived were now to be generated by the phrase structure rules themselves.

It is worth looking at a typical example in some detail. Let us consider the history of the treatment of definite pronouns (*it, he, her,* etc.). Earlier analyses assumed that pronouns replaced full noun phrases under identity with another noun phrase by means of a transformational rule (Lees and Klima 1963; Ross 1967; Langacker 1969). Thus it was assumed that (6.1a) underlay (6.1b), with the pronoun in (6.1b) arising from the transformational replacement of the second occurrence of *Harry* in (6.1a).

(6.1)   a. *Harry$_i$ thinks that Harry$_i$ should win the prize*
         b. *Harry$_i$ thinks that he$_i$ should win the prize*

However, by the end of the 1960s, generative semanticists and interpretivists alike acknowledged that such an approach faced insuperable difficulties. The most serious problem involved the analysis of the famous class of sentences discovered by Emmon Bach and Stanley Peters (and therefore called "Bach–Peters sentences") involving crossing coreference. (6.2) is an example from Bach (1970).

(6.2)   *[The man who shows he deserves it$_j$]$_i$ will get [the prize he$_i$ desires]$_j$*

If pronominalization were to be handled by a transformation that turned a full noun phrase into a pronoun, then sentence (6.2) would require a deep structure like (6.3), with an infinite number of embeddings, since each pronoun lies within the antecedent of the other.

(6.3)

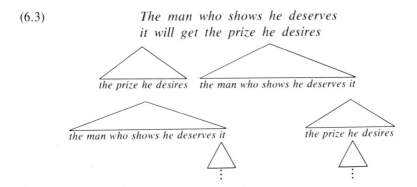

Interpretivists concluded from Bach–Peters sentences that infinite deep structures could be avoided only if definite pronouns were present in the deep structure, which, in turn, implied the existence of an interpretive rule to assign coreferentiality between those base-generated pronouns and the appropriate noun phrases.[2]

Four other well-known arguments supporting an interpretive over a transformational analysis of definite pronouns are paraphrased below.

Consider the sentences of (6.4):

(6.4)   a. *I wanted Charlie to help me, but the bastard wouldn't do it*
          b. *Although the bum tried to hit me, I can't really get too mad at Harry*

The anaphoric epithets *the bastard* and *the bum* are interpreted as coreferential to *Charlie* and *Harry*, respectively. As G. Lakoff (1976b) has shown, such epithets obey many of the same conditions on coreference as ordinary definite pronouns. But epithets surely are not transformationally derived from full NPs. What principle would decide which epithet an NP would be turned into? Therefore, since we need an interpretive rule for these epithets, it makes sense to utilize the same one for simple pronouns as well.

[Paraphrasing Jackendoff 1972, 110–111]

There are no reasonable candidates for full NPs to serve as syntactic antecedents for the pronouns in boldface. Therefore, it stands to reason that they should be generated in the base:

(6.5)   a. *Lips that touch liquor shall never touch **mine***
          b. *You can have an ice cream, a soda, or **both***
          c. *Each of Mary's sons hated **his** brothers*

[Paraphrasing Dougherty 1969, 490–501]

If pronouns replace full NPs, what would block *There*-Insertion from applying before Pronominalization, resulting in (6.6c)?

(6.6)   a. *some students$_i$ believe that some students$_i$ are running the show*
             THERE-INSERTION →

[2]Generative semanticists put forward the following transformational account of definite pronouns: they derived noun phrases from bound variables that substituted for indices in the clause representing the main propositional content of the sentence. Those indices remaining after the substitution rule would be realized as pronouns. Thus, they derived sentence (6.2) from semantic representation (i) below (see McCawley 1970c:177), thereby avoiding infinite regress.

(i)

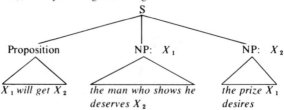

Such an approach to pronominalization was defended in Fauconnier (1973), Partee (1975a), and Jacobson (1980), and subject to a thoroughgoing critique in Wasow (1975).

b. *some students₁ believe that there are some students₁ running the show*
PRONOMINALIZATION →
c. **Some students believe that there are they running the show*
[PARAPHRASING BRESNAN 1970a, 122–123][3]

Consider (6.7).

(6.7)   *Ten errors were committed by the Red Sox and the Yankees, but it would never have happened with any two other teams*

Demanding a NP antecedent for *it* leads to the absurd conclusion that *ten errors were committed* is a noun phrase constituent. Since there is no other conceivable antecedent for *it* in the string, there is no possibility of deriving it transformationally.

[PARAPHRASING CHOMSKY 1971, 200]

The 1970s saw numerous attempts to state precisely the interpretive rule involved in admitting coreference between a definite pronoun and its antecedent. Among the most important are Dougherty (1969), Jackendoff (1972:108–177), Wasow (1972, 1979), Lasnik (1976), and Reinhart (1981). All assumed a rule of surface structure interpretation with the exception of Jackendoff, who argued that the interpretive rule applied at the end of each syntactic cycle.

6.1.2. The Interpretive Component in the EST

The earliest (late 1960s to early 1970s) versions of the EST hypothesized rules of semantic interpretation applying to both deep structure and surface structure (see Figure 6.1). These two types of rules can be illustrated through a reexamination of sentences (4.47a–b), repeated here as (6.8a–b).

(6.8)   a. *Many arrows did not hit the target*
         b. *The target was not hit by many arrows*

As was observed in Chapter 4, the scope of *many* and *not* differs in these two sentences and appears to be a function of their relative order in surface structure. Interpretivists thus posited a surface structure rule of semantic interpretation like the following to handle the facts:

If logical element A precedes logical element B in surface structure, then A is interpreted as having wider scope than B (where logical elements include quantifiers, negatives, and some modal auxiliaries).

The interpretations of (6.8a) and (6.8b) differ in another way: (a) is in some sense a sentence about arrows, while (b) is about targets, a fact that seems to correlate

---

[3]For critical remarks on Bresnan's argument, see Hankamer and Sag (1976:398–399) and Rando and Napoli (1978:310).

with the relative position of the two nouns in surface structure. Thus the discourse functioning of elements in a sentence, including their role in conveying such notions as "aboutness," old and new information, topic, presupposition, and so on were also assumed to be handled by surface structure rules of interpretation.

At the same time, interpretivists observed that the meanings of sentences like (6.8a) and (6.8b) are identical in an important aspect. In both sentences, the semantic relation between *arrows* and *hit* and between *target* and *hit* is the same. Since in the deep structure, the subject, verb, and object are in identical positions in both sentences, interpretivists assumed that the projection rule interpreting this semantic relation was stated at that level by a rule of semantic interpretion, as follows:

Interpret an animate deep structure subject of a sentence as the semantic agent of the verb.

For more complex examples of deep structure rules of semantic interpretation, see S. Anderson (1971b) and Jackendoff (1974a).

The most important treatment of semantics in the early EST was Ray Jackendoff's *Semantic Interpretation in Generative Grammar* (1972).[4] For Jackendoff, as for interpretivists in general, there was no single formal object called a "semantic representation." Rather, different types of rules filled in different aspects of the meaning. Jackendoff posited four distinct interpretive components that contributed to the complete semantic interpretation:

1. Functional structure: The main propositional content of the sentence (essentially, the semantic relationship between a verb and its noun phrase co-constituents within a clause.)
2. Modal structure: The specification of the scope of logical elements, such as negation and quantifiers, and of the referential properties of noun phrases.
3. The table of coreference: The specification of which noun phrases in a sentence are understood as coreferential.
4. Focus and presupposition: The designation of what information in the sentence is understood as new and what is understood as old.

Despite Jackendoff's work and the general importance that the counterexamples to the Katz–Postal hypothesis played in the development of the EST, most of the semantic analyses undertaken by generative grammarians before the mid 1970s were by generative semanticists. The neglect of semantics by interpretivists was partly a result of the all-absorbing work taking place constraining the syntactic rules, which seemed to be yielding such promising results. But it resulted as well from a lingering feeling that semantics was, for the time being at least, simply "not doable"—too nebulous and unsystemizable to admit formalization with the descriptive tools then available. Surely, the negative example of both the Katz–Fodor paper and the efforts of generative semanticists did much to reinforce this feeling

---

[4]This book incorporates and expands on several of his earlier papers (1968b; 1968c; 1969; 1971a; 1971b). For critiques of Jackendoff's work from interpretive viewpoints, see Gee (1974), Freidin (1975b), Lasnik (1976), and Hust and Brame (1976), and for a general critique of his theory of anaphora, see McCawley (1976c).

among interpretivists. While assertions like "sentence (43) is filtered out by the interpretive rules" (Dougherty 1969:499) fill the pages of the interpretivist literature, such rules were rarely even characterized, much less formalized.

By the mid 1970s, however, semantics began to be taken more seriously by interpretivists. The revival of interest was in part a result of the realization that the abandonment of transformational solutions to problems of grammatical analysis would necessitate semantic ones. And it was in part a result of the fact that trace theory (see Section 6.5) seemed to many interpretivists to provide a way of handling an interesting set of semantic relationships. And it was in part a result of the fact that as the achievements of model theoretic semantics (which were made largely outside the linguistic tradition) became known to linguists, the needed formal devices became available to express the desired generalizations about meaning. Hence, in the late 1970s, semantic studies flourished as never before. These studies are taken up in Section 6.5 and in Chapters 7 and 8.

6.2. CONSTRAINTS ON TRANSFORMATIONAL RULES

Except for the most hard core generative semanticists, syntacticians realized that the addition of transformational rules to the theory was a mixed blessing. On the one hand, such rules appeared to be vital to the adequate description of a wide variety of grammatical processes. But on the other, they vastly increased the expressive power of the theory. That is, they predicted the possibility of grammatical processes that never seemed to occur in any language in the world. The definition of a transformational rule as nothing more than a rule mapping a phrase marker into a phrase marker allows such rules to interchange the subject of a main clause with the indirect object of a subordinate clause, to state agreement between any two random elements in a sentence, and to perform other operations unknown to human language.

Chomsky had noted as early as 1955 in *The Logical Structure of Linguistic Theory* that the excessive power of transformational rules led to the theory making rather weak claims about what could or could not be a possible human language. As a consequence, even in the early and mid 1960s, proposals were mooted to restrict the power of such rules, among which were the condition on recoverability of deletion (see Section 3.2.6), the base recursion hypothesis (Section 3.5.1), and the A-over-A Principle (Section 6.2.1). The abstract syntacticians of the late 1960s recognized the importance of constraining transformations, and Ross's work along these lines was seminal (see Section 6.2.1). Nevertheless, in the 1970s, generative semanticists expanded the power of the transformational rule rather than restricting it, and the task of proposing constraints fell to the interpretivists.

There were two important classes of constraints on transformations proposed in the 1960s and 1970s: constraints on extraction, i.e., those preventing a transformational rule from moving an element from a particular position; and constraints on positioning, i.e., those preventing a transformational rule from moving an element to a particular position. They are discussed in Sections 6.2.1 and 6.2.2, respectively.

6.2.1. Constraints on Extraction

Chomsky (1964b) called attention to the ambiguity of (6.9).

(6.9)   *Mary saw the boy walking to the railroad station*

In one reading, bracketed below as (6.10a), *walking to the railroad station* is understood as a reduction of the relative clause *who was walking to the railroad station*. In the other, bracketed as (6.10b), it can be paraphrased *walk to the railroad station*.

(6.10)   a. *[_{NP}[_{NP}the boy] [walking to the railroad station]]*
          b. *[_{NP}the boy] [walking to the railroad station]*

He pointed out that if *the boy* is questioned, the resultant sentence is unambiguous, having only the second reading. Thus (6.11) does not have the reduced relative interpretation.

(6.11)   *Who did Mary see walking to the railroad station?*

He offered the following explanation for the nonambiguity of (6.11):

> The A-over-A Principle. If a transformational rule has the potential to apply both to a particular node and to another node of the same category which dominates it, only the dominating node may be affected by the rule.

Since the NP *the boy* in (6.10a) is itself dominated by an NP, the rule forming questions is unable to extract and question it. However *the boy* in (6.10b) may be extracted and questioned, since it is not dominated by an NP.

Apparent counterexamples like (6.12a–b) forced Chomsky to give up the A-over-A Principle very rapidly (Chomsky 1964b), and the matter was dropped for several years:

(6.12)   a. *[_{NP}who] would you approve of [_{NP}my seeing ____]*
          b. *[_{NP}what] are you uncertain about [_{NP}my giving ____ to John]*

However, the question of how extraction transformations might be constrained was returned to and treated in great detail in Ross's classic 1967 MIT dissertation, "Constraints on Variables in Syntax" (now published as Ross 1985). While Ross's work contains a wealth of observations, generalizations, and analyses of a number of syntactic topics, it centers on a set of constraints designed to do the work of the A-over-A Principle, without at the same time predicting the ungrammaticality of (6.12a–b). The four most important of Ross's constraints are the Complex Noun Phrase Constraint, the Coordinate Structure Constraint, the Left Branch Condition, and the Sentential Subject Constraint. These four constraints are given an informal statement below, accompanied by a diagram that gives a schematic illustration of their effect and a typical sentence whose ungrammaticality the constraint predicts:

Complex Noun Phrase Constraint. No element may be extracted from a sentence dominated by a noun phrase with a lexical head noun.

(6.13)

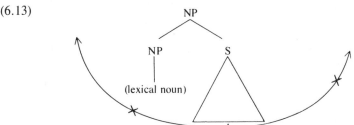

(6.14)　　*[_{NP}*who*] do you believe [_{NP}*the claim* [_{NP}*that Bill saw* ____]]*

Coordinate Structure Constraint. No conjunct in a coordinate structure may be moved, nor may any element in a conjunct be moved.

(6.15)

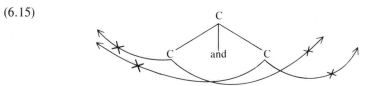

(6.16)　　*[_{NP}*what*] was John eating* [_{NP}[_{NP}*beans] and* ____]*

Left Branch Condition. No noun phrase on the left branch of another noun phrase may be extracted from that noun phrase.

(6.17)

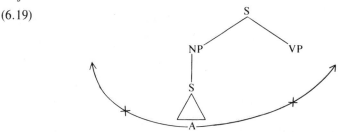

(6.18)　　*[_{NP}*whose*] did you like* [_{NP}* ____ [_{N}*book]]*

Sentential Subject Constraint. No element may be extracted from the sentential subject of a sentence.

(6.19)

(6.20)　　*[_{NP}*what*] [_{NP}[_{S}*that John will eat* ____]] is likely*

The importance of Ross's thesis is attested by the fact that throughout the 1970s it was second in number of citations only to Chomsky's *Aspects of the Theory of*

Syntax in publications dealing with syntax. Its Chapter 4, in which the bulk of the constraints are motivated, has served as a model in many a classroom for syntactic argumentation. And since the rules most relevant to the constraints (those involved in the formation of questions, relative clauses, and sentences with topicalized phrases) operate at fairly shallow levels of syntactic structure, Ross's own abstract syntactic–generative semantic biases at the time of writing did not serve to discredit his results even after generative semantics had fallen by the wayside.

Ross' constraints were so significant that their reanalysis was at the center of the major revision of the EST—the trace theory of movement rules. Since this revision has proved of such historical importance, Section 6.5 of this book is devoted to it. However, there have been quite a few other reanalyses of Ross's work within the EST that deserve mentioning. Among the most important are

(Grosu 1972). The Complex NP Constraint, the Coordinate Structure Constraint, and a constraint on extraction from adverbial subordinate clauses can be replaced by a single constraint making use of the notions "nucleus" and "satellite."

(Kuno 1973). The Sentential Subject Constraint can be generalized to exclude any extraction process that results in "incomplete" subjects.

(G. Horn 1977). Almost all of Ross's constraints can be replaced by a single one: no constituent can be extracted from a noun phrase.

(Cattell 1976). Most of Ross's constraints can be replaced by the NP Ecology Constraint: the number and identity of argument NPs within a syntactic configuration must remain constant under the operation of movement rules.

(Culicover 1976). The Binary Principle involving the structural notion "master of" can replace most of Ross's constraints.

(Shir 1977). Most of Ross's constraints have a semantic explanation: extraction can take place only out of clauses that are semantically dominant (not presupposed and without contextual reference).

(Bresnan 1976a). Ross's constraints can be reinterpreted essentially as a constraint involving unbounded movements or deletions and the COMP node.

(Wilkins 1979, 1980). The Variable Interpretation Convention, a condition on how phrase markers are analyzed, subsumes most movement constraints.

(Grosu 1981). Ross's constraints are explicable in terms of an interaction of syntactic, semantic, pragmatic, and perceptual factors.

While everyone agrees that Ross's original proposals are deficient in some respect, the continued use of the expression "Ross Constraint" to refer to constraints on extraction in general points to the importance and resilience of Ross's work. Anyone who wishes to convince the linguistic public that his or her approach to syntax represents a step forward is obligated to show how that approach measures up to the analyses first put forward by Ross in his dissertation.

6.2.2. Constraints on Positioning

In 1967, John Kimball, then a student at MIT, made an interesting observation. He noted that, by and large, cyclic transformations yield outputs that correspond to structures generable by the phrase structure rules (see Kimball 1972a). At the same time, his fellow students Stephen Anderson and Joseph Emonds made proposals that seemed to provide a means for capturing this insight. Anderson, in an effort to extend McCawley's (1968a) concept of the base component, suggested that (in effect) phrase structure rules "check" the output of each transformational rule (see S. Anderson 1976). And Emonds, noting the increasing length of derivations in this period of abstract syntax, put forward the idea (in unpublished work) that the phrase structure rules apply after the transformations, lest important generalizations about surface order go uncaptured.

Emonds's 1970 dissertation, *Root and Structure Preserving Transformations*, advanced a formal explanation within a nonabstract framework of why transformations have the property of preserving the structure provided by the phrase structure rules. Emonds devoted the next several years to a thoroughgoing revision of this work, the culmination of which is *A Transformational Approach to English Syntax* (1976), widely agreed to be the most impressive detailed analysis of English structure within the framework of transformational generative grammar.

The core of Emonds's analysis is the Structure Preserving Constraint. Put simply, this constraint states that a transformational rule can move an element of category C only into a position in a phrase marker held by a node of category C. The constraint is captured formally by allowing any deep structure node to remain unfilled (i.e., even phrasal categories such as NP, VP, S need not be expanded by the phrase structure rules). The resultant empty node (symbolized by Δ) may be filled by a transformationally moved element of the same category; if the empty node is unfilled in surface structure, the sentence is ungrammatical. To illustrate, consider Emonds's derivation (6.22a–b) of sentence (6.21).

(6.21)   *Germany was defeated by Russia*

(6.22)   a.

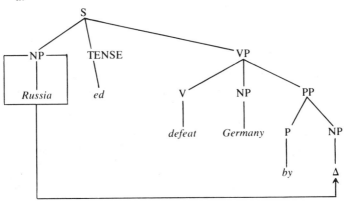

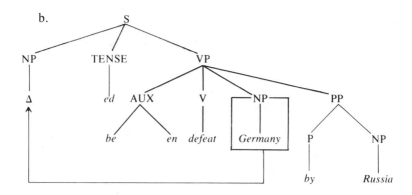

Passivization is accomplished by two separate operations. First, as illustrated in (6.22a), the deep structure subject, *Russia,* is postposed to fill the empty NP node following *by.* Second, as illustrated in (6.22b), *Germany* fills the now empty subject position without itself leaving behind an empty object node.

The constraining effect of this approach to movement can be appreciated from a consideration of the following ungrammatical sentences:

(6.23)   a. *Germany Russia was defeated by*
         b. *Germany was Russia defeated by*
         c. *Germany was by Russia defeated*
         d. *Germany was defeated Russia by*

Traditional treatments provide no explanation for the ungrammaticality of (6.23a–d) other than the formulation of the Passive transformation itself. The rule could be modified trivially to allow any one of them to be generated. But the Structure Preserving Constraint predicts their ungrammaticality from a general fact about English structure; none of these sentences corresponds to structures generated by independently motivated base rules.

There are two formally characterizable classes of transformations that are not structure preserving in Emonds's theory:

1. Root transformations: transformations that attach elements to a root sentence (essentially, the highest clause in the phrase marker). Topicalization is an example.[5]
2. Local transformations: transformations that refer to a single nonphrase node and one adjacent constituent. Particle Movement is an example.

Historically speaking, the Structure Preserving Constraint has had a somewhat paradoxical character. On the one hand, it was perhaps the best accepted of all interpretivist proposals in the 1970s, and the generalizations it expresses have been

---

[5]Hooper and Thompson (1973) argue that the effects of root transformations lend themselves to a purely discourse characterization, thus rendering unnecessary a structural definition of the notion "root sentence." Their claim is (in essence) defended in Bolinger (1977) and shown to be overstated in Green (1976).

incorporated into virtually all recent work. But on the other, it has seldom actually been utilized in deciding between competing analyses of syntactic phenomena. That is, while there are innumerable passages in the literature that read "we must reject the X analysis of Y because it violates such-and-such Ross Constraint," we almost never find "we must reject the X analysis of Y because it violates the Structure Preserving Constraint."

There are several reasons, I think, for the noncentral role that the Structure Preserving Constraint has played in linguistic argumentation. First, while the constraint excludes innumerable possible analyses, it barely restricts the class of plausible ones. In general, competing analyses of the same phenomenon all turn out to be structure preserving. By way of example, Emonds himself vastly revised his analysis of Extraposition between 1970 and 1976. Yet both alternatives are consistent with the constraint. Even a large percentage of the rules proposed by generative semanticists were structure preserving. Second, the claim that a rule is structure preserving is tantamount to the claim that its output could be base-generated without any great complication ensuing. For reasons discussed in Chapter 7, many linguists in the late 1970s began to favor, for a wide variety of constructions, base generation rather than transformational derivation, thereby diminishing the direct applicability of the constraint. And finally, some of the most problematic areas of English syntax, such as the analysis of Extraposition and *Wh*-Movement, have also been the most problematic for the Structure Preserving Constraint. Emonds's treatments of both have been widely criticized. In 1970 he analyzed the former by invoking the dubious device of "doubly filled nodes," and the latter by means of obligatorily empty deep structure nodes, which seemed equally dubious. In 1976 his treatment of the latter involved a significant weakening of the constraint itself, and that of the former necessitated an otherwise unmotivated local transformation. The perceived problems in both his earlier and his later solutions (see Higgins 1973; Hooper 1973; Freidin 1978b; Grimshaw 1979b) have prevented the Structure Preserving Constraint from playing an important role in choosing the correct analysis of these phenomena.

A set of constraints on positioning for the most part complementary to Emonds's was proposed in the late 1970s by Mark Baltin (see Baltin 1978, 1982). According to Baltin, a rule that moves an element to a defined structural position within a sentence can move that element only to either the left or right periphery of either V, VP, S, or S̄ (where S̄ is the constituent formed by a sentence along with its complementizer). Two examples are Extraposition, which moves an S̄ to the right periphery of VP, and *Wh*-Movement, which moves a *wh*-phrase to the left periphery of S̄. Baltin's "landing site" theory (as he called it) predicts, for example, that no element will be adjoined to an NP or moved into the center of any constituent.

6.3. CONSTRAINTS ON BASE RULES

The lexicalist hypothesis, by demanding base generation of constructions that had once been derived transformationally, resulted in an increased role for the phrase structure rules. Not surprisingly then, interpretivists in the 1970s saw it as important to constrain those rules, while simultaneously accomplishing the following five tasks:

1. Capturing the parallel internal structures of the phrasal categories (for discussion, see Section 4.5.1).
2. Capturing the fact that phrasal constructions in human language are invariably endocentric (see Chapter 4, footnote 14).
3. Allowing the grammar to express cross-categorial generalizations without demanding (à la generative semantics) the conflation of any two categories sharing a particular property. Examples of cross-categorial co-occurrence generalizations are given in Section 4.5.1. Below are paraphrased three examples that were adduced in the 1970s of grammatical rules applying to more than one category.[6]

Both Gapping (6.24a–b) and Verb Phrase Deletion (6.25a–b) generalize to apply to nouns (or noun phrases) as well as to verbs (or verb phrases).

(6.24)   a. *Max ate the apple and Sally* _____ *the hamburgers*
            b. *I bought three quarts of wine and two* _____ *of Clorox*

(6.25)   a. *Bill ate the peaches and Harry did* _____ *too*
            b. *I like John's yellow shirt, but not Max's* _____
                                    [PARAPHRASING JACKENDOFF 1971a, 21–36]

In French elevated speech, liaison is possible in contexts impossible in colloquial speech, namely between the inflected head of any phrase and its complement (ˆ indicates a liaison context).

(6.26)   a. *des [$_N$endroits]ˆobscurs*
            b. *des mois [$_A$féconds]ˆen événements*
            c. *il [$_V$vallait]ˆaccrocher le machin au mur*
                                    [PARAPHRASING SELKIRK 1974, 583–589]

Wh-Movement (6.27a–d), Comparative Deletion (6.28a–d), and Heavy-NP-Shift (6.29a–b) generalize to apply across major categories.

(6.27)   a. *[$_{NP}$what book] did you read* _____
            b. *[$_{Adj}$ ^{p}how long] is it* _____
            c. *[$_{Adv}$ ^{p}how quickly] did you read it* _____
            d. *[$_{QP}$how much] did it cost* _____

(6.28)   a. *it costs more than it weighs [$_{QP}$* _____*]*
            b. *it looks more costly than it is [$_{Adj}$ P* _____*]*
            c. *she drives more dynamically than he drives [$_{Adv}$ P*_____*]*
            d. *she had more friends than he had [$_{NP}$*_____*]*

(6.29)   a. *he considers stupid [$_{NP}$many of my best friends]*
            b. *he talked about their stupidity [$_{PP}$to many of my best friends]*
                                    [PARAPHRASING BRESNAN 1976c, 21–36]

[6]For other such cases, see Horvath's (1976) analysis of Hungarian focus; Napoli and Nespor's (1979) treatment of Italian consonant gemination; and Pierrehumbert's (1980) analysis of Finnish possessive suffixes.

4. Allowing for the assignment of feature specifications to phrasal categories as well as to lexical categories. In the *Aspects* model, there was no difficulty in subcategorizing a Noun for the feature NUMBER, yet there was no available mechanism for assigning a value for that feature to the entire Noun Phrase.
5. Eliminating the artificiality of the category–feature distinction. A syntactic theory admitting both categories and features as primitives is no more justified than a phonological theory with both indivisible segments and distinctive features. Yet, in the *Aspects* model, both categories and features are recognized as primitive.

X-bar theory, first proposed in Chomsky's "Remarks on Nominalization" paper (see Section 4.5.1), was designed to solve all these problems simultaneously. The principal base rules were replaced by (4.45), thus eliminating an infinite set of logically possible, but nonoccurring, phrase structure rules. The categories themselves were reduced to sets of distinctive features, thereby eliminating "syntactic category" as a notion of theoretical significance. And thus the possibility arose of any natural class of syntactic categories being represented by a smaller number of feature symbols than an unnatural one, thereby providing an elegant statement of cross-categorial generalizations.

As the 1970s progressed, an increasing amount of research was devoted to X-bar theory, and in its broadest outline it remains one of the most solid pillars of generative grammar. Yet at the same time it seems fair to say that advocates of the X-bar convention are still far from agreement on the answers to some of the most basic questions about the nature of the base rules and the proper means of constraining them. Among these questions are the following:

1. *How many levels are to be hypothesized for each category?* That is, if all phrase structure rules are of the form $X^n \rightarrow X^{n-1}$, what is the maximum value of n? There have been many answers to this question. In Chomsky's original formulation, n is 2 for nouns and 3 for verbs (assuming the verb to be the head of the sentence.) For Vergnaud (1974) and Siegel (1979), n equals 4, at least for nouns; in Jackendoff (1977), the most detailed exposition of X-bar theory, a uniform three-level analysis is proposed for all categories. Most syntacticians have moved away from an elaborate bar system, and typically posit only one, or at most two, bar levels for each category.
2. *Which categories participate in the X-bar system?* In Chomsky's original proposal, only N, V, and A participate, though he and most others later assumed that P had at least one bar level as well. Jackendoff (1977) assumes multiple bar levels for 10 categories in English, including M (modal), PRT (particle), Art (article), Q (quantifier), Deg (degree), and Adv (adverb), even though no rules at all applied to many of the 40 resultant categories.
3. *How do the categories S and $\bar{S}$ fit into the system?* Chomsky's original (1970) view was that S lay outside the X-bar system entirely, a position defended in Hornstein (1977) and Bresnan (1982a). Others, however, including Jackendoff (1977), Marantz (1980), Gazdar (1981b), and Borsley (1983) have ar-

gued that S is the maximal projection of V. For Williams (1975), Koster (1978b), and van Riemsdijk (1978a), S̄ is one higher projection of S within the V system. Chomsky (1981) and Safir (1982), on the other hand, consider INFL to be the head of both S and S̄, while Chomsky (1985) and Stowell (forthcoming) argue that INFL is the head of S and COMP of S̄.[7]

4. *How are the categories themselves subcategorized with respect to features?* In Bresnan (1976c), Chomsky and Lasnik (1977), and Gazdar, Klein, Pullum, and Sag (1985), verbs, nouns, adjectives, and prepositions are subcategorized as follows:

(6.30) $V = [+V, -N]$; $N = [-V, +N]$; $A = [+V, +N]$; $P = [-V, -N]$

But Jackendoff (1977) proposes a different (and quite incompatible) feature assignment:

(6.31) $V = [+SUBJ, +OBJ]$; $N = [+SUBJ, -OBJ]$; $A = [-SUBJ, -OBJ]$;
           $P = [-SUBJ, +OBJ]$

Most linguists today appear to support (6.30) over (6.31).

5. *How are structurally mixed languages to be handled?* Jackendoff (1977) points out that German, which has a verb-final VP but a noun-initial NP, poses a serious problem for the X-bar convention. The same can be said for any structurally mixed language (see Greenberg 1963 for a summary of data on many such languages).

Two important works have revised significantly earlier approaches to X-bar syntax. Emonds (1985) reanalyzes the distribution of syntactic categories in universal grammar and Stowell (forthcoming) attempts to derive many phrase structure generalizations through the interaction of independent principles.[8]

6.4. CONSTRAINTS ON SURFACE STRUCTURE

Ross, in Chapter 3 of his 1967 dissertation, observed a number of generalizations about English structure that seemed to defy statement in terms of either phrase structure or transformational rules. One example involved the surface structure order of the elements that can follow the verb within the verb phrase. Ross tentatively suggested that this ordering should be imposed by an output condition applying in a separate stylistic component that followed the transformational rules. While Ross never developed his proposal, the idea that a set of conditions should be applied to derived structure was defended at great length by David Perlmutter (1971). Perlmutter argued that the order of preverbial clitics in Spanish cannot be derived by any imaginable combination of transformational rules, but the output

---

[7]The various positions that have been taken on this question are summarized in Muysken (1982) and Gazdar, Klein, and Pullum (1983a).

[8]For an important critique of many popular formulations of X-bar theory, see Pullum (1985a).

condition (or, as he called it, "Surface Structure Constraint"), shown in (6.32), which requires that the clitics occur in the order represented, gives an elegant statement of the correct generalization (Roman numerals refer to grammatical person).

(6.32)   *se* II I III

By the mid 1970s, output conditions and surface structure constraints were being referred to universally as "filters," since they filter out derivations that survive the transformational rules. Below are paraphrased two examples of filters that were proposed on the grounds of the undesirability or impossibility of a transformational statement:

Ungrammatical sentences result from the application of Extraposition in (6.33) and Heavy-NP Shift in (6.34):

(6.33)   a. *That his fingernails were on my throat proves that he was unfond of me*
          b. **It proves that he was unfond of me that his fingernails were on my throat*

(6.34)   a. *We found the fact that she has blood on her hands indicative of the fact that she killed him*
          b. **We found indicative of the fact that she killed him the fact that she had blood on her hands*

Since it is undesirable to place the same condition on two rules, we must add the following filter to the grammar of English:
The Same Side Filter. No surface structure can have both complements of a bisentential verb on the same side of that verb.

[PARAPHRASING ROSS 1973c, 549–567]

In most cases, two consecutive words ending in *-ing* result in grammaticality violations:

(6.35)   a. *It is continuing raining*
          b. *I'm stopping watching it*
          c. *He's going drinking beer*

But in certain cases there is no violation:

(6.36)   a. *Waldo keeps molesting sleeping gorillas*
          b. *His avoiding contacting Harriet is understandable*
          c. *His having getting into college to consider is a drag*

As a result of the many interactions of rules that serve to create *-ing* . . . *-ing* sequences, there is no way to state the relevant constraint transformationally without loss of generality. However, it can be stated elegantly at the level of surface structure:
Double *-ing* Constraint. Surface sequences of V *-ing* are prohibited unless an NP boundary intervenes.

[PARAPHRASING EMONDS 1973, 39–62, itself a reinterpretation of ROSS 1972b]

Despite the fact that they are referred to as "surface structure constraints," filters in and of themselves do not have a constraining effect on the theory. Quite the contrary, they do no less than add a new descriptive device to the many already available. Perlmutter recognized the resultant weakening to linguistic theory of an unconstrained set of surface filters and therefore sought to provide a universal characterization of the phenomena to which they were applicable. For example, he suggested (1971) that the word is universally subject to surface structure constraints on morpheme order, expressed in positive output constraint notation. However, Emonds (1975), Kayne (1975), and Fiengo and Gitterman (1978) provided an essentially transformational account of clitic order in French, and today most syntacticians appear to take the position that clitic sequencing should be stated in the base (see, for example, Strozer 1976; Rivas 1977; Grimshaw 1982).

Chomsky and his associates in the 1970s proposed a rich set of surface filters (see Section 6.5.3). These were a necessary consequence of their attempt to remove as many undesirable ad hoc conditions as possible from the transformational rules. Recognizing that filters themselves are an undesirable addition to the theory, they have in recent years attempted to derive them from more general principles (see Section 8.2.2). On the other hand, some linguists have noted that the generalizations statable as filters mimic those expressible by phrase structure rules, a fact they feel indicates that filters and transformations alike should be eliminated in favor of an enormously increased phrase structure component (see Section 7.2.1).

6.5. THE TRACE THEORY OF MOVEMENT RULES

Chomsky published three papers in the early 1970s that were to redirect the course taken by syntactic studies within generative grammar. The first, "Remarks on Nominalization" (1970), challenged generative semantics by establishing the importance of a rich set of base rules. The second, "Deep Structure, Surface Structure, and Semantic Interpretation" (1971), sparked dozens of investigations probing the intimate connection between superficial levels of syntactic structure and meaning. But the paper that was undoubtedly most profound in its effect was "Conditions on Transformations," published in 1973. The "Conditions" paper, starting from a modest premise about the application of the transformational rules, was ultimately to alter dramatically not just the prevalent conception of the organization of the grammar, but also of the relationship between the grammar and other faculties involved in giving language its overall character. This paper, and those by Chomsky that followed it, were to trigger the first major schism in the interpretivist camp, a schism that survived into the 1980s.

6.5.1. Blind Application and Its Implications

In the earliest formulations, grammatical transformations were defined as applying "blindly" to factored strings, with no regard to grammatical relations or meaning, and without Boolean conditions on structural factors (for a precise, though highly technical, early characterizstion, see Chomsky 1961b:19). Chomsky in *Aspects* (1965) reiterated his view that "each transformation is fully defined by a structure index, which is a Boolean condition on Analyzability, and a sequence of elementary transformations" (pp. 142–143).

Yet very few transformations, as they were actually formulated, met this extremely restrictive condition. In particular, rules were often stated in terms of Boolean conditions on factors, as in one popular formulation of Extrapostion that required part of the structural analysis to be simultaneously "NP" and "*it* S" (see Burt 1971:94; Akmajian and Heny 1975:283). Rules were written with clause-mate conditions, identity conditions, and special ad hoc conditions that defied formalization.[9]

Chomsky, in a 1969 presentation (see Chomsky 1972a:118) and in "Conditions on Transformations" (written a year later, and published in 1973) reasserted the principle of blind application and explored its consequences further. They turned out to be cataclysmic. This principle, carried to its logical conclusion in today's government–binding theory, led ultimately to a model in which grammatical complexity is no longer captured by the application of a set of complexly stated language-particular rules; indeed, only one movement rule exists today: move α, where α is any category. In this theory, surface complexity is posited to result from the interaction of a set of very general principles that vary from language to language within definite bounds.

At the center of the "Conditions" paper lies the idea that not only is the principle of blind application desirable in itself, but it leads to a set of extremely restrictive (and therefore desirable) conditions on the application of transformational rules. Chomsky's first step in the long chain of argumentation was to point out that, given the principle, one would expect (without further assumptions) (6.37a) to be transformed by the rule of Passive into ungrammatical (6.37b). If rules apply blindly, then Passive could not "know" that the NP *the dog* is the subject of *is hungry* rather than the object of *believe*.

(6.37)   a. *I believe the dog is hungry*
           b. **The dog is believed is hungry (by me)*

Chomsky proposed to explain (6.37b) by the following constraint:

Tensed-S Condition. No rule can involve X,Y in the structure X . . . [α . . . Y . . .] . . . , where α is a tensed S.

There were still problems, however. Chomsky was assuming a rule of *Each Movement*, which transforms (6.38a) into (6.38b).

(6.38)   a. *The candidates each hated the other(s)*
           b. *The candidates hated each other*

The Tensed-S Condition correctly prevents this rule from moving *each* into tensed complements:

(6.39)   a. *The candidates each expected that the other would win*
           b. **The candidates expected that each other would win*

---

[9]Chomsky (1976:310) catalogs in detail the manner in which the principle of blind application had been violated in the literature, and Postal (1976a:151–152) lists a number of papers violating this principle.

But by what principle would this rule successfully transform (6.40a) into (6.40b), but fail to map (6.41a) into (6.41b)? Note that in both cases the embedded S is untensed:

(6.40) a. *The candidates each expected [$_s$PRO to defeat the other]*
        b. *The candidates expected to defeat each other*

(6.41) a. *The men each expected [$_s$the soldier to shoot the other]*
        b. **The men expected the soldier to shoot each other*

The crucial difference, Chomsky claimed, lies in the nature of the embedded subject. [10] In (6.40a) it is a null pronoun, controlled by (i.e., coreferential to) the higher subject. But in (6.41a), it is fully specified. The contrast between these sentences suggested to Chomsky the following constraint:

Specified Subject Condition. No rule can involve X,Y in the structure . . . X . . . [α . . . Z . . . −WYV . . .] . . . , where Z is the specified (i.e., uncontrolled) subject of WYV and α is a cyclic node (NP or $\bar{S}$).

As the following sentences illustrate, this constraint is sensitive to the subjects of noun phrases as well as sentences, thereby supporting Chomsky's hypothesis (see Section 4.5.1) that rules and grammatical relations generalize to apply within both noun phrases and sentences.

(6.42) a. *The men saw the pictures of each other*
        b. **The men saw John's pictures of each other*

But there appeared to be a very obvious counterexample to both the Tensed-S Condition and the Specified Subject Condition. Under previous treatments of *Wh*-Movement, this rule moved a *wh*-phrase over a variable to the left, transforming, for example, (6.43a) into (6.43b).

(6.43) a. *you told me that Bill saw who?*
        b. *Who did you tell me that Bill saw?*

Who appears to have been moved out of a tensed S and over a specified subject. To deal with this problem, Chomsky proposed his most radical revision of all analyses that were then current. First, he adopted the idea from Bresnan (1970b, 1972b) and

---

[10]In order for his constraints to be stated with maximum generality, it was necessary for Chomsky to consider PRO in (6.40a) and *the soldier* in (6.41a) to be the subjects of *defeat* and *shoot* respectively in derived as well as deep structure. That meant that the once-uncontroversial rule of Raising-to-Object (see Akmajian and Heny 1975:328–338), which operated to raise PRO and *the soldier* from embedded subject position to main clause object position, was impossible. Such a conclusion was particularly congenial to Chomsky, who felt that Raising-to-Object, as a rule performing a string-vacuous operation (i.e., one changing structure but not order) should be disallowed anyway (see Chomsky 1986 for a reaffirmation of this position). A 450-page defense of the rule of Raising-to-Object, Postal (1974), was subject to a critique by Bresnan (1976b). More recent commentary on string-vacuous rules and the rule of Raising-to-Object includes Cole and Hermon (1981), Lefebvre and Muysken (1982), and Clements, McCloskey, Maling, and Zaenen (1983).

Emonds (1970) that all sentences (main or subordinate) have a complementizer (COMP) node and that the landing site for the rule of *Wh*-Movement is restricted to COMP:

(6.44)   a. COMP *you saw who* →
          b. *who you saw* → *who did you see*

Chomsky further suggested that *Wh*-Movement could place a *wh*-phrase in any COMP node, not just one marked +WH, as assumed by Bresnan and others. Finally, he added a condition that an element can "escape" from a COMP only if it is moved into a COMP, without regard for whether either COMP is part of a tensed sentence or one with a specified subject. The COMP–COMP condition is known informally as the "Escape Clause":

Escape Clause. No rule can involve X,Y in the structure . . . X . . . [α . . . Z . . . −WYV . . .] . . . , where Y is in COMP and X is not in COMP and α is a cyclic node.

Under such assumptions, the derivation of (6.43) would proceed as follows:

(6.45)   a. COMP *you told me [$_{\bar{S}}$COMP Bill saw who]* →
          b. COMP *you told me [$_{\bar{S}}$who Bill saw]* →
          c. *who you told me Bill saw* →
          d. *who did you tell me Bill saw*

Chomsky went on to propose a particularly strong principle governing the application of transformational rules, the Principle of Subjacency:

Principle of Subjacency. Transformational rules are constrained to apply only within the domain of one cyclic node or the domain of two adjacent cyclic nodes.

Subjacency prohibits unbounded movement and unbounded deletion rules, i.e., rules that move an element indefinitely far from one place in a phrase marker to another or delete an element under identity to another indefinitely far away in the phrase marker. Subjacency, combined with the Escape Clause,[11] demands that in the derivation of (6.46a) from (6.46b), *who* moves repeatedly from COMP to COMP, one clause at a time, rather than being moved in a single step:

(6.46)   a. *Who do you think that Bill knows that Tom asked Mary to tell Sue to visit* ____
          b. COMP *you think* [COMP *Bill knows* [COMP *Tom asked Mary* [COMP PRO *tell Sue* [COMP PRO *visit who*]]]]

These principles combine to handle most of the phenomena covered by the Ross Constraints.[12] For example, consider (6.14), repeated below for convenience:

---

[11]Later work has shown that the Escape Clause can literally be derived from Subjacency and (an updated version of) the Specified Subject Condition (see Chomsky 1981 and the references therein).

[12]Chomsky also resurrected the A-over-A Principle, giving it a somewhat different interpretation from that in the (1964b) paper. He proposed several other conditions as well, of which space limiations prevent discussion.

(6.14)   *Who do you believe the claim that Bill saw?*

Its deep structure in the "Conditions" framework would be approximately (6.47).

(6.47)   COMP *you believe* [$_{NP}$*the claim* [$_S$COMP *Bill saw who*]

In the first cycle, *who* is moved into COMP position. But there is no way for it to escape from the lower clause since the next higher cyclic node, NP, does not have a COMP. Hence extraction is blocked, and the ungrammaticality of the sentence follows as a consequence. Most of Ross's Complex NP Constraint violations were handled in a similar fashion.

Likewise, Chomsky suggested that these principles could account for his earlier (1964a:44) observation that two *wh*-phrases originating in the same clause cannot both be fronted (a phenomenon that has at times been attributed to a distinct "Wh-Island Constraint.") Note

(6.48)   *what does he wonder where John put?*

The derivation of (6.48) would demand first that *where* be placed in COMP position in the lower sentence. But then *what* could not move into the now-filled lower COMP nor into the higher COMP by virtue of the above conditions. Hence (6.48) is underivable.

6.5.2. Early Trace Theory

In the middle of the "Conditions" paper, Chomsky observed a serious problem with the conditions as they had been formulated. They seemed incapable of blocking the following sentence:

(6.49)   *John seems to the men to like each other*

The movement of *each* violates neither the Tensed S Condition nor the Specified Subject Condition. Chomsky proposed to deal with the problem by assuming that every time a noun phrase moves, it leaves at the movement site a trace (t), which is co-indexed to the moved NP. This trace acts as a specified subject. The derivation of (6.49) thus proceeds as follows:

(6.50)   a. *it seems to each of the men [John to like the other]* →
          b. *John seems to each of the men **t** to like the other* →
          c. **John seems to the men to like each other* = (6.49)

The ungrammaticality of (6.49) thus follows from the movement of *each* over a specified subject.

The postulation of a trace of movement certainly worked in this situation, but how much independent motivation was there for such an idea? Chomsky was aware that if the only need for traces was to save the constraints and the principle of blind application that engendered them, then the entire principle would be in jeopardy. However, the trace theory of movement rules did not arise in a vacuum; numerous proposals in the years preceding and concurrent with the "Conditions" paper embodied the idea of leaving behind a marker of some sort at a movement or deletion site. For example, Postal (1970a) and Ross (1969c) had suggested that certain deletion rules leave behind a "doom marker" that later rules had the ability to refer to. And reference has already been made to the proposal of Emonds (1970) that movement rules leave an empty node at the site of movement (see also Perlmutter's 1972 "shadow pronoun" hypothesis). Finally, the Baker and Brame (1972) and Selkirk (1972) indexing proposals (see Section 5.3.4) also were, in a sense, antecedents of Chomsky's traces.

Chomsky and his early 1970s students set to work to find independent evidence for traces. An interesting argument is presented in Chomsky (1973:280–284) and developed in Wasow (1972) and Chomsky (1975c:99–100). They proposed that any trace left in the position occupied in deep structure by a moved *wh*-phrase be treated as a variable bound by the *wh*-phrase acting as a logical quantifier.[13] Given that assumptions, Wasow and Chomsky argued that it is transparently easy to convert surface structures with *wh*-phrases and traces directly to their logical forms. A relatively trivial interpretive rule maps (6.51a) onto (6.51b).

(6.51)   a. *the police knew who the FBI discovered that Bill shot t →*
         b. *the police know for which person x, the FBI discovered that*
            Bill shot x

The hypothesis that the site of *Wh*-Movement is marked by a trace interpreted as a logical variable suggested a solution to the crossover problem. Postal (1971) had observed that in sentences such as (6.52a), *who* and *him* can be interpreted as coreferential, while such an interpretation is not possible in (6.52b).

(6.52)   a. *Who said Mary kissed him?*
         b. *Who did he say Mary kissed?*

Postal offered an explanation based on the observation that in the derivation of (6.52b), but not (6.52a), coreferential NPs "cross" each other. But Wasow pointed out that trace theory explains this phenomenon without any additional assumptions.[14] Given that *Wh*-Movement leaves a trace, the surface structures of (6.52a–b) are (6.53a–b), respectively.

(6.53)   a. *who [t said Mary kissed him]*
         b. *who [he said Mary kissed t]*

These surface structures would be mapped into logical forms (6.54a–b), respectively.

---

[13]While neither Wasow nor Chomsky mentioned the fact, the idea that question words like *who* and *what* are logically equivalent to quantifiers is relatively old. As Bach (1977a) points out, this conception is found in the writings of Jespersen (1965:302–305), Carnap (1937:296), Reichenbach (1947:340), and, more recently, Bach (1968) and Baker (1970b).

[14]It should be pointed out that Postal invoked his principle to handle a number of other phenomena that did not lend themselves to explanation in terms of trace theory.

(6.54)   a. *for which person **x**, **x** said that Mary kissed him*
            b. *for which person **x**, he said that Mary kissed **x***

Now the coreferential reading in (6.52b) can be blocked by the same principle that excludes *he* and *John* from being coreferential in the sentence *he said Mary kissed John* (for discussion of this principle, see Ross 1967; Langacker 1969; and Reinhart 1981).

Syntactic motivation for traces was adduced in early work by Robert Fiengo (1974, 1977). Fiengo (1977:53) observed that by considering traces to fall into the same class as reflexive and reciprocal pronouns, an asymmetry in the types of movement rules could be explained. He pointed out that while transformations move NPs to a "higher" position within a clause (e.g., from object position to subject position) or raise them to the next higher clause, they seem not to move NPs to a "lower" position within a clause (i.e., from subject to object) or into a lower clause. That is, after movement we may have the trace-antecedent relations (6.55a–b), but not (6.56a–b).

(6.55)   a.

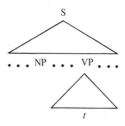

           b.

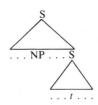

(6.56)   a.

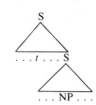

           b.

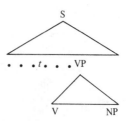

Fiengo argued that this asymmetry is an automatic consequence of the treatment of traces as bound anaphora. Just as, in surface structure, a reflexive may be c-commanded by, but may not c-command, its antecedent (contrast *John would like to shave himself* with **himself would like to shave John*), a trace is similarly restricted.[15]

6.5.3. From Conditions on Rules to Conditions on Representations

In the late 1970s, Chomsky's model developed in the following ways: many of the conditions, which were formulated originally to govern the application of grammatical rules, were reinterpreted to apply to grammatical representations; individual construction-specific movement transformations were replaced by one all-purpose rule "Move α"; and surface structure was accorded an even greater role in semantic interpretation. Figure 6.2 depicts the EST model developed by Chomsky and his

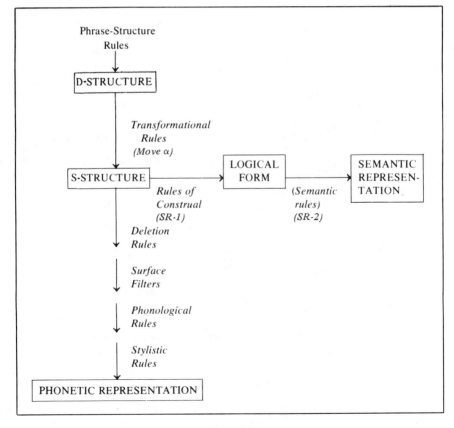

Figure 6.2

[15]C-command was defined as follows at that time: node α c-commands node β if the branching node most immediately dominating α also dominates β.

associates in this period, a model that, in its essential outline, remains their view of grammatical organization.

The hypothesis that surface structure contains traces of moved elements led directly to Chomsky's proposal (1976:319) that the conditions apply to representations rather than to rules (with the exception of Subjacency, which would still need to be a condition on rule application). Given traces in surface structure, the Specified Subject Condition could apply at that level to simultaneously rule ungrammatical the following sentences, thereby concretizing directly the idea that traces are instances of bound anaphora:

(6.57)   a. *Bill seems [John to like t]
          b. *Bill expected [Mary to like himself]
          c. *Bill expected [Mary to find his way home]

In order to solve some technical problems that had plagued earlier versions of trace theory, Chomsky, in his important paper "On Binding" (1980b), reinterpreted the Specified Subject Condition (renamed the Opacity Condition) and the Tensed-S Condition (renamed the Propositional Island Condition (PIC) and then the Nominative Island Condition (NIC)[16] as conditions on the occurrence of single anaphors, rather than as conditions on anaphor–antecedent pairings. The reformulated conditions were stated as follows:

Opacity Condition. An anaphor cannot be free in the domain of the subject of β,β minimal (β = NP,$\bar{S}$)
Nominative Island Condition. A nominative anaphor cannot be free in $\bar{S}$.

"Free," in this usage, means not co-indexed with a c-commanding antecedent (an antecedent in the same clause or a higher one.) Hence Opacity would exclude sentence (6.57a), since the trace is not co-indexed within the domain of the subject *John;* rather its antecedent (*Bill*) lies outside the $\bar{S}$ containing *John.*

In "On Binding," Chomsky proposed that the conditions apply at the level of logical form, though in subsequent work he returned to the idea of surface structure application (see Section 8.2.2).

Chomsky in 1976 suggested that all noun phrase movements could be subsumed under a single rule "Move NP," and in "On Binding" put forward the idea that this rule and all other movement transformations were simply instances of one all-purpose optionally applying rule "Move α," where α is a category. Needless to say, such a rule would overgenerate massively, placing moved elements where they never occur in grammatical sentences. Yet Chomsky was convinced that, by and

---

[16]These renamings were necessitated by slight changes in the formulations of the conditions. The PIC reflected the extension of the condition to languages like Korean which do not distinguish formally between tensed and untensed clauses, yet do manifest phenomena similar to those for which the Tensed-S Condition was originally proposed (see Kim 1976). And the NIC arose as a result of the realization that the case marking of the subject (and concomitant verbal agreement) was the crucial factor in the operation of the constraint. For early discussion and motivation of the NIC, see George and Kornfilt's (1981) study of Turkish gerunds and Rizzi's (1981) account of Italian infinitives.

large, independently motivated constraints would function to rule out those sentences with misplaced elements. Consider, for example, the sentences of (6.58), all of which would be produced by Move α.

(6.58)   a. *John is believed [t is incompetent]
         b.   John is believed [t to be incompetent]
         c. *John('s) was read [t book]
         d.   John seems [t to like Bill]
         e. *John seems [Bill to like t]
         f. *yesterday was lectured t
         g.   yesterday's lecture

As Chomsky (1976:314–318) noted, (6.58a) would be excluded by the Tensed-S Condition, (6.58c) by the A-over-A Principle, (6.58e) by the Specified Subject Condition, and (6.58f) (more vaguely) by a "principle of semantic interpretation of surface structures" (Chomsky 1976:317).

   In a surprising reanalysis of previous work, Chomsky (1977b) suggested that not just questions and relative clauses, but also comparative sentences, sentences with topicalized phrases, cleft sentences, and object-raised sentences ("*tough*-movements") all be derived by the movement of a *wh*-phrase, even though in these latter constructions no overt *wh*-morpheme appears in English. He motivated such an analysis by appealing to the fact that such constructions share a number of important properties with those containing overt *wh*-morphemes: they have gaps, they appear to ignore Subjacency and the Specified Subject and Tensed-S Conditions, they obey the Complex Noun Phrase Constraint, and they obey the *Wh*-Island Constraint (that is, they are impossible if a *wh*-phrase occurs in COMP). Likewise, these structures themselves create *wh*-islands that block further movement. By way of illustration, compare *wh*-questions and comparatives with respect to the aforementioned properties:

(6.59)   a. *who did you give the book to* ——
         b. *John is taller than Bill is* ——

(6.60)   a. *What did you tell John that Mary thought that Bill ate?*
         b. *The piece of pie is as big as any that John thought that Bill could ever eat*

(6.61)   a. **What do you believe the claim that John saw*
         b. **John is taller that I believed the claim that Bill was*

(6.62)   a. **What do you wonder where Bill put*
         b. **Mary isn't the same as I wonder whether she was five years ago*

(6.63)   a. **what do you wonder where Bill put* ——
         b. **who is John taller than* —— *is*

Instead of being derived by discrete rules, as had always been assumed, these constructions were postulated to result from the successive COMP-TO-COMP

movement of a *wh*-phrase by Move α. The (a) entries below illustrate the traditional analysis, the (b) entries Chomsky's revision:

(6.64)   Comparatives
          a. *John is taller than Mary is [tall]*
                             ⇓
                             Ø
          b. *John is taller than* [COMP↑] *Mary is what*
                                           |_____|

(6.65)   Topicalizations
          a. *I like beans* → *Beans I like*
          b. [TOP *beans*] [COMP↑] *I like what*
                                    |_____|

(6.66)   Cleft sentences
          a. *What I like are beans* → *It is beans that I like*
          b. *it is* [TOP *beans*] [COMP↑ *that*] *I like what*
                                               |_____|

(6.67)   Object-raised sentences (*tough*-movements)
          a. *It is easy to please John* → *John is easy to please*
          b. *John is easy* [COMP↑ *for*] PRO *to please who*
                                      |_____|

The fact that all of these constructions mimic *wh*-constructions now followed from
the hypothesis that they literally are *wh*-constructions.

The various conditions were able to block many of the ungrammatical sentences
resulting from the overgeneration produced by Move α, but not all of them. To take
an obvious example, a deletion rule was necessary to remove the nonoccurring *wh*-
phrases in the (b) sentences of (6.64–6.67) above. Chomsky furthermore needed a
set of filters (see Section 6.4) to exclude those ungrammatical sentences that were
unaffected by the constraints on movement. Chomsky and Lasnik (1977) proposed a
number of such filters, three of the most important of which are stated below (in
somewhat simplified form) along with examples of their effects:

(6.68)   a. *[NP NP tense VP]
          b. **the man met you is my friend*

(6.69)   a. *[α NP to VP], unless α = NP or follows V or P
          b. **it is unclear what John to do*

(6.70)   a. The "*that*-trace Filter": *[s̄ that [NP t] . . .]
          b. **who do you think that saw Bill*

Briefly, (6.68) accounts for the fact that in a relative clause structure, both COMP
and the subject position cannot be empty; (6.69) for the fact that the subject of an
infinitive cannot normally be lexically filled; and (6.70) for the fact that traces of
movement are normally impossible in subject position if immediately preceded by
the complementizer *that*.

Chomsky and Lasnik constructed an interesting argument to demonstrate that
filters have to follow deletion rules (see Figure 6.2). They observed that, super-

ficially, Spanish appears to violate the *that*-trace Filter; no overt element need intervene between the complementizer *que* and the tensed verb:

(6.71)   *Quién crees que ____ vio a Juan*

However, Spanish is a language that allows subject pronouns to be deleted freely. If subject deletion were to delete the subject trace, then the structural description of the subsequently applying filter would not be met, thereby predicting correctly the grammaticality of (6.71) and other Spanish sentences with complementizers followed by null subjects.[17]

While Chomsky and Lasnik recognized that filters were, in a sense, the "loose ends" of the theory, they regarded a theory embodying them and the optional rule Move α as a decided improvement over earlier theories. Filters took on the work of what had previously been expressed in terms of rule-ordering statements, in terms of conditions requiring that certain rules apply optionally and others obligatorily, and in terms of complex contextual-dependency conditions in the statement of individual rules. As they saw it, there was no a priori reason why filters, whose operation was restricted to exclude classes of surface structures, should be able to accomplish these tasks. The fact that they could do so seemed to indicate that their incorporation into grammatical theory was motivated.

In any event, by Chomsky's 1980 paper, "On Binding," progress had already been made in reducing the more complex filters to more general ones. It was in this paper that Chomsky first reinterpreted two traditional linguistic constructs, government and case. Jean-Roger Vergnaud had pointed out in a 1977 letter to Chomsky that it is a general feature of noun phrases that they must be in a position to be assigned case. Thus the [$_\alpha$ NP to VP] filter might be an automatic consequence of the fact that the subjects of infinitives are not (in the normal course of events) assigned case. He and Alain Rouveret developed this idea in published work (Rouveret and Vergnaud 1980) as did Chomsky, along somewhat different lines, in "On Binding." Both papers utilized a new principle, the Case Filter:

*N, if N has no case (where N is lexical)

Case is assigned under government, a notion defined as follows:

α is governed by β if α is c-commanded by β and no major category or major category boundary appears between α and β.

In the "On Binding" system, Tense governs the NP subject and assigns nominative Case[18] to it; V governs the NP object and assigns objective Case to it; and P governs an oblique NP object and assigns oblique Case to it (which in English is superficially identical to objective Case). Since the subject of an infinitive is not in a

---

[17]For an earlier approach to free subject deletion in Spanish and other languages, see Perlmutter (1971).

[18]Chomsky (1980a) began the practice of capitalizing the word "Case" to avoid possible confusion of the abstract theoretical construct with the surface marking and with the ordinary English word "case" (as "in this case").

position to be assigned Case of any kind, the $[_\alpha$ NP to VP] filter was thus reduced to the more general Case Filter.

Both government and Case were to play a crucial role in Chomsky's later work (see Sections 8.2.2 and 8.2.4).

The idea that surface structure is the sole syntactic input to all rules of semantic interpretation was first put forward in Chomsky (1975c:82) (though it must be pointed out that this was achieved in part by redefining surface structure—now called "S-Structure"—as the output of Move α, rather than as the output of the entire set of syntactic rules; see Figure 6.2). Since surface structures now contained traces of movement, the thematic roles borne by noun phrases could be computed directly from the surface; there was no longer a need for speical deep structure rules of semantic interpretation. Chomsky posited two classes of interpretive rules: SR-1 rules (or "rules of construal," as they were first called in Hale 1976), which map surface structure onto logical form (LF), and SR-2 rules, which take logical forms as input and, in interaction with other cognitive structures, give representations that indicate the contribution of beliefs, expectation, and so on to the full meaning and contain all information necessary "to determine role in inference, conditions of appropriate use, etc." (Chomsky 1976:306).

Among the rules of construal are the rule of Control (i.e., that which co-indexes *John* and the pronominal subject of *leave* in the sentence *John wants to leave now*) and the rule of Disjoint Reference (see Lasnik 1976 for early discussion), which disallows coreference in NP–pronoun pairs such as *the men* and *them* in *the men like them*.

LF incorporates "whatever features of sentence structure (1) enter directly into semantic interpretation of sentences and (2) are strictly determined by properties of (sentence-)grammar" (Chomsky 1976:305–306). Among its properties are the encoding of the scope and interpretation of logical constants and quantifiers, and the assignment of coreference, focus, and thematic relations. While LF representations are similar to those provided by standard forms of predicate calculus, given that they incorporate notions such as "sentence focus" and others not involved in determining truth conditions, they cannot be identified precisely with logical representations.

Chomsky has said little about the SR-2 mapping of LF onto meaning. However, he did give an interesting example (1976:323–324) of a rule that would necessarily apply in that component, the rule of anaphora associating simple definite pronouns with their antecedents, i.e., the rule of work in allowing coreference between *John* and *him* in (6.72).

(6.72)   *John thought that Mary knew that Sue had seen him*

The linking of *John* and *him* appears to violate Subjacency and both the Specified Subject and Tensed-S Conditions. This fact would be highly problematic if the rule involved were part of sentence grammar. But the fact that a definite pronoun and its antecedent need not be in the same sentence suggests that the rule belongs to SR-2 rather than SR-1. Observe that the antecedent of *him* in (6.73a–b) may be in a preceding sentence or even gleaned entirely from the pragmatic context (say, by observing the speaker point to the relevant individual):

(6.73) a. *I know one thing about John. Mary likes him*
  b. *Mary likes him*

Given the plausible assumption that discourse-based rules are not subject to the conditions, (6.72) does not present a problem for the theory.[19]

Syntactic rules having no effect on LF have been posited to apply in the mapping between surface structure and phonetic representation (see Figure 6.2). Aside from deletions and filters, these have included a set of stylistic rules, which, though syntactic, have been regarded as neither interacting with Move α nor being subject to conditions on syntactic representation. Rochemont (1978), the most comprehensive study of stylistic rules, exemplifies them in the derivation of (6.74) and (6.75) from their respective (a) sentences.

(6.74) a. *Sally walked in* $\rightarrow$
  b. *In walked Sally*

(6.75) a. *John asked a girl in a blue smock to dance with him* $\rightarrow$
  b. *John asked to dance with him a girl in a blue smock*

Chomsky followed "On Binding" with his book *Lectures on Government and Binding* (1981). The book's content and its impact on the field is discussed in Section 8.2.

---

[19]For discussion of discourse and anaphora within the EST, see Hankamer and Sag (1976), Williams (1977a, 1977b), and Grosu (1979).

Chapter 7

The New Consensus and the New Rift
in Generative Syntax

7.1. THE POST-GENERATIVE SEMANTICS CONSENSUS

The principal thrust of generative semantics had been to challenge two propositions: first, that the internal structure of the grammar of a language consists of a set of distinct components, each with its particular form and function; and second, that the principles of grammatical patterning are formulable without recourse to the extralinguistic context of the utterance. The abandonment by generative semantics of the level of deep structure represented the rejection of distinct syntactic and semantic components; by allowing phonological rules (such as contraction) global reference to syntax, generative semantics effectively negated the boundary between syntax and phonology. Furthermore, the late generative semantic conception of one homogeneous syntax–semantics–pragmatics rejected an assumption that had guided work in generative grammar since its inception, namely, that linguistic form is characterizable in terms of a set of primitives that themselves are strictly linguistic.

The collapse of generative semantics gave new life to the idea of an autonomous grammatical theory consisting of a set of distinct components. Since the late 1970s, virtually all work in generative grammar has presupposed (or defended) such an idea. The following sections review some work carried out in this general spirit. Section 7.1.1 outlines the widely accepted modular conception of language, and 7.1.2 reviews developments in pragmatics, which is now universally regarded as an area of study with princples distinct from those of formal grammar per se. 7.1.3 treats recent work in morphology, and 7.1.4 the evolution of thinking on the interface between syntax and phonology.

7.1.1. The Modular Conception of Language

Generative grammarians explain complex linguistic phenomena in terms of the interaction of the autonomous grammatical system with other systems involved in giving language its overall character. Such a "modular" conception can be represented schematically as in (7.1) (after S. Anderson 1981:494).

(7.1)

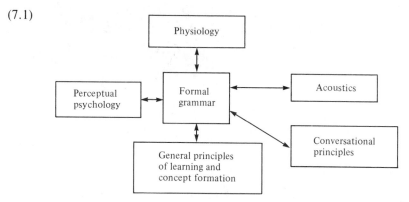

Even though modular explanations came into their own only in the mid 1970s, they were invoked in the earliest days of generative grammar. For example, Miller and Chomsky (1963) noted that sentences with multiple center embeddings are invariably unacceptable, as in (7.2).

(7.2)   *the rat [$_s$the cat [$_s$the dog chased] ate] died*

They demonstrated the implausibility of a strictly grammatical explanation of the unacceptability. For one thing, the deviance of (7.2) could hardly be due to a deep structure or semantic ill-formedness, since it is interpretable (if one is given time to work out its intricacies) and other sentences plausibly derived from the same deep structure are acceptable:

(7.3)   *The rat died that was eaten by the cat that the dog chased*

Nor could the unacceptability be a consequence of the filtering function of the transformational rules—no (relevant) transformations apply in the derivation of (7.2). And the only way to block (7.2) at the level of surface structure would be to incorporate into grammatical theory a device that would literally count the embeddings in the surface string, a device unlike any ever proposed to govern grammatical processes.

But there is an obvious reason, Miller and Chomsky argued, for the unacceptability of (7.2). Quite simply, the sentence is unacceptable because it is confusing. Without special aids (e.g., paper and pencil) it is difficult to figure out which subjects are paired with which predicates. They proposed a principle of sentence comprehension that states (essentially) that sentences are processed from left to right and that the processing mechanism cannot be interrupted more than once. Since the comprehension of (7.2) demands a double interruption of subject-verb pairing, the sentence is difficult to process.

In other words, sentence (7.2) is generated by the grammar, i.e., it is grammatical. Its unacceptability follows from the modular interaction of the grammatical principle of unlimited center embedding with the perceptual principle sketched above. Neither principle alone is sufficient to account for the unacceptability of (7.2) and the concomitant acceptability of (7.3).

The acceptance of modular explanations has been facilitated by the discovery that there is not a one-to-one mapping between particular linguistic forms and the particular communicative functions that language serves. Therefore, rather than attempt to "read off" the form from the function (or vice versa), it makes sense to seek a characterization of linguistic complexity in terms of the interaction of formal notions and functional ones. To give a concrete example, Green (1980), in her investigation of inverted subject constructions in English, (7.4a–d), found that each construction could play several discourse functions (among which were downplaying, foregrounding, anomaly resolution, and highlighting); furthermore, each of the discourse functions mentioned could be manifested grammatically in constructions other than the inverted subject one.

(7.4)   a. *Sitting down is Kevin Jones*
         b. *Scheduled to testify were representatives of RCA Global Communications, ITT World Communications, Western Union, Western Union International, as well as Joe R. Craig, a former FBI agent*
         c. *"She's too young to play," said Mrs. Rabbit*
         d. *Through the half-opened windows drifted the mingled smell of wood smoke and freshmen*

Green concluded from the many–many relation between form and function that the phenomena were best analyzed through the interaction of an autonomously functioning formal grammar and whatever systems are responsible for the organization of discourse.

Many investigators since the mid 1970s have demonstrated that it is desirable to abandon a grammatical account of phenomena that would previously have been handled by complex conditions on syntactic rules, and instead attribute them to systems outside of grammar itself. For example, Kuno (1976) showed that the statment of the rule of Gapping (illustrated by *John ate beans and Bill rice*) can be simplified if some of its complexities are attributed to general principles governing the appearance of old information in discourse, and Davison (1980) demonstrated that many of the cross-linguistic peculiarities of the passive construction are attributable to the interaction of a simple Passive rule with Grice's theory of conversational implicature (see Section 7.1.2). And Gazdar and Klein (1977) showed that phenomena for which Lakoff had proposed transderivational rules (see Section

5.2.1) can be handled elegantly by postulating the interaction of distinct formal principles of syntax and pragmatics.[1]

At the same time, many investigators have demonstrated that there is no hope of reducing syntax in its entirety to principles outside formal grammar. Prince (1976) and L. Horn (1978), for example, showed that the *Neg*-Raising construction (*I don't believe that he'll ever get here*) has certain properties that are strictly syntactic in nature, and Carden (1982) demonstrated that the conditions governing backward anaphora (*Because he_i was hungry, John_i opened the refrigerator*) are partly syntactic and partly discourse-derived.

The modular conception of language has received independent support from many diverse areas of investigation, in particular from studies of language acquisition, language–brain relationships, language processing, and language variation. For a summary of some of the most important evidence to that effect, see Newmeyer (1983). For an important discussion and defense of the modular conception of human cognitive functioning, see J. A. Fodor (1982), and for a discussion of general features of modular accounts of linguistic phenomena, see Bever (1974, 1975), Grosu (1981), Carroll (1981), Green (1981, 1982), and (especially) Sadock (1983).

7.1.2. Pragmatics

In the first decade of generative grammar, nobody had much faith in the possibility of constructing a theory of how language is used in communication. This pessimism was not simply a result of the belief in the prematurity of attempting such a theory, given the current state of knowledge, it was based in the belief in the principled impossibility of such an undertaking. Katz and Fodor (1963) stated the prevailing view succinctly: "But a complete theory of this kind is not possible in principle; for . . . it would be required that the theory represent all the knowledge speakers have about the world" (p. 178). The fact that such knowledge is not normally available to investigators tended to put a damper on studies of the pragmatic aspects of language.

But in the late 1960s, quite a few linguists reevaluated their self-imposed prohibition against the study of pragmatic phenomena. The most important factor in their change of mind was the work of a number of philosophers in the ordinary language tradition, especially J. L. Austin (1962), John Searle (1969), and H. P. Grice (1975). These philosophers were able to demonstrate that, beyond a shadow of a doubt, aspects of language use are systematic and amenable to study, without

---

[1]Despite the work cited in the above paragraph and that by a few others (see for example, Gundel 1977; Prince 1981; Reinhart 1982), treatments of discourse-based notions such as old and new information, topic and comment, and so on have been carried out largely by individuals hostile to grammatical theory. The papers in the anthologies edited by Charles Li (1976) and Talmy Givón (1979) illustrate this point. For critical discussion of discourse studies that attempt to bypass formal grammar, see Newmeyer (1983:chap. 4).

necessitating access to "all the knowledge speakers have about the world." They showed that strategies for successful communication are not only to a certain extent rule governed, but interact with what might be considered strictly grammatical phenomena in subtle and interesting ways. At the same time, the methodology that had come to characterize generative semantics (see especially Section 5.2.1) resulted in a climate highly receptive to the incorporation of these insights directly into grammatical theory. Since, to generative semanticists in this period, one's intuitions about, say, the correct use of honorifics (R. Lakoff 1972) carried the same theoretical weight as those about the surface order of auxiliary morphemes, there was no alternative to developing a full grammatical treatment of pragmatic phenomena. In fact, it does not seem unfair to say that the early 1970s saw many generative semanticists gradually transformed into ordinary language philosophers, as informal descriptions of language use replaced the construction of a grammatical theory as their immediate priority.

After generative semantics had died, the idea of an independent pragmatic theory was put on the research agenda. To many linguists, the most promising basis for such a theory seemed to be the work of Grice (1975, 1978, 1981), who developed principles of language use that were rooted in general principles of human cooperative interaction. The centerpiece of his theory is the COOPERATIVE PRINCIPLE: "Make your conversational contribution such as is required, at the stage at which it occurs, by the accepted purpose or direction of the talk exchange in which you are engaged" (1975:45). This principle embodies four maxims (pp. 45–46):

The Maxim of Quantity: (i) make your contribution as informative as is required (for the current purposes of the exchange). (ii) Do not make your contribution more informative than is required.

The Maxim of Quality: (i) Do not say what you believe to be false. (ii) Do not say that for which you lack adequate evidence.

The Maxim of Relation: Be relevant.

The Maxim of Manner: (i) Avoid obscurity of expression. (ii) Avoid ambiguity. (iii) Be brief. (iv) Be orderly.

Needless to say, participants in a conversation are no more bound to follow these maxims to the letter than humans are bound in general to behave cooperatively. The interest of the maxims, however, does not lie in their approximating descriptions of (or prescriptions for) human behavior. Rather, they seem to embody principles that one participant in a conversation will access when another is superficially behaving uncooperatively. For example, suppose that the following exchange takes place:

(7.5)   A: *I'm out of gasoline*
          B: *My house is just around the corner*

Given that A has no reason to believe that B is behaving uncooperatively, A invokes the Maxim of Relation to work out that B has communicated that B can provide A with gasoline that he keeps in his house. In Grice's terms, B has made a conversational implicature, a pragmatic device by which speakers, utilizing the Cooperative Principle, may convey more information than they literally utter.

An important way in which a pragmatic relation such as conversational implicature differs from a semantic (i.e., logical) relation such as entailment is that the former may be suspended or cancelled entirely. For example, B could have cancelled the implicature in (7.5) by responding

(7.5)   B′: *My house is just around the corner—but I'm afraid that the supply of gasoline that I keep there is used up*

Conversational implicature has been invoked in the explanation of a wide variety of linguistic phenomena. To take one example, L. Horn (1972), in his investigation of scalar predicates, observed the following contrasts:

(7.6)   a. *John is five years old, if not six*
          b. **John is five years old, if not four*

(7.7)   a. *Mary was seriously, if not critically, wounded*
          b. **Mary was critically, if not seriously, wounded*

(7.8)   a. *John can go—in fact, he will*
          b. **John will go—in fact, he can*

The relevant generalization appears to be that the lower bound of a scalar predicate is asserted and the upper bound is conversationally implicated by the Maxim of Quantity. Hence, as the (b) sentences above show, the lower bound of a scalar predicate cannot be suspended, while, as the (a) sentences show, the upper bound can be. Horn applied this generalization to the explanation of a number of seemingly unrelated phenomena. To cite only one example, he noted that expressions that can be conversationally implicated by others resist lexicalization, an idea that he employed in the explanation of the fact that there are lexical items corresponding to the (a) expressions of examples (7.9)–(7.11), but not to the (b) expressions.

(7.9)   a. *~some = no* or *none*
          b. *some~*

(7.10)   a. *~much = little*
          b. *much~*

(7.11)   a. *~frequently = rarely*
          b. *frequently~*

Given that scalar predicates are upper bounded by conversational implicature, it follows that (7.12a) implicates (7.12b), that is, it follows that "some" implicates "some not."

(7.12)   a. *Some have greatness thrust upon them*
          b. *Not all have greatness thrust upon them* (= some do not)

Hence, *some not,* (7.9b), has no lexcial item corresponding to it. But since no expression implicates *not some* (7.9a), it can be lexicalized (by *no* or *none*), as predicted.

Gricean implicature has also been invoked to simplify semantic description. There are many well-known cases of what seem to be discrepancies between the standard logical treatments of operators and the way that they function in natural language. For example, in the sentence *John went to the store and bought some groceries, and* appears to have a temporal sense ("and then") in addition its primary function as a logical conjunction. But it has been pointed out that the lexical entry of *and* need only specify its logical sense, since the fact that it can convey temporality follows from the Maxim of Manner (Be Orderly). Along the same lines, Gazdar and Pullum (1976) use the Maxim of Relevance to explain why all natural languages have such a small number of lexical items that correspond to truth-functional connectives.

Despite the above, not all linguists are convinced that Grice's theory is an adequate basis for an account of pragmatic phenomena. Some have called attention to the apparent fuzziness of its basic constructs and wonder if it makes genuinely contentful claims (Kroch 1972; Kiefer 1979).[2] Indeed, Richmond Thomason has remarked that "Grice's patterns of explanation have much more in common with the best and most rigorous literary criticism than with mathematical logic" (1973:4). Others have called attention to the difficulty of unequivocally identifying conversational implicature (Sadock 1978). And still others have attempted to subsume Grice's many disparate maxims into one or two unifying principles. For example, Deirdre Wilson and Dan Sperber propose to derive the maxims from one general principle of Relevance (Wilson and Sperber 1981; Sperber and Wilson 1986), and Laurence Horn (1984) reduces Grice's maxims to two types of forces: relation-based and quantity-based implicature.

The specific pragmatic topic that has received the greatest attention by far is presupposition. Work in the early 1970s contrasted two species of presupposition: logical (semantic) and pragmatic (see Keenan 1971). A sentence A was said to logically presuppose a sentence B if when A was true, B was true; when not A was true, B was true; and when B was false, A had no truth value. Keenan cited factive predicates (7.13a–b), definite names (7.14a–b), and cleft sentences (7.15a–b) as examples of constructions illustrating logical presupposition.

(7.13) a. (A) *John regrets that he left Seattle*
      b. (B) *John left Seattle*

(7.14) a. (A) *The mayor of Birmingham wears a hat*
      b. (B) *There exists a mayor of Birmingham*

(7.15) a. (A) *It was John who caught the thief*
      b. (B) *Someone caught the thief*

A pragmatic presupposition, on the other hand, was defined on the relation between the utterance of a sentence and its extralinguistic context. For example, the utterance of (7.16a) (by a Spanish speaker) pragmatically presupposes that the speaker is female; (7.16b) male.

---

[2]Kroch and Kiefer are rebutted in Gazdar (1979a:53) and (1980), respectively. In the former work, Gazdar proposes a formal account of Gricean implicature.

(7.16)   a. *Estoy cansada*
           b. *Estoy cansado*

Many linguists in recent years have challenged the existence of logical presupposition (see Kuroda 1974; Wilson 1975; Kempson 1975; Boër and Lycan 1976; Karttunen and Peters 1977; Gazdar 1979a; Atlas and Levinson 1981). They argue that presuppositions in simple affirmative clauses are really entailments, while those in negative clauses are pragmatic phenomena, perhaps conversational implicatures. A typical argument against the existence of logical presupposition has involved the citation of sentences like (7.17)–(7.19).

(7.17)   a. **John regrets that he left Seattle—but he didn't really leave*
           b. *John doesn't regret that he left Seattle—how could he? He never really left*

(7.18)   a. **The mayor of Birmingham wears a hat—but in fact there really is no such person*
           b. *The mayor of Birmingham doesn't wear a hat—in fact there really is no such person*

(7.19)   a. **It was John who caught the thief—actually, nobody did*
           b. *It wasn't John who caught the thief—actually, nobody did*

The (a) sentences of examples (7.17)–(7.19) are all internally contradictory, as one would expect if *John regrets that he left Seattle* entails *John left Seattle,* and so on. But the corresponding negative (b) sentences allow the propositions expressed to be cancelled, suggesting that the relationship between *John doesn't regret that he left Seattle* and *John left Seattle* is one of conversational implicature.

One important attempt to abandon presupposition as an independent property of sentences was put forward by Wilson and Sperber (1979). In their view, presuppositional behavior can be handled by a semantic theory in which the entailments of a sentence form an ordered, rather than an unordered, set of objects. Given this approach, presuppositions are really just background entailments.

The idea of logical presupposition, however, still has support and is defended in Katz and Langendoen (1976), Katz (1979), J. D. Fodor (1979), and S. Thomason (1979).

A great deal of attention has been devoted to what Langendoen and Savin (1971) called the "projection problem for presuppositions"—the question of how the presuppositions of complex sentences are determined from the presuppositions of their component parts. As Karttunen (1973) pointed out in an important early discussion of the topic, there are cases where presuppositions inherent in one subpart of a complex sentence fail to be inherited by the sentence as a whole and, conversely, cases where presuppositions of components survive, yet the entailments of these components do not.

There have been two major attempts to solve the projection problem. In the approach of Karttunen and Peters (1975, 1977) the presuppositions of complex sentences are built up in the compositional fashion of Montague grammar (see Section 7.2.3), and constituents contain "heritage expressions," whose function is to govern the projection of the presupposition to the next higher constituent. In an approach developed by Gadzar (1979a, 1979b) and modified by Soames (1979), the potential presuppositions of a sentence are distinguished from the actual presuppositions of an utterance in context, and a mechanism is proposed to filter out those potential presuppositions incompatible with the background information that is assumed at the time of utterance. Gazdar's solution, unlike Karttunen and Peters's, does not mention specific conjunctions or complement-taking verbs. Soames (1982) and Heim (1983) attempt to synthesize the desirable features of both accounts.

Finally, it should be mentioned that much attention has been devoted to establishing the boundary between pragmatics and semantics (for general discussion of this problem, see Levinson 1983: Chapter 1). Investigators have generally characterized the difference between the two systems in one of two ways: semantics deals with truth-conditional aspects of meaning, pragmatics with nontruth-conditional aspects; or semantics deals with conventionalized aspects of meaning, pragmatics with "natural" aspects, i.e., those that arise from systems outside language per se. Yet it is widely recognized that neither characterization is satisfactory. The principal problem is that there are aspects of meaning that are clearly conventional, yet do not affect the truth conditions of the sentence. Foremost among them are what Grice (1975) called "conventional implicatures." Such implicatures are illustrated by the role in interpretation played by words like *but, therefore, yet,* and *even.* They do not affect the truth conditions of the sentence (*John left* and *even John left* have the same truth conditions), yet their meanings are clearly conventional. To make matters worse, what start out (historically) as conversational implicatures (and are thus clearly pragmatic phenomena) can over time gradually become conventionalized (see Morgan 1978 for discussion). Hence a standard way of conveying a request, saying *Can you . . . ?,* occupies an intermediate position between being a conversational implicature and being wholly conventionalized.

For several years, the dominant trend was to attribute to pragmatics many phenomena that had previously been regarded as semantic (see the papers in Cole 1981). However, this idea of "radical pragmatics" has been successfully challenged (see Sadock 1984). In any event, establishing the boundary between semantics and pragmatics promises to be one of the central areas of investigation in both fields.[3]

7.1.3. Morphology

Early generative grammar stood in sharp contrast to prior structuralist approaches in an important respect: it contained no distinct component reserved for mor-

---

[3]This short section has failed to do justice to the many diverse areas of investigation that fall within the general rubric of pragmatics. Two more deserve attention, if only for the purpose of supplying literature citations: post-generative semantic work on speech acts and studies of deixis (i.e., indexical expressions). For the former, see Searle (1976a), Allwood (1976, 1977), Boër and Lycan (1980), Bach and Harnish (1979), Levinson (1980, 1983:chap. 5), Gazdar (1979a, 1981a), and Sadock and Zwicky (1985). For the latter, see Bar-Hillel (1970), Lyons (1977), Levinson (1979, 1983:chap. 2), and Anderson and Keenan (1985).

phological operations. Rather, processes of word formation were subsumed by the syntax and the phonology. Transformational rules attached derivational affixes as well as inflectional ones (e.g., *refusal* was derived from *refuse* by a transformational rule that affixed the *-al*) and, since morphophonemic and allophonic processes were treated identically in the *Sound Pattern of English* conception of phonology, phonological rules handled the alternations in such pairs as *sane–sanity, electric–electricity*, and so on.

But by the late 1960s, the stage was set for a separate place for morphology. For one thing, the lexicalist hyopthesis (see Section 4.5.1), which disallowed the transformation described above, demanded that the relationship between a verb and its corresponding nominalization be handled by a distinct process of word formation, hitherto unknown in generative grammar. And for another, as the highly abstract *Sound Pattern of English* phonological analyses began to be called into question, many began to explore the possibility of handling certain morphophonemic alternations in a word-formation component as well.

The first paper in generative grammar to propose explicit morphological rules as part of a word-formation component was Halle (1973). In Halle's view, the morphemes of a language were the input to rules of word formation, which generated all of that language's possible words. But since many possible words do not actually occur (for example, there is no **derival* or **refusion*), a filter was applied to the output of the word-formation rules to generate a dictionary. Finally, the words generated were fed into the syntax and then into the phonology.

In the years following the publication of the Halle paper, work in morphology was devoted primarily to two related questions: the structure of lexical entries and the processes by which words are formed. The former type of study is represented by Jackendoff (1975) and Hust (1978). For Jackendoff, all existing words were entered fully specified in the lexicon, rather than arising from word-formation rules such as Halle's. Jackendoff's entry for the noun *decision* (1975:643) for example, was the following:

$$(7.20) \quad \begin{bmatrix} \text{/dec\={\i}d + ion/} \\ +N \\ +[NP_1\text{'}s\underline{\quad}on\ NP_2] \\ \text{ABSTRACT RESULT OF ACT OF } NP_1\text{'S DECIDING } NP_2 \end{bmatrix}$$

Whether the structure of a particular word represented productive morphological processes was determined by the degree to which its information could be predicted by lexical redundancy rules (Jackendoff's static analogues of word-formation rules). Hust, on the other hand, took lexical entries to be functions of features representable on branching diagrams. Hence his entry for *decide* branched to bundles of features representing *decision, decidable, undecided*, and so on. In this approach, lexical redundancy rules served to fill in the redundant information at each branching point in the entry.

The major generative study devoted to the process by which new words are added to the language is Mark Aronoff's important work *Word Formation in Generative*

Grammar (1976). Aronoff argued for a word-based morphology, that is, for the idea that new words are formed only on the basis of already existing ones. (Words consisting entirely of combinations of nonfreely occurring stems and affixes, such as *carpenter, motion, repel,* do not count as counterexamples to this hypothesis, since they were added to the language as units.) However, subsequent work returned to Halle's idea that word-formation rules form part of the grammar itself and are not a device for extending the grammar by adding new words to the lexicon. As a consequence, the idea of word-based morphology has been dropped.

The greater part of Aronoff's book (the part that would bear most directly on subsequent work) was devoted to the particular properties of word-formation rules. Among his proposals were the following:

Word-formation rules

1. are always specified syntactically. For example, *-ness* attaches only to adjectives; *-ee* attaches only to transitive verbs taking animate objects (*payee,* but **goee, *tearee*).
2. always have as output a member of a major lexical category. Hence they can be represented, for example, as $[+[X]_V+ee]_N$.
3. can result in the loss of subcategorization information. Thus, *The glass broke into six pieces,* but **The glass is breakable into six pieces.*
4. can refer to abstract morphological features. Thus the suffix *-ity* must be specified as being attachable only to Latinate morphemes.
5. can perform complex transformational operations. *Nominee* is derived by suffixation of *-ee* to *nominate* with subsequent truncation of *-ate.*

The question of the position of word-formation rules in the grammar, particularly with respect to phonological rules, was taken up in Siegel (1979). Drawing on some observations made by Chomsky and Halle in *The Sound Pattern of English,* Siegel divided derivational affixes into two classes. Typical Class I affixes are the prefixes *in-* and *con-* and the suffixes *-ate* and *-ity;* typical Class II affixes are the prefixes *anti-* and *neo-* and the suffixes *-ness* and *-ful.* Siegel proposed that Class I affixation precede the cyclic stress-assignment rules while Class II affixation follow them. Among the various consequences of this proposal are the following: Class I affixes are affected by the stress rules, Class II affixes are not (contrast *fértile/fertílity/fértileness*); Class I affixes may not be affected by already assigned stress, Class II affixes may (the latter point is illustrated by the fact that *-ful* can attach only to nouns with final stress: *revengeful* but **judgmentful*).[4]

The dominant trend in morphology in the 1980s, represented in the most fully elaborated form by Lieber (1981) and Selkirk (1982), is to regard the process of word formation as essentially sublexical subcategorization. That is, there has been a move away from rules of word formation that build up words by adding affixes to

---

[4] The *-y* suffix of *beauty, bounty,* etc., is considered nonsyllabic. Hence, *beautiful* and *bountiful* are possible. Siegel's model is elaborated in M. Allen (1978). The notion that there exist two classes of affixes that interact in different ways with the phonology has been incorporated into the theory of lexical phonology (see Kiparsky 1982a, 1982b; Mohanan 1982; Kaisse and Shaw 1985).

stems toward a conception in which affixes themselves are entered in the lexicon and subcategorize for the stems they attach to, much as verbs, say, subcategorize for their complements. In Lieber's theory, the lexical entry of each morphological element contains the following information (1981:35–36; see Selkirk 1982:5 for a very similar view):

The category and conjugation or declension class of an item
Phonological representation
Semantic representation
Subcategorization
Diacritics
Insertion frames

These can be illustrated by her proposed entry for the suffix -*ize* (1981:37):

(7.21)   (phonological representation)
         semantic representation: causative
         category/subcategorization $]_N$ ____ $]_V$ (i.e., it is suffixed to a noun to
         form a verb)
         insertion frame: NP ____ (NP)
         diacritics: Level II (= Siegel's Class II)

The abandonment of word-formation rules for conditions on lexical insertion has led to a view of sublexical structure that mimics most of the important features of phrasal constituency. Indeed, Selkirk has gone so far as to claim that the words of a language (with their stems and affixes) are to be generated by a context-free rewriting system. Such a view is very much in the spirit of contemporary approaches to syntax that have abandoned transformational rules for a vastly expanded phrase structure component (see Sections 8.3 and 8.4). The broader consequences of this approach to morphology are worth calling attention to. In early generative grammar, both phrases and words were formed by identical means, namely by transformational rules. By postulating once again that words and phrases are formed by identical types of rules, Selkirk has, in a sense, brought the treatment of morphology full circle.

Below are sketched some of the major research questions of the mid 1980s in morphological theory:

Are Inflectional Processes Fundamentally Different in Nature from Derivational Processes? The EST of the 1970s recapitulated a distinction made by most traditional grammarians: that between inflectional and derivational morphology. In that period it was generally agreed that derivational affixes were present in the presyntactic representation of the word, while inflectional affixes (represented in English, for example, by the possessive, tense, and aspect morphemes) were adjoined transformationally.[5] Such an approach predicts that inflectional affixes lie

---

[5]An exception is Halle (1973), where both inflection and derivation are handled nontransformationally.

outside derivational ones: e.g., *temptation's path* but not **tempt'sation path*. However, numerous theoreticians have strengthened the lexicalist hypothesis to claim that both types of affix should be handled by the same type of (nontransformational) mechanism (see Lapointe 1980, 1981; Williams 1981b; Lieber 1981; Jensen 1981; Selkirk 1982). They have pointed out that, in many languages other than English, inflectional affixes are found inside both derivational affixes and compounds (Lieber, for example, cites German *Augenarzt* "eye doctor'), thereby calling into question the idea that derivational morphology is to inflectional morphology as base generation is to transformational derivation. They also point out that handling the two types of morphology by different rule types obscures the great number of formal similarities that they share.

Stephen Anderson (1984), however, argues at length that the traditional distinction is correct, as is the traditional analysis of attaching inflectional affixes by postlexical rules. He gives numerous examples from a variety of languages that indicate that a class of morphological processes, namely, those traditionally labeled "inflectional," need to refer to phrase-level syntactic structure and thus demand formulation in transformational terms. Anderson's "Extended Word and Paradigm" model of morphology, in which inflectional rules apply to S-structure representations with lexical items in place, has been elaborated by Thomas-Flinders (1982, 1983), Janda (1983) and subject to a critique by Lapointe (1983), Jensen and Strong-Jensen (1984), and Stump (1984).[6]

Can Word-Formation Rules Have Transformational Power? Many theoreticians who reject the idea of syntactic transformations performing morphological operations have nevertheless allowed processes of insertion, deletion, and so on to be performed in the lexicon. For example, Lieber (1981), building on work by Carrier (1979), argues that reduplication in Tagalog can be handled adequately only by a transformational word-formation rule. But others (e.g., McCarthy 1979) wish to deny word-formation rules such power. Even among those who agree that transformational power is necessary in the lexicon, there is disagreement over the extent to which it is needed. Roeper and Siegel (1978), Randall (1982), Janda (1982), and Keyser and Roeper (1984) present analyses in which the word-formation rules mimic important properties of syntactic transformations; Lieber (1983), however, argues that the degree of transformational power allowed in these analyses may be too great.

How Are Argument Structure and Word Formation Related? The argument structure of a lexical item is a listing of the thematic roles (i.e., semantic roles like agent, theme, patient, instrument) that can be borne by those items with which it co-occurs. Stephen Anderson (1977) was perhaps the first to suggest that argument structure and word formation are intimately related. One of his suggestions to this

---

[6]In Borer's (1984a, 1984b) government–binding approach to morphology, no formal distinction is made between inflection and derivation. The particular properties traditionally associated with each are claimed to fall out as a consequence of independently motivated interacting principles.

effect was that word-formation rules could be simplified by adding the following principle to the grammar:

Theme Rule. The Theme is to be found in subject position if the verb is intransitive, in direct object position if the verb is transitive.

Such a rule obviates the need, for example, to build subcategorization changes into the word-formation rule relating such pairs as transitive and intransitive *break, melt,* and *freeze.* The Theme Rule predicts that the theme will be the subject of the intransitive verb and the object of its transitive counterpart.

Wasow (1980), Williams (1981a), Bresnan (1982c), and Travis and Williams (1982) discuss specific ways in which morphological rules can affect the argument structure. Williams's central hypothesis is that all such rules must affect the external argument (very roughly, the subject) of the item undergoing the rule. One consequence of this proposal is that the rule of Dative Movement, illustrated in (7.22), cannot be a lexical rule, as suggested by Oehrle (1976), since it does not affect the external argument.

(7.22)   a. *John gave the book to Mary*
            b. *John gave Mary the book*

Given Williams's approach, it cannot be a rule of grammar of any kind.[7]

Lieber (1983) and Carrier-Duncan (1985) also explore the intimate relationship between argument structure and morphology, the former for English compounds, the latter for a variety of processes in Tagalog. Lieber's ingenious analysis is devoted to the explanation of why particular logically possible compounds in English do not exist, and why for others there are constraints on the thematic role that may be borne by their constituents. She explains, for example, why we find such constructions as *to hand weave cloth* but not **to cloth weave linen.*

To What Extent Is Word-Internal Syntax Like Phrase-Internal Syntax? Most work in the 1980s assumed that the syntax of words has at least some crucial properties in common with the syntax of entire phrases. For example, it is generally agreed that words as well as phrases are "headed" (see Lieber 1981; Hoekstra, van der Hulst, and Moortgat 1980a; Williams 1981b; Selkirk 1982; Zwicky 1985). Several investigators have discussed the possibility of applying X-bar principles (see Section 6.3) to word structure. Selkirk's (1982) X-bar approach retains the distinct categories "Root" and "Affix," while Walinska de Hackbeil (1983) dispenses with them in favor of a treatment in which the lexical categories are projected downward by means of minus bar levels (see Jensen 1981 for an earlier version of this idea). Finally, the "mirror principle" of M. Baker (1985) demands a direct correspondence between morphological and syntactic derivations.

---

[7]For critiques of Anderson (1977) and Williams (1981a), see Dryer (1985) and Poser (1982), respectively. B. Levin and Rappaport (1985) argue that, contrary to Williams, the argument structure of derived words need not be stipulated by distinct rules; rather it is predictable on the basis of the theta-Criterion and the Projection Principle (see Section 8.2.3) alone.

How Are "Bracketing Paradoxes" to Be Handled? Williams (1981b) pointed out the following paradox: Words like *hydroelectricity* and *set theoretic* are structurally *hydro-electricity* and *set-theoretic* respectively, but semantically *hydro-electric-ity* and *set theore-tic*. There have been two major attempts to deal with this problem. Pesetsky (1985), assuming the government–binding theory (see Section 8.2), argues that if words have distinct representations at the levels of S-Structure and Logical Form (LF) and that affixes are moved by the LF rule of Quantifier Raising, not only will the bracketing paradoxes be resolved, but a host of other problems of morphological analysis will be resolved as well.[8] And Sadock (1985), basing his proposals mainly on morphological facts drawn from Eskimo and other highly synthetic languages, presents a theory of "autolexical syntax," in which sentences are given fully distinct syntactic and morphological bracketings. In his approach, bracketing paradoxes arise as a consequence of the formulation of the principles relating the two levels of representation.

7.1.4. Syntax and Phonology

Generativists, in probing the interaction of syntax and phonology, have attempted to answer three distinct, though interrelated, questions:

1. What is the nature of the interface between the syntactic component and the phonological component of the grammar?
2. To what extent (if any) may syntactic rules have access to phonological information?
3. To what extent (if any) may phonological rules have access to syntactic information?

The earliest answer to the first question was that the boundary between the two components is sharp: "In short, the input to the phonological rules is identical to the output of the syntactic rules" (Postal 1968:xii). However, Chomsky and Halle were soon forced to recognize that things were not so simple: "Thus we have two concepts of surface structure: input to the phonological component and output of the syntactic component. It is an empirical question whether these two concepts coincide. In fact, they do coincide to a very significant degree, but there are also certain discrepancies" (Chomsky and Halle 1968:9). To handle these discrepancies, which involved the lack of correspondence between phonological phrases and the labeled bracketings provided by the syntactic component, they proposed readjustment rules to apply between the syntax and the phonology. Such rules are reinterpreted in a recent account by Selkirk (1984) as rules assigning a rhythmic structure, the metrical grid.

A drastic reanalysis of the syntax–phonology interface came with Joan Bresnan's (1971b) paper "Sentence Stress and Syntactic Transformations." Bresnan argued

---

[8]Pesetsky draws on earlier work relating morphology and logical form presented in Muysken (1981a, 1981b).

that stress-assignment rules had to precede the rule of *Wh*-Movement, and therefore must be ordered within the syntactic cycle. (While she did not emphasize it, this position entailed that all phonological rules be in the syntactic cycle, since stress-assignment rules and the rules of segmental phonology are interspersed.) She claimed, furthermore, that this provided independent support for the lexicalist hypothesis, since in order to work it demanded that stems and their derivational affixes be present in deep structure. A lively debate ensued in *Language,* with G. Lakoff (1972c), Bolinger (1972), and Berman and Szamosi (1972) attacking this view, followed by a defense by Bresnan (1972a). Lakoff (who defended a global account of the same facts) was correct in pointing out that Bresnan's position entailed a weakening of linguistic theory, since it allowed for the possibility that cyclic syntactic rules might refer to the stress levels of items in embedded clauses. Bresnan could only cite a highly controversial cliticization rule from her own unpublished work (1971a) that this was necessary.

While no elaborative work was done on Bresnan's proposal, most interpretivists at first seemed to assume its correctness. However, it was eventually rejected for two reasons: First, serious empirical difficulties were found with the generalizations underlying it (see Schmerling 1976, Ladd 1980). Second, it was incompatible with all current views of grammatical organization, from the government–binding theory, which makes no principled distinction between *Wh*-Movement and other types of movement, to generalized phrase structure grammar and (Bresnan's own) lexical–functional grammar, which allow no movement rules at all (see Chapter 8 for discussion of these models).

From time to time, syntactic rules have been proposed that have access to phonological information. Some rules, for example, have been formulated with conditions governing the "heaviness" (in terms, say, of the number of syllables) of an item affected by the rule, and syntactic rules of word formation (including cliticization) have often been given access to syllable structure and other phonological information. Zwicky (1969) and Pullum and Zwicky (forthcoming a,b) argue that the strong position that syntax is phonology-free can be maintained. In their view, heaviness restrictions can be attributed to pragmatic factors, and, in keeping with current sentiment, word-formation rules are more properly analyzed as morphological rather than syntactic.

Finally, it is generally assumed that phonological rules have very restricted access to syntactic structure. One such access is the apparent need for rules of sandhi to be sensitive to the syntactic configurational notion of "c-command" (see Kaisse 1985 for discussion).

7.2. THE NEW RIFT

There never really was a period of unity among generative grammarians after the mid 1960s. Even before the collapse of generative semantics, the interpretivist wing of the field had split into two camps. On the one side is Chomsky and his cothinkers, the progress of whose trace-theoretic model up to 1980 is charted in Section 6.5. On the other is a tendency that one might call "superlexicalist." Throughout the 1970s, its advocates resisted the trace theory of movement rules and the constraints that accompanied the theory. Their alternative involved narrowing steadily the scope of transformational operations to the point where, by the end of the decade, many had concluded that transformational rules did not exist.

Section 7.2.1 outlines the development of superlexicalism until 1980 and 7.2.2 sketches the specific criticisms that its advocates leveled against trace theory. Section 7.2.3 describes the framework of Montague grammar, another 1970s development that was regarded by many as an alternative to Chomsky's approach.

7.2.1. Superlexicalism

The roots of superlexicalism lie in Chomsky's two late 1960s papers, "Remarks on Nominalization" and "Deep Structure, Surface Structure and Semantic Interpretation." The twin thrusts of these papers are to diminish the role of the transformational component by enriching the lexicon and to increase the importance of the level of surface structure. Superlexicalism is, in its essentials, carrying the reasoning in these two papers to its logical conclusion.

What emerged from these two papers was a brief consensus on how transformational rules might be motivated. Two criteria must be met by any putative transformational rule. First, it was deemed necessary to demonstrate that an elegant treatment utilizing the more descriptively powerful transformations was available to replace a cumbersome analysis involving the base rules alone. The classic *Syntactic Structures* arguments for the various auxiliary transformations and Passive are of this type and were frequently cited as models for motivating transformations. Second, in keeping with the *Aspects* hypothesis that exceptionality and irregularity be localized in the lexicon, it was considered necessary that the process be fully productive. Part of the initial appeal of the EST was that those transformations that appeared to meet these two criteria also appeared to obey an extremely interesting set of constraints. That is, it seemed to be just those remaining rules that obeyed the Structure Preserving Constraint, that could be conflated under the X-bar convention, and that behaved in a unitary fashion in other respects. Furthermore, the deep structure level that served as input to those rules seemed at exactly the correct degree of abstractness to capture a host of syntactic generalizations.

But ironically, the twin criteria of simplification and productivity led a number of linguists ultimately to strike all (or virtually all) rules from the transformational roster. The first criterion mentioned above was effectively nullified by the Structure Preserving Constraint. Freidin (1974) was the first to point out that the structure-preserving quality of transformational rules undermines the most persuasive criterion for their existence, the overall simplification of the grammar (see also Jayaseelan 1979). Clearly, positing such processes as transformational could not lead to a simplification of the phrase structure rules because, figuratively speaking, these rules apply throughout the transformational derivation. That is, if passives are directly generated by the phrase structure rules, then any hypothesized Passive transformation would naturally appear to be structure preserving.[9]

The productivity argument for transformations was undermined in part by conflicting criteria for what constitutes a productive process. Consider once again, the case of derived nominals. Chomsky in *Aspects* argued that *destroy* and *destruction* are related transformationally on the basis of a productive relationship between them, while arguing that the unproductive *horror–horrid* relationship should be captured lexically. By the "Remarks" paper, however, his criteria for productivity had become more stringent. In that paper, he contrasted the nonproductivity of the *destroy–destruction* relationship with the productive active–passive relationship in concluding the former should be handled lexically.

In the 1970s many interpretivists took the productivity requirement so stringently that they found virtually all grammatical processes to be nonproductive and therefore nontransformational. For example, Freidin (1975a) argued against the rule of Passive on the basis of its lack of productivity, as illustrated by (7.23)–(7.25).[10]

(7.23)   a. *Max resembles Harry*
         b. **Harry is resembled by Max*

(7.24)   a. *The kimono fits Dorothy*
         b. **Dorothy is fit by the kimono*

(7.25)   a. *That picnic basket weighs a ton*
         b. **A ton is weighed by that picnic basket*

Along the same lines, Oehrle (1976) concluded from the contrasts in (7.26) and (7.27) that Dative Movement must be lexical rather than transformational.

(7.26)   a. *I'll get a ticket for you—I'll get you a ticket*
         b. *I'll obtain a ticket for you—*I'll obtain you a ticket*

(7.27)   a. *You should give back the package to the owner—you should give the owner back the package*
         b. *You should return the package to the owner—*You should return the owner the package*

Brame (1976) constructed different sorts of arguments to illustrate the lack of productivity (and therefore nonexistence) of the once widely accepted rule of Equi-NP Deletion. This rule had been posited to delete the subject of an embedded sentence under identity to a noun phrase in a higher sentence:

---

[9]Technically this is not correct, since Emonds' framework allows nonstructure-preserving insertions, to whose output a structure-preserving rule can apply (see Abbott 1982 for discussion).

[10]For the most thorough attack on the idea that passives are derived transformationally, see Bresnan (1982c).

(7.28)   a. *a few students tried [sfor a few students to be in class on time]*
          b. *a few students tried [vpto be in class on time]*

The existence of such a rule, Brame noted, demands that *try* take a sentential complement. But if so, he asked, what would prevent *There*-Insertion from applying in the embedded sentence to derive ungrammatical (7.29)?

(7.29)   **A few students tried for there to be a few students in class on time*

Brame suggested that if Equi were eliminated and (7.28b) considered the deep structure, this problem would not arise. But if so, as he pointed out, then the many rules that had been postulated to feed Equi, such as Passive, Raising, *There*-Insertion, and *Tough*-Movement, also could not exist as transformations.

By the late 1970s, there was considerable support for the idea that at least the transformations discussed in the above paragraphs should be reanalyzed as lexical rules and thus that the constructions derived by them should be generated directly by the phrase structure rules. Undoubtedly, many syntacticians would have come to such a conclusion in any event; nevertheless their doing so was facilitated by several independent developments. The most important derived from certain results in mathematical linguistics arrived at by Stanley Peters and Robert Ritchie (Peters and Ritchie 1969, 1971, 1973), who proved that transformational grammars, as they were conceived in that period, had the weak generative capacity of an unrestricted rewriting system (Turing machine). What this meant was that the then-current conception of transformational rules was so unconstrained that transformational grammar made no claim at all about any human language except that its sentences could be generated by some set of rules. They showed further that the situation was not alleviated by either the recoverability condition or the principle of cyclic application. The Peters–Ritchie results had repercussions on all wings of syntactic theory, and it was not uncommon in the 1970s to see the proposed formulation of some constraint on transformational rules appeal to them for justification. Not surprisingly, many concluded from the difficulties posed by unconstrained transformations that the best solution of all would be to avoid transformational analyses entirely, or at least wherever it seemed possible. Thus a dynamic developed in the 1970s that loaded the dice in favor of lexical solutions over transformational ones and therefore defined the criteria for the latter so stringently that by the end of the decade hardly a phenomenon existed that could meet them.

The superlexicalist tendency also drew on evidence from psycholinguistics, which seemed to indicate that the transformation-rich syntactic model of the early 1970s was inconsistent with the dominant contemporary view of the interface between the grammar and the processor. This view, the Derivational Theory of Complexity (DTC), posits an isomorphic relation between the grammatical steps involved in generating a sentence and the real-time steps of the processing mechanism. According to the DTC, if a certain sequence of operations (say, transformations) applies in the grammar in a particular order, then the processor's operations will mirror those steps. It was pointed out by a number of investigators that, given current assumptions about the way that the grammar was organized, this isomorphic relationship could not exist. For example, given a Passive transformation, the DTC predicts that passive sentences should take longer to process than actives. However, this was found by Slobin (1966) not to be the case. Along the same lines, Fodor and Garrett (1967) showed that phrases with prenominal modifiers such as *the red book* take no more time to parse than *the book that is red,* despite the then-current syntactic analyses of these phrases, in which two more transformations applied in the derivation of the former. Fodor and Garrett (1967) and Watt (1970) found that short passives such as *John was seen* are no more difficult to process than long passives such as *John was seen by someone,* despite the analysis that derived the former from the latter by transformation.

Superlexicalism drew further support from the branch of psycholinguistics that has come to be known as "learnability theory." This area, which was pioneered by Kenneth Wexler, Peter Culicover, and Henry Hamburger (Wexler, Culicover, and Hamburger 1975; Culicover and Wexler 1977; Wexler and Culicover 1980), asks the question: "What properties must grammars have in order to be learnable?" Interestingly, Wexler *et al.* were able to demonstrate that, given a finite amount of data, a child would have to have prior access to a principle very much like Subjacency (see Section 6.5.1) in order to acquire an *Aspects*-style grammar.[11] But C. L. Baker (1979) appealed to learnability considerations to argue against the existence of particular transformational rules that were generally assumed in the EST. He provided, for example, learnability support for Oehrle's conclusion, mentioned above, that there can be no Dative Movement transformation. Baker argued that given such a transformation, one would predict that children would overgeneralize it to *obtain* and *return* until given specific negative evidence that these verbs do not occur in the construction. But it appeared to be the case that neither the overgeneralization[12] nor the negative evidence ever took place, thus calling into question the possibility that Dative Movement was a transformation.

In one of the most important papers of the decade, "A Realistic Transformational Grammar," Joan Bresnan (1978) concluded from these facts that models of grammar containing transformations incompatible with the DTC were "psychologically unrealistic" (p. 2). Bresnan advocated abandoning those transformational rules (like Passive) that were particularly troublesome for the DTC. Instead, both active and passive forms of verbs were to be stored directly in the lexicon (thereby capturing the fact that it takes no longer to access passives than actives.) However, sentences with displaced *Wh*-phrases, which do take longer to process than sentences with undisplaced phrases, were still to be derived transformationally. By the closing years of the decade, Bresnan's "realistic" superlexicalist theory, which

---

[11]The original learnability paper that inspired all subsequent work in this area was Gold (1967). For later overviews of the results and problems in learnability theory, see Pinker (1979, 1984) and Culicover and Wilkins (1984:chap. 5).

[12]Mazurkewich and White (1984) later did report overgeneralization of the construction by children.

seemed to have psychological as well as internal linguistic support, posed itself as a promising alternative to the direction that Chomsky had taken the EST.[13]

7.2.2. The Resistance to Trace Theory

A large part of what fueled the development of superlexicalism was the conviction that the course Chomsky had charted with his "Conditions on Transformations" paper was thoroughly wrongheaded. Naturally, nobody objected in principle to the desirability of constraining transformational power to the fullest extent possible. But many linguists (e.g., Bresnan, 1976a; Bach 1977a) were quick to point out the reduction in power of the transformational rules, if accompanied by an increase in the power of other rule types, would not lead to a more constrained grammar overall. As Bresnan (1976a) put it:

> Nevertheless, a reduction in the class of possible TRANSFORMATIONS is not equivalent to a reduction in the class of permissible RULES, so for the above argument from restrictiveness to apply, it must be shown that the proposed restrictions on transformations are not offset by extensions of permissible rules elsewhere in the grammar. Otherwise, we have, not a "more restrictive" theory of grammar, but simply a different theory of grammar, for which there is no a priori preference. (p. 356)

Indeed, it seemed to many in the late 1970s that Chomsky had constrained the transformational component only by creating a new, unconstrained component of surface filters. Furthermore, many found the particular constraints Chomsky had proposed to govern blindly applying transformational rules to be empirically inadequate, or, as Brame (1978a:100) put it, "simply names for underlying problems." Subjacency, which prohibits unbounded movements and deletions, was the most severely criticized in this period. By going hand-in-hand with a reanalysis of all seemingly unbounded movements and deletions as instances of *Wh*-Movement applying on successive cycles, this principle flew in the face of analyses that had been assumed since the earliest days of transformational grammar. Not surprisingly, then, it was attacked incessantly. Support for the existence of unbounded movement and deletion rules was adduced from Modern English (Postal 1972b; Bresnan 1975, 1976a, 1977), Middle English (Grimshaw 1974), Old English (C. Allen 1980), Old Icelandic (Maling 1977), Modern Scandinavian (Maling 1978; Engdahl 1980), Basque (De Rijk 1972), Albanian (Morgan 1972), Polish (Borsley 1981), and Bulgarian (Rudin 1981).[14] Bresnan (1976a), for example, defended the claim

---

[13]I do not outline Bresnan's 1978 model here, since few analyses were published in it (but see G. Horn 1979) and since it developed rapidly into the theory of lexical–functional grammar (see Section 8.4.2). In the late 1970s, Michael Brame developed a superlexicalist model that shared many features with Bresnan's model (see Brame 1976, 1978a, 1979).

[14]On the other hand, there has been no lack of evidence presented in favor of the principle of Subjacency, which has been supported on the basis of data from French (Kayne and Pollock 1978), Norwegian (Taraldsen 1978), Chamorro (Chung 1982b), Hungarian (Horvath 1980), and Spanish (Torrego 1981). It seems fair to say that this evidence has dispelled much of the original skepticism toward the principle.

that sentences like (7.30) result from the rule of Comparative Deletion, a rule that deletes a noun phrase over a variable (i.e., is an unbounded rule), rather than from a local deletion after COMP-to-COMP movement, as Chomsky had suggested.

(7.30)   *he uttered more homilies than I'd ever listened to* ____ *in one sitting*

Her argument can be broken into steps (1)–(4):

(1) The obeying of constraints on extraction is not a diagnostic for movement. The second *Wh*-phrases in (7.31b) and (7.32b) were not subject to movement, yet both sentences are clearly constraint violations.

(7.31)   a. *Who saw pictures of whom?*
          b. **Who heard claims about pictures of whom?*

(7.32)   a. *Who has evidence about which crimes?*
          b. **Who has information about evidence of which crimes?*

Therefore the fact that Comparative Deletion obeys a constraint does not support Chomsky's claim that a movement rule applied in its derivation.

(2) The rule of Subdeletion, illustrated in (7.33), can be shown to be a special case of Comparative Deletion.

(7.33)   *they have many more enemies than we have* ____ *friends*

(3) But Subdeletion cannot possibly be a movement rule; if it were, it would violate the Left Branch Condition (see Section 6.2.1), a condition on movement.

(7.34)   *Maggie is as fine a doctor as her sister is* ____ *a lawyer*

(4) Therefore, Comparative Deletion cannot be a movement rule; it must be an unbounded deletion.

There have also been innumerable criticisms of another of Chomsky's conclusions, namely that many processes that previously had been analyzed as distinct rules be subsumed under *Wh*-Movement. A typical criticism was presented by Bach and Horn (1976), who called attention to a seeming problem with treating Topicalization as *Wh*-Movement: in almost all languages, topicalized elements appear to the left, even in Japanese, which has its COMP on the right.

But the deepest resistance to Chomsky's model was based on its incorporation of phonologically null elements, in particular traces. To a generation of students trained at MIT in the late 1960s and armed with rebuttals to generative semantics, it seemed that Chomsky himself had abandoned the fight against overly abstract analyses. Indeed, many looked upon the trace theory of movement rules as the *reductio ad absurdum* of the principle of blind application. If traces are the consequences of the principle, it was reasoned, then all the more reason to opt for transformationless grammar. Furthermore, some felt that traces caused as many problems as they solved. For example, several linguists (e.g., Bresnan 1976a; Bach 1977a) observed that the traces left in COMP as a result of iterative *Wh*-Movement have no semantic function whatever and might well complicate the retrieval of the underlying grammatical relations needed for interpretation from the enriched trace-containing surface structures.

What seemed to make matters worse was that as the decade progressed, Chomsky grew less and less explicit about the mechanics of his theory, rarely exploring the consequences of a particular proposed constraint for a wide variety of constructions and never presenting a formalized grammar fragment. As a result, he opened himself to attacks of linguists, Geoffrey Pullum and others, who were quick to show that a hazily adumbrated proposal of Chomsky's would fail to apply correctly in some crucial domain. For example, Pullum (1979a) demonstrated that the theory as it had been presented at the time predicted incorrectly the grammaticality of the sentence *who hit (with *who* understood as the object of *hit*), which was derivable as in (7.35).

(7.35)   a. $[_{\text{COMP}}[_{\text{NP1}} e]] \ [_S[_{\text{NP2}} e] \ hit[_{\text{NP3}} who]]$
b. $[_{\text{COMP}}[_{\text{NP1}} e]] \ [_S[_{\text{NP3}} who] \ hit[_{\text{NP3}} t]]$
c. $[_{\text{COMP}}[_{\text{NP3}} who]] \ [_S[_{\text{NP3}} t] hit[_{\text{NP3}} t]]$

Soon the call for rigorous formalism became the war cry of the superlexicalists, as, ironically, Chomsky's framework within generative syntax became the most informally presented one of them all.

7.2.3. Linguistics Meets Model-Theoretic Semantics

As syntactic theory developed in the 1970s, semantic theory did not keep pace with it. Despite the title of Chomsky's collection of papers, *Studies on Semantics in Generative Grammar* (1972b), most work in the EST dealt with semantic questions only in the most fragmentary way, mainly by the sporadic mention of a semantic implication of a particular syntactic proposal. At the same time, the earliest super-lexicalist work was more syntax-centered than even Chomsky's approach; the mid 1970s work by Bresnan and Brame, for example, did not raise the possibility of a comprehensive semantic theory within generative grammar.

As a consequence, logicians tended to scoff both at the linguists' seeming lack of interest in semantics and their approach to it. In their view, the abstract semantic representations of both the generativists and the interpretivists were not interpretations at all. Rather, they simply belonged to the syntax of another metalanguage into which the syntactic constructs of the theory were translated. David Lewis (1972) scornfully called this metalanguage ''Markerese'' and commented, ''But we can know the Markerese translation of an English sentence without knowing the first thing about the meaning of the English sentence: namely, the conditions under which it would be true. Semantics with no treatment of truth conditions is no semantics'' (p. 169). Logicians were also appalled at the lack of rigor in generativist descriptions. Richard Montague's (1970b) view was probably typical: ''One could also object to existing syntactical efforts by Chomsky and his associates on grounds of adequacy, mathematical precision, and elegance; but such criticism should perhaps await more definitive and intelligible expositions than are yet available'' (p. 373).

But the barriers between logicians and linguists began to break down in the early 1970s as many of the latter began to seek an adequate semantics for natural language. In particular, they became attracted to the method for carrying out the program of truth-conditional semantics known as ''model-theoretic semantics,'' in which, by means of a model, an arbitrary sentence of a language is assigned a truth value with respect to a possible state of affairs. Most agreed that the general approach of Montague seemed the most promising. Montague's work, as reinterpreted and redirected by his UCLA colleague Barbara Partee after his murder in 1971, began to attract a growing number of linguists, and by the end of the decade it had become one of the principal alternative models of syntactic–semantic description. Indeed, as early as 1977 Janet D. Fodor was able to write that ''the indications are that we are drawing to the end of the period in which semantic representations form an abstract uninterpreted system which can be connected with reality only by identifying its primitive terms with some universal innate mental entities'' (p. 61).

Montague broke with the two leading Anglo-American philosophical schools, the logical positivists and the ordinary language philosophers. The former, dismayed at the apparent chaotic nature of natural language, sought to ''do it one better'' by constructing artificial logical languages. The latter, believing artificial languages shed no light on real problems of linguistic philosophy, did study natural language, but highly informally. Montague, on the other hand, believed that natural languages themselves could be constructed as formal languages: ''I reject the contention that an important theoretical difference exists between formal and natural languages'' (1970a:189). In this view, the same formal devices suffice to describe the properties of both types of languages.

It needs to be stressed that Montague was no empirical scientist. That is, he was not constructing a model of linguistic competence with empirical constraints on its formulation. In fact, he had no real interest in syntax at all: ''I fail to see any great interest in syntax except as a preliminary to semantics'' (Montague 1970b:373). Nevertheless, his model, in the hands of Partee and others, lent itself easily to reinterpretation as a competence model, and from this fact derives its interest to linguists and its significance for linguistics.[15] By the mid and late 1970s, many linguists besides Partee with a history of research in transformational grammar had begun to publish Montague analyses (see, for example, Karttunen and Peters 1975; Dowty 1976; Bach 1976; Schmerling 1979).

Montague grammar, in most versions, has three components:[16]

1. The Lexicon. This consists of a list of the lexical items in the language, each provided with a syntactic category and a translation into intensional logic.

---

[15]Not all Montague grammarians have interested themselves in constructing models of linguistic competence. The philosopher Richmond Thomason (1974), for example, considers Montague grammar to be a branch of mathematics, not linguistics.

[16]For an introduction to Montague grammar, see Dowty, Wall, and Peters (1981).

2. A Set of Syntactic Rules. These build a sentence from the bottom up, in the manner of categorial grammar (see Ajdukiewicz 1935; Bar Hillel 1953). Each has the form given in (7.36) where α, β, and γ are strings of terminal symbols and A, B, and C are syntactic categories.

(7.36)   If $\alpha \in A$ and $\beta \in B$, then $\gamma \in C$, where $\gamma = F_i(\alpha, \beta)$

For Montague, F_i was normally simple concatenation. However, he also proposed some transformation-like rules to handle quantification. All rules are assumed to apply in mixed and variable orders, and thus there is no level resembling deep structure.

3. A Set of Semantic Rules. For each syntactic rule, there is precisely one translation rule, which gives the translation of the resulting phrase into intensional logic as a specified function of the translations of its parts. The second stage of interpretation is the model-theoretic semantics for the intensional logic.

What linguists have found most interesting about Montague grammar is its claim that for each syntactic rule there exists a semantic rule.[17] Partee (1973), for example, maintained that the hypothesis of syntactic rule–semantic rule association is very strong, allowing for the principled selection of only one out of a number of competing analyses of the same phenomenon. For example, (7.37a) and (7.37b) had long been put forward as alternative analyses for relative clauses (using *the boy who lives in the park* as an illustration).

(7.37)   a. $[_{NP}[_{NP}$*the boy*$] [_S$*who lives in the park*$]]$
             b. $[_{NP}$*the* $[_{NOM}$*boy who lives in the park*$]]$

She argues that if each syntactic rule must have semantic consequences, then the phrase has to have structure (7.37b), not (7.37a). Only in (7.37b) are

> the two class-denoting phrases [*boy* and *who lives in the park*] . . . first combined to form a complex class-denoting phrase, which can be interpreted as denoting the intersection of the two classes, namely the class of entities which both live in the park and are boys; combining *the* with the results leads to the correct assertion that it is that class that has one and only one member. (Partee 1973:512)

Others have thought, however, that the claim of semantic rule–syntactic rule pairing might not be so strong after all, since in principle there is nothing to prevent a "stubborn" (i.e., semantically nonunified) syntactic rule from being split into two or more parts, each part being assigned its own corresponding semantic rule. And in the very case of relative clauses, Bach and Cooper (1978) demonstrated that a Montague semantics for the NP–S structure could be provided.

---

[17]Bach (1976), in his discussion of certain formal similiarties between Montague grammar and pre-*Aspects* transformational grammar, points out that the idea of a semantic rule for each syntactic rule appeared in the 1963–1965 model. Each of the generalized transformations in that model had an accompanying P2 projection rule (see Section 3.3.2). In fact, under one interpretation of the Katz–Fodor (1963) P1 projection rules, each phrase structure rule corresponds to a different P1 rule, resulting in a model even more strikingly like Montague grammar.

There are many ways in which Partee and others brought Montague grammar closer to mainstream generative grammar in the 1970s.[18] Most importantly, Partee (1975b:258) proposed that rules be stated in terms of labeled bracketed structures, rather than simply in terms of strings, as in Montague's original conception. Furthermore, she (1975b) and Emmon Bach (1979) added operations virtually identical to transformations to the stock of syntactic rules. While they are interspersed with the concatenatory rules, their formal properties are nevertheless much like the standard transformations familiar to linguists. And David Dowty has proposed Montague analogues to the lexical rules of the EST (Dowty 1978a, 1978b, 1979).

The move to incorporate model-theoretic semantics into linguistic theory was challenged as early as 1975 by Chomsky, who rejected its underlying assumptions and questioned whether such an approach could, in any sense, further our understanding of meaning in language. Chomsky's resistance to Montague grammar grew stronger perhaps as a consequence of one of the most significant developments of the late 1970s—the marriage of Montague grammar with superlexicalism. This marriage, which produced an alternative to Chomsky's model that has proved to be far more potent than superlexicalism in and of itself, is discussed in the following chapter.

---

[18]There is an interesting discussion in McCawley (1977a) of the evolutionary parallels between Montague grammar and transformational grammar.

Chapter 8

Current Approaches to Syntax

8.1. WORK IN PROGRESS

It is not easy to treat the present as history. Lacking the advantage of at least a few years hindsight, I run the risk in this chapter of distorting the importance of some current development by assigning it (by virtue of too great or too little coverage) a significance that history will show it does not deserve. Nevertheless, I do my best in the following pages to survey what are generally recognized to be the major contemporary currents in syntactic theory.

8.2. THE GOVERNMENT–BINDING THEORY

In April of 1979, Chomsky delivered a series of lectures at a conference held at the Scoula Normale Superiore in Pisa, Italy. The point of departure of the "Pisa lectures" (as they came to be known) was his paper "On Binding," which, though not published until 1980, had been written two years earlier and was widely available in mimeographed form. But the Pisa lectures were far more than an elaboration of the "On Binding" model; they represented the most important step forward in Chomsky's thinking since the "Conditions" paper of almost a decade earlier. These lectures were revised and greatly expanded in Chomsky's 1981 book *Lectures on Government and Binding* (*LGB*), which, of all of Chomsky's publications, compares only to *The Logical Structure of Linguistic Theory* in scope and level of detail. The government–binding (GB) theory presented engendered renewed interest in generative grammar the world over and won back many one-time followers of Chomsky who had remained unconvinced about the adequacy of the late 1970s EST. Indeed, the most interesting sociological fact about GB is that the number of its adherents in Europe (a high percentage of whom worked out its technical details on their own) comes close to equaling those in the United States.[1] GB has been modified considerably since 1981, in three books by Chomsky (1982b, 1985, 1986), in several dozen other books, and in literally hundreds of journal articles and unpublished papers. Nevertheless, the basic outline of the theory as presented in *LGB* is still intact, and forms the basis of the following presentation of GB.

8.2.1. Core Grammar, Markedness, and Parameterized Principles

By 1980, the idea that the complexity of language could be explained by recourse to the modular interaction of formal grammar with principles from physiology, cognition, sociology, and so on had become well accepted, at least by those who saw any place for formal grammar at all. The central guiding principle of GB is that the internal structure of the grammar is modular as well. That is, syntactic complexity results from the interaction of grammatical subsystems, each characterizable in terms of its own set of general principles. The central goal of syntactic theory thus becomes to identify such systems and characterize the degree to which they may vary from language to language.

Most early work in generative syntax was rather nonmodular in character. Essentially, each construction had its own associated rule: passives were derived by the Passive transformation, subject-raised sentences by the Raising transformation, and so on. But as the work on constraints on rules accelerated throughout the 1970s, it became clear that at least some of the complexities of particular constructions could be attributed to general principles, rather than having to be stated ad hoc in particular rules. As noted in Section 6.2.2, for example, the Structure Preserving Constraint predicts the ungrammaticality of such passives as *Germany Russia was defeated by, *Germany was Russia defeated by,* and *Germany was by Russia defeated,* since such sentences do not have structures that could have been generated by independently motivated phrase structure rules. This and other constraints allowed the simplification of the structural description of Passive to the point where it could be collapsed with other rules moving noun phrases. Thus the complexities of the passive construction now resulted from the modular interaction of the generalized movement rule and the constraints. In GB, grammar-internal modularity is carried as far as it can go; with some minor exceptions, all syntactic complexity results from the interaction of the following grammatical subsystems (Chomsky 1981:5):

bounding theory, which sets limits on the domain of movement rules
government theory, which defines the relation between the head of a construction
    and those categories dependent upon it

---

[1] "Generative Linguists of the Old World" (GLOW), an organization of European linguists that meets yearly at a different university, has boosted GB and the enthusiasm of its supporters the way that the CLS meetings of the early 1970s boosted generative semantics. The foundational document of the organization, the "GLOW Manifesto," does not merely endorse generative grammar in general, but specifically points to "Conditions on Transformations" as "epoch-making" and states that "a significant number of members of GLOW have found their common ground in the research program that grew out of 'Conditions'" (Koster, van Riemsdijk, and Vergnaud 1978:5).

Θ-theory, which deals with the assignment and functioning of thematic roles
binding theory, which links grammatical elements such as pronouns, anaphors,
names, and variables with their antecedents
Case theory, which deals with the assignment of abstract Case and its morphological realization
control theory, which determines the potential for reference of the abstract pronominal element PRO
X-bar theory, which constrains the base component of the grammar

Each of these subsystems is treated below.

What many have found most appealing about GB is that it incorporates a program
of comparative syntax, that is, it provides a theoretical foundation for linguistic
typology. In the GB view, what appear on the surface to be major structural
differences among languages result from each language setting slightly different
values (''parameters'') for each of the various grammatical subsystems. Such an
approach to cross-linguistic variation was first taken in an extremely important
paper that Luigi Rizzi wrote in 1978 (Rizzi 1982c). As Rizzi pointed out, Italian at
first glance appears to be very different from English, in that several constraints on
the extraction of *wh*-elements that work for English seem to be violated in Italian.
But Rizzi showed the relevant difference between Italian and English to be no more
than a difference in setting for the bounding parameter in the two languages: in
English, the bounding nodes relevant for subjacency are both S and S̄, for Italian S̄
alone.

The attempt to attribute differences among languages to different parameter set-
tings has proved most intense (and, possibly, most fruitful) where languages differ
from each other in terms of a clustering of properties. For example, Italian and
Spanish differ from English and French in that the former manifest the following
constellation of syntactic properties not found in the latter:

missing subject in simple sentences; Italian *ho trovato il libro,* 'have found the
book'
free inversion in simple sentences: *ha mangiato Giovanni,* 'has eaten Giovanni'
''long *wh*-movement'' of subject: *l'uomo che mi domando chi abbia visto,* 'the
man who I wonder who [someone has] seen'
empty resumptive pronouns in embedded clauses: *ecco la ragazza che mi domando chi crede che possa. . . ,* 'this is the girl who I wonder who thinks that she
may . . .'
apparent violations of the *that*-trace filter: *chi credi che partirà,* 'who do you
think that will leave'

More work in GB has been devoted to linking this clustering of properties to a single
parameter setting than to any other single issue. While the complexities of the issues
involved in setting this so-called pro-drop (or null subject) parameter prevent a
literature review, the following publications are among the most important: Taraldsen (1980), Chomsky (1981:240–275, 1982b:78–89), Jaeggli (1982:chap. 4),
Rizzi (1982b), Safir (1985), Suñer (1982), Zubizarreta (1982b), Belletti (1982),

Franks (1982), Montalbetti and Saito (1983), Picallo (1984), Huang (1984), Contreras (1984b), Borer (1984a:chap. 6), Bouchard (1984:chap. 4), and Kenstowicz (1984).

A second familiar typological division that has received a great deal of attention by GB is that between those languages in which word order and hierarchic constituent structure play important roles (English and Hebrew are typical examples) and those with fairly free word order and seemingly "flat" constituent structure (Japanese and the Dravidian and Australian languages are examples). Hale (1982, 1983) and Farmer (1984) are among the works devoted to the exploration of what parameter or set of parameters might be involved in distinguishing the former "configurational" languages from the latter "nonconfigurational" ones.[2]

Other studies that attribute cross-linguistic differences to parametic variation are represented by Borer's (1984a) treatment of clitics in various languages; Huang's (1982a, 1982b) division of languages into those that have syntactic *Wh*-Movement and those (like Chinese) that have it only in LF and thus do not evidence it on the surface and his (1984) attribution of certain empty subjects in Japanese, Chinese, and other languages to their allowing "zero topics"; Kayne's (1984e) proposal linking a set of differences between English and French to the different ways that prepositions can govern in the two languages; and Muysken's (1982) idea that languages vary according to how heads of constructions are defined.

Chomsky, however, sees no hope of attributing all plausibly grammatical features of all languages to interacting subsystems of principles. As he puts it, a language incorporates "a periphery of borrowings, historical residues, inventions, and so on, which we can hardly expect to . . . incorporate within a principled theory of UG [universal grammar]" (1981:8). As a consequence, each language contains a periphery of marked constructions, i.e., those that defy characterization in terms of the principles of UG alone. Two suggested candidates for membership in the marked periphery are English sentences with stranded prepositions like *Who did you write about?* (van Riemsdijk 1978a; Hornstein and Weinberg 1981) and restrictive relative clauses in a variety of languages that deviate from canonical [$_{NP}$NP S] structure (Cinque 1982). The product of the interaction of the subsystems of principles forms the core grammar of the language. Acquiring a language, then, involves both setting the correct parameters of its core grammar, and identifying (and learning) those aspects that belong to the periphery.

While the overall geometry of the grammar in terms of the interrelationships of the various components is essentially the same in GB as in its antecedent approaches, (i.e., the grammar is still organized as in Figure 6.2),[3] there have been a

---

[2]Much of the groundwork for a generative account of the differences between the two types of languages was laid in Staal (1967). It should be pointed out that there has been considerable criticism of the idea, developed in greatest detail in Farmer (1984), that Japanese belongs unequivocally in the class of nonconfigurational languages (for discussion, see Kiss 1981; Saito and Hoji 1983; Kuroda 1983), and even of the idea that any language can truly be described as nonconfigurational (see Pullum 1982; Sproat 1985; Horvath 1985; Stowell forthcoming).

[3]Mention should be made of two alternative approaches with different geometries: the L-model of van Riemsdijk and Williams (1981), in which logical form is an intermediate level between two distinct

TABLE 8.1

	Overt NPs	Empty NPs
+ANA,−PRON	reciprocals, reflexives	NP trace
−ANA,+PRON	pronouns	missing subjects in Spanish, Italian, etc. (symbolized "pro")
+ANA,+PRON	——	the understood subject in *John wants___to go*, etc. (symbolized PRO)
−ANA,−PRON	ordinary nonpronominal NPs	variables, including traces of *Wh*-Movement

number of attempts to derive what in the past had been regarded as idiosyncratic features of particular components from principles governing the grammar as a whole. The most ambitious by far is Stowell (forthcoming), who defends the idea that the categorial (base) component of the grammar can be eliminated entirely, along with many of the features traditionally incorporated into X-bar theory. Stowell makes recourse to the full set of interacting GB principles, in particular to Case theory.

8.2.2. The Binding Conditions and the Empty Category Principle

One of the most important advances of the GB theory over its antecedents is its imposition of order on the previously chaotic treatment of empty NPs. Earlier work had proposed a number of such elements, including traces, unindexed dummy elements, and empty pronominals (i.e., PRO), yet no clear overall picture had emerged of their properties, their distribution, or their relationship to overt (i.e., lexically specified) NPs. Such chaos tended to call into question the very need for empty elements.

A major step toward a unified approach to empty elements was the division of all NPs, whether overt or empty, into the following classes (Chomsky 1981:101):

anaphors: those that lack intrinsic reference (and therefore must have an antecedent)

pronominals: those which contain no intrinsic features other than person, number, and gender (and therefore may, but need not necessarily, have an antecedent)

R-expressions (i.e., referring expressions): those that are potentially referential.

The anaphor–pronominal distinction suggested two feature specifications: ±ANA(PHORIC) and ±PRON(OMINAL), resulting in the partition of NPs into four natural classes (Chomsky 1982b:78) as shown in Table 8.1.

Given this classification of NPs, the following three principles, collectively referred to as the "binding theory," account for their distribution (Chomsky 1981:188):

---

syntactic levels and S-Structure, and the model presented in Koster (1978b, 1981), in which S-Structures are base generated.

(A) An anaphor is A-bound in its governing category
(B) A pronominal is A-free in its governing category
(C) An R-expression is A-free (everywhere)

The terms "A-bound," "A-free," and "governing category" require some explanation. An element is A-bound if it is co-indexed with an argument (essentially, a subject or object) that c-commands it, A-free if it is not. Thus a trace of *Wh*-Movement, for example, which is co-indexed with an element in COMP, is A-free. A governing category is the minimal NP or S containing an element and its governor.[4]

Since PRO (the controlled subject in sentences like *John wants ___ to go*) is both a pronominal and an anaphor, it would seem to have to be subject to both conditions (A) and (B) simultaneously. Chomsky concluded from the apparent necessity for PRO to be both A-free and A-bound in its governing category that it cannot have a governing category at all, i.e., that PRO can occur only in ungoverned position. This was certainly the desired result, and one that had followed from no independent principles in earlier work. The ungoverned nature of pronominal anaphors was also put forward as an explanation of the apparent fact that there is no overt analog to PRO (see Table 8.1). An ungoverned overt element would not be assigned Case; hence, any sentence containing such an element would violate the Case Filter (see Section 6.5.3).

Some, though by no means all, of the predictions of the binding theory can be illustrated by sentence (8.1a) and its representation (8.1b) (*e* represents an empty element).

(8.1)   a. *Who does Mary think wants to shave himself?*

The anaphor *himself* is A-bound in its governing category (S_3) to the subject of its clause e_i. This e_i itself is interpreted as a PRO controlled by (i.e., coreferential to) the empty subject of *want* in S_2. As predicted, it occurs in ungoverned position (the INFL node of S_3, being untensed, does not govern the subject). The subject of *want* is the trace of *Wh*-Movement. As a *wh*-trace it is A-free: its antecedent, *who*, is in COMP (as a matter of fact, condition C predicts that a *wh*-phrase will never move to subject or object position). Finally, the overt R-expression, *Mary*, is A-free.[5]

By appealing to the notion of government as the unifying factor, the binding

---

[4]To handle arguments within NPs, a somewhat more complex definition of governing category is required (see Chomsky 1981:207–218). Given the analysis of small clauses in Stowell (1983) and Manzini (1983), governing category can be generalized from S and NP to all syntactic categories.

For rough definitions of the notions "c-command" and "govern," see Chapter 6.

[5]For more detailed derivations, see Chomsky (1981:188f). Zagona (1982) and Koopman (1984) suggest that traces of verbal elements, as well as those of NPs, are subject to the binding theory. It is generally agreed that the binding theory has been somewhat less successful in accounting for the distribution of empty elements within noun phrases than within full sentences. For attempts to solve some of the problems involved, see Chung (1982a), Harbert (1982, 1983), Huang (1983), Clark (1984), Kayne (1984g), and Bouchard (1985).

(8.1)   b.

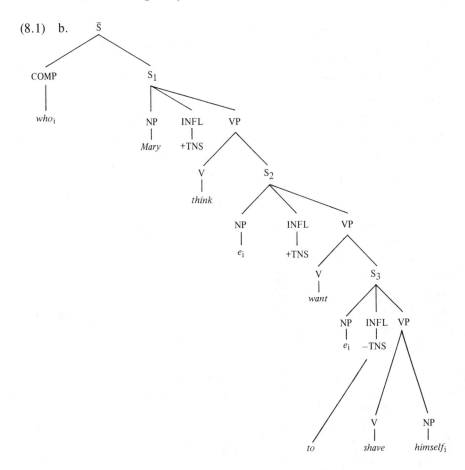

theory succeeded for the first time in unifying the Nominative Island and Specified Subject Conditions. This was a major advance, since these two conditions (and their descendents) had to be stipulated separately throughout the 1970s.

The conceptual break that made the binding theory possible was the realization that traces of NP Movement and those of *Wh*-Movement behave quite differently in a number of respects. Earlier treatments had subsumed both under the same sets of conditions. Persuaded by Freidin and Lasnik's (1981) and Rizzi's (1982c) demonstration that *wh*-traces ignore the two conditions, Chomsky treated them along with names under condition C of the binding theory, a decision facilitated by the fact that variables function, in a sense, as place holders for names (Chomsky 1982b:23).

Nevertheless, there were well-known cases of *Wh*-Movement that did appear to be subject to the Nominative Island Condition, as for example, sentence (8.2), in which *who* has been extracted from a tensed clause.

(8.2)   **who do you wonder [t how [t solved the problem]]*

Indeed, the apparent success of this condition in predicting the ungrammaticality of (8.2) led Taraldsen (1980), Pesetsky (1982a), and Kayne (1984d) to suggest that *that*-trace Filter violations like (8.3) could be subsumed under the Nominative Island Condition as well:

(8.3)   *who do you think [t that [t saw Bill]]

In the *LGB* reanalysis, (8.2) and (8.3) are indeed handled by the same principle, but not by the binding theory. Rather, they are both treated as violations of a novel construct, the Empty Category Principle (ECP):

ECP: A trace must be properly governed,

where proper government is defined as follows:

Proper Government: α properly governs β if and only if α governs β, and
  (i) α is N, V, or A or
  (ii) α is co-indexed with β

(8.2) and (8.3) are ECP violations since the traces in their most deeply embedded clauses are not properly governed: the tensed INFL nodes that govern them do not properly govern them (INFL is not a proper governor),[6] while the traces in COMP that are co-indexed with them do not govern them.

By subsuming the *that*-trace Filter, the residue of Nominative Island Condition violations not falling under the binding theory, and several other (not very general) principles that previously had to be stipulated ad hoc, the ECP was immediately regarded as one of the most appealing features of GB.

Among advocates of GB, there is general—perhaps universal—agreement that the generalizations expressed by the binding theory and the ECP are valid ones. Nevertheless, it seems fair to say that at the level of specifics, there have been markedly different proposals for how the binding theory and the ECP should be formulated. These differences have furthermore been exacerbated by the fact that there is fundamental disagreement on how the constructs underlying them (government, governing category, co-indexing, argument, and so on) should themselves be defined. Some of the most important questions pertaining to the binding theory and the ECP are cataloged below:

At What Levels Do the Binding Theory and the ECP Apply? Chomsky (1981, 1982b) argues that binding applies at S-Structure and the ECP at LF (for supporting evidence that the ECP applies at LF, see Koopman 1982, 1983; Rizzi 1982a; Jaeggli 1982; and Kayne 1984d, 1984f). However, in *Knowledge of Language,* Chomsky (1985) suggests that the binding theory applies at LF. Aoun (1982, 1985) develops a comprehensive theory of "generalized binding," in which

---

[6]One approach to "pro-drop" languages such as Spanish and Italian, however, considers INFL to be a proper governor in those languages (see Chomsky 1982b for discussion and literature citations). The notion "proper government" is subject to detailed formulation and discussion in Lasnik and Saito (1984).

binding principles are stated at both S-Structure and LF. This, he argues, allows the binding theory to subsume the ECP. Aoun's theory is defended in Safir (1983) and Hornstein (1984) and is subject to a critique in Bouchard (1984). On the other hand, Jaeggli (1982) and Huang (1982a) state the ECP at both S-Structure and LF, and Chung (1983) and Contreras (1984b) argue that the ECP applies at S-Structure alone.

How Is Government Best Defined? Chomsky (1980a, 1981:165), Rouveret and Vergnaud (1980), Lasnik and Freidin (1981), and Aoun and Sportiche (1983) each present definitions that, despite their small differences, have major consequences for the functioning of the binding theory and the ECP. Some (but not all) of these definitions incorporate the notion c-command, which itself has been defined in various ways (for a summary, see Saito 1984), and for some (Stowell 1983; Kayne 1984a; Koopman 1984; Travis 1984, Horvath 1985) the definition has a directional parameter. In addition, Belletti and Rizzi (1981) suggest that the head of a phrase can be governed from outside the phrase, and Safir and Pesetsky (1981), Safir (1982), Jaeggli (1982), Reuland (1983), and Kayne (1984c) develop the idea that government can be transmitted (or percolated, to use a popular term) from one node to another.

How Can the Classification of Empty Categories Be Improved? A number of researchers have questioned the classifications of empty elements depicted in Table 8.1. The two most ambitious revisions, Aoun (1983) and Bouchard (1984), develop a significantly revised set of binding principles. Other departures from the *LGB* account of empty categories are presented in Suñer (1983), Brody (1985), Koster (1984), Hornstein (1984:chap. 4), J. Levin (1984), Byrne (1985), and Cinque (forthcoming). More recent work has also recognized a class of implicit arguments (see Roeper 1987, in press).

How Can the ECP Be Simplified or Generalized to Cover a Broader Range of Data? A number of proposals have been put forward to eliminate the disjunction in the definition of the ECP (see Bennis 1981; Jaeggli 1982; Stowell forthcoming). Kayne (1984c) extends the ECP to subsume subjacency, a position criticized by Freidin and Lasnik (1981), Aoun (1985), and Stowell (forthcoming). And Kayne (1984a, 1984g), Pesetsky (1982b), Longobardi (1985), and May (1985) derive many ECP effects by appealing to the paths of nodes running from one member of a structural relation to another.

8.2.3. The Projection Principle and the Θ-Criterion

In addition to constraints on individual levels of representation like the binding conditions and the ECP, *LGB* introduced two conditions that have to be met by entire derivations: the Projection Principle and the Θ-Criterion. The Projection Principle can be thought of as a vastly strengthened Structure Preserving Constraint, in that it demands that the subcategorization properties of lexical items be maintained at all three syntactic levels (D-Structure, S-Structure, and LF). Thus it insures that the phrase structure configuration of a particular sentence remain constant throughout the derivation. Both trace theory and the existence of a strong parallelism in the distribution of empty and overt categories are natural complements to the Projection Principle: given the principle, it follows that movement must leave behind an empty element to maintain the prior structural configuration; likewise, the principle invites the conclusion that the differences between overt and empty categories are superficial and predictable, since it demands that NP positions remain constant.

Chomsky (1982b) added a clause to the original Projection Principle demanding that all clauses have subjects. This Extended Projected Principle was unified in Rothstein (1983, 1984).[7]

Chomsky (1981:36) placed the following constraint on the distribution of arguments:

Θ-Criterion: Each argument bears one and only one Θ-role and each Θ-role is assigned to one and only one argument.

The Θ-Criterion represented the first major utilization of thematic roles in syntactic theory since the work of Fillmore, Gruber, and Jackendoff in the late 1960s and early 1970s.

One interesting consequence of the Θ-Criterion, first pointed out in Borer (1980), is the fact that the "landing site" of a movement rule is always a position to which no Θ-role is assigned (e.g., COMP, the subject of a passive verb, the subject position of predicates like *likely, happen,* and so on). If movement were to take place to a position assigned a Θ-role, then the combination of that Θ-role and the one possessed by the moved element would lead to a Θ-Criterion violation.[8]

While the Θ-Criterion has been invoked in the analysis of a wide variety of linguistic phenomena, only a few GB analyses make reference to particular Θ-roles (e.g., Zubizarreta 1982a; Giorgi 1984; Stowell forthcoming). Indeed, Hoekstra (1984) and B. Levin and Rappaport (1985) suggest that such information is not utilized in syntactic or morphological descriptions.

8.2.4. Case and Control

Two (not very closely related) subsystems of principles remain to be discussed: Case and control. *LGB* abandoned the idea that English has distinct oblique Case,

---

[7]Other interesting modifications of the Projection Principle are made in Hirschbühler and Rivero (1983), where it is suggested that it might have to be parameterized; in Borer (1984a), where it is treated as a condition on features, not relational configurations; and in Pesetsky (1985), where it is argued to be sensitive to thematic, rather than categorial, information. For criticisms of the principle, see Carden, Gordon, and Munro (1982), Bresnan and Kaplan (1982:li), and McCloskey (1984).

[8]The Θ-Criterion strengthens an earlier proposal by Freidin (1978a). It is subject to modification and extension in Burzio (1985), Taraldsen (1981a), Williams (1983, 1984), Safir (1983, 1985), Pesetsky (1985), and Chomsky (1985). Stowell (forthcoming), Zubizarreta (1982a), and Chomsky (1985) allow for the compounding of θ-roles; Marantz (1984) and Schein (forthcoming) attempt to circumvent the θ-Criterion entirely.

subsuming oblique into objective. A major Case-related problem taken up in that book concerns the assignment of exceptional objective Case in sentences such as *I believe her to be smart*. Chomsky's analysis involves the pruning (or "deletion," as he misleadingly terms it) of the S̄ node below *believe*, thereby allowing *believe* to govern the subject of the infinitive and assign it objective Case (for a different account of exceptional Case marking, see Kayne 1984e). The class of case assigners is open to some debate; for example, Platzack (1982) argues that adjectives in Swedish assign Case. Case has been called upon to account for the distribution of argument NPs, PPs, and S̄s (Stowell forthcoming) and of PRO (Sportiche 1983; Bouchard 1984), and to play a role in the definition of empty categories (Chomsky 1982b).

Chomsky (1981:339, 1982b:6, 1985) has argued that the Case Filter can be derived from the Θ-Criterion. However, Borer (1984a:chap. 3) provides evidence that this is not possible.

Control theory remains the most poorly developed subsystem of GB. Most discussions of control have attempted to reduce it (or much of it) to the binding theory or the ECP (see Manzini 1983; Bouchard 1984; Sportiche 1983; Jones 1984; Koster 1984). Chomsky (1981), following Jackendoff (1972), has suggested that Θ-role is relevant to the determination of the possible controller, a position developed in Ruzicka (1983), Chierchia (1983), Nishigauchi (1984), and Culicover and Wilkins (1986).[9]

8.2.5. Logical Form

GB expanded the role of the Logical Form (LF) component of the grammar.[10] In particular, the goal of many GB theorists became to show that what might at first be assumed semantic generalizations, and therefore outside of sentence grammar per se, lend themselves to more adequate syntactic formulation within LF. Indeed, the principal theme of Norbert Hornstein's *Logic as Grammar* (1984) is that "much of what we would pretheoretically call 'meaning phenomena' can only be accounted for in terms of a syntactic theory, where laws exploit the grammatical distinctions of language that are arbitrary from any natural semantic point of view" (p. 104). For example, Hornstein argues that the natural semantic class of quantifiers containing *any, a certain, every, a,* and so on do not pattern in a uniform way syntactically. *Every* and *a,* but not *any* and *a certain,* are subject to the LF rule of Quantifier Raising (QR), which removes the quantifier from its surface position and adjoins it to the S node that contains it (for discussion of this rule, now generally considered to be subsumed under Move α, see May 1977).[11] Furthermore, the structures

---

[9]For other approaches to control within GB, see Huang (1984) and Yang (1985).

[10]"Logical Form" has come to be used ambiguously to refer both to a set of rules applying to S-Structure and to the level defined by the output of those rules. The major GB studies of LF rules are May (1977, 1985), Hornstein (1984), and Higginbotham (1985b).

[11]The idea that certain types of quantifiers appear not to undergo QR is also explored in Aoun, Hornstein, and Sportiche (1981).

containing these raised quantifiers are then subject to the ECP, a syntactic constraint. Given the traditional logical analysis, which would treat all quantified phrases as having operator-variable form, there is no reason to expect such a result, particularly since *any* and *every* have general interpretations, whereas *a* and *a certain* do not.

The topic pertaining to LF that has generated the greatest amount of discussion concerns "crossover" phenomena, mentioned in Section 6.5.2. Actually, there are two categories of crossover phenomena, strong crossover, illustrated by (8.4), in which the subject of the sentence is co-indexed with the moved *wh*-phrase, and weak crossover, illustrated by (8.5), in which a phrase contained within the subject is co-indexed with the moved phrase.

(8.4)   *who_i did he_i see t_i

(8.5)   *who_i did his_i mother see t_i

As far as strong crossover is concerned, the analysis presented in Section 6.5.2 carries over directly to GB: (8.4) violates Principle C of the binding theory since the trace of *Wh*-Movement, a variable and therefore an R-expression, is not A-free (it is co-indexed with the subject). A different binding theory analysis was presented by Koopman and Sportiche (1982), who argued that if the relation between the pronoun and the *wh*-phrase is taken into account, the violation might be attributable to Principles A and B (but see Sportiche 1985 for problems with this approach).

Weak crossover has generated far more discussion than strong crossover. One of the earliest proposals designed to handle such cases was the Leftness Condition proposed in Chomsky (1976:342).

Leftness Condition: A variable cannot be the antecedent of a pronoun to its left.

Since the *wh*-trace (a variable) in (8.5) is the antecedent of the pronoun *his*, the indicated reading is impossible.[12]

Koopman and Sportiche (1982) present a quite different LF condition to rule out weak crossover violations: the Bijection Principle:

Bijection Principle: An operator (essentially, an element in COMP) can bind and only one element in argument position.

Since the *wh*-phrase in COMP in (8.5) binds both the pronoun *his* and its own trace, the intended reading is impossible.

Neither the Leftness Condition nor the Bijection Principle have been found to be unproblematic. For discussion, see Safir (1984), Sells (1984), Goodall (1984), Sportiche (1985), and Contreras (1986).[13]

---

[12]For further discussion of this condition and its interaction with other LF principles, see Higginbotham (1980a, 1980b) and Higginbotham and May (1981).

[13]The most famous Bijection Principle violation is the "parasitic gap" construction, first described in Taraldsen (1981b) and Engdahl (1983). A typical example is *which paper$_i$ did you file t_i without reading e_i*. Chomsky (1982b:36–77) devotes an entire chapter to attempting to derive the nuances of the construction entirely from independent principles. For further remarks on parasitic gaps, see Sag (1982a, 1983), Engdahl (1984), Contreras (1984a), van der Wilt (1984), Haegeman (1984), Bennis and Hoekstra (1985), Huybregts and van Riemsdijk (1985), and Cowper (1985).

An ongoing debate concerns whether rules in the LF component obey Subjacency. In May's original (1977) treatment of QR, the rule crucially obeys this bounding condition. Huang (1982a), however, derived a set of facts about Chinese from the assumption that the LF analogue to *Wh*-Movement in that language does not obey Subjacency (see also Aoun, Hornstein, and Sportiche 1981 for a similar conclusion drawn from French and English data). But other work by Huang (1982b) and Pesetsky (forthcoming) suggests that LF rules are constrained by Subjacency. It seems fair to say that no clear picture has yet emerged on the applicability of bounding theory to LF.

8.3. GENERALIZED PHRASE STRUCTURE GRAMMAR

The most successful current alternative to GB is the framework known as "generalized phrase structure grammar" (GPSG). Indeed, GPSG and GB stand together as the only models of syntactic description that have won more than a small handful of recruits beyond their leading members' immediate circle.

GPSG represents the logical conclusion of the superlexicalist movement of the late 1970s (see Section 7.2.1). As we have seen, the attempt to constrain the power of transformational rules led one such rule after another to be eliminated; GPSG was born in the conviction that all transformations could be dispensed with. In the words of Gerald Gazdar, whose work provided the framework with much of its early impetus: "The strongest way to constrain a component is to eliminate it" (1982:132). Transformationless models had, in fact, been proposed before 1980;[14] the impact of GPSG resulted, then, not so much from the claim that such rules were dispensible, but rather from Gazdar's startling resurrection of a well-understood and highly constrained alternative to them: context-free phrase structure grammar (CF-PSG). Gazdar argued not only that a CF-PSG is able to generate all and only the grammatical sentences of any natural language, but to assign to them their correct structural descriptions as well. Since it was generally acknowledged that Chomsky had demonstrated the impossibility of such a grammar accomplishing even the weaker of the two tasks (see Section 2.2.2), the shock value alone of this claim was sufficient to guarantee that the field would take notice of the version of CF-PSG that Gazdar and his coworkers formalized under the name "generalized phrase structure grammar."

GPSG purports to have developed an explanatory theory of language more constrained than transformational grammar. Put simply, it has played the game by Chomsky's rules and claims to have beaten him at it. Certainly the belief among some linguists that it has been successful in doing so (or their suspicion that it might have been) accounts to a considerable degree for its relative success. But GPSG has proved attractive for other reasons as well. Most importantly, it is committed to a model theoretic account of natural language semantics. By providing a semantic

---

[14]See, for example, Starosta (1971), Hudson (1976), Brame (1976), and Kac (1978).

translation for each syntactic rule,[15] GPSG carries out the program of Montague grammar, and thus, independently of its treatment of syntax per se, has provided a pole of attraction for those discontent with the relative lack of attention to semantic questions in the EST and its successor models. Finally, GPSG is rigorously formalized, which appeals not only to those frustrated with the informality of most GB presentations, but also to those committed to studying the implementation of grammar in a model of language processing (human or computer).

In terms of concrete analyses of particular grammatical phenomena, it was Gadzar's demonstration (1981b, 1982) that a CF-PSG account can be provided for unbounded dependencies that attracted the most attention to GPSG. It had long been assumed that the dependent relation between fronted *wh*-phrases (8.6a), topicalized phrases (8.6b), and so on, and their associated gaps was unstatable within CF-PSG (or at least unamenable to an elegant account). Thus such constructions had always been regarded as providing the primary motivation for transformational rules.

(8.6)   a. *who$_i$ do you think Mary asked Bill to tell Tom to see* ____$_i$
          b. *that book$_i$, I want to ask Mary to tell Tom to read* ____$_i$

The trick to a CF-PSG account was to allow for two types of syntactic categories: basic categories of the familiar sort (S, NP, VP, etc.) and derived (or, more commonly, "slash") categories, represented by S/NP, VP/NP, NP/S, etc. The category S/NP, for example, denotes an S with an NP missing, VP/NP a VP with an NP missing, and so on. The set of phrase structure rules is devised so that any slash category is carried down the tree from its first appearance to the level of terminal elements. At this point, a slash category with the same symbol on both sides of the slash may be rewritten as the empty element *e*. Thus, sentence (8.6b) is represented roughly as (8.8). In other words, the slash-category device allows unbounded dependencies to be reduced to a linked series of mother–daughter correspondences.[16]

Subcategorization correspondences that the EST would handle transformationally are captured in GPSG by the device of the metarule, which is, essentially, a rule for generating other rules. Take the active–passive relationship as an example. Standard transformational grammar includes a statement like (8.7).

(8.7)   Map the structures underlying active transitive sentences into structures underlying their corresponding passive sentences.

The GPSG metarule for passive, on the other hand, represented in (8.9), simply expands a verb's subcategorization frame. It allows any verb that subcategorizes for a direct object to occur in passive form with an optional *by*-phrase.

---

[15]Indeed, phenomena granted a syntactic account in all prior frameworks are reanalyzed as semantic in GPSG. The rule of Raising, for example, is defined on the argument structures of the relevant verbs and adjectives, an argument structure itself being a complex model-theoretic object (see Sag 1982b; Gazdar *et al.* 1985:chap. 10; and, for general discussion, McCloskey 1984).

[16]For detailed discussion of long distance dependencies in GPSG, see Jacobson (1984); Gazdar *et al.* (1985:chap. 7).

(8.8)

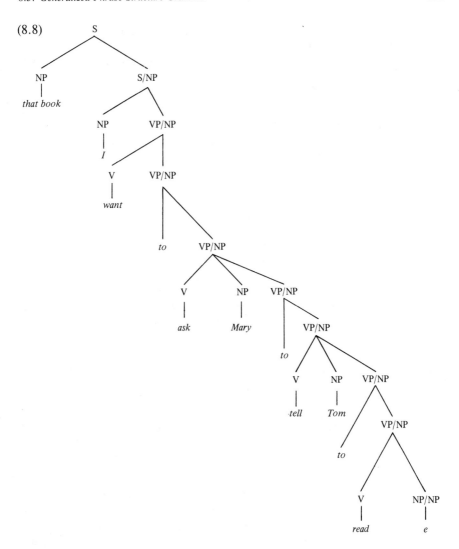

(8.9)   VP → V, NP, X
        ⇓
    VP[PAS] → V, (PP[*by*]), X

The metarule, unlike the transformation, is no more than a novel rule-collapsing device, and thus does not take the power of GPSG beyond that of a CF-PSG.

   GPSG has correspondingly given a very different account of syntactic constraints: it has reanalyzed what had previously been analyzed as constraints on transformational rules as constraints on configurations of categories and features generable by phrase structure rules. Consider, for example, an interesting GPSG reanalysis of the Coordinate Structure Constraint (see Section 6.2.1), which in a transformational account handles the ungrammaticality of sentences like (8.10).

(8.10)   *Beans, I ate rice and

However, Gazdar (1982) attributed the ungrammaticality of this sentence to the principle that only like categories can be conjoined. In (8.11), a GPSG phrase structure representation of (8.10), the nonidentical categories NP and NP/NP are conjoined, thus explaining the ungrammaticality of the sentence.[17]

(8.11)

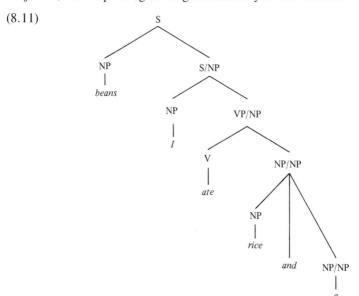

Along the same lines, the A-over-A Principle, the Left Branch Condition, and the Complex Noun Phrase Constraint have been reinterpreted as constraints prohibiting particular phrase structure configurations of categories and features.

GPSG has undergone a number of important changes. Most strikingly, there are now no longer any phrase structure rules as such; instead, the class of admissible structural descriptions is determined by a component of rules that, strictly speaking, are not themselves CF-PSG rules. In particular, rules governing the structural relations of dominance are separated from those governing linear precedence.[18]

---

[17]See Gazdar et al. 1985:chap. 8 for a later GPSG account of the same phenomenon. The ability of GPSG to handle coordination has been the single most extensively debated issue pertaining to that framework. For discussion, see Gazdar (1981b), Pesetsky (1982b), Williams (1981c), Schachter and Mordechay (1983), Goodall (1984), Schachter (1984), and Sag, Gazdar, Wasow, and Weisler (1985).

[18]See Gazdar and Pullum (1981) and Stucky (1982). As Gazdar et al. (1985:47) point out, the idea of separating these two types of rules has a long history within generative grammar.

(8.12) is an example of an immediate dominance (ID) rule and is interpreted to mean that A dominates B, C, and D, the relative ordering of which is unspecified.

(8.12)   A → B,C,D

(8.13) typifies a linear precedence (LP) rule; B must precede C, which must precede D.

(8.13)   B < C < D

Thus rule set (8.14) from a conventionally formulated CF-PSG is rephrased as (8.15a–b) in ID–LP format.

(8.14)   S → NP VP
          S → AUX NP VP
          VP → AUX VP
          VP → V VP
          VP → V NP
          VP → V NP VP

(8.15)   a. S → NP, VP
             S → AUX, NP, VP
             VP → AUX, VP
             VP → V, VP
             VP → V, NP
             VP → V, NP, VP
          b. AUX < NP
             V < NP
             NP < VP

Many benefits are claimed to accrue from separating ID from LP rules. One is that this separation allows a natural account of nonconfigurational languages, since the output of ID rules is unordered and LP rules are not required to apply (for discussion of such languages in GPSG, see Pullum 1982; Stucky 1982, 1983). Also, this separation facilitates the expression of the generalization that the order of lexical heads and their complements is, in most languages, the same across phrases (e.g., English, in which verbs, nouns, adjectives, and prepositions all precede their complements). All that is necessary is an LP statement like (8.16), which means that items that contain the subcategorization feature [SUBCAT] (i.e., heads of phrases) must precede those that do not (i.e., nonheads).

(8.16)   [SUBCAT] < ~ [SUBCAT]

Flickinger (1983) has proposed to constrain metarules by allowing them to map only from lexical ID rules (i.e., those that introduce lexical nodes) to other lexical ID rules. This has the effect of saying that metarules serve solely to express generalizations about the subcategorization possibilities of lexical heads, thereby capturing directly the superlexicalist notion that passive and related rules are essentially lexical in nature.[19] Given Flickinger's constraint, Passive metarule (8.9) can be simplified to (8.17): there is no longer a need to mention the verbal head of the VP explicitly in the rule.

(8.17)   VP → W, NP
               ⇓
           VP[PAS] → W, (PP[*by*])

Another trend in GPSG has been the development of an extremely rich set of syntactic features, along with a set of principles governing their assignment and distribution. Generalizations that were once stated by reference to atomic categories or metarules are now expressed in feature notation. Space does not permit a discussion of their intricacies; however, they are presented and defended in great detail in Gazdar, Klein, Pullum, and Sag (1985).

Finally, and surprisingly, a number of practitioners of GPSG have abandoned the idea that human languages are context free. This is particularly remarkable when one considers that in the first few years of the framework, one of its principal thrusts was to rebut the many arguments that CF-PSGs are inadequate (for the most important set of rebuttals, see Pullum and Gazdar 1982). But incontrovertible evidence mounted against strict CF-PSG accounts of human language. Bresnan, Kaplan, Peters, and Zaenen (1982) argue that a Dutch construction containing cross-serial dependencies cannot be strongly generated by a CF-PSG, though they concede that such constructions could be weakly generated by one. But apparently CF-PSG fails on the grounds of weak generative capacity as well; Culy (1985) and Shieber (1985) have proven that a reduplication construction in Bambara and a cross-serial dependency construction in a dialect of Swiss German, respectively, are beyond the bounds of CF-PSG description.[20]

Given the historical importance of Gazdar's original hypothesis about the context-free quality of natural language, one might think that its falsification would have been greeted by the advocates of GSPG with dismay. Such is, however, not the case. For one thing, they point out that the constructions referred to above are still generable by a device far more restrictive in its generative capacity than one with transformational rules. For another, their rhetorical emphasis has shifted from the restrictiveness of GPSG to its elegance. In particular, they stress that many universals of language that would have to be stipulated in other frameworks (e.g., GB) follow from the basic architecture of GPSG. The most consistent theme of Gazdar *et al.* (1985) is that the rich deductive structure of the theory allows universals to be stated within the metalanguage itself.

---

[19]In the development of GPSG called "head-driven phrase structure grammar" (HPSG) (Pollard 1984, 1985), lexical ID rules are eliminated, and subcategorization is stated as a property of lexical heads. HPSG thus represents, in a certain sense, a convergence between GPSG and GB, since in the latter framework more and more global features of syntactic derivations are being analyzed as projections from lexical entries (see especially Stowell forthcoming).

[20]Not all attacks on the noncontext-free nature of human language are uncontroversial, however. Higginbotham (1984), for example, offers a proof based on the English *such that* construction, which has been subject to a rebuttal in Pullum (1985b), which itself has been challenged in Higginbotham (1985a).

GPSG analyses have now appeared on about two dozen languages, from Dutch (Moortgat 1984), to Hungarian (Farkas 1984), to Welsh (Borsley 1983, Harlow 1983) (for a complete listing, see Gazdar *et al.* 1985:15).

8.4. RELATIONALLY BASED MODELS OF GRAMMAR

Two important frameworks for grammatical analysis, relational grammar and lexical–functional grammar, take grammatical relations such as subject and direct object to be primitive theoretical terms.

8.4.1. Relational Grammar

In the *Aspects* model, grammatical relations were not only wholly derivative notions, but they were also thought not to play an important role in any grammatical process. But as the scope of grammatical analysis deepened in the early 1970s, syntacticians from all quarters began to realize that they were more central than had previously been believed. Chomsky's crucial Specified Subject Condition, for example, not only refers to the notion Subject, but, if the condition has any claim to universality, demands a universal characterization of that notion. And on the basis of extensive empirical research, Edward Keenan and Bernard Comrie discovered numerous processes in numerous languages that seem to pay attention to grammatical relations. They postulated for example (see Keenan and Comrie 1977, 1979) that relative clause formation is universally subject to the hierarchy in (8.18). All languages relativize from subject position; if a language relativizes from a position lower on the hierarchy, it will also relativize from higher positions.

(8.18)   Subject > Direct Object > Indirect Object > Major Oblique Case NP > Genitive NP > Object of Comparison

Others have found this Accessibility Hierarchy to be relevant to a variety of grammatical processes. For example, it has been claimed to play a role in determining the grammatical relation assumed by embedded subjects after clause-merging causative transformations apply (Comrie 1976) and in selecting the particular NP affected by rules that change grammatical relations (Johnson 1974; Trithart 1975).

While working together at IBM in the summer of 1972, David Perlmutter and Paul Postal began to investigate the possibility of a theory in which these relations are taken to be the primitives and in which linear order is derivative and predicted on the basis of the grammatical relations borne by the elements in the sentence. Their work developed into a nascent theory called ''relational grammar'' (RG), which soon gained the reputation of being an important alternative to all varieties of standard transformational grammar.[21]

RG quickly won a sizeable number of adherents, a fact that was not due merely to

---

[21]John Kimball in the late 1960s pointed out that the class of cyclic rules and the class of rules affecting grammatical relations is roughly coextensive (see Kimball 1972a). The first proposal known to

the prestige of its formulators. The greatest attraction of the theory was that it seemed to be able to capture universal generalizations about language unstatable in linear-order-based models. Most importantly, it made possible a universal rule inventory that seemed to defy statement in nonrelational terms. Consider the rule of Passive as an example. Standard transformational grammar would seemingly have to handle it very differently from language to language. In some languages (e.g., English) the rule appears to move the object to the left and the subject to the right. In others (e.g., Chinese) the object moves to the left of the verb, while in Japanese it moves to the left of the subject. And in others (e.g., Cebuano) no movement takes place at all. One might conclude, then, that Passive admits no universal statement in terms of change in linear order. But Perlmutter and Postal (1977) argued that if grammatical relations are basic, Passive can be stated universally as (8.19), with all language-independent surface orderings following from principles needed independently for the language in question.

(8.19)   Direct Object → Subject

The most attractive feature of RG was the significant number of putatively universal laws stated in relational terms that Postal, Perlmutter, and others were able to formulate. The following three (from around 1974) were among the most important, though well over a dozen were proposed.[22]

The Relational Succession Law. When a rule turns an NP bearing a particular grammatical relation in a lower clause into a relation bearer in a higher clause, that NP assumes the grammatical relation of the NP that originally dominated it. For example, the rule of Raising-to-Subject in English moves an NP out of a clause that is in subject position; the rule of Raising-to-Object moves an NP out of a clause that is in object position. This law predicts that derived higher subjects cannot be raised from object clauses, nor higher objects from subject clauses.

The Relational Annihilation Law. When a NP, NP_i, assumes the grammatical relations borne by another NP, NP_j, then NP_j ceases to bear any grammatical relation whatever. (Hence the displaced subjects from Passive, *There*-Insertion, etc., cannot partake in any rules sensitive to grammatical relations.)

The Reranking Law. A rule that applies within a particular clause to alter the grammatical relation of an NP can only increase the hierarchic rank of the NP on (8.18). (Hence there are rules that turn direct objects into subjects, but none that turn subjects into direct objects.)

An important reason for the immediate popularity of RG was that it seemed able to capture directly the descriptions of the great traditional grammarians in a way that

---

me for stating the rules in terms of grammatical relations was put forward in class lectures at the University of Illinois by Jerry Morgan in the fall of 1971. While Morgan did not follow up this idea immediately, his lectures inspired David Johnson's 1974 Illinois dissertation *Toward a Theory of Relationally Based Grammar* (Johnson 1976). Johnson later joined Postal at IBM. The first published hint of the developing theory is in Postal (1974), in which relational solutions are briefly sketched.

[22]At the expense of slight misrepresentation, I have simplified the statement of these laws and recast them in more familiar terminology.

standard transformational grammar did not. By and large, Jespersen, Poutsma, Curme, and others described rules in terms of changes of grammatical relations, not linear order; hence relational grammarians felt that they had more right to claim such luminaries as their direct predecessors than did the mainstream transformational grammarians.[23]

Finally, RG appealed to many by virtue of the easily tested universal claims about linguistic structure that it makes, which have encouraged an intensive empirical investigation of numerous languages.

The crowning moment of RG was the 1974 LSA Summer Institute in Amherst. There Postal and Perlmutter jointly taught the fundamentals of the framework to hundreds in the best-attended Institute class since Chomsky's at UCLA in 1966.

The Postal–Perlmutter lecture series was complemented by the publication of Sandra Chung's paper "An Object-Creating Rule in Bahasa Indonesia" (1976), widely agreed to be the most compelling defense of RG in print. Chung argues that if rules are sensitive to linear order rather than grammatical relations, then there is no non-ad hoc way to block dative-moved NPs in Indonesian from subsequently undergoing a number of transformations. However, the Relational Annihilation Law predicts that these NPs will be immune to any subsequent relation-affecting transformations.

The earliest work in RG bore a close resemblance to classical transformational grammar in the sense that much of the formalism of the latter was simply carried over to the former. Indeed, the only major change was that transformations began to be stated in terms of grammatical relations rather than linear order. However, with Perlmutter and Postal (1977), sentences began to be represented in terms of relational networks, which represent the grammatical relations that elements of a sentence bear to each other and the syntactic level(s) at which those relations hold. The relational network for sentence (8.20a), for example, is represented (in simplified form) as (8.20b).

(8.20)　　a. *That book was reviewed by Louise*
　　　　　b.

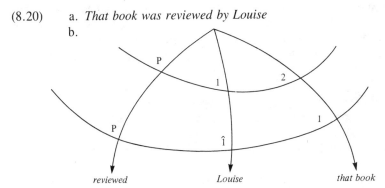

---

[23]Although Fiengo and Lasnik (1976) pointed out that Jespersen considered *John* in both (i) and (ii) to be the indirect object.

(i) *Mary gave the book to John*
(ii) *Mary gave John the book*

The first stratum consists of the predicate (P) *reviewed* and two terms (relation-bearing elements): *Louise*, the subject (represented as 1) and *that book*, the direct object (represented as 2). In the second stratum, *that book* is now a subject, while *Louise* ceases to bear any grammatical relation at all; it has become a *chômeur*, as is indicated by the symbol 1̂.

RG began to lose momentum in the late 1970s and has never regained it. There seem to be several reasons for its not fulfilling its initial promise. The first is Postal and Perlmutter's long delay in publishing a concise outline of the theory. Nothing couched in a relational framework appeared in a printed journal or book until Postal (1977), and even in the photo-litho format of the parajournals put out by the linguistic societies, nothing appeared until Aissen and Perlmutter (1976). Neither of these articles gives an account of the theory as a whole. While Johnson (1976) partially filled the gap, the transmission of word-of-mouth (and word-of-ditto ma-chine) of relational principles in the mid 1970s seriously impeded the acceptance and general credibility of the theory.[24] Even today, published material is fairly meager. Aside from Johnson and Postal's mammoth *Arc-Pair Grammar* (1979), in which a version of the theory is minutely outlined and formalized, the only books that give general overviews of RG are the anthologies edited by Perlmutter (1983) and Perlmutter and Rosen (1984).

Second, many linguists, already exasperated with the style of the generative semanticists (see Section 5.4.3), groaned to see many of the same traits reappear in RG. These traits, which manifested themselves in the preciously cute and ever-changing technical vocabulary of the theory, were another impediment to its wide-spread adoption by the linguistic public.

Third, relational grammar ran counter to the renewed interest in semantics in the late 1970s. While its partisans have claimed (Permutter and Postal 1977; Perlmutter 1978) that initial grammatical relations are semantically determined, the major paper devoted to probing this question, Rosen (1984) has not found "any reliable homomorphism" (p. 73) between them and semantic roles (for other work on this topic, see Rhodes 1977; Hermon 1981; and Aissen 1984). In fact, Newmeyer (1976b) has argued that only rather low-level syntactic processes give support to the model, suggesting an intimate connection between RG and autonomous syntax. If this is correct, then the situation is not without irony, given the generative seman-tics-oriented background of some leading relational grammarians.

Finally and most importantly, RG lost appeal because a large percentage of the universal laws proposed within the framework were falsified or weakened. Signifi-cantly, many challenges to RG principles were put forward by linguists highly sympathetic to the model or even working with it. For example, the Accessibility

[24]The cause of this seems to have been the favoring of different research strategies by the two linguists. Perlmutter's priorities were to begin by carrying out intensive cross-language studies of relational phenomena; Postal's to begin by developing and refining the formalism in which relational generalizations might be expressed and proposing candidate laws on the basis of the known facts of English and other well-known languages. These different priorities impeded collaboration at the level necessary to publish a synopsis of the theory.

Hierarchy was attacked by Cole (1976a, 1976b), Stratal Uniqueness and the Relational Annihilation Law by Dalgish and Sheintuch (1976) and Gary and Keenan (1977). No framework exists, of course, whose principles have not undergone constant revision. But the public perception, at least, of RG is that those challenged principles were not replaced by any of equal or greater generality.

Nevertheless, RG continues to attract a certain number of bright students of linguistics, who in turn continue to develop its conceptions. Its lasting contribution to the field will undoubtedly be the wealth of phenomena in the wealth of languages that its practitioners have called attention to and analyzed. No one doubts that work of the quality of Aissen's on Tzotzil (1983), Davies's on Choctaw (1984, 1985), Gerdts's on Halkomelem (1980, 1984), Gibson's on Chamorro (1980), A. Harris's on Georgian (1982, 1984), and Rosen's on Italian (1981, 1982) will retain its value whatever the ultimate fate of relational grammar.

8.4.2. Lexical–Functional Grammar

The origins and development of the other major relationally based framework, lexical–functional grammar (LFG), are quite different from those of RG. Whereas RG was conceived and developed primarily by one-time generative semanticists in the period of the collapse of that framework, LFG was a direct outgrowth of the superlexicalist alternative to trace theory. In fact, it is descended directly from the framework outlined in Joan Bresnan's "Realistic Transformational Grammar" paper (see Section 7.2.1). And unlike RG, LFG had no difficulty in creating an active and stable constituency.

LFG shares with RG the notion of the universality, centrality, and primitiveness of grammatical relations, which it refers to as "grammatical functions." In LFG, as in RG, functions such as subject, direct object, and indirect object are basic, in the sense that they cannot be expressed in terms of invariant tree configurations across languages. But LFG differs profoundly from RG in that it accords a central role to the lexicon and carries over the superlexicalist conception that, in general, lexical analyses are preferable to nonlexical ones. In fact, advocates of LFG have continued to adduce arguments for lexical, as opposed to transformational, solutions for a variety of syntactic phenomena. The centrality of the lexicon in LFG is assured by its principle of direct syntactic encoding (Bresnan 1982c:6), which requires that every nonlexical rule of grammar preserve function assignments. Hence the rule of Passive, the paradigm case of a function-changing rule, could only be lexical.

LFG differs from the pre-GB Extended Standard Theory and from GPSG in the importance it attaches to the predicate argument structures of lexical items, namely the relationship between a predicate and the semantic roles with which it can be associated. Kaplan and Bresnan (1982:174), in fact, have identified the "fundamental problem" for a theory of syntax as "to characterize the mapping between semantic predicate-argument relationships and surface word and phrase configurations by which they are expressed." Unlike semantically based theories such as generative semantics, LFG rejects the idea that predicate-argument structure directly determines (or is determined by) syntactic constituent structure (for defense of this position, see Grimshaw's 1979a treatment of concealed questions and its summary in Newmeyer 1983:10). However, LFG does see close connections between the number and kinds of arguments that a predicate takes (its "polyadicity"[25]) and the grammatical functions it can represent. For example, an argument is represented in predicate argument structure only if it can be associated with a grammatical function (hence the inherent semantic object of *homer,* 'to hit a home run (in baseball),' is not represented as an argument in predicate argument structure, while the inherent semantic object of *crane* in 'crane one's neck' is so represented. And an important principle in LFG is that of function-argument biuniqueness, which prevents the same grammatical function from being assigned to different predicate arguments and different grammatical functions from being assigned to the same predicate argument. Thus biuniqueness disallows, say, the subject of a sentence being represented by two noun phrases bearing different thematic roles or by a single argument functioning simultaneously as both subject and object. While this condition might appear superficially to resemble the Θ-Criterion of GB, the Θ-Criterion is, in fact, inexpressible in LFG: any rule that might have the potential to alter the polyadicity of a predicate (and thus be subject to the Θ-Criterion) would, by the principle of direct syntactic encoding, necessarily be a lexical rule.

The level of functional structure, at which the most important syntactic generalizations are expressed, is built up in several stages.[26] First, the constituent structure (c-structure) of the sentence is defined by a context-free phrase structure grammar whose major nodes are annotated in highly configurational languages such as English by the grammatical functions that they perform and in freer word order languages such as Latin in terms of morphological case (the exact mechanism for this annotation is determined by language-particular redundancy rules). Thus the c-structure for sentence (8.21a) can be represented by (8.21b).

(8.21)   a. *Fred handed a toy to the baby*

b.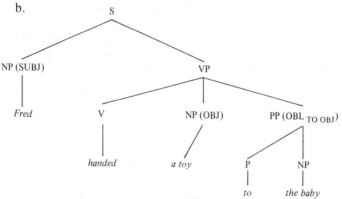

[25]Michael Covington (1983:405) suggests that "polyadicity" may be the only word in English analyzable as a prefix followed by three suffixes with no intervening root.
[26]The following account glosses over a number of important points of notation and terminology. For the most extensive overview of the mechanics of an LFG derivation, see Kaplan and Bresnan (1982).

Second, the grammatical functions of each lexical entry are linked with its predicate argument structure by lexical rules. For the verb *hand* in the example above, the following would result:

(8.22)

Functional structures (f-structures), which encode the meaningful grammatical relations of an entire sentence and provide sufficient information for the semantic component to determine the appropriate predicate-argument formulas, are built up from information provided by the lexicon and the c-structures. Each f-structure consists of two columns enclosed in large brackets. The left column contains attributes, the right column values. An attribute is the name of a grammatical function or feature (SUBJ, PRED, OBJ, NUM, CASE, etc.) and a value can be either a simple symbol, a semantic form governing the process of semantic interpretation, or can itself be a subsidiary f-structure representing complexes of internal functions. The f-structure for sentence (8.21a), for example, is represented by (8.23).

(8.23)

$$
\begin{bmatrix}
\text{SUBJ} & \begin{bmatrix} \text{PRED} & \text{'FRED'} \\ \text{SPEC} & \text{A} \\ \text{NUM} & \text{SG} \end{bmatrix} \\
\text{TENSE} & \text{PAST} \\
\text{PRED} & \text{'HAND} <\text{(SUBJ) (OBJ) (TO OBJ)}>\text{'} \\
\text{OBJ} & \begin{bmatrix} \text{PRED} & \text{'TOY'} \\ \text{SPEC} & \text{A} \\ \text{NUM} & \text{SG} \end{bmatrix} \\
\text{TO} & \begin{bmatrix} \text{PCASE} & \text{TO} \\ \text{OBJ} & \begin{bmatrix} \text{PRED} & \text{'BABY'} \\ \text{SPEC} & \text{THE} \\ \text{NUM} & \text{SG} \end{bmatrix} \end{bmatrix}
\end{bmatrix}
$$

Lexical rules operate strictly in terms of lexical information. Thus, given the existence of the "dativizing" rule (8.24a–b) in the grammar of English, it is predicted that a lexical entry containing the specifications (OBJ) and (TO OBJ) may have another entry in which (OBJ2) appears in place of (OBJ) and (OBJ) appears in place of (TO OBJ). In other words, the rule predicts the existence of both functional structure (8.25) as well as (8.23).

(8.24)   a. (OBJ) → (OBJ2)
          b. (TO OBJ) → (OBJ)

(8.25)

$$
\begin{bmatrix}
\text{SUBJ} & \begin{bmatrix} \text{PRED} & \text{`FRED'} \\ \text{SPEC} & \text{A} \\ \text{NUM} & \text{SG} \end{bmatrix} \\
\text{TENSE} & \text{PAST} \\
\text{PRED} & \text{`HAND} <(\text{SUBJ}) (\text{OBJ2}) (\text{OBJ})>' \\
\text{OBJ} & \begin{bmatrix} \text{PRED} & \text{`BABY'} \\ \text{SPEC} & \text{THE} \\ \text{NUM} & \text{SG} \end{bmatrix} \\
\text{OBJ2} & \begin{bmatrix} \text{PRED} & \text{`TOY'} \\ \text{SPEC} & \text{A} \\ \text{NUM} & \text{SG} \end{bmatrix}
\end{bmatrix}
$$

The level of f-structure, as should be apparent from (8.23) and (8.25), embodies no aspects of the syntactic constituency nor linear ordering of the elements in the sentence. Since such is a universal property of f-structures (indeed, f-structure attributes are invariant across languages, though in some languages not all are expressed), LFG claims that it can provide a more elegant account of nonconfigurational languages than can other frameworks, which demand that these notions be encoded at all syntactic levels (for the most extensive defense of this idea, see Mohanan 1982a).

The order-free nature of f-structure has led to the claim that it is a more suitable level for input to semantic interpretation than the logical-form level of GB or the surface constituency of GPSG. Exploiting this property, Halvorsen (1983) has proposed a detailed model-theoretic interpretation for f-structure and L. Levin (1982) has suggested that this level is optimal for stating constraints on discourse phenomena.

Many other phenomena accorded a configurational treatment in other frameworks are handled at f-structure under LFG. Perhaps the most important is control. In her detailed treatment of this phenomenon, Bresnan proposes the control hierarchy in (8.26) for English (1982a:322).

(8.26)   OBJ2 > OBJ > SUBJ

That is, if there is an OBJ2, it will be the controller. If there is an OBJ, but no OBJ2, the former will be the controller. Otherwise, the SUBJ is the controller. This treatment extends to an explanation of Visser's generalization, namely, that verbs whose complements are predicated of their subjects do not passivize (see Visser 1963–1973, part III.2:2118). Note the following contrast:

(8.27)   a. *He strikes his friends as pompous*
           b. **His friends are struck (by him) as pompous*

(8.28)   a. *Mary promised Frank to leave*
         b. **Frank was promised to leave (by Mary)*

Since the lexical rule of Passive turns a SUBJ into an oblique object, which cannot be a controller, it follows that the passive form of a subject-control verb will not be able to control the understood subject of its complement.

The treatment of "long-distance" dependencies involving displaced *Wh*-phrases and topicalized phrases remains the least worked out aspect of LFG. Topicalized phrases and fronted *wh*-phrases are base generated in their surface positions and associated with the functions TOPIC and FOCUS, respectively. Dependencies are then stated as binding relations between these functions and the grammatical functions representing the gap; constraints are expressed by particular syntactic configurations or lexical items blocking binding between the two.[27]

Practitioners of LFG have followed the spirit of Bresnan's "Realistic Transformational Grammar" paper in defending the model on psycholinguistic grounds. Supporting evidence for LFG has been adduced from the area of first language acquisition (Pinker 1982, 1984), language comprehension (Ford, Bresnan, and Kaplan 1982), and language production (Ford 1982). LFG places an extremely strong (and controversial) condition on grammatical models, the strong competence hypothesis: every rule of the grammar must be interpreted in a model of some behavior (Bresnan and Kaplan 1982:xxxi). As one might expect, Bresnan and Kaplan argue that of all grammatical frameworks, only LFG obeys this condition.

LFG accounts have now been provided for about two dozen languages. Perhaps the most extensively treated outside of English is Modern Icelandic (Zaenen 1980; L. Levin and Simpson 1981; Andrews 1982a, 1982b; Zaenen, Maling, and Thráinsson 1985). The complex interplay between surface case, grammatical functions, and constituent structure in that language seems ideally suited for exhibiting the various mechanisms of LFG in their fullest flower. Other studies have dealt with Russian case agreement (Neidle 1982), Malayalam relational structure (Mohanan 1982a), Romance reflexive clitics (Grimshaw 1982), Warlpiri control (Simpson and Bresnan 1982), Japanese anaphora (Kameyama 1985), Japanese complex predicates (Ishikawa 1985), and English auxiliaries (Falk 1984).

Most of the important papers in LFG are assembled in two collections: Bresnan (1982b) and L. Levin, Rappaport, and Zaenen (1983).

8.5. THE CURRENT DEBATE WITHIN GENERATIVE SYNTAX

In the United States today, somewhat more than two-thirds of the generative syntactic analyses published adopt the GB framework, about one-fifth GPSG, and

---

[27]In a major revision of the LFG account of long-distance dependencies, Zaenen (forthcoming) states island constraints in terms of functional information.

the remainder RG, LFG, and other frameworks too recently developed or commanding too few supporters to merit discussion here.[28] Outside of the United States, GB commands an even larger slice of the generative syntactic pie.

The first question one must address is why GB is so popular. The obvious answer is to attribute its success wholly or largely to Chomsky's influence. One might take it for granted that a syntactician would naturally gravitate into Chomsky's orbit, given his persuasiveness, his fame, and his charisma. However, the obvious answer is seriously flawed, as a review of earlier developments attests. Twice in the past have linguists flocked away from Chomsky and his current framework. In the late 1960s, after the publication of *Aspects of the Theory of Syntax,* Chomsky's prestige was at its peak. Yet, as we have seen, by 1970 he hardly had a supporter outside of his home institution. In the late 1970s, as the EST became bogged down in the Filters and Control phase, there was a corresponding drift to other frameworks, albeit not as dramatic a one as earlier. Clearly, Chomsky waves no magic wand that places the linguists of the world under his spell.

GB is popular, first and foremost, because a great number of syntacticians find its premises convincing and its results impressive. What other explanations could there be for the fact that more than a few established linguists, who have no need to adopt one particular framework in order to appease a Ph.D. or tenure committee, have taken the initiative to learn the intricacies of the framework and publish analyses in it?[29]

Many have found the most exciting aspect of GB to lie at the heart of its research program: the "tinker-toy" approach to linguistic complexity, which involves stripping language down to a half dozen or so component parts and reassembling these parts in slightly different ways to derive the particulars of individual languages. And the special lure is that anybody can do it, at least anybody who has invested the time to master *LGB*s 371 densely packed pages. GB gives the second-year graduate student the opportunity to be a theoretician who can discover a new parameter or modify an already proposed one in the light of data from another language. GPSG and LFG, by contrast, whose research programs give priority to detailed analyses of specific constructions, are perceived by many students to offer them little more than a chance to tinker with formalism or apply current formalism to a new set of facts.

The GB research program of concentrating on the big picture at the expense of constructing formalized grammar fragments has been subject to a barrage of criticism. Partisans of every alternative framework have lit into Chomsky for his indisputable deemphasis of formalism. Criticisms have ranged from Cooper's respectfully phrased observation that "if we collect a huge set of examples without trying to formalize grammars to account for them, I think we might be preparing

---

[28]Four of which are the theories of binding and fusion (Brame 1981), phrase linking grammar (Peters 1982), function unification grammar (Kay 1985), and tree adjoining grammar (Kroch and Joshi 1985). Categorial grammar is also enjoying a renewal of interest (Bach 1983; Flynn 1983; Steedman 1985; Oehrle, Bach, and Wheeler 1986).

[29]See, for example, Chung (1983), Contreras (1984a), Kenstowicz (1984), Bickerton (1985), McCloskey (1985), and Newmeyer (1986b).

more headaches than anything else for future generations of linguists" (1980:20) to Gadzar, Klein, Pullum, and Sag's refusal to apply the label "generative grammar" to GB, since it gives "few signs of any commitment to the explicit specification of grammars or theoretical principles in this genre of linguistics" (1985:6).

Chomsky has defended his inattention to formalism by asserting that the principles that engage him do not lend themselves at the current time to it (1982a:28) and remarks, "I do not see any point in formalizing for the sake of formalizing. You can always do that" (1982a:101).[30] But his opponents are quick to argue that this inattentiveness to formal detail gives GB a deceptive simplicity, which, given Chomsky's penchant for rhetorical flourishes, has given the field the impression that it has accomplished far more than is actually the case. As a consequence, a literary genre has developed whose goal is to demolish GB by attempting to make precise some of its plausibly exaggerated claims about its accomplishments within a particular domain and to show that they lead to internal self-contradictions or false predictions. Geoffrey Pullum, the undisputed master of this genre, has thus taken GB to task for its oft-repeated claim that its principles explain the thorny facts governing the contraction of *want to* to *wanna* (see Postal and Pullum 1982, 1986 and the citations therein), for its (astounding) claim that there are a finite number of core grammars (Pullum 1983),[31] and for conveying the impression that there actually exists a coherent X-bar theory, whose central features GB has been able to derive from framework-internal principles (Pullum 1985a).

And yet, this line of attack on GB has proved singularly unsuccessful at daunting its supporters. The reason is simple: the short-term goal of GB is not to provide a descriptive account of all the facts pertaining to some circumscribed domain of grammar, rather it is to probe the properties of universal grammar. Such a goal involves, of course, calling attention to suggestive facts from diverse areas of grammar and, needless to say, ultimately GB hopes to derive the full set of linguistic facts from a small set of basic principles (to the extent that it is possible to do so). Nevertheless, Chomsky and other GB practitioners feel that, given our present knowledge, the kind of descriptive detail demanded by their critics is premature. Thus Postal and Pullum's irony-laden charge that GB seems to have achieved "descriptive failure, but explanatory 'success' " (1982:134) does not squarely address the heart of the GB strategy. Aoun and Lightfoot note in response that Postal and Pullum

---

[30]Contrast these remarks with the following from the Preface to *Syntactic Structures:*

The search for rigorous formulation in linguistics has a much more serious motivation than mere concern for logical niceties or the desire to purify well-established methods of linguistic analysis. Precisely constructed models for linguistic structure can play an important role, both negative and positive, in the process of discovery itself. By pushing a precise but inadequate formulation to an unacceptable conclusion, we can often expose the exact source of this inadequacy and, consequently, gain a deeper understanding of the linguistic data. More positively, a formalized theory may automatically provide solutions for many problems other than those for which it was explicitly designed. (1957:5)

[31]The finiteness claim is presented in Chomsky (1981:12) and (1982b:13).

find it theoretically suspicious that trace theory advocates can claim to have achieved explanatory success when in fact their descriptions fail. We would argue that one can explain some facts even if others are left undescribed; it is unreasonable to say that one has no explanation until all facts are described. In order to have an explanation (of greater or lesser depth) one needs to describe the RELEVANT facts. It is important to note that there is no theory-independent way of establishing which facts are relevant. (1984:472)

Furthermore, GB supporters point to the vast arrays of new facts that keep being discovered in studies carried out in the GB research paradigm on countless languages and assert that GB is overwhelmingly more productive in bringing new facts into the literature than any other framework. Moreover, because of GBs approach to parametric variation, new facts cited from an exotic language are more likely to have repercussions for established analyses of other languages than they are likely to have in GPSG or LFG.

The Aoun–Lightfoot response is rare; by and large GB supporters have ignored criticism from other frameworks and rarely acknowledge that opposition demands to be taken seriously. Such is perhaps natural, given their numerical advantage. A feeling among many GB supporters is that GPSG, LFG, and the other surface-oriented frameworks are just a (small) step up from being empiricist approaches to language, bogged down in superficial detail, and lacking a genuine commitment to the construction of an explanatory theory.[32] This is unfair, however: abstract explanatory principles abound in both GPSG and LFG. Nevertheless, their research program does open them to the charge and no doubt deters potential supporters from adopting their framework.

One factor that confuses the interframework debate is the proper treatment of semantics. Chomsky has always taken a hard-and-fast stand against truth-conditional approaches to meaning and sees no place for its constructs within a theory of language.[33] He is willing to admit a few indisputably semantic notions such as thematic roles into linguistic theory, but is otherwise reluctant to acknowledge that linguists have much at all to say about meaning. Indeed, it seems fair to say that Chomsky holds to some version of a use theory of meaning, which allows for a rich grammatical component to language, as well as a set of pragmatic principles (perhaps of a Gricean sort), but no discrete semantics at all.

One selling point of the rival frameworks (in particular GPSG) is their commitment to formal semantics. Yet, there is no question that Chomsky's view of meaning can easily be divorced from the approach he takes to grammatical theory. There is no reason why a model-theoretic account of meaning could not be grafted into GB, just as it has been incorporated into GPSG and LFG. And, in fact, there are

---

[32]No comprehensive GB critique of GPSG exists. However, the GPSG claim that the restrictiveness of that theory leads ipso facto to a more adequate theory of language is challenged in Chomsky (1982a:65) and Berwick and Weinberg (1982). The major GB-oriented critiques of LFG are Berwick and Weinberg (1984), in which the LFG claim to be a psychologically realistic theory is rejected and Marantz (1984) and Williams (1984), which argue against grammatical relations being primitives.

[33]See Chomsky (1975b, 1979:141–144, 1982a:90–94) and Hornstein (1984) for an approach to semantics quite similar in spirit to Chomsky's.

linguists who have begun to carry out just such a program (see Enç 1983; Heim 1982). Nevertheless, a popular perception is that the GB package includes a rejection of currently popular semantic approaches, a perception that has boosted the fortunes of the opponents of that framework.

The fortunes of GPSG and LFG have also been boosted by the perception—in this case, a correct one—that these models are more computationally tractable than GB, that is, that they are more amenable to computer applications. For example, computer scientists in private industry, in cooperation with linguists, have written programs that process written English well enough to understand questions of some degree of complexity, to search for an answer to them in a computerized data base, and to respond in written English. Overwhelmingly, it has been the formalized theories of GPSG and LFG that have been applied to this task, not GB. While generativists of all persuasions are rejoicing that the principles of this approach to language are being applied successfully to practical goals (as well as creating new jobs for those trained in them), many see the danger that for the first time the needs of industry could significantly distort the nature of basic research in the field. This would happen, of course, if students perceived that their developing proficiency in a linguistically and psychologically inadequate framework would help insure them a decently paying job upon graduation. And disturbingly, at least one case has been reported of students at a GB-oriented department requesting that an introduction to GPSG be added to the curriculum for this very reason.

The danger should not be exaggerated, however. There is no inherent defect of GB that renders it in principle useless for computer applications, and, in fact, Wehrli (1983) has developed and implemented a GB-based parser for French. As work within GB advances, and with it the requisite degree of formalism, such applications will no doubt increase.

When one considers the number of seemingly plausible approaches to grammar (to say nothing of the possible ones), GB, GPSG, and LFG are really very close to each other. Certainly the distance between these frameworks is incomparably less than that between generative and interpretive semantics 15 years ago. Its partisans attend the same conferences, can (and do) make helpful suggestions about each other's work, and are often able to incorporate specific generalizations from one framework into another with ease. While it is, perhaps, premature to speak of a convergence of research lines within generative syntax, the distance between the various approaches is, in any event, growing no greater.

8.6. THE STATUS OF GENERATIVE GRAMMAR

This study was focused almost entirely on developments within generative grammar, while ignoring the question of the changing status of generative grammar as a whole within the field of linguistics. It seems appropriate, therefore, to conclude our discussion with some remarks addressed to this latter point.

As has already been noted, the 1960s were heady days for generative grammar, as it quickly surpassed the once-hegemonic post-Bloomfieldian approach in importance and triggered new research programs in fields as diverse as philosophy, psychology, language pedagogy, anthropology, and computer science. But the next decade saw a decline in its relative importance, both within linguistics as a whole and among those outside it who wished to apply the conceptions and results of the field to their own concerns. This was partly a function of its rather narrow domain of investigation, which was disquieting to those students of language whose interests were broader than the working out of the principles governing grammatical patterning. The political atmosphere of the late 1960s and early 1970s contributed to this feeling of discontent and was a major factor in drawing many serious students of language into adopting the generative semantic program, which, by combining work on formal grammar with concern for the use of language in the real world, promised to satisfy their intellectual interests as well as the demands of their social conscience. George Lakoff was undoubtedly correct when he wrote, "Nowadays students are interested in generative semantics because it is a way for them to investigate the nature of human thought and social interaction" (1974a:172). Not surprisingly, then, in this period the proportion of students attracted to sociolinguistics grew relatively faster than did that attracted to generative grammar, with a consequent relative decline in importance of the latter.

The 1970s also saw the growth of a functionalist alternative to generative grammar (for representative work, see the volumes edited by Charles Li 1975, 1976, 1977). While functionalism had always been an important trend in Europe, it is only in this period that the attempt began in earnest in the United States to bypass formal grammar in favor of an approach that attempted to ground grammatical patterning in communicative function.

At the same time, many scholars outside the field became disillusioned with generative grammar. For example, the hoped-for payoffs in improved methods of language teaching did not materialize, leading some to the conclusion that the Chomskyan view of language was seriously flawed; naturally a misconceived theory could not be expected to lead to fruitful applications. John Lamendella (1969) offered a popular explanation for the failure of the attempted applications: transformational generative grammar was simply "irrelevant" to pedagogy.

While applied linguists deplored the theory's seeming inability to aid language teaching, psycholinguists began to express increasing dissatisfaction with Chomsky's claims about the innate basis of grammar. Alternative hypotheses were formulated that, it was hoped, could deal with the same range of facts without the need for the innate syntactic principles that many found jarring to common sense. In the early 1970s, more and more psycholinguists abandoned Chomsky's conception of innate grammatical universals and turned to the Piagetian idea that language acquisition results from the interaction of all-purpose cognitive skills with external environmental stimuli.

As a result of the combined weight of the above factors, the prestige of generative grammar fell to an all-time low around 1975. Since then, its relative importance within the field has gradually increased. The greatest part of its renewed success must be attributed to advances in the theory of grammar. The government–binding theory, in particular, by succeeding in unifying a number of disparate and seemingly recalcitrant grammatical phenomena into a conceptually simple and elegant overall framework of principles, attracted the interest of many of those who had dismissed the importance of formal grammar and had turned instead to other ways of looking at language.

Dramatic developments within psycholinguistics and neurolinguistics as well have led to rekindled interest in generative grammar.[34] Recent discoveries have provided independent corroboration for the generativist view that the form of language exists independently of its content (i.e., competence independently of performance), thereby shattering the functionalist view that the two are inseparable. For example, neurologists have found that the grammatical properties of language are represented in the brain separately from its functional properties, including those pragmatic aspects that generativists would ascribe to performance. Under pathological conditions, form and function can even become disassociated from each other; many cases are documented in which, as a result of some cerebral trauma, a patient has maintained grammatical abilities, yet has lost the ability to use language communicatively, or vice versa. Psychologists report cases of abnormal language acquisition, where form and function have become dissociated. Such findings have suggested to many that a generative grammar is more than the product of the manipulation of a set of arcane symbols—it is a model of the human language faculty.

As a result of these developments, the position of generative grammar is more secure than at any time since the 1960s. In the United States, a substantial majority of those committed to the explanation of grammatical phenomena take its basic premises for granted. Outside the United States, far fewer do so, though the percentage has increased substantially in the past decade.

But the impact of generative grammar cannot be measured simply by the percentage of linguists who practice it. A better measure is the fact that any linguist, not just in the United States, but abroad as well, who wishes to put forward a new theory of language feels obligated to demonstrate how that theory is superior to the generativist one. Judging from the lack of success enjoyed by the alternatives to generative grammar, it seems reasonable to conclude that the research program based on the idea that at the center of language lies an autonomous competence characterized by formal, discrete, and interacting rules and constraints will direct the field for years to come.

[34]The subject matter of this paragraph is e   . See also
Newmeyer (1986a) for commentary on the rela   he field of
linguistics.

References

Abbott, Barbara. 1982. "Isomorphic Structure Preservation." *Linguistic Analysis* 10:119–130.

Aissen, Judith. 1973. "Shifty Objects in Spanish." *Papers from the Ninth Regional Meeting of the Chicago Linguistic Society*, pp. 11–22.

Aissen, Judith. 1974. "Verb Raising." *Linguistic Inquiry* 5:325–366.

Aissen, Judith. 1983. "Indirect Object Advancement in Tzotzil." In *Studies in Relational Grammar 1*, edited by D. Perlmutter, pp. 272–302.

Aissen, Judith. 1984. "Theme and Absolutives: Some Semantic Rules in Tzotzil." In *Syntax and Semantics 16: The Syntax of Native American Languages*, edited by E. D. Cook and D. Gerdts, pp. 1–20. New York: Academic Press.

Aissen, Judith, and Hankamer, Jorge. 1972. "Shifty Subjects: A Conspiracy in Syntax?" *Linguistic Inquiry* 3:501–504.

Aissen, Judith, and Perlmutter, David. 1976. "Clause Reduction in Spanish." *Papers from the Second Annual Meeting of the Berkeley Linguistics Society*, pp. 1–30.

Ajdukiewicz, Kasimierz. 1935. "Die Syntaktische Konnexität." *Studia Philosophica* 1:1–27.

Akmajian, Adrian. 1984. "Sentence Types and the Form-Function Fit." *Natural Language and Linguistic Theory* 2:1–24.

Akmajian, Adrian, and Heny, Frank. 1975. *An Introduction to the Principles of Transformational Syntax*. Cambridge, MA: MIT Press.

Allen, Cynthia. 1980. "Movement and Deletion in Old English." *Linguistic Inquiry* 11:261–324.

Allen, Harold B., ed. 1958. *Readings in Applied English Linguistics*. New York: Appleton-Century-Crofts.

Allen, Margaret. 1978. *Morphological Investigations*. Ph.D. dissertation, University of Connecticut.

Allwood, Jens. 1976. *Linguistic Communication in Action and Cooperation*. Gothenberg Monographs in Linguistics 2.

Allwood, Jens. 1977. "A Critical Look at Speech Act Theory." In *Logic, Pragmatics, and Grammar*, edited by Östen Dahl, pp. 53–59. University of Gothenberg, Department of Linguistics.

Anderson, John. 1971. *The Grammar of Case: Towards a Localist Theory*. London: Cambridge University Press.

Anderson, John. 1977. *On Case Grammar*. London: Croom Helm.

Anderson, Stephen. 1971a. "On the Linguistic Status of the Performative/Constative Distinction." Indiana University Linguistics Club Publication.

Anderson, Stephen. 1971b. "On the Role of Deep Structure in Semantic Interpretation." *Foundations of Language* 7:387–396.

Anderson, Stephen. 1976 (1967). "Concerning the Notion 'Base Component of a Transformational Grammar.' " In *Syntax and Semantics*, vol. 7, edited by James McCawley, pp. 113–128. New York: Academic Press.

Anderson, Stephen. 1977. "Comments on the Paper by Wasow." In *Formal Syntax*, edited by Peter Culicover, *et al.*, pp. 361–378. New York: Academic Press.

Anderson, Stephen. 1981. "Why Phonology Isn't 'Natural.' " *Linguistic Inquiry* 12:493–540.

Anderson, Stephen. 1984. "Where's Morphology?" *Linguistic Inquiry* 13:571–612.

Anderson, Stephen. 1985. *Phonology in the Twentieth Century*. Chicago: University of Chicago Press.

Anderson, Stephen, and Chung, Sandra. 1977. "On Grammatical Relations and Clause Structure in Verb-Initial Languages." In *Syntax and Semantics*, vol. 8, edited by Peter Cole and Jerrold Sadock, pp. 1–26. New York: Academic Press.

Anderson, Stephen, and Keenan, Edward. 1985. "Deixis." In *Language Typology and Syntactic Description Volume III: Grammatical Categories and the Lexicon*, edited by Timothy Shopen, pp. 259–308. Cambridge: Cambridge University Press.

Anderson, Stephen, and Kiparsky, Paul, eds. 1973. *A Festschrift for Morris Halle*. New York: Holt, Rinehart and Winston.

Andrews, Avery. 1971. "Case Agreement of Predicate Modifiers in Ancient Greek." *Linguistic Inquiry* 2:127–152.

Andrews, Avery. 1982a. "Long Distance Agreement in Modern Icelandic." In *The Nature of Syntactic Representation*, edited by Pauline Jacobson and Geoffrey Pullum, pp. 1–34. Dordrecht: Reidel.

Andrews, Avery. 1982b. "The Representation of Case in Modern Icelandic." In *The Mental Representation of Grammatical Relations*, edited by Joan Bresnan, pp. 427–503. Cambridge, MA: MIT Press.

Aoun, Joseph. 1982. "On the Logical Nature of the Binding Principles." *Proceedings of NELS 12*, pp. 16–35.

Aoun, Joseph. 1983. "A Symmetric Theory of Anaphoric Relations." *Proceedings of NELS 13*, pp. 1–10.

Aoun, Joseph. 1985. *A Grammar of Anaphora*. Cambridge, MA: MIT Press.

Aoun, Joseph, Hornstein, Norbert, and Sportiche, Dominique. 1981. "Some Aspects of Wide Scope Quantification." *Journal of Linguistic Research* 1:69–96.

Aoun, Joseph, and Lightfoot, David. 1984. "Government and Contraction." *Linguistic Inquiry* 15:465–473.

Aoun, Joseph, and Sportiche, Dominique. 1983. "On the Formal Theory of Government." *Linguistic Review* 2:211–236.

Aronoff, Mark. 1976. *Word Formation in Generative Grammar*. Cambridge, MA: MIT Press.

Atlas, J. D. and Levinson, Stephen. 1981. "*It*-Clefts, Informativeness, and Logical Form: Radical Pragmatics (Revised Standard Version)." In *Radical Pragmatics*, edited by Peter Cole, pp. 1–61. New York: Academic Press.

Austin, J. L. 1962. *How to Do Things with Words*. Oxford: Oxford University Press.

Bach, Emmon. 1962. "The Order of Elements in a Transformational Grammar of German." *Language* 38:263–269.

Bach, Emmon. 1964a. *An Introduction to Transformational Grammars*. New York: Holt, Rinehart and Winston.

Bach, Emmon. 1964b. "Subcategories in Transformational Grammars." In *Proceedings of the Ninth International Congress of Linguists*, edited by H. Lunt, pp. 672–677. The Hague: Mouton.

Bach, Emmon. 1965. "Structural Linguistics and the Philosophy of Science." *Diogenes* 51:111–128.

Bach, Emmon. 1968. "Nouns and Noun Phrases." In *Universals in Linguistic Theory*, edited by Emmon Bach and Robert Harms, pp. 91–124. New York: Holt, Rinehart and Winston.

Bach, Emmon. 1970. "Problominalization." *Linguistic Inquiry* 1:121–122.

Bach, Emmon. 1976. "An Extension of Classical Transformational Grammar." In *Problems in Linguistic Metatheory*. East Lansing, MI: Michigan State University.

Bach, Emmon. 1977a. "Comments on the Paper by Chomsky." In *Formal Syntax,* edited by Peter Culicover, Thomas Wasow, and Adrian Akmajian, pp. 133–156. New York: Academic Press.

Bach, Emmon. 1977b (1974). " 'The Position of Embedding Transformations in a Grammar' Revisited." In *Linguistic Structures Processing,* edited by A. Zampolli, pp. 31–54. New York: North-Holland.

Bach, Emmon. 1979. "Control in Montague Grammar." *Linguistic Inquiry* 10:515–532.

Bach, Emmon. 1983. "Generalized Categorial Grammars and the English Auxiliary." In *Linguistic Categories,* edited by F. Heny and B. Richards, pp. 101–120. Dordrecht: Reidel.

Bach, Emmon, and Cooper, Robin. 1978. "The NP-S Analysis of Relative Clauses and Compositional Semantics." *Linguistics and Philosophy* 2:145–150.

Bach, Emmon, and Harms, Robert, eds. 1968. *Universals in Linguistic Theory.* New York: Holt, Rinehart and Winston.

Bach, Emmon, and Horn, George. 1976. "Remarks on 'Conditions on Transformations.' " *Linguistic Inquiry* 7:265–279.

Bach, Kent, and Harnish, Robert. 1979. *Linguistic Communication and Speech Acts.* Cambridge, MA: MIT Press.

Bailey, Charles-James, and Shuy, Roger, eds. 1973. *New Ways of Analyzing Variation in English.* Washington: Georgetown University Press.

Baker, C. L. 1970a. "Double Negatives." *Linguistic Inquiry* 1:169–186.

Baker, C. L. 1970b. "Notes on the Descriptions of English Questions: The Role of an Abstract Question Morpheme." *Foundations of Language* 6:179–219.

Baker, C. L. 1979. "Syntactic Theory and the Projection Problem." *Linguistic Inquiry* 10:533–582.

Baker, C. L., and Brame, Michael. 1972. "Global Rules: A Rejoinder." *Language* 48:51–77.

Baker, C. L., and McCarthy, John, eds. *The Logical Problem of Language Acquisition.* Cambridge, MA: MIT Press.

Baker, Mark. 1985. "The Mirror Principle and Morphosyntactic Explanation." *Linguistic Inquiry* 16:373–416.

Baltin, Mark. 1978. *Toward a Theory of Movement Rules.* Ph.D. dissertation, MIT.

Baltin, Mark. 1982. "A Landing Site Theory of Movement Rules." *Linguistic Inquiry* 13:1–38.

Banfield, Ann. 1973a. "Narrative Style and the Grammar of Direct and Indirect Speech." *Foundations of Language* 10:1–40.

Banfield, Ann. 1973b. *Stylistic Transformations in "Paradise Lost."* Ph.D. dissertation, University of Wisconsin.

Bar-Hillel, Yehoshua. 1953. "A Quasi-Arithmetical Notation for Syntactic Description." *Language* 29:47–58.

Bar-Hillel, Yehoshua. 1970. *Aspects of Language.* Amsterdam: North-Holland.

Belletti, Adriana. 1982. " 'Morphological' Passive and Pro-Drop: The Impersonal Construction in Italian." *Journal of Linguistic Research* 2:1–34.

Belletti, Adriana, Brandi, Luciana, and Rizzi, Luigi, eds. 1981. *Theory of Markedness in Generative Grammar.* Pisa: Scoula Normale Superiore di Pisa.

Belletti, Adriana, and Rizzi, Luigi. 1981. "The Syntax of "ne": Some Theoretical Implications." *Linguistic Review* 1:117–154.

Bennis, Hans. 1981. "A Note on Government and Binding." In *Levels of Syntactic Representation,* edited by J. Koster and R. May, pp. 1–8. Dordrecht: Foris.

Bennis, Hans, and Hoekstra, Teun. 1985. "Parasitic Gaps in Dutch." *Proceedings of NELS 15,* pp. 1–14.

Berman, Arlene. 1974. "On the VSO Hypothesis." *Linguistic Inquiry* 5:1–37.

Berman, Arlene, and Szamosi, Michael. 1972. "Observations on Sentential Stress." *Language* 48:304–325.

Berwick, Robert, and Weinberg, Amy. 1982. "Parsing Efficiency, Computational Complexity, and the Evaluation of Grammatical Theories." *Linguistic Inquiry* 13:165–192.

Berwick, Robert, and Weinberg, Amy. 1984. *The Grammatical Basis of Linguistic Performance.* Cambridge, MA: MIT Press.

Bever, Thomas. 1974. "The Ascent of the Specious; or, There's a Lot We Don't Know about Mirrors." In *Explaining Linguistic Phenomena,* edited by David Cohen, pp. 173–200. Washington, DC: Hemisphere.

Bever, Thomas. 1975. "Functional Explanations Require Independently Motivated Functional Theories." In *Papers from the Parasession on Functionalism,* edited by Robin Grossman, L. J. San, and Timothy Vance, pp. 580–609.

Bever, Thomas, Katz, Jerrold, and Langendoen, D. Terence, eds. 1976. *An Integrated Theory of Linguistic Ability.* New York: Crowell.

Bickerton, Derek. 1985. "Argument Domains as Binding Categories." *Proceedings of the Fourth West Coast Conference on Formal Linguistics* (in press).

Bierwisch, Manfred, and Heidolph, Karl, eds. 1970. *Progress in Linguistics.* The Hague: Mouton.

Bloch, Bernard. 1941. "Phonemic Overlapping." *American Speech* 16:278–284. Reprinted in *Readings in Linguistics,* edited by Martin Joos (1958), pp. 93–96. Washington: American Council of Learned Societies.

Bloch, Bernard. 1946. "Studies in Colloquial Japanese II: Syntax." *Language* 22:200–248. Reprinted in *Readings in Linguistics,* edited by Martin Joos (1958), pp. 154–185. Washington: American Council of Learned Societies.

Bloch, Bernard. 1947. "English Verb Inflection." *Language* 23:399–418. Reprinted in *Readings in Linguistics,* edited by Martin Joos (1958), pp. 243–254. Washington: American Council of Learned Societies.

Bloch, Bernard. 1948. "A Set of Postulates for Phonemic Analysis." *Language* 24:3–46.

Bloch, Bernard. 1950. "Studies in Colloquial Japanese IV: Phonemics." *Language* 26:86–125.

Bloomfield, Leonard. 1933. *Language.* New York: Holt, Rinehart and Winston.

Bloomfield, Leonard. 1939a. *Linguistic Aspects of Science. International Encyclopedia of Unified Science,* vol. 1, no. 4. Chicago: University of Chicago Press.

Bloomfield, Leonard. 1939b. "Menomini Morphophonemics." *Travaux du Cercle Linguistique de Prague* 8:105–115.

Boër, Steven, and Lycan, William. 1976. *The Myth of Semantic Presupposition.* Indiana University Linguistics Club Publication.

Boër, Steven, and Lycan, William. 1980. "A Performadox in Truth-Conditional Semantics." *Linguistics and Philosophy* 4:71–100.

Bolinger, Dwight. 1972. "Accent Is Predictable (If You're a Mind–Reader)." *Language* 48:633–644.

Bolinger, Dwight. 1977. "Another Glance at Main Clause Phenomena." *Language* 53:511–519.

Boole, George. 1854. *The Laws of Thought.* London: Walton.

Borer, Hagit. 1980. "Empty Subjects in Modern Hebrew and Constraints on Thematic Relations." *Proceedings of NELS 10,* pp. 25–38.

Borer, Hagit. 1984a. *Parametric Syntax.* Dordrecht: Foris.

Borer, Hagit. 1984b. "The Projection Principle and Rules of Morphology." *Proceedings of NELS 14,* pp. 16–33.

Borkin, Ann. 1972. "Where the Rules Fail: A Student's Guide. An Unauthorized Appendix to M. K. Burt's *From Deep to Surface Structure.*" Indiana University Linguistics Club Publication.

Borsley, Robert. 1981. "*Wh*-Movement and Unbounded Deletion in Polish Equatives." *Journal of Linguistics* 17:271–288.

Borsley, Robert. 1983. "A Welsh Agreement Process and the Status of VP and S." In *Order, Concord, and Constituency,* edited by Gerald Gazdar, Ewen Klein, and Geoffrey Pullum, pp. 57–74. Dordrecht: Foris.

Bouchard, Denis. 1984. *On the Content of Empty Categories.* Dordrecht: Foris.

Bouchard, Denis. 1985. "The Binding Theory and the Notion of Accessible SUBJECT." *Linguistic Inquiry* 16:117–134.

Bowers, John. 1970. "A Note on 'Remind.'" *Linguistic Inquiry* 1: 559–560.

Brame, Michael. 1976. *Conjectures and Refutations in Syntax and Semantics.* New York: North-Holland.

Brame, Michael. 1978a. *Base Generated Syntax.* Seattle: Noit Amrofer Press.

Brame, Michael. 1978b. "Binding and Discourse without Transformations." *Linguistic Analysis* 4:321–360.

Brame, Michael. 1979. "Realistic Grammar." Paper presented at the Conference on Current Approaches to Syntax, Milwaukee, Wisconsin.

Brame, Michael. 1981. "The General Theory of Binding and Fusion." *Linguistic Analysis* 7:277–325.

Brekle, H. E. 1969. Review of N. Chomsky, *Cartesian Linguistics. Linguistics* 49:74–91.

Bresnan, Joan. 1970a. "An Argument against Pronominalization." *Linguistic Inquiry* 1:122–123.

Bresnan, Joan. 1970b. "On Complementizers: Towards a Syntactic Theory of Complement Types." *Foundations of Language* 6:297–321.

Bresnan, Joan. 1971a. "Contraction and the Transformational Cycle in English." Unpublished manuscript.

Bresnan, Joan. 1971b. "Sentence Stress and Syntactic Transformations." *Language* 47:257–281.

Bresnan, Joan. 1972a. "Stress and Syntax: A Reply." *Language* 48:326–342.

Bresnan, Joan. 1972b. *Theory of Complementation in English Syntax.* Ph.D. dissertation, MIT.

Bresnan, Joan. 1975. "Comparative Deletion and Constraints on Transformations." *Linguistic Analysis* 1:25–74.

Bresnan, Joan. 1976a. "Evidence for a Theory of Unbounded Transformations." *Linguistic Analysis* 2:353–394.

Bresnan, Joan. 1976b. "Nonarguments for Raising." *Linguistic Inquiry* 7:485–501.

Bresnan, Joan. 1976c. "On the Form and Functioning of Transformations." *Linguistic Inquiry* 7:3–40.

Bresnan, Joan. 1977. "Variables in the Theory of Transformations." In *Formal Syntax,* edited by Peter Culicover, Thomas Wasow, and Adrian Akmajian, pp. 157–196. New York: Academic Press.

Bresnan, Joan. 1978. "A Realistic Transformational Grammar." In *Linguistic Theory and Psychological Reality,* edited by Morris Halle, Joan Bresnan, and George Miller, pp. 1–59. Cambridge, MA: MIT Press.

Bresnan, Joan. 1982a. "Control and Complementation." In *The Mental Representation of Grammatical Relations,* edited by Joan Bresnan, pp. 282–390. Cambridge, Massachusetts: MIT Press. Also published in *Linguistic Inquiry* 13:343–434.

Bresnan, Joan, ed. 1982b. *The Mental Representation of Grammatical Relations.* Cambridge, MA: MIT Press.

Bresnan, Joan. 1982c. "The Passive in Lexical Theory." In *The Mental Representation of Grammatical Relations,* edited by Joan Bresnan, pp. 3–86. Cambridge, MA: MIT Press.

Bresnan, Joan and Kaplan, Ronald M. 1982. "Introduction." In *The Mental Representation of Grammatical Relations,* edited by Joan Bresnan, pp. i–lii. Cambridge, MA: MIT Press.

Bresnan, Joan, Kaplan, Ronald M., Peters, Stanley, and Zaenen, Annie, 1982. "Cross-Serial Dependencies in Dutch." *Linguistic Inquiry* 13:613–636.

Bright, William. 1975. "Editor's Report." *LSA Bulletin* 64:11–14.

Brody, Michael. 1985. "On the Complementary Distribution of Empty Categories." *Linguistic Inquiry* 16:505–546.

Burt, Marina. 1971. *From Deep to Surface Structure.* New York: Harper and Row.

Burzio, Luigi. 1985. *Italian Syntax: A Government-Binding Approach.* Dordrecht: Reidel.

Byrne, Francis. 1985. "Pro-arb in Saramaccan." *Linguistic Inquiry* 16:313–319.

Cantrall, William. 1970. "If You Hiss or Anything, I'll Do It Back." *Papers from the Sixth Regional Meeting of the Chicago Linguistic Society,* pp. 168–177.

Carden, Guy. 1968. "English Quantifiers." In *The Computation Laboratory of Harvard University, Mathematical Linguistics and Automatic Translation,* Report No. NSF-20 to the National Science Foundation, pp. IX1–IX45.

Carden, Guy. 1982. "Backwards Anaphora in Discourse Context." *Journal of Linguistics* 18:361–388.

Carden, Guy, Gordon, Lynn, and Munro, Pamela. 1982. "A Critique of the Projection Principle." Paper presented to the Annual Meeting of the Linguistic Society of America, San Diego.

Carnap, Rudolf. 1937 (1934). *The Logical Syntax of Language.* London: Routledge and Kegan Paul.

Carrier, Jill. 1979. *The Interaction of Morphological and Phonological Rules in Tagalog.* Ph.D. dissertation, MIT.

Carrier-Duncan, Jill. 1985. "Linking of Thematic Roles in Derivational Word Formation." *Linguistic Inquiry* 16:1–34.

Carroll, John B. 1953. *The Study of Language.* Cambridge, MA: Harvard University Press.

Carroll, John M. 1981. *Modularity and Naturalness in Cognitive Science.* IBM Research Report #39482.

Cattell, Ray. 1976. "Constraints on Movement Rules." *Language* 52:18–50.

Chafe, Wallace. 1970. *Meaning and the Structure of Language.* Chicago: University of Chicago Press.

Chao, Yuen-Ren. 1934. "The Non-Uniqueness of Phonemic Solutions of Phonetic Systems." *Bulletin of the Institute of History and Philology, Academia Sinica,* vol. IV, part 4. pp. 363–397. Reprinted in *Readings in Linguistics,* edited by Martin Joos (1958), pp. 38–54. Washington: American Council of Learned Societies.

Chapin, Paul. 1967. *The Syntax of Word-Derivation in English.* Bedford, MA: MITRE Corporation Information System Language Studies No. 16.

Chierchia, Gennaro. 1983. "Outline of a Semantic Theory of (Obligatory) Control." *Proceedings of the Second West Coast Conference on Formal Linguistics,* pp. 19–31.

Chomsky, Noam. 1951. *Morphophonemics of Modern Hebrew.* M.A. thesis, University of Pennsylvania. Published under the same title, 1979. New York: Garland.

Chomsky, Noam. 1953. "Systems of Syntactic Analysis." *Journal of Symbolic Logic* 18:242–256.

Chomsky, Noam. 1955. *The Logical Structure of Linguistic Theory.* Mimeographed. Cambridge, MA: MIT.

Chomsky, Noam. 1956. "Three Models for the Description of Language." *IRE Transactions on Information Theory,* pp. II-2, 113–124.

Chomsky, Noam. 1957. *Syntactic Structures.* The Hague: Mouton.

Chomsky, Noam. 1959a. "On Certain Formal Properties of Grammars." *Information and Control* 2:2.

Chomsky, Noam. 1959b. Review of B. F. Skinner, *Verbal Behavior. Language* 35:26–57. Reprinted in *The Structure of Language: Readings in the Philosophy of Language,* edited by Jerry A. Fodor and Jerrold Katz (1964), pp. 547–578. Englewood Cliffs, NJ: Prentice-Hall; and in *Readings in the Psychology of Language,* edited by Leon Jakobovits and Murray Miron (1967), pp. 142–171. Englewood Cliffs, NJ: Prentice-Hall.

Chomsky, Noam. 1961a. "On the Notion 'Rule of Grammar.'" In *Structure of Language and Its Mathematical Aspects. Proceedings of Symposia in Applied Mathematics,* vol. XII, edited by Roman Jackobson, pp. 6–24. Providence, RI: American Mathematical Society. Reprinted in *The Structure of Language: Readings in the Philosophy of Language,* edited by Jerry A. Fodor and Jerrold Katz (1964), pp. 119–136. Englewood Cliffs, NJ: Prentice-Hall.

Chomsky, Noam. 1961b. "Some Methodological Remarks on Generative Grammar." *Word* 17:219–239.

Chomsky, Noam. 1962a. "Explanatory Models in Linguistics." In *Logic, Methodology, and the Philosophy of Science,* edited by E. Nagel, P. Suppes, and A. Tarski, pp. 528–550. Stanford: Stanford University Press.

Chomsky, Noam. 1962b (1958). "A Transformational Approach to Syntax." In *Proceedings of the Third Texas Conference on Problems of Linguistic Analysis in English,* edited by Archibald Hill (1962), pp. 124–158. Austin, TX: University of Texas Press. Reprinted in *The Structure of Language: Readings in the Philosophy of Language,* edited by Jerry A. Fodor and Jerrold Katz (1964), pp. 211–245. Englewood Cliffs, NJ: Prentice-Hall.

Chomsky, Noam. 1964a. *Current Issues in Linguistic Theory.* The Hague: Mouton. (A slightly different version appears in *The Structure of Language: Readings in the Philosophy of Language,* edited by Jerry A. Fodor and Jerrold Katz (1964), pp. 50–118. Englewood Cliffs, NJ: Prentice-Hall.)

Chomsky, Noam. 1964b. "The Logical Basis of Linguistic Theory." In *Proceedings of the Ninth International Congress of Linguists,* edited by H. Lunt, pp. 914–978. The Hague: Mouton. (A revised version was published as Chomsky 1964a.)

Chomsky, *65, 70, 72, 77, 81, 82, 86, 92*

Chomsky, Noam. 1965. *Aspects of the Theory of Syntax.* Cambridge, MA: MIT Press.

Chomsky, Noam. 1966a. *Cartesian Linguistics.* New York: Harper and Row.

Chomsky, Noam. 1966b. *Topics in the Theory of Generative Grammar.* The Hague: Mouton.

Chomsky, Noam. 1967. "The Formal Nature of Language." In *Biological Foundations of Language,* edited by Eric Lenneberg, pp. 397–442. New York: Wiley.

Chomsky, Noam. 1968. *Language and Mind.* (First ed.) New York: Harcourt.

Chomsky, Noam. 1970 (1967). "Remarks on Nominalization." In *Readings in English Transformational Grammar,* edited by Roderick Jacobs and Peter Rosenbaum (1970), pp. 184–221.Waltham, MA: Ginn. Reprinted in Noam Chomsky, *Studies on Semantics in Generative Grammar,* (1972b), pp. 11–61. The Hague: Mouton.

Chomsky, Noam. 1971 (1969). "Deep Structure, Surface Structure, and Semantic Interpretation." In *Semantics: An Interdisciplinary Reader,* edited by Danny Steinberg and Leon Jakobovits (1971), pp. 183–216. Cambridge: Cambridge University Press. Reprinted in Noam Chomsky, *Studies on Semantics in Generative Grammar* (1972b), pp. 62–119. The Hague: Mouton.

Chomsky, Noam. 1972a (1969). "Some Empirical Issues in the Theory of Transformational Grammar." In *Goals of Linguistic Theory,* edited by S. Peters (1972), pp. 63–130. Reprinted in Noam Chomsky, *Studies on Semantics in Generative Grammar* (1972b), pp. 120–202. The Hague: Mouton.

Chomsky, Noam. 1972b. *Studies on Semantics in Generative Grammar.* The Hague: Mouton.

Chomsky, Noam. 1973. "Conditions on Transformations." In S. Anderson and P. Kiparsky, pp. 232–286. Reprinted in Noam Chomsky, *Essays on Form and Interpretation* (1977a), pp. 81–162. Amsterdam: North-Holland.

Chomsky, Noam. 1975a (1955). *The Logical Structure of Linguistic Theory* (with a new Introduction). New York: Plenum.

Chomsky, Noam. 1975b. "Questions of Form and Interpretation." *Linguistic Analysis* 1:75–109. Reprinted in Noam Chomsky, *Essays on Form and Interpretation* (1977a), pp. 25–62. New York: North-Holland.

Chomsky, Noam. 1975c. *Reflections on Language.* New York: Pantheon.

Chomsky, Noam. 1976. "Conditions on Rules of Grammar." *Linguistic Analysis* 2:303–351. Reprinted in Noam Chomsky, *Essays on Form and Interpretation* (1977a), pp. 163–210. New York: North-Holland.

Chomsky, Noam. 1977a. *Essays on Form and Interpretation.* New York: North-Holland.

Chomsky, Noam. 1977b. "On *Wh*-Movement." In *Formal Syntax,* edited by Peter Culicover, Thomas Wasow, and Adrian Akmajian, pp. 71–132. New York: Academic Press.

Chomsky, Noam. 1979. *Language and Responsibility.* New York: Pantheon.

Chomsky, Noam. 1980a. "On Binding." *Linguistic Inquiry* 11:1–46.

Chomsky, Noam. 1980b. *Rules and Representations.* New York: Columbia University Press.

Chomsky, Noam. 1981. *Lectures on Government and Binding.* Dordrecht: Foris.

Chomsky, Noam. 1982a. *The Generative Enterprise.* Dordrecht: Foris.

Chomsky, Noam. 1982b. *Some Concepts and Consequences of the Theory of Government and Binding.* Cambridge, MA: MIT Press.

Chomsky, Noam. 1985. *Knowledge of Language.* New York: Praeger.

Chomsky, Noam. 1986. *Barriers.* Cambridge, MA: MIT Press.

Chomsky, Noam, and Halle, Morris. 1960. "The Morphophonemics of English." *MIT Research Laboratory of Electronics Quarterly Progress Report,* p. 58.

Chomsky, Noam, and Halle, Morris. 1965. "Some Controversial Questions in Phonological Theory." *Journal of Linguistics* 1:97–138.

Chomsky, Noam, and Halle, Morris. 1968. *The Sound Pattern of English.* New York: Harper and Row.

Chomsky, Noam, Halle, Morris, and Lukoff, Fred. 1956. "On Accent and Juncture in English." In Morris Halle, Horace Lunt, Hugh McLean, and Cornelis van Schooneveld (compilers), *For Roman Jakobson,* pp. 65–80. The Hague: Mouton.

Chomsky, Noam, and Lasnik, Howard. 1977. "Filters and Control." *Linguistic Inquiry* 8:425–504.

Chomsky, Noam, and Miller, George. 1963. "Introduction to the Formal Analysis of Natural Languages." In *Handbook of Mathematical Psychology,* edited by P. Luce, R. Bush, and E. Galanter, vol. II, pp. 269–322. New York: Wiley.

Chung, Sandra. 1976. "An Object-Creating Rule in Bahasa Indonesia." *Linguistic Inquiry* 7:41–88.

Chung, Sandra. 1982a. "On Extending the Null-Subject Parameter to NPs." *Proceedings of the West Coast Conference on Formal Linguistics* 1:125–136.

Chung, Sandra. 1982b. "Unbounded Dependencies in Chamorro Grammar." *Linguistic Inquiry* 13:39–78.

Chung, Sandra. 1983. "The ECP and Government in Chamorro." *Natural Language and Linguistic Theory* 2:207–244.

Cinque, Guglielmo. 1982. "On the Theory of Relative Clauses and Markedness." *Linguistic Review* 1:247–296.

Cinque, Guglielmo. Forthcoming. "A-Bar Bound PRO Versus Variable." *Linguistic Inquiry.*

Clark, Robin. 1984. "Control into NP." *Proceedings of the West Coast Conference on Formal Linguistics* 3:40–47.

Clements, G. N., McCloskey, James, Maling, Joan, and Zaenen, Annie. 1983. "String-Vacuous Rule Application." *Linguistic Inquiry* 14:1–18.

Cohen, David, ed. 1972. *Limiting the Domain of Linguistics.* Milwaukee: University of Wisconsin at Milwaukee Linguistics Group.

Cole, Peter. 1976a. "An Apparent Asymmetry in the Formation of Relative Clauses in Modern Hebrew." In *Studies in Modern Hebrew-Syntax and Semantics,* edited by P. Cole, pp. 231–247. Amsterdam: North-Holland.

Cole, Peter. 1976b. "The Interface of Theory and Description." *Language* 53:563–583.

Cole, Peter, ed. 1978. *Syntax and Semantics,* vol. 9. New York: Academic Press.

Cole, Peter, ed. 1981. *Radical Pragmatics.* New York: Academic Press.

Cole, Peter, and Hermon, Gabriella. 1981. "Subjecthood and Islandhood: Evidence from Quechua." *Linguistic Inquiry* 12:1–30.

Cole, Peter, and Morgan, Jerry, eds. 1975. *Syntax and Semantics,* vol. 3. New York: Academic Press.

Cole, Peter, and Sadock, Jerrold, eds. 1977. *Syntax and Semantics,* vol. 8. New York: Academic Press.

Comrie, Bernard. 1976. "The Syntax of Causative Constructions: Cross-Language Similarities and Divergences." In *Syntax and Semantics,* vol. 6, edited by Masayoshi Shibatani, pp. 261–312. New York: Academic Press.

Contreras, Heles. 1984a. "A Note on Parasitic Gaps." *Linguistic Inquiry* 15:698–701.

Contreras, Heles. 1984b. Review of P. Jaeggli, *Topics in Romance Syntax. Language* 60:143–148.

Contreras, Heles. 1986. "Conditions on A-bar Chains." *Proceedings of the West Coast Conference on Formal Linguistics,* 5.

Cooper, Robin. 1980. "Montague's Syntax." In *Syntax and Semantics, Volume 13: Current Approaches to Syntax,* edited by E. Moravcsik and J. Wirth, pp. 19–44. New York: Academic Press.

Corum, Claudia, Smith-Stark, T. Cedric, and Weiser, Ann. eds. 1973. *You Take the High Node and I'll Take the Low Node.* Chicago: Chicago Linguistic Society.

Covington, Michael. 1983. Review of T. Hoekstra, *et al., Lexical Grammar. Language* 59:402–406.

Cowper, Elizabeth. 1985. "Parasitic Gaps, Coordinate Structures, and the Subjacency Condition." *Proceedings of NELS 15,* pp. 75–86.

Culicover, Peter. 1976. *Syntax.* New York: Academic Press.

Culicover, Peter. 1977. "An Invalid Evaluation Metric." *Linguistic Analysis* 3:65–100.

Culicover, Peter, Wasow, Thomas, and Akmajian, Adrian, eds. 1977. *Formal Syntax.* New York: Academic Press.

Culicover, Peter, and Wexler, Kenneth. 1977. "Some Syntactic Implications of a Theory of Language Learnability." In *Formal Syntax,* edited by Peter Culicover, Thomas Wasow, and Adrian Akmajian, pp. 7–60. New York: Academic Press.

Culicover, Peter, and Wilkins, Wendy. 1984. *Locality in Linguistic Theory.* New York: Academic Press.

Culicover, Peter, and Wilkins, Wendy. 1986. "Control, PRO, and the Projection Principle." *Language.* 62:120–153.

Culy, Christopher. 1985. "The Complexity of the Vocabulary in Bambara." *Linguistics and Philosophy* 8:345–352.

Dalgish, Gerard, and Sheintuch, Gloria. 1976. "On the Justification for Language-Specific Sub-Grammatical Relations." *Studies in the Linguistic Sciences* 6:2.

Darden, Bill. 1974. "Introduction." In *Papers from the Parasession on Natural Phonology,* edited by A. Bruck, R. Fox, and M. LeGaly. Chicago: Chicago Linguistic Society.

Davidson, Donald, and Harmon, Gilbert, eds. 1972. *Semantics of Natural Language.* Dordrecht: D. Reidel.

Davies, William. 1984. "Antipassive: Choctaw Evidence for a Universal Characterization." In *Studies in Relational Grammar 2,* edited by D. Perlmutter and C. Rosen, pp. 311–376. Chicago: University of Chicago Press.

Davies, William. 1985. *Choctaw Verb Agreement and Universal Grammar.* Dordrecht: Reidel.

Davis, Steven, and Mithun, Marianne, eds. 1979. *Linguistics, Philosophy, and Montague Grammar.* Austin: University of Texas Press.

Davison, Alice. 1980. "Peculiar Passives." *Language* 56:42–66.

De George, Richard, and De George, Fernande, eds. 1972. *The Structuralists: From Marx to Lévi-Strauss.* Garden City, NY: Doubleday.

De Rijk, Rudolf. 1972. *Studies in Basque Syntax: Relative Clauses.* Ph.D. dissertation, MIT.

Directory of Programs in Linguistics in the United States and Canada. 1984. Number 12. Washington: Linguistic Society of America.

Dixon, R. M. W. 1963a. *Linguistic Science and Logic.* The Hague: Mouton.

Dixon, R. M. W. 1963b. "A Trend in Semantics." *Linguistics* 1:30–57.

Dixon, R. M. W. 1964. "A Trend in Semantics—A Rejoinder." *Linguistics* 3:19–22.

Dixon, R. M. W. 1970. "Olgolo Syllable Structure and What They Are Doing about It." *Linguistic Inquiry* 1:273–276.

Dixon, R. M. W. 1972. *The Dyirbal Language of North Queensland.* Cambridge: Cambridge University Press.

Dixon, R. M. W. 1977. "Some Phonological Rules in Yidin." *Linguistic Inquiry* 8:1–34.

Dougherty, Ray. 1969. "An Interpretive Theory of Pronominal Reference." *Foundations of Language* 5:488–519.

Dougherty, Ray. 1970a. "A Grammar of Conjoined Coordinate Structures." *Language* 46:850–898; 47:298–339.

Dougherty, Ray. 1970b. "Recent Studies on Language Universals." *Foundations of Language* 6:505–561.

Dougherty, Ray. 1974. "Generative Semantic Methods: A Bloomfieldian Counterrevolution." *International Journal of Dravidian Linguistics* 3:255–286.

Dowty, David. 1976. "Montague Grammar and the Lexical Decomposition of Causative Verbs." In *Montague Grammar,* edited by Barbara Partee, pp. 201–246. New York: Academic Press.

Dowty, David. 1978a. "Applying Montague's Views on Linguistic Metatheory to the Structure of the Lexicon." In *Papers from the Parasession on the Lexicon,* edited by D. Farkas, W. Jacobsen, and K. Todrys, pp. 97–137. Chicago: Chicago Linguistic Society.

Dowty, David. 1978b. "Governed Transformations as Lexical Rules in a Montague Grammar." *Linguistic Inquiry* 9:393–426.

Dowty, David. 1979. "Dative 'Movement' and Thomason's Extensions of Montague Grammar." In *Linguistics, Philosophy, and Montague Grammar,* edited by S. Davis and M. Mithun, pp. 153–222. Austin: University of Texas Press.

Dowty, David, Wall, Robert, and Peters, Stanley. 1981. *Introduction to Montague Semantics.* Dordrecht: Reidel.

Dryer, Matthew. 1985. "The Role of Thematic Relations in Adjectival Passives." *Linguistic Inquiry* 16:320–326.

Emonds, Joseph. 1970. *Root and Structure-Preserving Transformations.* Indiana University Linguistics Club Publication.

Emonds, Joseph. 1973. "Alternatives to Global Constraints." *Glossa* 7:39–62.

Emonds, Joseph. 1975. "A Transformational Analysis of French Clitics without Positive Output Constraints." *Linguistic Analysis* 1:3–24.

Emonds, Joseph. 1976. *A Transformational Approach to English Syntax.* New York: Academic Press.

Emonds, Joseph. 1985. *A Uniform Theory of Syntactic Categories.* Dordrecht: Foris.

Enç, Mürvet. 1983. "Anchored Expressions." *Proceedings of the West Coast Conference on Formal Linguistics* 2:79–88.

Engdahl, Elisabet. 1980. "Wh-Constructions in Swedish and the Relevance of Subjacency." *Proceedings of NELS 10,* pp. 89–108.

Engdahl, Elisabet. 1983. "Parasitic Gaps." *Linguistics and Philosophy* 6:5–34.

Engdahl, Elisabet. 1984. "Why Some Empty Subjects Don't License Parasitic Gaps." *Proceedings of the West Coast Conference on Formal Linguistics* 3:91–104.

Falk, Yehuda. 1984. "The English Auxiliary System." *Language* 60:483–509.

Farkas, Donka. 1984. "The Status of VP in Hungarian." *Papers from the Twentieth Regional Meeting of the Chicago Linguistic Society,* pp. 65–76.

Farmer, Ann. 1984. *Modularity in Syntax.* Cambridge, MA: MIT Press.

Fauconnier, Giles. 1973. "Cyclic Attraction into Networks of Coreference." *Language* 49:1–18.

Fiengo, Robert. 1974. *Semantic Conditions on Surface Structure.* Ph.D. dissertation, MIT.

Fiengo, Robert. 1977. "On Trace Theory." *Linguistic Inquiry* 8:35–61.

Fiengo, Robert, and Gitterman, Martin. 1978. "Remarks on French Clitic Order." *Linguistic Analysis* 4:115–148.

Fiengo, Robert, and Lasnik, Howard. 1976. "Some Issues in the Theory of Transformations." *Linguistic Inquiry* 7:182–192.

Fillmore, Charles. 1963. "The Position of Embedding Transformations in a Grammar." *Word* 19:208–231.

Fillmore, Charles. 1965 (1962). "Indirect Object Constructions and the Ordering of Transformations." *Project on Syntactic Analysis, Report No. 1,* pp. 1–49. The Hague: Mouton.

Fillmore, Charles. 1966. "A Proposal Concerning English Prepositions." *Monograph Series on Languages and Linguistics* 19:19–34.

Fillmore, Charles. 1968. "The Case for Case." In *Universals in Linguistic Theory,* edited by Emmon Bach and Robert Harms, pp. 1–90. New York: Holt, Rinehart and Winston.

Fillmore, Charles. 1969a. "Toward a Modern Theory of Case." In *Modern Studies in English,* edited by David Reibel and Sanford Schane, pp. 361–375. Englewood Cliffs, NJ: Prentice-Hall.

Fillmore, Charles. 1969b. "Verbs of Judging: An Exercise in Semantic Description." *Papers in Linguistics* 1:91–117. Reprinted in *Studies in Linguistic Semantics,* edited by Charles Fillmore and D. Terence Langendoen (1971), pp. 273–290. New York: Holt, Rinehart and Winston.

Fillmore, Charles, ed. 1971a. *Ohio State University Working Papers in Linguistics,* No. 10.

Fillmore, Charles. 1971b. "Some Problems for Case Grammar." *Monograph Series on Languages and Linguistics* 24:35–56.

Fillmore, Charles. 1971c. "Types of Lexical Information." In *Semantics: An Interdisciplinary Reader,* edited by Danny Steinberg and Leon Jakobovits, pp. 370–392. Cambridge: Cambridge University Press.

Fillmore, Charles. 1972 (1969). "On Generativity." In *Goals of Linguistic Theory,* edited by Stanley Peters, pp. 1–20. Englewood Cliffs, New Jersey: Prentice-Hall.

Fillmore, Charles. 1977. "The Case for Case Reopened." In *Syntax and Semantics,* vol. 8, edited by Peter Cole and Jerrold Sadock, pp. 59–82. New York: Academic Press.

Fillmore, Charles, and Langendoen, D. Terence, eds. 1971. *Studies in Linguistic Semantics.* New York: Holt, Rinehart and Winston.

Flickinger, Daniel. 1983. "Lexical Heads and Phrasal Gaps." *Proceedings of the West Coast Conference on Formal Linguistics* 2:89–101.

Flynn, Michael. 1983. "A Categorial Theory of Structure Building." In *Order, Concord, and Constituency,* edited by G. Gazdar, E. Klein, and G. Pullum, pp. 139–174. Dordrecht: Foris.

Fodor, Janet Dean. 1977. *Semantics: Theories of Meaning in Generative Grammar.* New York: Crowell.

Fodor, Janet Dean. 1979. "In Defense of the Truth Value Gap." In *Syntax and Semantics, Volume 11: Presupposition*, edited by C. Oh and D. Dinneen, pp. 199–224. New York: Academic Press.

Fodor, Jerry A. 1961. "Projection and Paraphrase in Semantics." *Analysis* 21:73–77.

Fodor, Jerry A. 1970. "Three Reasons for Not Deriving 'Kill' from 'Cause to Die.' " *Linguistic Inquiry* 1:429–438.

Fodor, Jerry A. 1982. *The Modularity of Mind*. Cambridge, MA: MIT Press.

Fodor, Jerry A., and Garrett, Merrill. 1967. "Some Syntactic Determinants of Sentential Complexity." *Perception and Psychophysics* 2:289–296.

Fodor, Jerry A., and Katz, Jerrold, eds. 1964. *The Structure of Language: Readings in the Philosophy of Language*. Englewood Cliffs, NJ: Prentice-Hall.

Ford, Marilyn. 1982. "Sentence Planning Units: Implication for the Speaker's Representation of Meaningful Relations Underlying Sentences." In *The Mental Representation of Grammatical Relations*, edited by Joan Bresnan, pp. 797–828. Cambridge, MA: MIT Press.

Ford, Marilyn, Bresnan, Joan, and Kaplan, Ronald. 1982. "A Competence-Based Theory of Syntactic Closure." In *The Mental Representation of Grammatical Relations*, edited by Joan Bresnan, pp. 727–796. Cambridge, MIT Press.

Francis, W. Nelson. 1958. *The Structure of American English*. New York: Ronald Press.

Franks, Steven. 1982. "Is There a Pro-Drop Parameter for Slavic?" *Papers from the Eighteenth Regional Meeting of the Chicago Linguistic Society*, pp. 140–155.

Frantz, Donald. 1974. "Generative Semantics: An Introduction, with Bibliography." Indiana University Linguistics Club Publication.

Fraser, Bruce. 1974 (1969). "An Examination of the Performative Analysis." *Papers in Linguistics* 7:1–40.

Freidin, Robert. 1974 (1972). "Transformations and Interpretive Semantics." In *Towards Tomorrow's Linguistics*, edited by Roger Shuy and C. J. Bailey, pp. 12–22. Washington: Georgetown University Press.

Freidin, Robert. 1975a. "The Analysis of Passives." *Language* 51:384–405.

Freidin, Robert. 1975b. Review of R. Jackendoff, *Semantic Interpretation in Generative Grammar*. *Language* 51:189–204.

Freidin, Robert. 1978a. "Cyclicity and the Theory of Grammar." *Linguistic Inquiry* 9:519–550.

Freidin, Robert. 1978b. Review of J. Emonds, *A Transformational Approach to English Syntax*. *Language* 54:407–415.

Freidin, Robert, and Lasnik, Howard. 1981. "Disjoint Reference and *Wh*-trace." *Linguistic Inquiry* 12:39–54.

Friedrich, Paul. 1974. "Annual Report by the Chairman of the Program Committee." *LSA Bulletin* 60:15–16.

Fujimura, Osamu, ed. 1973. *Three Dimensions of Linguistic Theory*. Tokyo: TEC Corporation.

Gary, Judith, and Keenan, Edward. 1977. "On Collapsing Grammatical Relations in Universal Grammar." In *Syntax and Semantics*, vol. 8, edited by Peter Cole and Jerrold Sadock, pp. 83–120. New York: Academic Press.

Gazdar, Gerald. 1979a (1977). *Pragmatics: Implicature, Presupposition and Logical Form*. New York: Academic Press.

Gazdar, Gerald. 1979b. "A Solution to the Projection Problem." In *Syntax and Semantics, Volume 11: Presupposition*, edited by C. Oh and D. Dinneen, pp. 57–90. New York: Academic Press.

Gazdar, Gerald. 1980. "Reply to Kiefer." *Linguisticae Investigationes* 3:375–377.

Gazdar, Gerald. 1981a. "Speech Act Assignment." In *Elements of Discourse Understanding*, edited by A. Joshi, Bonnie Webber, and Ivan Sag, pp. 64–83. Cambridge: Cambridge University Press.

Gazdar, Gerald. 1981b. "Unbounded Dependencies and Coordinate Structure." *Linguistic Inquiry* 12:155–184.

Gazdar, Gerald. 1982. "Phrase Structure Grammar." In *The Nature of Syntactic Representation*, edited by P. Jacobson and G. Pullum, pp. 131–186. Dordrecht: Reidel.

Gazdar, Gerald, and Klein, Ewan. 1977. "Context Sensitive Transderivational Constraints and Conventional Implicature." *Papers from the Thirteenth Regional Meeting of the Chicago Linguistic Society,* pp. 137–146.

Gazdar, Gerald, and Klein, Ewan. 1978. Review of E. Keenan, ed. *Formal Semantics of Natural Language. Language* 54:661–667.

Gazdar, Gerald, Klein, Ewan, and Pullum, Geoffrey. 1983a. "Introduction." In *Order, Concord, and Constituency,* edited by G. Gazdar, Ewan Klein, and Geoffrey Pullum, pp. 1–8. Dordrecht: Foris.

Gazdar, Gerald, Klein, Ewan, and Pullum, Geoffrey, eds. 1983b. *Order, Concord, and Constituency.* Dordrecht: Foris.

Gazdar, Gerald, Klein, Ewan, Pullum, Geoffrey, and Sag, Ivan. 1985. *Generalized Phrase Structure Grammar.* Cambridge, MA: Harvard University Press.

Gazdar, Gerald, and Pullum, Geoffrey. 1976. "Truth Functional Connectives in Natural Language." *Papers from the Twelfth Regional Meeting of the Chicago Linguistic Society,* pp. 220–234.

Gazdar, Gerald, and Pullum, Geoffrey. 1981. "Subcategorization, Constituent Order, and the Notion 'Head.'" In *The Scope of Lexical Rules,* edited by M. Moortgat, H. van der Hulst, and T. Hoekstra, pp. 107–124. Dordrecht: Foris.

Gee, James. 1974. "Jackendoff's Thematic Hierarchy Condition and the Passive Construction." *Linguistic Inquiry* 5:304–308.

George, Leland, and Kornfilt, Jaklin. 1981. "Finiteness and Boundedness in Turkish." In *Binding and Filtering,* edited by F. Heny, pp. 105–128. Cambridge, MA: MIT Press.

Gerdts, Donna. 1980. "Causal to Object Advancement in Halkomelem." *Papers from the Sixteenth Regional Meeting of the Chicago Linguistic Society,* pp. 83–101.

Gerdts, Donna. 1984. "A Relational Analysis of Halkomelem Causals." In *Syntax and Semantics, Volume 16: The Syntax of Native American Languages,* edited by E. Cook and D. Gerdts, pp. 169–204. New York: Academic Press.

Gibson, Jeanne. 1980. *Clause Union in Chamorro and Universal Grammar.* Ph.D. dissertation, University of California, San Diego.

Gildin, Bonny. 1978. "Concerning Radios in Performative Clauses." *Pragmatics Microfiche* 3:4.

Giorgi, Alessandra. 1984. "Toward a Theory of Long Distance Anaphors: A GB Approach." *Linguistic Review* 3:307–362.

Givón, Talmy, ed. 1979. *Syntax and Semantics, Volume 12: Discourse and Syntax.* New York: Academic Press.

Gleason, Henry. 1955 (Second ed. 1961). *An Introduction to Descriptive Linguistics.* New York: Holt, Rinehart and Winston.

Gold, E. M. 1967. "Language Identification in the Limit." *Information and Control* 16:447–474.

Goodall, Grant. 1984. "Across-the Board Movement, the ECP, and the Bijection Principle." *Proceedings of the Western Conference on Linguistics* 3:129–138.

Gordon, David, and Lakoff, George. 1971. "Conversational Postulates." *Papers from the Seventh Regional Meeting of the Chicago Linguistic Society,* pp. 63–84. Reprinted in *Syntax and Semantics,* vol. 3, edited by Peter Cole and Jerry Morgan (1975), pp. 83–106. New York: Academic Press.

Green, Georgia. 1972. "Some Observations on the Syntax and Semantics of Instrumental Verbs." *Papers from the Eighth Regional Meeting of the Chicago Linguistics Society,* pp. 83–97.

Green, Georgia. 1975. "How to Get People to Do Things with Words: The Whimperative Question." In *Syntax and Semantics,* vol. 3, edited by Peter Cole and Jerry Morgan, pp. 107–142. New York: Academic Press.

Green, Georgia. 1976. "Main Clause Phenomena in Subordinate Clauses." *Language* 52:382–397.

Green, Georgia. 1980. "Some Wherefores of English Inversions." *Language* 56:582–602.

Green, Georgia. 1981. "Pragmatics and Syntactic Description." *Studies in the Linguistic Sciences* 11:27–38.

Green, Georgia. 1982. "Linguistics and the Pragmatics of Language Use." In *Neurolinguistics and Cognition,* edited by R. Buhr, pp. 81–102. New York: Academic Press.

Greenberg, Joseph, ed. 1963. *Universals of Language.* Cambridge, MA: MIT Press.

Greenberg, Joseph. 1973. "Linguistics as a Pilot Science." In *Themes in Linguistics: The 1970's*, edited by E. Hamp, pp. 45–60. The Hague: Mouton.

Greene, Judith. 1972. *Psycholinguistics: Chomsky and Psychology*. Harmondsworth: Penguin.

Grice, H. P. 1975 (1967). "Logic and Conversation." In *Syntax and Semantics*, vol. 3, edited by Peter Cole and Jerry Morgan, pp. 41–58. New York: Academic Press.

Grice, H. P. 1978. "Further Notes on Logic and Conversation." In *Syntax and Semantics, Volume 9: Pragmatics*, edited by P. Cole, pp. 113–128.

Grice, H. P. 1981. "Presupposition and Conversational Implicature." In *Radical Pragmatics*, edited by P. Cole, pp. 183–198.

Grimshaw, Jane. 1974. "Evidence for Relativization by Deletion in Chaucerian Middle English." *Proceedings of NELS 5*, pp. 216–224.

Grimshaw, Jane. 1979a. "Complement Selection and the Lexicon." *Linguistic Inquiry* 10:279–326.

Grimshaw, Jane. 1979b. "The Structure-Preserving Constraint: A Review of *A Transformational Approach to English Syntax* by J. E. Emonds." *Linguistic Analysis* 5:313–343.

Grimshaw, Jane. 1982. "On the Lexical Representation of Romance Reflexive Clitics." In *The Mental Representation of Grammatical Relations*, edited by J. Bresnan, pp. 87–149. Cambridge, MA: MIT Press.

Grinder, John, and Elgin, Suzette. 1973. *Guide to Transformational Grammar*. New York: Holt, Rinehart and Winston.

Grossman, Robin, San, L. J., and Vance, Timothy, eds. 1975. *Papers from the Parasession on Functionalism*. Chicago: Chicago Linguistic Society.

Grosu, Alexander. 1972. "The Strategic Nature of Island Constraints." *Ohio State University Working Papers in Linguistics* 13:1–225.

Grosu, Alexander. 1979. Review of N. Chomsky, *Essays on Form and Interpretation. Journal of Linguistics* 15:356–364.

Grosu, Alexander. 1981. *Approaches to Island Phenomena*. Amsterdam: North-Holland.

Gruber, Jeffrey. 1976 (1965–1967). *Lexical Structures in Syntax and Semantics*. New York: North-Holland.

Guide to Programs in Linguistics: 1974–1975 and *1978–1979*. Arlington, VA: Center for Applied Linguistics and Linguistic Society of America.

Gundel, Jeanette. 1977. *Role of Topic and Comment in Linguistic Theory*. Indiana University Linguistics Club Publication.

Haegeman, Liliane. 1984. "Parasitic Gaps and Adverbial Clauses." *Journal of Linguistics* 20:229–232.

Hagège, Claude. 1976. *La Grammaire Générative: Réflexions Critiques*. Paris: Presses Universitaires de France.

Hale, Kenneth. 1976. "Linguistic Autonomy and the Linguistics of Carl Voegelin." *Anthropological Linguistics* 18:120–128.

Hale, Kenneth. 1982. "Preliminary Remarks on Configurationality." *Proceedings of NELS 12*, pp. 86–96.

Hale, Kenneth. 1983. "Warlpiri and the Grammar of Non-configurational Languages." *Natural Language and Linguistic Theory* 1:5–48.

Hall, Robert. 1946. "The State of Linguistics: Crisis or Reaction?" *Italica* 23:33–34.

Hall, Robert. 1951. "American Linguistics, 1925–1950." *Archivum Linguisticum* 3:101–125.

Hall, Robert. 1977. Review of C. Hagège, *La Grammaire Générative: Réflexions Critiques. Forum Linguisticum* 2:75–79.

Halle, Morris. 1959. *The Sound Pattern of Russian*. The Hague: Mouton.

Halle, Morris. 1962. "Phonology in Generative Grammar." *Word* 18:54–72. Reprinted in *The Structure of Language*, edited by Jerry A. Fodor and Jerrold Katz (1964), pp. 334–352. Englewood Cliffs, NJ: Prentice-Hall.

Halle, Morris. 1973. "Prolegomena to a Theory of Word Formation." *Linguistic Inquiry* 4:3–16.

Halle, Morris, Bresnan, Joan, and Miller, George, eds. 1978. *Linguistic Theory and Psychological Reality.* Cambridge, MA: MIT Press.

Halvorsen, Per-Kristian. 1983. "Semantics for Lexical Functional Grammar." *Linguistic Inquiry* 14:567–616.

Hankamer, Jorge. 1972. "Analogical Rules in Syntax." *Papers from the Eighth Regional Meeting of the Chicago Linguistic Society,* pp. 111–123.

Hankamer, Jorge. 1973. "Unacceptable Ambiguity." *Linguistic Inquiry* 4:17–68.

Hankamer, Jorge, and Sag, Ivan. 1976. "Deep and Surface Anaphora." *Linguistic Inquiry* 7:391–428.

Harbert, Wayne. 1982. "Should Binding Refer to SUBJECT?" *Proceedings of NELS 12,* pp. 116–131.

Harbert, Wayne. 1983. "On the Definition of Governing Category." *Proceedings of the West Coast Conference on Formal Linguistics* 2:102–113.

Harlow, Stephen. 1983. "Celtic Relatives." *York Papers in Linguistics* 10:77–121.

Harris, Alice. 1982. "Georgian and the Unaccusative Hypothesis." *Language* 58:290–306.

Harris, Alice. 1984. "Inversion as a Rule of Universal Grammar: Georgian Evidence." In *Studies in Relational Grammar 2,* edited by D. Perlmutter and C. Rosen, pp. 259–291. Chicago: University of Chicago Press.

Harris, Zellig. 1946. "From Morpheme to Utterance." *Language 22:*161–183. Reprinted in *Readings in Linguistics,* edited by Martin Joos (1958), pp. 142–153. Washington: American Council of Learned Societies.

Harris, Zellig. 1951. *Methods in Structural Linguistics.* Chicago: University of Chicago Press.

Harris, Zellig. 1952a. "Discourse Analysis." *Language* 28:1–30.

Harris, Zellig. 1952b. "Discourse Analysis: A Sample Text." *Language* 28:474–494.

Harris, Zellig. 1955. "From Phoneme to Morpheme." *Language* 31:190–222.

Harris, Zellig. 1957. "Co-Occurrence and Transformation in Linguistic Structure." *Language* 33:283–340.

Harris, Zellig. 1965. "Transformational Theory." *Language* 41:363–401.

Haugen, Einar. 1951. "Directions in Modern Linguistics." *Language* 27:211–222.

Heal, Jane. 1977. "Ross and Lakoff on Declarative Sentences." *Studies in Language* 1:337–362.

Heim, Irene. 1982. *The Semantics of Definite and Indefinite Noun Phrases.* Ph.D. dissertation, University of Massachusetts.

Heim, Irene. 1983. "On the Projection Problem for Presuppositions." *Proceedings of the West Coast Conference on Formal Linguistics* 2:114–125.

Hempel, Carl. 1950. "Problems and Changes in the Empiricist Criterion of Meaning." *Revue Internationale de Philosophie* 11:41–63.

Hempel, Carl. 1951. "The Concept of Cognitive Significance: A Reconsideration." *Proceedings of the American Academy of Arts and Sciences* 80:61–77.

Hempel, Carl. 1965. "Empiricist Criteria of Cognitive Significance: Problems and Changes." In *Aspects of Scientific Explanation,* edited by Carl Hempel, pp. 101–122. New York: Free Press.

Heny, Frank, ed. 1981. *Binding and Filtering.* Cambridge, MA: MIT Press.

Hermon, Gabriella. 1981. "The Relationship of Meaning and Underlying Grammatical Relations. *Proceedings of the Seventh Annual Meeting of the Berkeley Linguistics Society,* pp. 68–81.

Higginbotham, James. 1980a. "Anaphora and GB: Some Preliminary Remarks." *Proceedings of NELS 10,* pp. 223–236.

Higginbotham, James. 1980b. "Pronouns and Bound Variables." *Linguistic Inquiry* 11:679–708.

Higginbotham, James. 1984. "English is Not a Context-Free Language." *Linguistic Inquiry* 15:225–234.

Higginbotham, James. 1985a. "Reply to Pullum." *Linguistic Inquiry* 16:298–304.

Higginbotham, James. 1985b. "On Semantics." *Linguistic Inquiry* 16:547–594.

Higginbotham, James, and May, Robert. 1981. "Questions, Quantifiers, and Crossing." *Linguistic Review* 1:41–80.

Higgins, F. Roger. 1973. "On J. Emonds' Analysis of Extraposition." In *Syntax and Semantics,* vol. 2, edited by John Kimball, pp. 149–196. New York: Seminar Press.

Hill, Archibald. 1958. *Introduction to Linguistic Structures.* New York: Harcourt, Brace and World.

Hill, Archibald, ed. 1962 (1958). *Proceedings of the Third Texas Conference on Problems of Linguistic Analysis in English.* Austin: University of Texas Press.

Hill, Archibald. 1980. "How Many Revolutions Can a Linguist Live Through?" In *First Person Singular,* edited by B. Davis and R. O'Cain, pp. 69–78. Amsterdam: John Benjamins.

Hirschbühler, Paul and Rivero, María-Luisa. 1983. "Non-Matching Concealed Questions in Catalan and Spanish and the Projection Principle." *Linguistic Review* 2:331–364.

Hockett, Charles. 1942. "A System of Descriptive Phonology." *Language* 18:3–21. Reprinted in *Readings in Linguistics,* edited by Martin Joos (1958), pp. 97–108. Washington: American Council of Learned Societies.

Hockett, Charles. 1951. Review of A. Martinet, *Phonology as Functional Phonetics. Language* 27:333–341.

Hockett, Charles. 1952. Review of *Travaux du Cercle Linguistique de Copenhague, V: Recherches Structurales. IJAL* 18:86–89.

Hockett, Charles. 1953. Review of C. Shannon and W. Weaver, *The Mathematical Theory of Communication. Language* 29:69–93.

Hockett, Charles. 1954. "Two Models of Grammatical Description." *Word* 10:210–231. Reprinted in *Readings in Linguistics,* edited by Martin Joos (1958), pp. 386–399. Washington: American Council of Learned Societies.

Hockett, Charles. 1955. *A Manual of Phonology.* Baltimore: Waverly Press.

Hockett, Charles. 1958. *A Course in Modern Linguistics.* New York: Macmillan.

Hockett, Charles. 1965. "Sound Change." *Language* 41:185–204.

Hockett, Charles. 1966. *Language, Mathematics, and Linguistics.* The Hague: Mouton.

Hockett, Charles. 1968. *The State of the Art.* The Hague: Mouton.

Hoekstra, Teun. 1984. *Transitivity: Grammatical Relations in Government-Binding Theory.* Dordrecht: Foris.

Hoekstra, Teun, van der Hulst, Harry, and Moortgat, Michael. 1980a. "Introduction." In *Lexical Grammar,* edited by T. Hoekstra, H. van der Hulst, and M. Moortgat, pp. 1–48. Dordrecht: Foris.

Hoekstra, Teun, van der Hulst, Harry, and Moortgat, Michael, eds. 1980b. *Lexical Grammar.* Dordrecht: Foris.

Hooper, Joan. 1973. "A Critical Look at the Structure Preserving Constraint." *UCLA Papers in Syntax* 4:34–72.

Hooper, Joan, and Thompson, Sandra. 1973. "On the Applicability of Root Transformations." *Linguistic Inquiry* 4:465–497.

Horn, George. 1977 (1974). *The Noun Phrase Constraint.* Indiana University Linguistics Club Publication.

Horn, George. 1979. *A Lexical Interpretive Approach to Some Problems in Syntax.* Indiana University Linguistics Club Publication.

Horn, Laurence. 1969. "A Presuppositional Analysis of *Only* and *Even.*" *Papers from the Fifth Regional Meeting of the Chicago Linguistic Society,* pp. 98–107.

Horn, Laurence. 1970. "Ain't It Hard (Anymore)?" *Papers from the Sixth Regional Meeting of the Chicago Linguistics Society,* pp. 318–327.

Horn, Laurence. 1972. *On the Semantic Properties of Logical Operators in English.* Indiana University Linguistics Club Publication.

Horn, Laurence. 1978. "Remarks on Neg-Raising." In *Syntax and Semantics, Volume 9: Pragmatics,* edited by P. Cole, pp. 129–220. New York: Academic Press.

Horn, Laurence. 1984. "Toward a New Taxonomy for Pragmatic Inference: Q- and R-Based Implicature." In *Meaning, Form, and Use in Context: Linguistic Applications,* edited by D. Schiffrin, pp. 11–41. Washington: Georgetown University Press.

Hornstein, Norbert. 1977. "S and X-Bar Convention." *Linguistic Analysis* 3:137–176.

Hornstein, Norbert. 1984. *Logic as Grammar.* Cambridge, MA: MIT Press.

Hornstein, Norbert, and Lightfoot, David, eds. 1981. *Explanation in Linguistics.* London: Longman.

Hornstein, Norbert, and Weinberg, Amy. 1981. "Case Theory and Preposition Stranding." *Linguistic Inquiry* 12:55–92.

Horvath, Julia. 1976. "Focus in Hungarian and the X-Bar Notation." *Linguistic Analysis* 2:175–198.

Horvath, Julia. 1980. "Successive Cyclic *Wh*-Movement: Evidence from Hungarian." Unpublished paper, UCLA.

Horvath, Julia. 1985. *Focus in the Theory of Grammar and the Syntax of Hungarian*. Dordrecht: Foris.

Householder, Fred. 1957. "Rough Justice in Linguistics." *Monograph Series on Languages and Linguistics* 7:153–160.

Householder, Fred. 1965. "On Some Recent Claims in Phonological Theory." *Journal of Linguistics* 1:13–34.

Householder, Fred. 1973. "On Arguments from Asterisks." *Foundations of Language* 10:365–376.

Huang, James. 1982a. *Logical Relations in Chinese and the Theory of Grammar*. Ph.D. dissertation, MIT.

Huang, James. 1982b. "Move *Wh* in a Language Without *Wh*-Movement." *Linguistic Review* 1:369–416.

Huang, James. 1983. "A Note on the Binding Theory." *Linguistic Inquiry* 14:554–560.

Huang, James. 1984. "On the Distribution and Reference of Empty Pronouns." *Linguistic Inquiry* 15:531–574.

Hudson, Richard. 1976. *Arguments for a Non-Transformational Grammar*. Chicago: University of Chicago Press.

Hull, Clark. 1943. *Principles of Behavior*. New York: Appleton-Century-Crofts.

Hust, Joel. 1978. "Lexical Redundancy Rules and the Unpassive Construction." *Linguistic Analysis* 4:61–89.

Hust, Joel, and Brame, Michael. 1976. "Jackendoff on Interpretive Semantics." *Linguistic Analysis* 2:243–278.

Huybregts, Riny, and van Riemsdijk, Henk. 1985. "Parasitic Gaps and ATB." *Proceedings of NELS 15*, pp. 168–187.

Hymes, Dell. 1964. "Directions in (Ethno-)linguistic Theory." In *Transcultural Studies in Cognition*, edited by A. Romney and R. D'Andrade, pp. 6–56. Washington: American Anthropological Association.

Hymes, Dell. 1971. "Competence and Performance in Linguistic Theory." In *Language Acquisition: Models and Methods*, edited by R. Huxley and E. Ingram, pp. 3–24. New York: Academic Press.

Hymes, Dell, and Fought, John. 1981 (1975). *American Structuralism*. Mouton: The Hague.

Ishikawa, Akira. 1985. *Complex Predicates and Lexical Operations in Japanese*. Ph.D. dissertation, Stanford.

Jackendoff, Ray. 1968a. *An Interpretive Theory of Pronouns and Reflexives*. Indiana University Linguistics Club Publication.

Jackendoff, Ray. 1968b. "Quantifiers in English." *Foundations of Language* 4:422–442.

Jackendoff, Ray. 1969. "An Interpretive Theory of Negation." *Foundations of Language* 5:218–241.

Jackendoff, Ray. 1971a. "Gapping and Related Rules." *Linguistic Inquiry* 2:21–36.

Jackendoff, Ray. 1971b. "Modal Structure in Semantic Representation." *Linguistic Inquiry* 2:479–538.

Jackendoff, Ray. 1971c. "On Some Questionable Arguments about Quantifiers and Negation." *Language* 47:282–297.

Jackendoff, Ray. 1972 (1966–1969). *Semantic Interpretation in Generative Grammar*. Cambridge, MA: MIT Press.

Jackendoff, Ray. 1974a. "A Deep Structure Projection Rule." *Linguistic Inquiry* 5:481–505.

Jackendoff, Ray. 1974b. *Introduction to the X-Bar Convention*. Indiana University Linguistics Club Publication.

Jackendoff, Ray. 1975. "Morphological and Semantic Regularities in the Lexicon." *Language* 51:639–671.

Jackendoff, Ray. 1977. *X-Bar Syntax: A Study of Phrase Structure*. Cambridge, MA: MIT Press.

Jacobs, Roderick, and Rosenbaum, Peter, eds. 1970. *Readings in English Transformational Grammar.* Waltham, MA: Ginn.

Jacobson, Pauline. 1980 (1977). *The Syntax of Crossing Coreference Sentences.* New York: Garland.

Jacobson, Pauline. 1984. "Connectivity in Phrase Structure Grammar." *Natural Language and Linguistic Theory* 1:535–582.

Jacobson, Pauline, and Neubauer, Paul. 1976. "Rule Cyclicity: Evidence from the Intervention Constraint." *Linguistic Inquiry* 7:429–462.

Jacobson, Pauline, and Pullum, Geoffrey, eds. 1982. *The Nature of Syntactic Representation.* Dordrecht: Reidel.

Jaeggli, Osvaldo. 1982. *Topics in Romance Syntax.* Dordrecht: Foris.

Jakobovits, Leon, and Miron, Murray, eds. 1967. *Readings in the Psychology of Language.* Englewood Cliffs, NJ: Prentice-Hall.

Jakobson, Roman. 1941. *Kindersprache, Aphasie und allgemeine Lautgesetze.* Uppsala Universitets Aarsskrift. (Translated as *Child Language, Aphasia and Phonological Universals.* 1968. The Hague: Mouton.)

Jakobson, Roman, ed. 1961. *Structure of Language and Its Mathematical Aspects* (=*Proceedings of Symposia in Applied Mathematics,* volume XII). Providence, RI: American Mathematical Society.

Jakobson, Roman. 1979. "The Twentieth Century in European and American Linguistics: Movements and Continuity." In *The European Background of American Linguistics,* edited by H. Hoenigswald, pp. 161–174. Dordrecht: Foris.

Jakobson, Roman, Fant, Gunnar, and Halle, Morris. 1952. *Preliminaries to Speech Analysis.* Cambridge, MA: MIT Press.

Jakobson, Roman, and Halle, Morris. 1956. *Fundamentals of Language.* The Hague: Mouton.

Janda, Richard. 1982. "On Limiting the Form of Morphological Rules." *Proceedings of NELS 12,* pp. 140–152.

Janda, Richard. 1983. "Morphemes Aren't Something that Grow on Trees." In *The Interplay of Phonology, Morphology, and Syntax,* edited by J. Richardson, M. Marks, and A. Chukerman, pp. 79–95. Chicago: Chicago Linguistic Society.

Jayaseelan, Karattuparambil. 1979. "On the Role of the Empty Node in the Structure-Preserving Hypothesis." *Linguistic Analysis* 5:247–292.

Jensen, John T. 1981. "X-Bar Morphology." *Proceedings of NELS 11,* pp. 155–172.

Jensen, John T., and Strong-Jensen, Margaret. 1984. "Morphology is in the Lexicon!" *Linguistic Inquiry* 15:474–498.

Jespersen, Otto. 1965 (1924). *The Philosophy of Grammar.* New York: Norton.

Johnson, David. 1974. "Prepaper on Relational Constraints on Grammars." Unpublished manuscript.

Johnson, David. 1976 (1974). *Toward a Theory of Relationally Based Grammar.* Indiana University Linguistics Club Publication.

Johnson, David, and Postal, Paul. 1979. *Arc-Pair Grammar.* Princeton: Princeton University Press.

Jones, Charles. 1984. "Under Control: Where is the Controlled Element?" *Papers from the Twentieth Regional Meeting of the Chicago Linguistic Society,* pp. 218–227.

Jones, Lyle, Lindzey, Gardner, and Coggeshall, Porter, eds. 1982. *An Assessment of Research-Doctorate Programs in the United States: Humanities.* Washington: National Academy Press.

Joos, Martin, ed. 1958. *Readings in Linguistics.* Washington: American Council of Learned Societies.

Joos, Martin. 1961. "Linguistic Prospects in the United States." In *Trends in European and American Linguistics, 1939–1960,* edited by C. Mohrmann, A. Sommerfelt, and J. Whatmough, pp. 11–20. Utrecht: Spectrum.

Joos, Martin. 1964. *The English Verb.* Madison: University of Wisconsin Press.

Joshi, Aravind, Webber, Bonnie, and Sag, Ivan, eds. 1981. *Elements of Discourse Understanding.* Cambridge, Cambridge University Press.

Kac, Michael. 1972. "Action and Result: Two Aspects of Predication in English." In *Syntax and Semantics,* vol. 1, edited by John Kimball, pp. 117–124. New York: Seminar Press.

Kac, Michael. 1978. *Corepresentation of Grammatical Structure*. Minneapolis: University of Minnesota Press.

Kaisse, Ellen. 1985. *Connected Speech*. New York: Academic Press.

Kaisse, Ellen, and Shaw, Patricia. 1985. "On the Theory of Lexical Phonology." *Phonology Yearbook* 2:1–30.

Kameyama, Megumi. 1985. *Zero Anaphora: The Case of Japanese*. Ph.D. dissertation, Stanford.

Kaplan, Ronald, and Bresnan, Joan. 1982. "Lexical-Functional Grammar: A Formal System for Grammatical Representation." In *The Mental Representation of Grammatical Relations*, edited by J. Bresnan, pp. 173–281. Cambridge, MA: MIT Press.

Karttunen, Lauri. 1973. "Presuppositions of Compound Sentences." *Linguistic Inquiry* 4:169–193.

Karttunen, Lauri, and Peters, Stanley. 1975. "Conventional Implicature and Montague Grammar." *Papers from the First Annual Meeting of the Berkeley Linguistics Society*, pp. 266–278.

Kartunen, Lauri, and Peters, Stanley. 1977. "Requiem for Presupposition." *Papers from the Third Annual Meeting of the Berkeley Linguistics Society*, pp. 360–371.

Katz, Jerrold. 1962. "A Reply to 'Projection and Paraphrase in Semantics.'" *Analysis* 22:36–41.

Katz, Jerrold. 1967. "Recent Issues in Semantic Theory." *Foundations of Language* 3:124–194.

Katz, Jerrold. 1972. *Semantic Theory*. New York: Harper and Row.

Katz, Jerrold. 1979. "A Solution to the Projection Problem for Presupposition." In *Syntax and Semantics, Volume 11: Presupposition*, edited by C. Oh and D. Dinneen, pp. 91–126. New York: Academic Press.

Katz, Jerrold, and Bever, Thomas. 1976. "The Fall and Rise of Empiricism." In *An Integrated Theory of Linguistic Ability*, edited by Thomas Bever, Jerrold Katz, and D. Terence Langendoen, pp. 11–64. New York: Crowell.

Katz, Jerrold, and Fodor, Jerry. 1963. "The Structure of a Semantic Theory." *Language* 39:170–210. Reprinted in *The Structure of Language*, edited by Jerry A. Fodor and Jerrold Katz, pp. 479–518. Englewood Cliffs, NJ: Prentice-Hall.

Katz, Jerrold, and Langendoen, D. Terence. 1976. "Pragmatics and Presupposition." *Language* 52:1–17.

Katz, Jerrold, and Postal, Paul. 1964. *An Integrated Theory of Linguistic Descriptions*. Cambridge, MA: MIT Press.

Kay, Martin. 1985. "Parsing in Functional Unification Grammar." In *Studies in Natural Language Processing*, pp. 251–278. Cambridge: Cambridge University Press.

Kayne, Richard. 1975. *French Syntax*. Cambridge, MA: MIT Press.

Kayne, Richard. 1984a. "Connectedness. In *Connectedness and Binary Branching*, edited by Richard Kayne, pp. 165–192. Dordrecht: Foris. Reprinted from *Linguistic Inquiry* (1983) 14:223–250.

Kayne, Richard. 1984b. *Connectedness and Binary Branching*. Dordrecht: Foris.

Kayne, Richard. 1984c (1981). "ECP Extensions." In *Connectedness and Binary Branching*, edited by Richard Kayne, pp. 47–86. Dordrecht: Foris. Reprinted from *Linguistic Inquiry* (1981) 12:93–134.

Kayne, Richard. 1984d. "Extensions of Binding and Case-Marking." In *Connectedness and Binary Branching*, edited by Richard Kayne, pp. 1–22. Dordrecht: Foris. Reprinted from *Linguistic Inquiry* (1980) 11:75–96.

Kayne, Richard. 1984e (1981). "On Certain Differences Between French and English." In *Connectedness and Binary Branching*, edited by Richard Kayne, pp. 103–124. Dordrecht: Foris. Reprinted from *Linguistic Inquiry* (1981) 12:349–372.

Kayne, Richard. 1984f. "Two Notes on the NIC." In *Connectedness and Binary Branching*, edited by Richard Kayne, pp. 23–46. Dordrecht: Foris.

Kayne, Richard. 1984g. "Unambiguous Paths." In *Connectedness and Binary Branching*, edited by Richard Kayne, pp. 129–164. Dordrecht: Foris.

Kayne, Richard, and Pollock, Jean-Yves. 1978. "Stylistic Inversion, Successive Cyclicity, and Move NP in French." *Linguistic Inquiry* 9:595–622.

Keenan, Edward. 1971. "Two Kinds of Presupposition in Natural Language." In *Studies in Linguistic*

Semantics, edited by Charles Fillmore and D. Terence Langendoen, pp. 45–54. New York: Holt, Rinehart and Winston.

Keenan, Edward, ed. 1975. *Formal Semantics of Natural Language.* London: Cambridge University Press.

Keenan, Edward, and Comrie, Bernard. 1977 (1972). "Noun Phrase Accessibility and Universal Grammar." *Linguistic Inquiry* 8:63–99.

Keenan, Edward, and Comrie, Bernard. 1979. "Data on the Noun Phrase Accessibility Hierarchy." *Language* 55:333–351.

Kempson, Ruth. 1975. *Presupposition and the Delimitation of Semantics.* Cambridge: Cambridge University Press.

Kenstowicz, Michael. 1984. "The Null-Subject Parameter in Modern Arabic Dialects." *Proceedings of NELS 14,* pp. 207–219.

Keyser, S. Jay, ed. 1978. *Recent Transformational Studies in European Languages.* Cambridge, MA: MIT Press.

Keyser, S. Jay, and Roeper, Thomas. 1984. "On the Middle and Ergative Constructions in English." *Linguistic Inquiry* 15:381–416.

Kiefer, Ferenc. 1979. "What Do Conversational Maxims Explain?" *Linguisticae Investigationes* 3:57–74.

Kim, W. C. 1976. *The Theory of Anaphora in Korean Syntax.* Ph.D. dissertation, MIT.

Kimball, John, 1972a. "Cyclic and Linear Grammars." In *Syntax and Semantics,* vol. 1, edited by John Kimball, pp. 63–80. New York: Seminar Press.

Kimball, John, ed. 1972b. *Syntax and Semantics,* vol. 1. New York: Seminar Press.

Kimball, John, ed. 1973. *Syntax and Semantics,* vol. 2. New York: Seminar Press.

King, Harold. 1970. "On Blocking the Rules for Contraction in English." *Linguistic Inquiry* 1:134–136.

Kiparsky, Paul. 1982a. "From Cyclic Phonology to Lexical Phonology." In *The Structure of Phonological Representations,* Part 1, edited by H. van der Hulst and N. Smith, pp. 131–176. Dordrecht: Foris.

Kiparsky, Paul. 1982b. "Lexical Phonology and Morphology." In *Linguistics in the Morning Calm,* edited by I. S. Yang, pp. 3–91. Seoul: Hanshin.

Kiss, Katalin. 1981. "On the Japanese 'Double Subject' Construction." *Linguistic Review* 1:155–170.

Klima, Edward. 1964. "Negation in English." In *The Structure of Language,* edited by Jerry A. Fodor and Jerrold Katz, pp. 246–323. Englewood Cliffs, NJ: Prentice-Hall.

Koerner, E. F. K. 1983. "The 'Chomskyan Revolution' and its Historiography: A Few Critical Remarks." *Language and Communication* 3:147–169.

Koopman, Hilda. 1982. "Theoretical Implications of the Distribution of *Quoi.*" *Proceedings of NELS 12,* pp. 153–162.

Koopman, Hilda. 1983. "ECP Effects in Main Clauses." *Linguistic Inquiry* 14:346–351.

Koopman, Hilda. 1984. *The Syntax of Verbs.* Dordrecht: Foris.

Koopman, Hilda, and Sportiche, Dominique. 1982. "Variables and the Bijection Principle." *Linguistic Review* 2:139–160.

Koster, Jan. 1978a. "Conditions, Empty Nodes, and Markedness." *Linguistic Inquiry* 9:551–594.

Koster, Jan. 1978b. *Locality Principles in Syntax.* Dordrecht: Foris.

Koster, Jan. 1978c. "Why Subject Sentences Don't Exist." In *Recent Transformational Studies in European Languages,* edited by S. Jay Keyser, 53–64. Cambridge, MA: MIT Press.

Koster, Jan. 1981. "Configurational Grammar." In *Levels of Syntactic Representation,* edited by J. Koster and R. May, pp. 185–206. Dordrecht: Foris.

Koster, Jan. 1984. "On Binding and Control." *Linguistic Inquiry* 15:417–460.

Koster, Jan, and May, Robert, eds. 1981. *Levels of Syntactic Representation.* Dordrecht: Foris.

Koster, Jan, van Riemsdijk, Henk, and Vergnaud, Jean Roger. 1978. "GLOW Manifesto." *GLOW Newsletter* 1:2–5.

Kroch, Anthony. 1972. "Lexical and Inferred Meanings for Some Time Adverbs." *Quarterly Progress Report of the MIT Research Laboratory of Electronics* 104.

Kroch, Anthony, and Joshi, Aravind. 1985. *The Linguistic Relevance of Tree Adjoining Grammar.* Department of Computer and Information Science, University of Pennsylvania.

Kroeber, A. L. 1952. "Culture." In *Papers of the Peabody Museum in American Archaeology and Ethnology,* edited by A. L. Kroeber and C. H. Kluckhohn, vol. 47, pp. 103–136.

Kuhn, Thomas. 1970. *The Structure of Scientific Revolutions* (second edition, enlarged). Chicago: University of Chicago Press.

Kuno, Susumu. 1973. "Constraints on Internal Clauses and Sentential Subjects." *Linguistic Inquiry* 4:363–386.

Kuno, Susumu. 1974. "The Position of Relative Clauses and Conjunctions." *Linguistic Inquiry* 5:117–136.

Kuno, Susumu. 1976. "Gapping: A Functional Analysis." *Linguistic Inquiry* 7:318–330.

Kuroda, S.-Y. 1969 (1965). "Attachment Transformations." In *Modern Studies in English,* edited by David Reibel and Sanford Schane, pp. 331–351. Englewood Cliffs, NJ: Prentice-Hall.

Kuroda, S.-Y. 1972. "Anton Marty and the Transformational Theory of Grammar." *Foundations of Language* 9:1–37.

Kuroda, S.-Y. 1974. "Geach and Katz on Presupposition." *Foundations of Language* 12:177–200.

Kuroda, S.-Y. 1983. "What Can Japanese Say About Government and Binding?" *Proceedings of the West Coast Conference on Formal Linguistics* 2, pp. 153–164.

La Barre, Weston. 1958. "What Linguists Tell Anthropologists." *Monograph Series on Languages and Linguistics* 9:73–78.

Ladd, Robert. 1980. *The Structure of Intonational Meaning.* Bloomington: Indiana University Press.

Lakoff, George. 1968a (1966). *Deep and Surface Grammar.* Indiana University Linguistics Club Publication.

Lakoff, George. 1968b. "Instrumental Adverbs and the Concept of Deep Structure." *Foundations of Language* 4:4–29.

Lakoff, George. 1968c. "Some Verbs of Change and Causation." In *The Computation Laboratory of Harvard University, Mathematical Linguistics and Automatic Translation, Report No. NSF-20 to the National Science Foundation,* pp. III-1–III-27.

Lakoff, George. 1969a. "Empiricism without Facts." *Foundations of Language* 5:118–127.

Lakoff, George. 1969b. "On Derivational Constraints." *Papers from the Fifth Regional Meeting of the Chicago Linguistic Society,* pp. 117–139.

Lakoff, George. 1970a. "Global Rules." *Language* 46:627–639.

Lakoff, George. 1970b (1965). *Irregularity in Syntax.* New York: Holt, Rinehart and Winston.

Lakoff, George. 1970c. "Pronominalization, Negation, and the Analysis of Adverbs." In *Readings in English Transformational Grammar,* edited by Roderick Jacobs and Peter Rosenbaum, pp. 145–165. Waltham, MA: Ginn.

Lakoff, George. 1971a (1969). "On Generative Semantics." In *Semantics,* edited by Danny Steinberg and Leon Jakobovits, pp. 232–296. Cambridge: Cambridge University Press.

Lakoff, George. 1971b. "Presupposition and Relative Well-Formedness." In *Semantics,* edited by Danny Steinberg and Leon Jakobovits, pp. 329–340. Cambridge: Cambridge University Press.

Lakoff, George. 1971c. "The Role of Deduction in Grammar." In *Studies in Linguistic Semantics,* edited by Charles Fillmore and D. Terence Langendoen, pp. 63–72. New York: Holt, Rinehart and Winston.

Lakoff, George. 1972a. "The Arbitrary Basis of Transformational Grammar." *Language* 48:76–87.

Lakoff, George. 1972b. "Forward" to "Where the Rules Fail" edited by Ann Borkin, pp. i–v. Indiana University Linguistics Club Publication.

Lakoff, George. 1972c. "The Global Nature of the Nuclear Stress Rule." *Language* 48:285–303.

Lakoff, George. 1972d. "Hedges: A Study in Meaning Criteria and the Logic of Fuzzy Concepts." *Papers from the Eighth Regional Meeting of the Chicago Linguistic Society,* pp. 183–228.

Lakoff, George. 1972e. "Linguistics and Natural Logic." In *Semantics of Natural Language,* edited by Donald Davison and Gilbert Harmon, pp. 545–665. Dordrecht: Reidel.

Lakoff, George. 1972f. Quotation from *The New York Times,* 10 September 1972.

Lakoff, George. 1973. "Fuzzy Grammar and the Performance/Competence Terminology Game." *Papers from the Ninth Regional Meeting of the Chicago Linguistic Society,* pp. 271–291.

Lakoff, George. 1974a. "Interview." In *Discussing Language,* by Herman Parret, pp. 151–178. The Hague: Mouton.

Lakoff, George. 1974b. "Notes Toward a Theory of Global Transderivational Well-Formedness Grammar." Unpublished manuscript.

Lakoff, George. 1975a. "Dual-Hierarchy Grammar." Unpublished manuscript.

Lakoff, George. 1975b (1973). "Pragmatics in Natural Logic." In *Formal Semantics of Natural Language,* edited by Edward Keenan, pp. 253–286. London: Cambridge University Press. Reprinted in *Proceedings of the Texas Conference,* edited by Andy Rogers, Bob Wall, and John P. Murphy, pp. 107–134. Arlington: Center for Applied Linguistics.

Lakoff, George. 1976a (1968). "Pronouns and Reference." In *Syntax and Semantics,* vol. 7, edited by James McCawley, pp. 275–335. New York: Academic Press.

Lakoff, George. 1976b (1963). "Toward Generative Semantics." In *Syntax and Semantics,* vol. 7, edited by James McCawley, pp. 43–62. New York: Academic Press.

Lakoff, George. 1977. "Linguistic Gestalts." *Papers from the Thirteenth Regional Meeting of The Chicago Linguistic Society,* pp. 236–287.

Lakoff, George, and Peters, Stanley. 1969. "Phrasal Conjunction and Symmetric Predicates." In *Modern Studies in English,* edited by David Reibel and Sanford Schane, pp. 113–142. Englewood Cliffs, NJ: Prentice-Hall.

Lakoff, George, and Ross, John R. 1976 (1967). "Is Deep Structure Necessary?" In *Syntax and Semantics,* vol. 7, edited by James McCawley, pp. 159–164. New York: Academic Press.

Lakoff, George, and Thompson, Henry. 1975. "Introducing Cognitive Grammar." *Papers from the First Annual Meeting of the Berkeley Linguistics Society,* pp. 295–313.

Lakoff, Robin. 1968. *Abstract Syntax and Latin Complementation.* Cambridge, MA: MIT Press.

Lakoff, Robin. 1971. "If's, And's and But's about Conjunction." In *Studies in Linguistic Semantics,* edited by Charles Fillmore and D. Terence Langendoen, pp. 115–150. New York: Holt, Rinehart and Winston.

Lakoff, Robin. 1972. "Language in Context." *Language* 48:907–927.

Lakoff, Robin. 1974. "Pluralism in Linguistics." In *Berkeley Studies in Syntax and Semantics,* vol. 1, pp. XIV-1–XIV-36. Berkeley: Department of Linguistics, University of California.

Lamb, Sidney. 1963. "On Redefining the Phoneme." Paper presented to Linguistic Society of America.

Lamendella, John. 1969. "On the Irrelevance of Transformational Grammar to Second Language Pedagogy." *Language Learning* 19:255–270.

Lane, Michael. 1970. *Introduction to Structuralism.* New York: Basic Books.

Langacker, Ronald. 1969 (1966). "On Pronominalization and the Chain of Command." In *Modern Studies in English,* edited by David Reibel and Sanford Schane, pp. 160–186. Englewood Cliffs, NJ: Prentice-Hall.

Langendoen, D. Terence, and Savin, Harris. 1971. "The Projection Problem for Presuppositions." In *Studies in Linguistic Semantics,* edited by C. Fillmore and D. T. Langendoen, pp. 55–62. New York: Holt, Rinehart and Winston.

Lapointe, Steven. 1980. *A Theory of Grammatical Agreement.* Ph.D. dissertation, University of Massachusetts.

Lapointe, Steven. 1981. "The Representation of Inflectional Morphology within the Lexicon." *Proceedings of NELS 11,* pp. 190–204.

Lapointe, Steven. 1983. "A Comparison of Two Recent Theories of Agreement." In *The Interplay of Phonology, Morphology, and Syntax,* edited by J. Richardson, M. Marks, and A. Chuckerman, pp. 122–134. Chicago: Chicago Linguistic Society.

Lasnik, Howard. 1976. "Remarks on Coreference." *Linguistic Analysis* 2:1–22.

Lasnik, Howard, and Freidin, Robert. 1981. "Core Grammar, Case Theory, and Markedness." In *Theory of Markedness in Core Grammar,* edited by A. Belletti, L. Brandi, and L. Rizzi, pp. 407–422. Pisa: Scuola Normale Superiore di Pisa.

Lasnik, Howard, and Saito, Mamoru. 1984. "On the Nature of Proper Government." *Linguistic Inquiry* 15:235–290.

Lawler, John. 1973. "Tracking the Generic Toad." *Papers from the Ninth Regional Meeting of the Chicago Linguistic Society*, pp. 320–331.

Lawler, John. 1977. "A Agrees with B in Achinese: A Problem for Relational Grammar." In *Syntax and Semantics*, vol. 8, edited by Peter Cole and Jerrold Sadock, pp. 219–248. New York: Academic Press.

Lees, Robert B. 1953. "The Basis of Glottochronology." *Language* 29:113–127.

Lees, Robert B. 1957. Review of Noam Chomsky, *Syntactic Structures*. *Language* 33:375–408.

Lees, Robert B. 1960. *The Grammar of English Nominalizations*. The Hague: Mouton.

Lees, Robert B. 1961. "Grammatical Analysis of the English Comparative Construction." *Word* 17:171–185. Reprinted in *Modern Studies in English*, edited by David Reibel and Sanford Schane (1969), pp. 303–315. Englewood Cliffs, NJ: Prentice-Hall.

Lees, Robert B. 1963. "Analysis of the 'Cleft Sentence in English.'" *Zeitschrift für Phonetik* 16:311–388.

Lees, Robert B. 1964. "On Passives and Imperatives in English." *Gengo Kenkyu* 46:28–41.

Lees, Robert B., and Klima, Edward. 1963. "Rules for English Pronominalization." *Language* 39:17–28. Reprinted in *Modern Studies in English*, edited by David Reibel and Sanford Schane (1969), pp. 145–159. Englewood Cliffs, NJ: Prentice-Hall.

Lefebvre, Claire, and Muysken, Pieter. 1982. "Raising as Move Case." *Linguistic Review* 2:161–210.

Lehmann, Winfred. 1978. "The Great Underlying Ground-Plans." In *Syntactic Typology*, edited by W. Lehmann, pp. 3–56. Austin: University of Texas Press.

Le Page, R. B. 1964. *The National Language Question*. London: Oxford University Press.

Lévi-Strauss, Claude. 1953. "Remarks." In *An Appraisal of Anthropology Today*, edited by Sol Tax, *et al.*, pp. 349–352. Chicago: University of Chicago Press.

Levin, Beth, and Rappaport, Malka. 1985. *The Formation of Adjectival Passives*. MIT Lexicon Working Papers #2.

Levin, Juliette. 1984. "Government Relations and the Distribution of Empty Operators." *Proceedings of NELS 14*, pp. 294–305.

Levin, Lori. 1982. "Sluicing: A Lexical Interpretation Procedure." In *The Mental Representation of Grammatical Relations*, edited by J. Bresnan, pp. 590–654. Cambridge, MA: MIT Press.

Levin, Lori, Rappaport, Malka, and Zaenen, Annie, eds. 1983. *Papers in Lexical-Functional Grammar*. Indiana University Linguistics Club Publication.

Levin, Lori, and Simpson, Jane. 1981. "Quirky Case and the Structure of Icelandic Lexical Entries." *Papers from the Seventeenth Regional Meeting of the Chicago Linguistic Society*, pp. 185–196.

Levin, Samuel R. 1965. "Langue and Parole in American Linguistics." *Foundations of Language* 1:83–94.

Levinson, Stephen. 1979. "Pragmatics and Social Deixis." *Proceedings of the Fifth Annual Meeting of the Berkeley Linguistics Society*, pp. 206–223.

Levinson, Stephen. 1980. "Speech Act Theory: The State of the Art." *Language and Language Teaching Abstracts* 13:5–24.

Levinson, Stephen. 1983. *Pragmatics*. Cambridge: Cambridge University Press.

Levy, Mary, Carroll, John B. and Roberts, A. Hood. 1976. *Present and Future Needs for Specialists in Linguistics and the Uncommonly Taught Languages*. Arlington, VA: Center for Applied Linguistics and Linguistic Society of America.

Lewis, David. 1972. "General Semantics." In *Semantics of Natural Language*, edited by Donald Davidson and Gilbert Harmon, pp. 169–218. Dordrecht: Reidel. Reprinted in *Montague Grammar*, edited by Barbara Partee (1976), pp. 1–50. New York: Academic Press.

Li, Charles, ed. 1975. *Word Order and Word Order Change*. Austin: University of Texas Press.

Li, Charles, ed. 1976. *Subject and Topic*. New York: Academic Press.

Li, Charles, ed. 1977. *Mechanisms of Syntactic Change*. Austin: University of Texas Press.

Lieber, Rochelle. 1981. *On the Organization of the Lexicon*. Indiana University Linguistics Club Publication.

Lieber, Rochelle. 1983. "Argument Linking and Compounds in English." *Linguistic Inquiry* 14:251–286.

Lightfoot, David. 1976. "Trace Theory and Twice-Moved NPs." *Linguistic Inquiry* 7:559–582.

Lightfoot, David. 1979. Review of C. Li, *Mechanisms of Syntactic Change. Language* 55:381–395.

Locke, William N. 1955. "Machine Translation to Date." *Monograph Series on Language and Linguistics* 6:101–113.

Longobardi, Giuseppe. 1985. "Connectedness and Island Constraints." In *Grammatical Representation*, edited by J. Guéron, H. G. Obenauer, and J.-Y. Pollock, pp. 117–146. Dordrecht: Foris.

Lyons, John. 1968. *Introduction to Theoretical Linguistics*. Cambridge: Cambridge University Press.

Lyons, John. 1977. "Deixis and Anaphora." In *The Development of Conversation and Discourse*, edited by T. Myers, pp. 88–103. Edinburgh: Edinburgh University Press.

Maclay, Howard. 1973. "Linguistics and Psycholinguistics." In *Issues in Linguistics: Papers in Honor of Henry and Renee Kahane*, edited by B. Kachru, *et al.*, pp. 569–587. Urbana: University of Illinois Press.

Maling, Joan. 1977. "Old Icelandic Relative Clauses: An Unbounded Deletion Rule." *Proceedings of NELS 7*, pp. 175–188.

Maling, Joan. 1978. "An Asymmetry with Respect to *Wh*-Islands." *Linguistic Inquiry* 9:75–88.

Manzini, Maria Rita. 1983. "On Control and Control Theory." *Linguistic Inquiry* 14:421–446.

Marantz, Alec. 1980. "English S is the Maximal Projection of V." *Proceedings of NELS 10*, pp. 303–314.

Marantz, Alec. 1984. *On the Nature of Grammatical Relations*. Cambridge, MA: MIT Press.

Martinet, André. 1953. "Structural Linguistics." In *Anthropology Today*, edited by A. L. Kroeber, *et al.*, pp. 574–586. Chicago: University of Chicago Press.

Martinet, André. 1960. *Elements de Linguistique Générale*. Paris: Librarie Armand Colin.

Matthews, G. H. 1961. "Analysis by Synthesis of Sentences of Natural Language." *First International Conference on Machine Translation*. Teddington, England.

May, Robert. 1977. *The Grammar of Quantification*. Ph.D. dissertation, MIT.

May, Robert. 1985. *Logical Form: Its Structure and Derivation*. Cambridge, MA: MIT Press.

Mazurkewich, Irene, and White, Lydia. 1984. "The Acquisition of the Dative Alternation: Unlearning Overgeneralizations." *Cognition* 16: 261–283.

McCarthy, John. 1979. *Formal Problems in Semitic Phonology and Morphology*. Ph.D. dissertation, MIT.

McCawley, James. 1968a. "Concerning the Base Component of a Transformational Grammar." *Foundations of Language* 4:243–269. Reprinted in *Grammar and Meaning*, by James McCawley (1976), pp. 35–58. New York: Academic Press.

McCawley, James. 1968b. "Lexical Insertion in a Transformational Grammar without Deep Structure." *Papers from the Fourth Regional Meeting of the Chicago Linguistic Society*, pp. 71–80. Reprinted in *Grammar and Meaning*, by James McCawley (1976), pp. 155–166. New York: Academic Press.

McCawley, James. 1968c. "The Role of Semantics in Grammar." In *Universals in Linguistic Theory*, edited by Emmon Bach and Robert Harms, pp. 125–170. New York: Holt, Rinehart and Winston. Reprinted in *Grammar and Meaning*, by James McCawley (1976), pp. 59–98. New York: Academic Press.

McCawley, James. 1970a. "English as a VSO Language." *Language* 46:286–299. Reprinted in *Grammar and Meaning*, by James McCawley (1976), pp. 211–228. New York: Academic Press.

McCawley, James. 1970b. "Semantic Representation." In *Cognition: A Multiple View*, edited by P. Garvin, pp. 227–247. New York: Spartan Books. Reprinted in *Grammar and Meaning*, by McCawley (1976), pp. 240–256. New York: Academic Press.

McCawley, James. 1970c. "Where Do Noun Phrases Come From?" In *Readings in English Transformational Grammar*, edited by Roderick Jacobs and Peter Rosenbaum, pp. 166–183. Waltham, MA: Ginn. Reprinted in *Grammar and Meaning*, by James McCawley (1976), pp. 133–154. New York: Academic Press.

McCawley, James. 1971. "Interpretive Semantics Meets Frankenstein." *Foundations of Language* 7:285–296. Reprinted in *Grammar and Meaning*, by James McCawley (1976), pp. 333–342. New York: Academic Press.

McCawley, James. 1972. "On Interpreting the Theme of This Conference." In *Limiting the Domain of Linguistics*, edited by David Cohen, n.p. Milwaukee: University of Wisconsin Linguistics Group.

McCawley, James. 1974 (1972). "Interview." In *Discussing Language*, by Herman Parret, pp. 249–278. The Hague: Mouton.

McCawley, James. 1975. "Review of N. Chomsky, *Studies on Semantics in Generative Grammar*." *Studies in English Linguistics* 3:209–311.

McCawley, James. 1976a. *Grammar and Meaning*. New York: Academic Press.

McCawley, James. 1976b. "Madison Avenue, Si, Pennsylvania Avenue, No!" In *The Second LACUS Forum*, edited by Peter Reich, pp. 1–20. Reprinted in *Adverbs, Vowels, and Other Objects of Wonder* by J. McCawley (1979), pp. 223–234. Chicago: University of Chicago Press.

McCawley, James, 1976c. "Notes on Jackendoff's Theory of Anaphora." *Linguistic Inquiry* 7: 319–341

McCawley, James, ed. 1976d. *Syntax and Semantics, Volume 7: Notes from the Linguistic Underground*. New York: Academic Press.

McCawley, James. 1977a. "Evolutionary Parallels between Montague Grammar and Transformational Grammar." *Proceedings of NELS 7*, pp. 219–232.

McCawley, James. 1977b. "The Nonexistence of Syntactic Categories." In *Second Annual Linguistic Metatheory Conference Proceedings*, pp. 212–222. East Lansing: Department of Linguistics, Michigan State University.

McCawley, James. 1979. *Adverbs, Vowels, and Other Objects of Wonder*. Chicago: University of Chicago Press.

McCloskey, James. 1984. "Raising, Subcategorization, and Selection in Modern Irish." *Natural Language and Linguistic Theory* 1:441–486.

McCloskey, James. 1985. "Case, Movement, and Raising in Irish." *Proceedings of the Fourth West Coast Conference on Formal Linguistics* (in press).

Mehta, Ved. 1971. *John Is Easy to Please*. New York: Farrar, Strauss and Giroux.

Mellema, Paul. 1974. "A Brief Against Case Grammar." *Foundations of Language* 11:39–76.

Miller, George, and Chomsky, Noam. 1963. "Finitary Models of Language Users." In *Handbook of Mathematical Psychology*, vol. II, edited by P. Luce, R. Bush, and E. Galanter, pp. 419–492. New York: Wiley.

Miller, George, Galanter, E., and Pribram, K. 1960. *Plans and the Structure of Behavior*. New York: Holt, Rinehart and Winston.

Mohanan, K. P. 1982a. "Grammatical Relations and Clause Structure in Malayalam." In *The Mental Representation of Grammatical Relations*, edited by J. Bresnan, pp. 504–589. Cambridge, MA: MIT Press.

Mohanan, K. P. 1982b. *Lexical Phonology*. Indiana University Linguistics Club Publication.

Montague, Richard. 1970a. "English as a Formal Language." In *Linguaggi nella Societa e nella Tecnica*, edited by B. Visentini *et al.*, pp. 189–224. Milan: Edizioni di Communita. Reprinted in *Formal Philosophy*, edited by Richmond Thomason (1974), pp. 188–221. New Haven: Yale University Press.

Montague, Richard. 1970b. "Universal Grammar." *Theoria* 36:373–398. Reprinted in *Formal Philosophy*, edited by Richmond Thomason (1974), pp. 222–246. New Haven: Yale University Press.

Montalbetti, Mario, and Saito, Mamoru. 1983. "On Certain (Tough) Differences between Spanish and English." *Proceedings of NELS 13*, pp. 191–198.

Moortgat, Michael. 1984. "A Fregean Restriction on Metarules." *Proceedings of NELS 14*, pp. 306–325.

Moortgat, Michael, van der Hulst, Harry, and Hoekstra, Teun, eds. 1981. *The Scope of Lexical Rules*. Dordrecht: Foris.

Moravcsik, Edith, and Wirth, Jessica, eds. 1980. *Syntax and Semantics, Volume 13: Current Approaches to Syntax.* New York: Academic Press.

Morgan, Charles Grady, and Pelletier, Francis Jeffry. 1977. "Some Notes Concerning Fuzzy Logics." *Linguistics and Philosophy* 1:79–98.

Morgan, Jerry. 1969a. "On Arguing about Semantics." *Papers in Linguistics* 1:49–70.

Morgan, Jerry. 1969b. "On the Treatment of Presupposition in Transformational Grammar." *Papers from the Fifth Regional Meeting of the Chicago Linguistic Society,* pp. 167–177.

Morgan, Jerry. 1972. "Some Aspects of Relative Clauses in English and Albanian." In *The Chicago Which Hunt,* edited by P. Peranteau, J. Levi, and G. Phares, pp. 63–72. Chicago: Chicago Linguistic Society.

Morgan, Jerry. 1973a. "How Can You Be in Two Places at Once, When You're Not Anywhere at All?" *Papers from the Ninth Regional Meeting of the Chicago Linguistic Society,* pp. 410–427.

Morgan, Jerry. 1973b. "Sentence Fragments and the Notion 'Sentence.'" In *Issues in Linguistics: Papers in Honor of Henry and Renee Kahane,* edited by B. Kachru, *et al.,* pp. 719–751. Urbana: University of Illinois Press.

Morgan, Jerry. 1975. "Some Interactions of Syntax and Pragmatics." In *Syntax and Semantics,* vol. 3, edited by Peter Cole and Jerry Morgan, pp. 289–304. New York: Academic Press.

Morgan, Jerry. 1977. "Conversational Postulates Revisited." *Language* 53:277–284.

Morgan, Jerry. 1978. "Two Types of Convention in Indirect Speech Acts." In *Syntax and Semantics,* vol. 9, edited by Peter Cole, pp. 261–280. New York: Academic Press.

Murray, Stephen. 1980. "Gatekeepers and the 'Chomskyan Revolution.'" *Journal of the History of the Behavioral Sciences* 16:73–88.

Muysken, Pieter. 1981a. "Quechua Causatives and Logical Form: A Case Study in Markedness." In *Theory of Markedness in Generative Grammar,* edited by A. Belletti, L. Brandi, and L. Rizzi, pp. 445–474. Pisa: Scuola Normale Superiore.

Muysken, Pieter. 1981b. "Quechua Word Structure." In *Binding and Filtering,* edited by Frank Heny, pp. 279–328. Cambridge, MA: MIT Press.

Muysken, Pieter. 1982. "Parameterizing the Notion 'Head.'" *Journal of Linguistic Research* 2:57–76.

Napoli, Donna Jo, and Nespor, Marina. 1979. "The Syntax of Word-Initial Consonant Germination in Italian." *Language* 55:812–841.

National Research Council, Commission on Human Resources. 1975–1984. *Summary Report, Doctorate Recipients from United States Universities.* Washington, D.C.: National Academy Press.

Neidle, Carol. 1982. "Case Agreement in Russian." In *The Mental Representation of Grammatical Relations,* edited by Joan Bresnan, pp. 391–426. Cambridge, MA: MIT Press.

Newman, Paul. 1978. Review of C. Hagège, *La Grammaire Générative. Language* 54:925–929.

Newmeyer, Frederick. 1971. "The Source of Derived Nominals in English." *Language* 47:786–796.

Newmeyer, Frederick. 1975 (1969). *English Aspectual Verbs.* The Hague: Mouton.

Newmeyer, Frederick. 1976a. "The Precyclic Nature of Predicate Raising." In *Syntax and Semantics,* vol. 6, edited by Mayayoshi Shibatani, pp. 131–164. New York: Academic Press.

Newmeyer, Frederick. 1976b. "Relational Grammar and Autonomous Syntax." *Papers from the Twelfth Regional Meeting of the Chicago Linguistic Society,* pp. 506–515.

Newmeyer, Frederick. 1977. "Review of F. Rossi-Landi, *Linguistics and Economics." Language* 53:254–256.

Newmeyer, Frederick. 1983. *Grammatical Theory: Its Limits and Its Possibilities.* Chicago: University of Chicago Press.

Newmeyer, Frederick. 1986a. "Has There been a 'Chomskyan Revolution' in Linguistics?" *Language* 62:1–18.

Newmeyer, Frederick. 1986b. "Minor Movement Rules." In *Rhetorica, Phonologica, Syntactica: Papers Presented to Robert P. Stockwell by his Friends and Colleagues,* edited by C. Duncan-Rose, J. Fisiak, and T. Vennemann (in press). Amsterdam: Benjamins.

Newmeyer, Frederick. In press. *The Politics of Linguistics.* Chicago: University of Chicago Press (hardcover) and New York: Pantheon Books (paperbound).

Newmeyer, Frederick, ed. Forthcoming. *Linguistics: The Cambridge Survey.* Cambridge: Cambridge University Press.

Newmeyer, Frederick, and Emonds, Joseph. 1971. "The Linguist in American Society." *Papers from the Seventh Regional Meeting of the Chicago Linguistic Society,* pp. 285–306.

Newmeyer, Frederick, and Weinberger, Steven. Forthcoming. "The Ontogenesis of the Field of Second Language Learning Research." In *Proceedings of the M.I.T. Conference on Linguistic Theory and Second Language Learning,* edited by S. Flynn and W. O'Neil. Dordrecht: Reidel.

Nishigauchi, Taisuke. 1984. "Control and Thematic Domain." *Language* 60:215–250.

Oehrle, Richard. 1976. *The Grammatical Status of the English Dative Alternation.* Ph.D. dissertation, MIT.

Oehrle, Richard. 1977. Review of G. Green, *Semantics and Syntactic Regularity. Language* 53:198–208.

Oehrle, Richard, Bach, Emmon, and Wheeler, Deirdre, eds. 1986. *Categorial Grammars and Natural Language Structures.* Dordrecht: Reidel.

Oh, Choon-Kyu, and Dinneen, David, eds. 1979. *Syntax and Semantics, Volume 9: Presupposition.* New York: Academic Press.

Olmstead, David. 1955. Review of C. Osgood and T. Sebeok, *Psycholinguistics. Language* 31:46–59.

Osgood, Charles, and Miron, Murray. 1963. *Approaches to the Study of Aphasia.* Urbana: University of Illinois Press.

Osgood, Charles, and Sebeok, Thomas. 1954. *Psycholinguistics.* Indiana University Publications in Anthropology and Linguistics, Memoir 10 of the *International Journal of American Linguistics.* Bloomington: Indiana University Press.

Parret, Herman. 1974. *Discussing Language: Interviews with [Various Linguists].* The Hague: Mouton.

Partee, Barbara. 1970 (1968). "Negation, Conjunction, and Quantifiers: Syntax vs. Semantics." *Foundations of Language* 6:153–165.

Partee, Barbara. 1971. "On the Requirement That Transformations Preserve Meaning." In *Studies in Linguistic Semantics,* edited by Charles Fillmore and D. Terence Langendoen, pp. 1–22. New York: Holt, Rinehart and Winston.

Partee, Barbara. 1973. "Some Transformational Extensions of Montague Grammar." *Journal of Philosophical Logic* 2:509–534. Reprinted in *Montague Grammar,* edited by Barbara Partee (1976), pp. 51–76. New York: Academic Press.

Partee, Barbara. 1975a. "Deletion and Variable Binding." In *Formal Semantics of Natural Language,* edited by Edward Keenan, pp. 16–34. London: Cambridge University Press.

Partee, Barbara. 1975b. "Montague Grammar and Transformational Grammar." *Linguistic Inquiry* 6:203–300.

Partee, Barbara, ed. 1976. *Montague Grammar.* New York: Academic Press.

Pelletier, Francis Jeffry. 1977. "How/Why Does Linguistics Matter to Philosophy?" *Southern Journal of Philosophy* 15:393–426.

Peranteau, Paul, Levi, Judith, and Phares, Gloria, eds. 1972. *The Chicago Which Hunt.* Chicago: Chicago Linguistic Society.

Percival, W. Keith. 1971. Review of P. Salus, *Linguistics. Language* 47:181–185.

Perlmutter, David. 1971 (1968). *Deep and Surface Structure Constraints in Syntax.* New York: Holt, Rinehart and Winston.

Perlmutter, David. 1972. Evidence for Shadow Pronouns in French Relativization." In *The Chicago Which Hunt,* edited by Paul Peranteau, Judith Levi, and Gloria Phares, pp. 73–105. Chicago: Chicago Linguistic Society.

Perlmutter, David. 1978. "Impersonal Passives and the Unaccusative Hypothesis." *Papers from the Fourth Annual Meeting of the Berkeley Linguistics Society,* pp. 157–189.

Perlmutter, David, ed. 1983. *Studies in Relational Grammar 1.* Chicago: University of Chicago Press.

Perlmutter, David, and Postal, Paul. 1977. "Toward a Universal Characterization of Passive." *Papers from the Third Annual Meeting of the Berkeley Linguistics Society,* pp. 394–417.

Perlmutter, David, and Rosen, Carol, eds. 1984. *Studies in Relational Grammar 2.* Chicago: University of Chicago Press.

Pesetsky, David. 1982a (1979). "Complementizer-Trace Phenomena and the Nominative Island Condition." *Linguistic Review* 1:297–344.

Pesetsky, David. 1982b. *Paths and Categories.* Ph.D. dissertation, MIT.

Pesetsky, David. 1985. "Morphology and Logical Form." *Linguistic Inquiry* 16:193–246.

Pesetsky, David. Forthcoming. Paper to appear in *The Representation of Indefiniteness,* edited by E. Reuland and A. ter Meulen. Cambridge, MA: MIT Press.

Peters, Stanley, ed. 1972. *Goals of Linguistic Theory.* Englewood Cliffs, NJ: Prentice-Hall.

Peters, Stanley. 1982. "Phrase Linking Grammar." Unpublished manuscript, Stanford.

Peters, Stanley, and Ritchie, Robert. 1969. "A Note on the Universal Base Hypothesis." *Journal of Linguistics* 5:150–152.

Peters, Stanley, and Ritchie, Robert. 1971. "On Restricting the Base Component of Transformational Grammars." *Information Sciences* 6:49–83.

Peters, Stanley, and Ritchie, Robert. 1973. "On the Generative Power of Transformational Grammars." *Information Sciences* 6:49–83.

Picallo, M. Carme. 1984. "The INFL Node and the Null Subject Parameter." *Linguistic Inquiry* 15:75–102.

Pierrehumbert, Janet. 1980. "The Finnish Possessive Suffixes." *Language* 56:603–621.

Pike, Kenneth. 1947a. "Grammatical Prerequisites to Phonemic Analysis." *Word* 3:155–172.

Pike, Kenneth. 1947b. "On the Phonemic Status of English Diphthongs." *Language* 23:151–159.

Pike, Kenneth. 1952. "More on Grammatical Prerequisites." *Word* 8:106–172.

Pike, Kenneth. 1954. *Language in Relation to a Unified Theory of the Structure of Human Behavior.* Glendale, CA: Summer Institute of Linguistics.

Pike, Kenneth. 1958. "Discussion." *Proceedings of the Eighth International Congress of Linguists.* Oslo: Oslo University Press.

Pinker, Steven. 1979. "Formal Models of Language Learning." *Cognition* 1:217–283.

Pinker, Steven. 1982. "A Theory of the Acquisition of Lexical Interpretive Grammars." In *The Mental Representation of Grammatical Relations,* edited by J. Bresnan, pp. 655–726.

Pinker, Steven. 1984. *Language Learnability and Language Development.* Cambridge, MA: Harvard University Press.

Platzack, Christer. 1982. "Transitive Adjectives in Swedish: A Phenomenon with Implications for the Theory of Abstract Case." *Linguistic Review* 2:39–56.

Pollard, Carl. 1984. *Generalized Phrase Structure Grammars, Head Grammars, and Natural Language.* Ph.D. dissertation, Stanford.

Pollard, Carl. 1985. "Phrase Structure Grammar without Metarules." *Proceedings of the West Coast Conference on Formal Linguistics* 3, pp. 246–261.

Pool. I. de Sola. 1959. *Trends in Content Analysis.* Urbana: University of Illinois Press.

Poser, William. 1982. "Lexical Rules May Exchange Internal Arguments." *Linguistic Review* 2:97–100.

Postal, Paul. 1962. *Some Syntactic Rules in Mohawk.* Ph.D. dissertation, Yale University.

Postal, Paul. 1964a. *Constituent Structure: A Study of Contemporary Models of Syntactic Description.* The Hague: Mouton.

Postal, Paul. 1964b. "Limitations of Phrase Structure Grammars." In *The Structure of Language,* edited by Jerry A. Fodor and Jerrold Katz, pp. 137–151. Englewood Cliffs, NJ: Prentice-Hall.

Postal, Paul. 1964c. "Underlying and Superficial Linguistic Structure." *Harvard Educational Review* 34:246–266.

Postal, Paul. 1966. Review of R. M. W. Dixon, *Linguistic Science and Logic. Language* 42:84–92.

Postal, Paul. 1968. *Aspects of Phonological Theory.* New York: Harper and Row.

Postal, Paul. 1969. "Anaphoric Islands." *Papers from the Fifth Regional Meeting of the Chicago Linguistic Society,* pp. 205–239.

Postal, Paul. 1970a. "On Coreferential Complement Subject Deletion." *Linguistic Inquiry* 1:439–500.

Postal, Paul. 1970b. "On the Surface Verb 'Remind.'" *Linguistic Inquiry* 1:37–120. Reprinted in *Studies in Linguistic Semantics,* edited by Charles Fillmore and D. Terence Langendoen (1971), pp. 181–272. New York: Holt, Rinehart and Winston.

Postal, Paul. 1971 (1967). *Cross-Over Phenomena.* New York: Holt, Rinehart and Winston.

Postal, Paul. 1972a (1969). "The Best Theory." In *Goals of Linguistic Theory,* edited by Stanley Peters, pp. 131–170. Englewood Cliffs, NJ: Prentice-Hall.

Postal, Paul. 1972b. "On Some Rules That Are Not Successive Cyclic." *Linguistic Inquiry* 3:211–222.

Postal, Paul. 1974. *On Raising.* Cambridge, MA: MIT Press.

Postal, Paul. 1976a. "Avoiding Reference to Subject." *Linguistic Inquiry* 7:151–181.

Postal, Paul. 1976b. (1967). "Linguistic Anarchy Notes." In *Syntax and Semantics,* vol. 7, edited by James McCawley, pp. 201–226. New York: Academic Press.

Postal, Paul. 1977. "Antipassive in French." *Lingvisticae Investigationes* 1:333–374.

Postal, Paul, and Pullum, Geoffrey. 1982. "The Contraction Debate." *Linguistic Inquiry* 13:122–138.

Postal, Paul, and Pullum, Geoffrey. 1986. "Misgovernment." *Linguistic Inquiry* 17:104–110.

Price, P. J. 1983. "The Status of Women in Linguistics." Unpublished manuscript, MIT.

Prince, Ellen. 1976. "The Syntax and Semantics of NEG-Raising with Evidence from French." *Language* 52:404–426.

Prince, Ellen. 1981. "Toward a Taxonomy of Given-New Information." In *Radical Pragmatics,* edited by Peter Cole, pp. 223–256. New York: Academic Press.

Pullum, Geoffrey. 1979a. "The Nonexistence of the Trace-Binding Algorithm." *Linguistic Inquiry* 10:356–362.

Pullum, Geoffrey. 1979b (1976). *Rule Interaction and the Organization of Grammar.* New York: Garland.

Pullum, Geoffrey. 1982. "Free Word Order and Phrase Structure Rules." *Proceedings of NELS 12,* pp. 209–220.

Pullum, Geoffrey. 1983. "How Many Possible Human Languages Are There?" *Linguistic Inquiry* 14:447–468.

Pullum, Geoffrey. 1985a. "Assuming Some Version of X-Bar Theory." *Papers from the Twenty-First Regional Meeting of the Chicago Linguistic Society,* pp. 323–353.

Pullum, Geoffrey. 1985b. "*Such that* Clauses and the Context-Freeness of English." *Linguistic Inquiry* 16:291–297.

Pullum, Geoffrey, and Gazdar, Gerald. 1982. "Natural Languages and Context-Free Languages." *Linguistics and Philosophy* 4:471–504.

Pullum, Geoffrey, and Postal, Paul. 1979. "On an Inadequate Defense of 'Trace Theory.'" *Linguistic Inquiry* 10:689–706.

Pullum, Geoffrey, and Zwicky, Arnold. Forthcoming (a). *The Syntax-Phonology Interface.* New York: Academic Press (in press).

Pullum, Geoffrey, and Zwicky, Arnold. Forthcoming (b). "The Syntax-Phonology Interface." In *Linguistics: The Cambridge Survey,* edited by F. Newmeyer. Cambridge: Cambridge University Press (in press).

Quicoli, A. C. 1972. *Aspects of Portuguese Complementation.* Ph.D. dissertation, State University of New York at Buffalo.

Quicoli, A. C. 1982. *The Structure of Complementation.* Ghent: E. Story-Scientia.

Randall, Janet. 1982. "A Lexical Approach to Causatives." *Journal of Linguistic Research* 2:77–105.

Rando, Emily, and Napoli, Donna Jo. 1978. "Definites in *There*-Sentences." *Language 54:300–313.*

Reibel, David, and Schane, Sanford, eds. 1969. *Modern Studies in English.* Englewood Cliffs, NJ: Prentice-Hall.

Reichenbach, Hans. 1947. *Elements of Symbolic Logic.* New York: Macmillan.

Reichling, Anton. 1961. "Principles and Methods of Syntax: Cryptanalytical Formalism." *Lingua* 10:1–17.

Reinhart, Tanya. 1981 (1976). "Definite NP Anaphora and C-Command Domains." *Linguistic Inquiry* 12:605–636.

Reinhart, Tanya. 1982. *Pragmatics and Linguistics: An Analysis of Sentence Topics.* Indiana University Linguistics Club Publication.

Reuland, Eric. 1983. "Governing *-ing.*" *Linguistic Inquiry* 14:101–136.

Rhodes, Richard. 1977. "Semantics in a Relational Grammar." *Papers from the Thirteenth Regional Meeting of the Chicago Linguistic Society,* pp. 503–514.

Rivas, Alberto. 1977. *A Theory of Clitics.* Ph.D. dissertation, MIT.

Rizzi, Luigi. 1981. "Nominative Marking in Italian Infinitives and the Nominative Island Constraint." In *Binding and Filtering,* edited by F. Heny, pp. 129–158. Cambridge, MA: MIT Press.

Rizzi, Luigi. 1982a. *Issues in Italian Syntax.* Dordrecht: Foris.

Rizzi, Luigi. 1982b. "Negation, *Wh*-Movement, and the Null Subject Parameter." In *Issues in Italian Syntax,* by L. Rizzi, pp. 117–184. Dordrecht: Foris.

Rizzi, Luigi. 1982c. "Violations of the *Wh*-Island Constraint and the Subjacency Condition." In *Issues in Italian Syntax* by Luigi Rizzi, pp. 49–76. Dordrecht: Foris.

Robinson, Jane. 1970. "Dependency Structures and Transformational Rules." *Language* 46:259–385.

Rochemont, Michael. 1978. *A Theory of Stylistic Rules in English.* Ph.D. dissertation, University of Massachusetts.

Rodman, Robert. 1975. "The Nondiscrete Nature of Islands." Indiana University Linguistics Club Publication.

Roeper, Thomas. 1987. "Implicit Arguments." *Linguistic Inquiry* (in press).

Roeper, Thomas, and Siegel, Muffy. 1978. "A Lexical Transformation for Verbal Compounds." *Linguistic Inquiry* 9:199–260.

Rogers, Andy. 1974. "A Transderivational Constraint on Richard?" *Papers from the Tenth Regional Meeting of the Chicago Linguistic Society,* pp. 551–558.

Rogers, Andy, Wall, Bob, and Murphy, John P., eds. 1977 (1973). *Proceedings of the Texas Conference on Performatives, Presuppositions, and Implicatures.* Arlington, VA: Center for Applied Linguistics.

Ronat, Mitsou. 1972 (1970). *A Propos du Verbe 'Remind' selon P. M. Postal, La Sémantique Générative: Une Réminiscence du Structuralisme?* Padova: Liviana Editrice.

Rosch, Eleanor. 1973. "On the Internal Structure of Perceptual and Semantic Categories." In *Cognitive Development and the Acquisition of Language,* edited by T. Moore, pp. 111–144. New York: Academic Press.

Rosen, Carol. 1981. *The Relational Structure of Reflexive Clauses: Evidence From Italian.* Ph.D. dissertation, Harvard.

Rosen, Carol. 1982. "The Unaccusative Hypothesis and the 'Inherent Clitic' Phenomenon in Italian." *Papers from the Eighteenth Regional Meeting of the Chicago Linguistic Society,* pp. 530–541.

Rosen, Carol. 1984. "The Interface between Semantic Roles and Initial Grammatical Relations." In *Studies in Relational Grammar 2,* edited by D. Perlmutter and C. Rosen, pp. 38–80. Chicago: University of Chicago Press.

Rosenbaum, Peter. 1967 (1965). *The Grammar of English Predicate Complement Constructions.* Cambridge, MA: MIT Press.

Ross, John R. 1967. "On the Cyclic Nature of English Pronominalization." In *To Honor Roman Jakobson,* 1669–1682. The Hague: Mouton. Reprinted in *Modern Studies in English,* edited by David Reibel and Sanford Schane (1969), pp. 187–200. Englewood Cliffs, NJ: Prentice-Hall.

Ross, John R. 1968 (1967). *Constraints on Variables in Syntax.* Indiana University Linguistics Club Publication.

Ross, John R. 1969a. "Adjectives as Noun Phrases." In *Modern Studies in English,* edited by David Reibel and Sanford Schane, pp. 352–360. Englewood Cliffs, NJ: Prentice-Hall.

Ross, John R. 1969b. "Auxiliaries as Main Verbs." In *Studies in Philosophical Linguistics 1,* edited by W. Todd, pp. 77–102. Evanston, IL: Great Expectations Press.

Ross, John R. 1969c. "Guess Who?" *Papers from the Fifth Regional Meeting of the Chicago Linguistic Society*, pp. 252–286.

Ross, John R. 1970 (1967). "On Declarative Sentences." In *Readings in English Transformational Grammar*, edited by Roderick Jacobs and Peter Rosenbaum, pp. 222–272. Waltham, MA: Ginn.

Ross, John R. 1972a. "Act." In *Semantics of Natural Language*, edited by Donald Davidson and Gilbert Harmon, pp. 70–126. Dordrecht: D. Reidel.

Ross, John R. 1972b. "Doubl-ing." *Linguistic Inquiry* 3:61–86. Reprinted in *Syntax and Semantics*, vol. 1, edited by John Kimball (1972), pp. 157–186. New York: Seminar Press.

Ross, John R. 1973a. "A Fake NP Squish." In *New Ways of Analyzing*, edited by Charles-James Bailey and Roger Shuy, pp. 96–140. Washington: Georgetown University Press.

Ross, John R. 1973b. "Nouniness." In *Three Dimensions of Linguistic Theory*, edited by Osamu Fujimura, pp. 137–258. Tokyo: TEC Corporation.

Ross, John R. 1973c. "The Same Side Filter." *Papers from the Ninth Regional Meeting of the Chicago Linguistic Society*, pp. 549–567.

Ross, John R. 1973d. "Slifting." In *The Formal Analysis of Natural Language*, edited by M. Gross, Morris Halle, and M. Schützenberger, pp. 133–172. The Hague: Mouton.

Ross, John R. 1974. "Three Batons for Cognitive Psychology." In *Cognition and the Symbolic Processes*, edited by D. Palermo and W. Weimar, pp. 63–124. Washington: V. H. Winston.

Ross, John R. 1975. "Clausematiness." In *Formal Semantics of Natural Language*, edited by Edward Keenan, pp. 422–475. London: Cambridge University Press.

Ross, John R. 1985 (1967). *Infinite Syntax*. Norwood, NJ: Ablex.

Rothstein, Susan. 1983. *The Syntactic Forms of Predication*. Ph.D. dissertation, MIT.

Rothstein, Susan. 1984. "On the Conceptual Link Between Clauses I and II of the Extended Projection Principle." *Proceedings of the Tenth Annual Meeting of the Berkeley Linguistics Society*, pp. 266–273.

Rouveret, Alain, and Vergnaud, Jean-Roger. 1980. "Specifying Reference to the Subject: French Causatives and Conditions on Representations." *Linguistic Inquiry* 11:97–202.

Rudin, Catherine. 1981. " 'Who What to Whom Said?': An Argument from Bulgarian Against Cyclic *Wh*-Movement." *Papers from the Seventeenth Regional Meeting of the Chicago Linguistic Society*, pp. 353–360.

Ruzicka, Rudolf. 1983. "Remarks on Control." *Linguistic Inquiry* 14: 309–324.

Sadock, Jerrold. 1969. "Hypersentences." *Papers in Linguistics* 1:283–370.

Sadock, Jerrold. 1970. "Whimperatives." In *Studies Presented to Robert B. Lees by His Students*, edited by J. Sadock and A. Vanek, pp. 223–238. Edmonton: Linguistic Research Inc.

Sadock, Jerrold. 1972. "Speech Act Idioms." *Papers from the Eighth Regional Meeting of the Chicago Linguistic Society*, pp. 329–339.

Sadock, Jerrold. 1974. *Toward a Linguistic Theory of Speech Acts*. New York: Academic Press.

Sadock, Jerrold. 1975. "The Soft Interpretive Underbelly of Generative Semantics." In *Syntax and Semantics*, vol. 3, edited by Peter Cole and Jerry Morgan, pp. 383–396. New York: Academic Press.

Sadock, Jerrold. 1977. "Aspects of Linguistic Pragmatics." In *Proceedings of the Texas Conference*, edited by Andy Rogers, Bob Wall, and John P. Murphy, pp. 67–78. Arlington, VA: Center for Applied Linguistics.

Sadock, Jerrold. 1978. "On Testing for Conversational Implicature." In *Syntax and Semantics, Volume 9: Pragmatics*, edited by P. Cole, pp. 281–298. New York: Academic Press.

Sadock, Jerrold. 1983. "The Necessary Overlapping of Grammatical Components." In *The Interplay of Phonology, Morphology, and Syntax*, edited by J. Richardson, M. Marks, and A. Chukerman, pp. 198–221. Chicago: Chicago Linguistic Society.

Sadock, Jerrold. 1984. "Whither Radical Pragmatics?" In *Meaning, Form, and Use In Context: Linguistic Applications*, edited by D. Schiffrin, pp. 88–114. Washington: Georgetown University Press.

Sadock, Jerrold. 1985. "Autolexical Syntax." *Natural Language and Linguistic Theory* 3:379–440.

Sadock, Jerrold, and Zwicky, Arnold. 1985. "Sentence Types." In *Language Typology and Syntactic Description*, edited by T. Shopen, pp. 23–63. Cambridge: Cambridge University Press.

Safir, Ken. 1982. "Inflection Government and Inversion." *Linguistic Review* 1:417–467.

Safir, Ken. 1983. "Missing Subjects, Post-Verbal Subjects, and the Definiteness Effect." *Proceedings of NELS 13*, pp. 229–242.

Safir, Ken. 1984. "Multiple Variable Binding." *Linguistic Inquiry* 15:603–638.

Safir, Ken. 1985. *Syntactic Chains and the Definiteness Effect*. Cambridge: Cambridge University Press.

Safir, Ken, and Pesetsky, David. 1981. "Inflection, Inversion, and Subject Clitics." *Proceedings of NELS 11*, pp. 331–344.

Sag, Ivan. 1982a. "On Parasitic Gaps." *Proceedings of the First West Coast Conference on Formal Linguistics*, pp. 35–46.

Sag, Ivan. 1982b. "A Semantic Theory of 'NP Movement' Dependencies." In *The Nature of Syntactic Representation*, edited by P. Jacobson and G. Pullum, pp. 427–466. Dordrecht: Reidel.

Sag, Ivan. 1983. "On Parasitic Gaps." *Linguistics and Philosophy* 6:35–46.

Sag, Ivan, Gazdar, Gerald, Wasow, Thomas, and Weisler, Steven. 1985. "Coordination and How to Distinguish Categories." *Natural Language and Linguistic Theory* 3:117–172.

Saito, Mamoru. 1984. "On the Definition of C-Command and Government." *Proceedings of NELS-14*, pp. 402–417.

Saito, Mamoru, and Hoji, Hajime. 1983. "Weak Crossover and Move Alpha in Japanese." *Natural Language and Linguistic Theory* 1:245–260.

Sampson, Geoffrey. 1976. Review of D. Cohen, ed., *Explaining Linguistic Phenomena*. *Journal of Linguistics* 12:177–181.

Sapir, Edward. 1921. *Language*. New York: Harcourt, Brace and World.

Sapir, Edward. 1922. "Takelma." In *Handbook of American Indian Languages*, edited by F. Boas, pp. 3–296. Washington: Bureau of American Ethnology.

Saussure, Ferdinand de. 1959. *Course in General Linguistics*. New York: McGraw-Hill. (Translation of *Cours de Linguistique Générale*. 1916. Paris: Payot.)

Schachter, Paul. 1962. Review of R. B. Lees, *The Grammar of English Nominalizations*. *IJAL* 28:134–145.

Schachter, Paul. 1984. "A Note on Syntactic Categories and Coordination in GPSG." *Natural Language and Linguistic Theory* 2:269–282.

Schachter, Paul, and Mordechay, Susan. 1983. "A Phrase-Structure Account of 'Nonconstituent' Conjunction." *Proceedings of the West Coast Conference on Formal Linguistics* 2, pp. 260–274.

Scheffler, Israel. 1963. *The Anatomy of Inquiry*. New York: Knopf.

Schein, Barry. Forthcoming. "Small Clauses and Predication." *Linguistic Inquiry*.

Schlick, Moritz. 1936. "Meaning and Verification." *Philosophical Review* 45:339–369. Reprinted in *Theory of Meaning*, edited by A. and K. Lehrer (1970), pp. 98–112. Englewood Cliffs, NJ: Prentice-Hall.

Schmerling, Susan. 1973. "Subjectless Sentences and the Notion of Surface Structure." *Papers from the Ninth Regional Meeting of the Chicago Linguistic Society*, pp. 577–586.

Schmerling, Susan. 1976. *Aspects of English Sentence Stress*. Austin: University of Texas Press.

Schmerling, Susan. 1979. "A Categorial Analysis of Dyirbal Ergativity." *Texas Linguistic Forum* 13:96–112.

Searle, John. 1969. *Speech Acts*. Cambridge: Cambridge University Press.

Searle, John. 1972. "Chomsky's Revolution in Linguistics." *The New York Review*, 29 June 1972, pp. 16–24.

Searle, John. 1975. "Indirect Speech Acts." In *Syntax and Semantics*, vol. 3, edited by Peter Cole and Jerry Morgan, pp. 59–82. New York: Academic Press.

Searle, John. 1976a. "The Classification of Illocutionary Acts." *Language in Society* 5:1–24.

Searle, John. 1976b. Review of J. Sadock, *Toward a Linguistic Theory of Speech Acts*. *Language* 52:966–971.

Sebeok, Thomas, ed. 1960. *Style in Language*. Cambridge, MA: MIT Press.

Seegmiller, Milton. 1974. *Lexical Insertion in a Transformational Grammar*. Ph.D. dissertation, New York University.

Selkirk, Elisabeth. 1972. *The Phrase Phonology of English and French*. Ph.D. dissertation, MIT.

Selkirk, Elisabeth. 1974. "French Liason and the 'X-Bar' Notation." *Linguistic Inquiry* 5:573–590.

Selkirk, Elisabeth. 1982. *The Syntax of Words*. Cambridge, MA: MIT Press.

Selkirk, Elisabeth. 1984. *Phonology and Syntax: The Relation Between Sound and Structure*. Cambridge, MA: MIT Press.

Sells, Peter. 1984. "Resumptive Pronouns and Weak Crossover." *Proceedings of the West Coast Conference on Formal Linguistics*, 3, pp. 252–262.

Shannon, Claude E., and Weaver, Warren. 1949. *The Mathematical Theory of Communication*. Urbana: University of Illinois Press.

Shibatani, Masayoshi, ed. 1976. *Syntax and Semantics*, vol. 6. New York: Academic Press.

Shieber, Stuart. 1985. "Evidence Against the Context-Freeness of Natural Language." *Linguistics and Philosophy* 8:333–344.

Shir, Nomi Erteschik. 1977 (1973). *On the Nature of Island Constraints*. Indiana University Linguistics Club Publication.

Shopen, Timothy, ed. 1985. *Language Description and Syntactic Typology*. Cambridge: Cambridge University Press.

Siegel, Dorothy. 1979 (1974). *Topics in English Morphology*. New York: Garland.

Simpson, Jane, and Bresnan, Joan. 1982. "Control and Obviation in Warlpiri." *Proceedings of the West Coast Conference on Formal Linguistics* 1, pp. 280–291.

Skinner, B. F. 1957. *Verbal Behavior*. New York: Appleton-Century-Crofts.

Sklar, Robert. 1968. "Chomsky's Revolution in Linguistics." *The Nation*, 9 September 1968, pp. 213–217.

Sledd, James. 1955. Reviews of G. Trager and H. L. Smith, *An Outline of English Structure* and C. C. Fries, *The Structure of English*. *Language* 31:312–345.

Slobin, Daniel. 1966. "Grammatical Transformations and Sentence Comprehension in Childhood and Adulthood." *Journal of Verbal Learning and Verbal Behavior* 5:219–227.

Smith, Carlota. 1964. "Determiners and Relative Clauses in a Generative Grammar of English." *Language* 40:37–52. Reprinted in *Modern Studies in English*, edited by David Reibel and Sanford Schane (1969), pp. 247–263. Englewood Cliffs, NJ: Prentice-Hall.

Smith, Neil, and Wilson, Deirdre. 1979. *Modern Linguistics: The Results of Chomsky's Revolution*. Bloomington: Indiana University Press.

Soames, Scott. 1979. "A Projection Problem for Speaker Presuppositions." *Linguistic Inquiry* 10:623–666.

Soames, Scott. 1982. "How Presuppositions Are Inherited: A Solution to the Projection Problem." *Linguistic Inquiry* 13:483–546.

Sommerstein, Alan. 1977. *Modern Phonology*. London: Edward Arnold.

Sperber, Daniel, and Wilson, Deirdre. 1986. *Relevance*. Oxford: Blackwell.

Spitzer, Leo. 1946. "The State of Linguistics: Crisis or Reaction?" *Modern Language Notes* 71:497–502.

Sportiche, Dominique. 1983. *Structural Invariance and Symmetry in Syntax*. Ph.D. dissertation, MIT.

Sportiche, Dominique. 1985. "Remarks on Crossover." *Linguistic Inquiry* 16:460–470.

Sproat, Richard. 1985. "Welsh Syntax and VSO Structure." *Natural Language and Linguistic Theory* 3:173–216.

Staal, J. F. 1967. *Word Order in Sanskrit and Universal Grammar*. Dordrecht: Reidel.

Stalker, Douglas. 1973. "Some Problems with Lakoff's Natural Logic." *Foundations of Language* 10:527–544.

Starosta, Stanley. 1971. "Lexical Derivation in Case Grammar." *University of Hawaii Working Papers in Linguistics* 3:83–101.

Starosta, Stanley. 1973. "The Faces of Case." *Language Sciences* 25:1–14.

Steedman, Mark. 1985. "Dependency and Coordination in the Grammar of Dutch and English." *Language* 61:523–568.

Steinberg, Danny, and Jakobovits, Leon, eds. 1971. *Semantics: An Interdisciplinary Reader.* Cambridge: Cambridge University Press.

Stockwell, Robert. 1960. "The Place of Intonation in a Generative Grammar of English." *Language* 36:360–367.

Stockwell, Robert, and Schachter, Paul. 1962. "Rules for a Segment of English Syntax." Mimeographed. Los Angeles: University of California.

Stockwell, Robert, Schachter, Paul, and Partee, Barbara. 1973 (1969). *The Major Syntactic Structures of English.* New York: Holt, Rinehart and Winston.

Stowell, Timothy. 1983. "Subjects Across Categories." *Linguistic Review* 2:285–312.

Stowell, Timothy. Forthcoming (1981). *Origins of Phrase Structure.* Cambridge, MA: MIT Press.

Strozer, Judith. 1976. *Clitics in Spanish.* Ph.D. dissertation, UCLA.

Stucky, Susan. 1982. "Linearization Rules and Typology." *Proceedings of the West Coast Conference on Formal Linguistics* 1, pp. 60–70.

Stucky, Susan. 1983. "Verb Phrase Constituency and Linear Order in Makua." In *Order, Concord, and Constituency,* edited by G. Gazdar, Ewan Klein, and Geoffrey Pullum, pp. 75–94. Dordrecht: Foris.

Stump, Gregory. 1984. "Agreement vs. Incorporation in Breton." *Natural Language and Linguistic Theory* 2:289–348.

Suñer, Margarita. 1982. "On Null Subjects." *Linguistic Analysis* 9:55–78.

Suñer, Margarita. 1983. "Pro$_{arb}$." *Linguistic Inquiry* 14:188–191.

Swadesh, Morris. 1947. "On the Analysis of English Syllabics." *Language* 23:137–150.

Taraldsen, K. T. 1978. "The Scope of *Wh*-Movement in Norwegian." *Linguistic Inquiry* 9:623–640.

Taraldsen, K. T. 1980. "On the NIC, Vacuous Application, and the *that*-Trace Filter." Indiana University Linguistics Club Publication.

Taraldsen, K. T. 1981a. "Remarks on Government, Thematic Structure, and the Distribution of Empty Categories." In *Levels of Syntactic Representation,* edited by J. Koster and R. May, pp. 253–292. Dordrecht: Foris.

Taraldsen, K. T. 1981b. "The Theoretical Interpretation of a Class of Marked Exceptions." In *Theory of Markedness in Generative Grammar,* edited by A. Belletti, L. Brandi, and L. Rizzi, pp. 475–516. Pisa: Scuola Normale Superiore.

Thomas, Owen. 1965. *Transformational Grammar and the Teacher of English.* New York: Holt, Rinehart and Winston.

Thomas-Flinders, Tracy. 1982. "On the Notions 'Head of a Word' and 'Lexically Related': Evidence from Maricopa Verbal Morphology." *Proceedings of the West Coast Conference on Formal Linguistics* 1, pp. 168–178.

Thomas-Flinders, Tracy. 1983. *Morphological Structures.* Ph.D. dissertation, UCLA.

Thomason, Richmond. 1973. "Semantics, Pragmatics, Conversation, and Presupposition." Unpublished manuscript, University of Pittsburgh.

Thomason, Richmond, 1974. Introduction to *Formal Philosophy: Selected Papers of Richard Montague,* pp. 1–17. New Haven: Yale University Press.

Thomason, S. K. 1979. "Truth-Value Gaps, Many Truth Values, and Possible Worlds." In *Syntax and Semantics, Volume 11: Presupposition,* edited by C. Oh and D. Dinneen, pp. 357–370. New York: Academic Press.

Thorne, James. 1965. Review of P. Postal, *Constituent Structure. Journal of Linguistics,* 1:73–76.

Torrego, Esther. 1981. "More Effects of Successive Cyclic Movement." *Linguistic Inquiry* 14:561–565.

Torrego, Esther. 1984. "On Inversion in Spanish and Some of Its Effects." *Linguistic Inquiry* 15:103–130.

Trager, George L., and Bloch, Bernard. 1941. "The Syllabic Phonemes of English." *Language* 17:223–246.

Trager, George L., and Smith, Henry Lee. 1951. *An Outline of English Structure.* Studies in Linguistics: Occasional Papers, no. 3. Norman, OK: Battenberg Press.

Travis, Lisa. 1984. *Parameters and Effects of Word Order Variation.* Ph.D. dissertation, MIT.

Travis, Lisa, and Williams, Edwin. 1982. "Externalization of Arguments in Malayo-Polynesian Languages." *Linguistic Review* 2:57–78.

Trithart, Lee. 1975. "Relational Grammar and Chicewa Subjectivization Rules." *Papers from the Eleventh Regional Meeting of the Chicago Linguistic Society,* pp. 615–624.

Trubetskoi, N. S. 1939. *Grundzüge der Phonologie. Travaux du Cercle Linguistique de Prague* 7. (Translated by Christiane A. M. Baltaxe as *Principles of Phonology.* 1969. Los Angeles: University of California Press.)

Uhlenbeck, E. M. 1963. "An Appraisal of Transformational Theory." *Lingua* 12:1–18.

U.S. Department of Health, Education, and Welfare, U.S. National Center for Educational Statistics. 1957–1984. *Earned Degrees Conferred.* Washington, DC: U.S. Government Printing Office.

U.S. Department of Health, Education, and Welfare, U.S. National Center for Educational Statistics. 1962–1977. *Enrollment for Advanced Degrees.* Washington, DC: U.S. Government Printing Office.

van der Wilt, Koos. 1984. "Two Remarks on Parasitic Gaps in Dutch." *Linguistic Analysis* 13:145–155.

van Riemsdijk, Henk. 1978a. *A Case Study in Syntactic Markedness.* Lisse: Peter de Ridder Press.

van Riemsdijk, Henk. 1978b. "On the Diagnosis of *Wh* Movement." In *Recent Transformational Studies in European Languages,* edited by S. Jay Keyser, pp. 189–206. Cambridge, MA: MIT Press.

van Riemsdijk, Henk, and Williams, Edwin. 1981. "NP-Structure." *Linguistic Review* 1:171–218.

Vergnaud, J.-R. 1974. *French Relative Clauses.* Ph.D. dissertation, MIT.

Visser, F. T. 1963–1973. *An Historical Syntax of the English Language.* Leiden: F. J. Brill.

Voegelin, C. F. 1958. Review of Noam Chomsky, *Syntactic Structues. International Journal of American Linguistics* 24:229–231.

von Humboldt, Wilhelm. 1836. *Über die Verschiedenheit des menschlichen* Sprachbaues; facsimile ed. F. Dümmlers Verlag. Bonn. 1960.

Walinska de Hackbeil, Hanna. 1983. "X-Bar Categories in Morphology." In *The Interplay of Phology, Morphology, and Syntax,* edited by J. Richardson, M. Marks, and A. Chuckerman, pp. 301–313. Chicago: Chicago Linguistic Society.

Wasow, Thomas. 1972. *Anaphoric Relations in English.* Ph.D. dissertation, MIT.

Wasow, Thomas. 1975. "Anaphoric Pronouns and Bound Variables." *Language* 51:368–373.

Wasow, Thomas. 1976. "McCawley on Generative Semantics." *Linguistic Analysis* 2:279–301.

Wasow, Thomas. 1979. *Anaphora in Generative Grammar.* Ghent: E. Story-Scientia.

Wasow, Thomas. 1980. "Major and Minor Rules in Lexical Grammar." In *Lexical Grammar,* edited by T. Hoekstra, H. van der Hulst, and M. Moortgat, pp. 285–312. Dordrecht: Foris.

Watt, William. 1970. "On Two Hypotheses Concerning Psycholinguistics." In *Cognition and the Development of Language,* edited by J. Hayes, pp. 137–220. New York: Wiley.

Wehrli, Eric. 1983. "A Modular Parser for French." *Proceedings of the Eighth International Joint Conference on Artificial Intelligence,* pp. 686–689. Palo Alto: William Kaufmann.

Weinreich, Uriel. 1966. "Explorations in Semantic Theory." In *Current Trends in Linguistics,.* vol. 3, edited by T. Sebeok, pp. 395–478. The Hague: Mouton.

Wells, Rulon. 1945. "The Pitch Phonemes of English." *Language* 21:27–39.

Wells, Rulon. 1947. "Immediate Constituents." *Language* 23:81–117. Reprinted in *Readings in Linguistics,* edited by Martin Joos (1958), pp. 186–207. Washington: American Council of Learned Societies.

Wexler, Kenneth, and Culicover, Peter. 1980. *Formal Principles of Language Acquisition.* Cambridge, MA: MIT Press.

Wexler, Kenneth, Culicover, Peter, and Hamburger, Henry. 1975. "Learning Theoretic Foundations of Linguistic Universals." *Theoretical Linguistics* 2:213–253.

Whitehall, Harold. 1951. *Structural Essentials of English.* New York: Harcourt, Brace.

Wilkins, Wendy. 1979. *The Variable Interpretation Convention.* Indiana University Linguistics Club Publication.

Wilkins, Wendy. 1980. "Adjacency and Variables in Syntactic Transformations." *Linguistic Inquiry* 11:709–758.

Williams, Edwin. 1974. *Rule Ordering in Syntax.* Ph.D. dissertation, MIT.

Williams, Edwin. 1975. "Small Clauses in English." In *Syntax and Semantics, Volume 4,* edited by John Kimball, pp. 249–274.

Williams, Edwin. 1977a. "Discourse and Logical Form." *Linguistic Inquiry* 8:101–139.

Williams, Edwin. 1977b. "On Deep and Surface Anaphora." *Linguistic Inquiry* 8:692–696.

Williams, Edwin. 1980. "Abstract Triggers." *Journal of Linguistic Research* 1:71–82.

Williams, Edwin. 1981a. "Argument Structure and Morphology." *Linguistic Review* 1:81–114.

Williams, Edwin. 1981b. "On the Notions 'Lexically Related' and 'Head of a Word.'" *Linguistic Inquiry* 12:245–274.

Williams, Edwin. 1981c. "Transformationless Grammar." *Linguistic Inquiry* 12:645–654.

Williams, Edwin. 1983. "Against Small Clauses." *Linguistic Inquiry* 14:287–308.

Williams, Edwin. 1984. "Grammatical Relations." *Linguistic Inquiry* 15:639–674.

Wilson, Deirdre. 1975. *Presupposition and Non-Truth Conditional Semantics.* London: Academic Press.

Wilson, Deirdre, and Sperber, Daniel. 1979. "Ordered Entailments: An Alternative to Presuppositional Theories." In *Presuppositions. Syntax and Semantics,* vol. 11, edited by C. K. Oh and D. Dinneen, pp. 299–323. New York: Academic Press.

Wilson, Deirdre, and Sperber, Daniel. 1981. "On Grice's Theory of Conversation." In *Conversation and Discourse,* edited by P. Werth, pp. 155–178. London: Croom Helm.

Winter, Werner. 1965. "Transforms without Kernels?" *Language* 41:484–489.

Wittgenstein, Ludwig. 1953. *Philosophical Investigations.* London: Blackwell.

Yang, Dong-Whee. 1985. "On the Integrity of Control Theory." *Proceedings of NELS 15,* pp. 389–408.

Yngve, Victor. 1960. "A Model and an Hypothesis for Language Structure." *Proceedings of the American Philosophical Society* 104:444–466.

Yngve, Victor. 1961. "The Depth Hypothesis." In *Structure of Language and Its Mathematical Aspects,* edited by Roman Jakobson, pp. 130–138. Providence, RI: American Mathematical Society.

Zadeh, Lofti. 1965. "Fuzzy Sets." *Information and Control* 8:338–353.

Zadeh, Lofti. 1971. "Quantitative Fuzzy Semantics." *Information Sciences* 3:159–176.

Zaenen, Annie. 1980. *Extraction Rules in Icelandic.* Ph.D. dissertation, Harvard.

Zaenen, Annie. Forthcoming. "Island Constraints and Grammatical Functions."

Zaenen, Annie, Maling, Joan, and Thráinsson, H. 1985. "Case and Grammatical Functions: The Icelandic Passive." *Natural Language and Linguistic Theory* 3:441–484.

Zagona, Karen. 1982. *Government and Proper Government of Verbal Projections.* Ph.D. dissertation, University of Washington.

Zubizarreta, Maria Luisa. 1982a. *On the Relationship of the Lexicon to Syntax.* Ph.D. dissertation, MIT.

Zubizarreta, Maria Luisa. 1982b. "Theoretical Implications of Subject Extraction in Portuguese." *Linguistic Review* 2:79–96.

Zwicky, Arnold. 1969. "Phonological Constraints in Syntactic Description." *Papers in Linguistics* 1:411–463.

Zwicky, Arnold. 1985. "Heads." *Journal of Linguistics* 21:1–30.

Name Index

Subject Index

273